W9-ADP-855

STALIN AND THE LITERARY INTELLIGENTSIA, 1928–39

STALIN AND THE LITERARY INTELLIGENTSIA, 1928–39

A. Kemp-Welch

Lecturer in Politics
University of Nottingham

MACMILLAN

First published 1991 by
THE MACMILLAN PRESS LTD
Houndmills, Basingstoke, Hampshire RG21 2XS
and London
Companies and representatives
throughout the world

ISBN 0–333–27770–8

A catalogue record for this book is available
from the British Library.

Printed in Great Britain by
Antony Rowe Ltd
Chippenham, Wiltshire

Reprinted 1994

Contents

Acknowledgements

This book is based on unpublished Soviet archives of the 1920s and 1930s. My first debts are to the custodians of these unique collections, notably those of the Soviet Academy of Sciences' Institute of World Literature in Moscow. A full description of these and other archives consulted is appended. My second acknowledgement is owed to Harvard University for hospitality while I explored the Trotsky Exile Papers (released in 1980) and photocopies of the Smolensk Archive, made for Merle Fainsod and his team.

I learned much at the London School of Economics, particularly from Leonard Schapiro, who introduced me to the study of Soviet politics, and from Peter Reddaway who (in 1971) first suggested the 1930s as a subject for research. Then followed a post-doctoral fellowship in the Russian Centre at St Antony's College, Oxford, where I had the good fortune to be encouraged and guided by the late Max Hayward and Mr H.T. Willetts. The subsequent work was mostly done in the Taylorian Institution Slavonic Library in Oxford. I am immensely grateful to Mr David Howells and his assistants for access to their magnificent collection.

The conclusion was finally reached in the Library of King's College, Cambridge, during sabbatical leave from the University of Nottingham. I would like to thank Mrs Angela Fullerton and Mrs Anne Macdonald for their miraculous transcriptions of my many drafts, and Tim Farmiloe of Macmillan for his patience. I was saved from many errors at the last minute by Julian Graffy. Those which remain are entirely my own.

A. K-W.
October 1990

1 The Revolution

A Russian writer should never live in friendship with a Russian
Government

Gorky, 1902

Theoretically, the Russian writer was an independent critic of the
state. When the state acted, the writer submitted its policies to
careful scrutiny; when, as was more frequent, the state did nothing,
writers attempted to goad it into activity. But, while regularly in
opposition to the authorities, the writers of the nineteenth century
found themselves increasingly critical of Russian society and found in
its ignorance, backwardness, violence, litigiousness and *Oblomovism*, plenty of material for literary expression. Caught in a limbo
between society and the state, such writers began to be regarded as
an intelligentsia[1] whose rootlessness was treated as a unique vantage
point from which to articulate the 'social interest' as a whole. To the
frequent charge that the intelligentsia 'lacks conviction', its members
liked to reply that 'on the contrary, only we are free to have intellectual convictions', untramelled by social or financial position. Despite
the numerous cases of compromises with the authorities, the notion
developed that the intelligentsia occupied the unique position of
custodian of cultural and ethical values against the infringements of
the state. Although the term cannot be equated solely with 'left-wing'
opposition, it was in politics that it had the most vital consequences,
the outcome of which, it would be scarcely an exaggeration to say,
was the Russian Revolution itself.

The first response of writers to the February Revolution was
characterised in the classic account as 'an endless flood of talk'. The
'fullest liberty had been declared and there was no power that could
have enforced restrictions, even if they had existed'.[2] Their first
concern was to protect the past. A meeting assembled in Gorky's
apartment in early March to organise protection for the country's
historic monuments. At the next session, the Gorky Commission
advanced further objectives: the erection of statues to 'fighters for
freedom' and other measures for the 'development of Russian art'.[3]
They also approached the Petrograd Soviet which agreed to issue an
appeal to Russian citizens to protect national monuments. Gorky's
Commission obtained offices in the Winter Palace and was attached,

1

as a special advisory board on cultural matters, to the Provisional Government. But neither Gorky's rapid elevation nor the priorities he proposed passed without challenge from the rest of the artistic community. Some 1,400 members attending a mass meeting at the Mikhailovsky Theatre on 12 March called for 'complete freedom in the arts' and protested against any form of governmental intervention in this sphere. It condemned Gorky's Commission in this connection.

In reply, Gorky emphasised the purely practical role of his Commission to protect historical monuments and denied that it harboured any aspirations to a commanding role in the arts.[4] His audience was unconvinced. Fundamental objections even to such limited activities were raised by a 'freedom of art' group formed the previous day. Although broadly based, a significant minority of its founding members were 'leftists' such as Meyerhold and the art critic Punin. Their spokesman Mayakovsky called for a complete separation of the arts from central government and the passing of both teaching and organisational matters such as financing to local levels. This too failed to sway the meeting which became hopelessly split between the 'leftists', an unofficial 'rightist bloc' headed by F. Sologub, and a centrist group. But none of these managed to muster sufficient votes to elect an organisational structure.[5] The meeting achieved a negative result in discouraging even the minimal cooperation with the Provisional Government suggested by Gorky, who felt obliged to disband his Commission shortly afterwards.

This inability to act together was deeply perturbing to many sections of the intelligentsia. Long accustomed to consider themselves the most advanced part of the nation, the intelligentsia was perplexed to find itself left behind by a radical Revolution which its earlier actions and writings had, in part unwittingly, done so much to engender. A crisis of confidence ensued which led in turn to a re-examination of the intelligentsia's own role and to a search for fresh identities and expressions. One response was patriotism. Already, in March 1917, the writer Bunin had made an ill-fated attempt to organise a campaign against Bolshevik anti-war policy. Soon afterwards a 'league of Russian culture' was announced. Ostensibly non-political and dedicated to the cultural traditions that 'unite all Russians', it was in practice a Kadet venture in which the former Marxist P. Struve was prominent. A number of patriotic rallies were held to coincide with the Provisional Government's June offensive. The military débâcle that followed put paid to these assemblies.[6]

Thus attempts by the liberal intelligentsia to assert a leading role in this time of crisis proved entirely ineffective.

During the 'July days', with its abortive coups from both right and left, the intelligentsia experienced even more sharply its own helplessness. Bely complained to a correspondent 'time is outstripping us: it is almost impossible to catch up'.[7] In an attempt to find a positive role for the intelligentsia, Sologub advanced the view that it was not simply neutral towards the struggle between capital and labour but that it actually formed a third class between the proletariat and the bourgeoisie.[8] This came close to the suggestion that the intelligentsia might use its own superior education and knowledge to foster its self-interest. In Russian history this is associated with Jan Machajski (Vol'skii), who considered that the intelligentsia accumulated a 'capital' of knowledge and education, and predicted that 'as long as the working class is condemned to ignorance, the intelligentsia will rule through workers' deputies'.[9] Such self-criticism was not uncommon among the Russian intelligentsia, and gave rise to an anti-intellectualism known as *makhaevshchina*, about which more was to be learned under Stalinism.

The October Revolution was welcomed by only a small section of the intelligentsia. As the Soviet historian Fedyukin puts it, 'many members of the intelligentsia were gripped with a deep pessimism, taking the collapse of the rule of the bourgeoisie, a class which they considered to be the only bearer of culture, as the death of culture in general'.[10] But while there were strikes amongst teachers and doctors, there were few stoppages in the artistic world. Even those theatres that had cancelled performances in the immediate aftermath of October, soon resumed their normal programmes. A more typical response was to carry on regardless of the new state authorities and to ignore their official representatives. Artists, especially in Petrograd, were bent on autonomy: theatres formerly financed by the state now sought self-management. Lunacharsky, as Commissar for Education and the Arts, described these aspirations as 'syndicalist' and proposed instead to constitute a state Soviet on artistic affairs, whose membership would be drawn jointly from representatives of the arts and from the Soviets of workers, soldiers and peasants' deputies.[11] It was rejected unanimously, with even Lunacharsky's intermediary Punin voting against it. A further approach to propose cooperation between Lunacharsky's Commissariat and the Union of Artists on the protection of art treasures – as uncontroversial a proposal as could possibly have been made – was similarly rejected by 68 votes to nil with two abstentions. One abstainer, Mayakovsky, explained that in his opinion the stationing of sentries would suffice to perform this task.[12] During December a minor poet, Ivnev, had the idea of organising a pro-Bolshevik rally of the intelligentsia and invited Lunacharsky, Kollontai, Blok, Meyerhold, and Esenin to speak. But a sequel arranged for January did not materialise. The advertised speakers, such as Blok, made known that their names had been included without their permission and none of them attended.[13]

For a significant group of writers – such as Bunin, Kuprin, Z. Gippius and Khodasevich – the Revolution was a parting of the ways. They left the country at the earliest opportunity and helped to found a parallel stream of Russian 'literature in emigration'.[14] Some of those who stayed behind began to be regarded as 'internal emigres'. Russian writers began to separate themselves on political lines into 'ours' or 'theirs'[15] and to ostracise each other accordingly. Thus the solidarity of the literary intelligentsia, always fragile, was shattered by the Revolution.

The first Ode to October came, paradoxically, from the group which had previously been most aloof from the political arena: Russian Symbolism. Reacting against the didactic criticism and realist prose that had dominated *belles-lettres* for half a century, Russian writers of the last two decades before the First World War entered a phase of feverish experiment, sometimes referred to as a Silver Age. This movement, of which the principal medium was poetry, attempted to educate the public in 'symbolic' language which emphasised the musical and mystical at all costs, including some critics thought, lucidity. It used to meet weekly at Vyacheslav Ivanov's 'Tower' for recitations and for lengthy discussion, of which one critic commented 'they are hopelessly given to ratiocination and their awareness that something new must be said far exceeds their ability to say it'.[16] Partly under such criticism and the further accusation of evading social responsibility, particularly in the more politically charged atmosphere that followed 1905, Symbolism began to edge toward commitment. Its second generation of poets gave greater attention to reality, though still retorting to charges of escapism that their art proceeded beyond mere 'symbols' into the higher world of revelation. With Bely, the leading Russian follower of Rudolph Steiner, this became pessimism, cynicism and deep despair, punctuated by wild anarchic moments as seen in his novel *Petersburg*.

Such fluctuating moods were also characteristic of Blok, the great-est of the Symbolists. He was obsessed by the 'inevitable catastrophe that overshadows us'. He warned Ivanov's meetings that the common people would wreak vengeance for 'our apathy, for our falsity, for the evening we have just spent, for your poetry and for mine'. The 'Tower' seemed to him 'the last act of the tragic estrangement between the intelligentsia and the people'.[16] He noted that the rumble of popular discontent was 'growing so fast that with every passing year we can hear it more distinctly'. He added in 1915 that 'the days of all manner of cosy "privileged" institutions are over: it is now too late to think on the lines of it'll see out our time'.[17] Here guilt and self-doubt are mingled with the conviction that subterranean currents were already moving in society and would inevitably push the intelligentsia aside. And yet, despite all these forebodings, Blok wrote the first literary tribute to the Russian Revolution. His famous poem, *The Twelve*, relates the saga of a dozen robber-heroes on their murderous progress through Petrograd. That they are Red Guards is confirmed by their dispatch to close the Constituent Assembly. Yet such shoddy characters, with their disorderly accoutrements of dis-ease and drink, are suddenly transfigured in the final stanza by the unseen materialisation of a mysterious Christ-figure at their head. This unexpected analogy, which atheist Bolsheviks felt able to ac-cept, was not one Blok himself managed to explain. He merely commented 'unfortunately Christ and no-one else'. The poet was not a professing Christian, and had used the same image in previous works. It was probably intended to impose order on the revolution-ary events, transforming them from mere chaos into an extraordinary and ambivalent apocalypse.[18]

An accompanying article, 'Intelligentsia and Revolution', reiter-ates the stormy landscape: tempests and hurricanes, fierce torna-does 'like snowstorms' and other natural elements conspire with popular forces to bring about a Revolution which 'despite everything, invariably concerns that which is great'. Bolshevism is associated with a colossal refurbishment of the old culture to which the author seemed reconciled. It was possible to endure the loss of 'Kremlin's palaces, pictures and books' because the human imagination could recreate them. To overthrow the old culture was to purge and to exact retribution for social injustices for which an ineffective intel-ligentsia was principally to blame.[19] Blok's poem thus becomes familiar Russian messianism. God is brought forth by nature and the *Narod*': it pushes intellectuals aside and ushers in a new order embodying a higher truth before which all must bow. Blok evidently believed that this ousting of the intelligentsia would be temporary and that a 'musical reconciliation' would follow, which individualism, now purified, would blend harmoniously into the 'new unison' of eternity. Most other Symbolists were horrified by Blok's poem and his ambiguous interpretation. They broke off personal relations with him. Only Bely offered a comparable, though artistically much inferior, welcome to the Revolution.

His poem *Christ is Risen* (also of early 1918) does not describe the Revolution directly, yet the sounds of revolution intrude. We hear machine-gun fire and the internationale, we encounter a 'bespectacled enfeebled intellectual' reminiscent of Blok's 'bourgeois at the crossroads' and are shown a railwayman shot and left bleeding on the track, whose body is identified with Christ's. Beneath the drab exterior of a country at war, Bely perceives a national reawakening, a coming of the *Narod*. He, too, believed this cataclysm to be portended by catastrophes: a tornado sweeping away old forces, an explosion, an earthquake, thunder and lightening, a stretching of nature 'beyond its limits', disorders to which the intelligentsia must, helplessly, submit. In the last section, the God-bearing Russian people overcome the evil serpent and extend their hands towards the Second Coming. The Revolution thus becomes a form of resurrection. But this was not something that Bely believed the politicians, who imagined they made the Revolution, could understand.[20]

Such ideas were 'Scythian'.[21] This school of thought maintained the October Revolution should be 'deepened' and extended from the political into the social sphere. It was intended to bring about a new synthesis consisting of the intelligentsia's individualism and creativeness, together with a sense of community and spiritual maximalism. Moreover the Scythians were convinced – as were the Bolsheviks – that the Russian Revolution had global significance. To the Scythians its importance was second only to the birth of Christ. Backward Russia had brought 'new ecumenical ideas' into the world, just as backward Judea had given birth to Christianity. Central to these new ideas was that socialism combined 'the recognition of the supreme value of the individual personality with great social activity' and 'posed with new force the old eternal question about East and West, Russia and Europe'.[22] The Revolution thus raised the perennial question of whether Russia could fulfil a universal civilising mission. Such Slav messianism assumed a highly patriotic form following the renewed German advance of February 1918. The placating of the 'savage Hun', at the punitive settlement of Brest-Litovsk, caused the Scythians dismay. Their political sympathisers, the Left SRs, withdrew from Lenin's 'coalition' government.[23]

The Scythians also included two peasant poets. The senior of these, hailed by Ivanov-Razumnik as the Scythians' main theorist, was Klynev, 'the first profound poet of the people'.[24] The second, Esenin, addressed the Revolution through gentle blasphemy. *Inoniya*, dedicated to Jeremiah, disdains the old God and threatens to pull his beard and to 'lick the faces of saints' from icons. The poet proclaims a post-revolutionary peasant paradise in which a saviour rides into the new Nazareth of cornfields, huts and his ancient mother. *Jordan Dove* declared Esenin a Bolshevik. Equating October with the defeat of the wicked west and its machinery, it anticipated a rural utopia in which the Virgin Mary was a familiar everyday figure. Bolsheviks must have been astonished by this prospect for the countryside.[25] A further poem, *Celestial Drummer*, explained that the earth and village were feminine while the sun and town were masculine, notions which Bukharin described as 'metaphysical claptrap' and *Pravda* rejected as 'incoherent nonsense: unsuitable'.[26]

Several Scythians were accused of taking part in a 'Left-S.R. conspiracy'. Those arrested included Ivanov-Razumnik and several writers whose names were found in his notebook. One such, the writer and critic Zamyatin, caused confusion by admitting to former membership of the Bolshevik party and lecturing his interrogator: 'if you were a real Marxist, you would know that the stratum of Bolsheviks' petty-bourgeois fellow-travellers tends to disintegrate and that only the workers are the unswerving class supporters of communism. As I belong to the class of petty-bourgeois intellectuals, I fail to understand why you should be surprised'.[27] He was released forthwith. It was also difficult for Blok to deny the alleged 'conspiracy' since some of his work had been published in the Left SR newspaper. It took some hours of cross-examination before this could be cleared up. Partly under the influence of such treatment, Blok found that his earlier enthusiasm for the Revolution had waned. Thus he wrote at the height of the Petrograd siege by foreign intervention forces: 'One thing one must grant the Bolsheviks is the unique ability to stamp out custom and to liquidate the individual. I do not know if that is particularly bad or not but it is a fact'.[28] He began to distance himself from the new regime, withdrawing from government committees or sitting through their work in silence.

In his last months, Blok pondered on the incompatibility of art with 'any forcible measures by the powers that be'. His Pushkin lecture rejected the imposition of authority on art. It urged 'those bureaucrats to beware of a worse name than rabble who are preparing to direct poetry along some particular channel'. Poetry was characteristically defined as 'bringing harmony into the world'. He now feared that the authorities might seek to 'muddy the very sources of harmony', adding 'it is uncertain what prevents them: lack of inventiveness, reticence, or conscience. Or perhaps such methods are already being sought?'[29] After failing to secure exit visas to visit Finland with his wife for treatment, Blok died in Petrograd in August 1921 from premature arteriosclerosis. He was forty. The whole of 'literary Petersburg' attended the funeral. Zamyatin, a pall bearer, noted 'only then did it become apparent how few remained'.[30]

After Blok's death, the mantle of poet-witness to the revolution passed to the Acmeists, an informal group in existence since 1912. The moving spirits were Gumilev, Akhmatova (whom he had married in 1910) and Mandelstam who wrote the manifestoes.[31] Utterly unlike the Symbolists – such as Vyacheslav Ivanov and Bryusov – who assumed the role of high priests soaring above ordinary life, the Acmeists kept their feet on the ground. Mandelstam explained 'the earth is not an encumbrance or an unfortunate accident but a God-given palace'. Renouncing the Symbolist 'cult of the poet' with its principle that 'all is permitted to one who dares', the Acmeists found inspiration in everyday life. They saw themselves as craftsmen: the builders or masons who could mould the most mundane material into artistic or architectural form.[32] The Symbolist period was described in a lecture by Mandelstam as an experiment with apostasy, a turning-away from Christianity to Buddhism and theosophy. In his view, a Christian art communicates directly with God and acts throughout as a preparation for life's triumphant apex: death. The lecture linked Scriabin's death with that of Pushkin as 'two transformations of the same sun'. He explained that they died full deaths 'as one lives a full life'. In dying they had 'twice gathered the Russian people' and bore witness through a 'public (*sobornii*) Russian death'.[33]

For Mandelstam the Revolution was an enormous event. He tried to grasp its elemental qualities and subterranean forces, while remaining sharply aware that the only judge of its outcome could be the Russian people themselves. Perhaps his most direct comment on the Revolution is *Twilight of Freedom* published in May 1918. The poet's ambivalence is found even in his title, which may apply either to the period of semi-darkness after sunset (dusk) or that preceding sunrise (dawn).[34] Here an acceptance of history is accompanied by claustrophobia and foreboding. The poet sees that the Revolution had both positive and negative potentialities although which would prevail could not yet be foretold. Akhmatova, by contrast, lamented that no-one would want poetry in the 'dark days' to come. She predicted that the poet would be bound to wander 'like a beggar' from door to door.[35] In this the fate of Mandelstam is accurately foretold.

Akhmatova has recorded their journeys together across the 'unbelievable potholes of the revolutionary winter, among the famous bonfires which were kept alight almost till May, to the crackle of rifle fire coming from Lord knows where'.[36] Although the old shop signs were still in place, there was behind them nothing but dust, darkness and gaping emptiness. She describes the typhus, famine, pitch dark flats, damp firewood and people so swollen as to be unrecognisable. Even the famous wooden blocks with which the streets of Petersburg had been paved were finally rotting away.[37] Yet while the city had so altered its external appearance as to turn into its opposite, public demand for poetry remained unchanged. The thought of emigration appears in her writings of the early twenties. Sunlight still shining in the west is contrasted with Russian death that had already marked out its victims and summoned up its raven harbingers. But she pitied the exile's lot, condemned like a criminal or leper to homelessness, and declared proudly in 1922 'I am not one of those who left the land'.[38]

Pasternak, too, bore witness to the daily impact of Revolution. Though unaffiliated apart from some association with the 'centrifuge' group before the Revolution, he accepted the Acmeist assumptions that true art expressed the essence of life and could dispense with allegories, symbols and other trappings. Long after, he recalled of October how 'simple people unburdened their hearts and talked about what mattered most, about how to live and what to live for'. Their elation 'erased the boundary between human beings and nature'. No longer dormant, nature itself seems to participate in the political commotion: 'roads, trees and stars held meetings and made speeches too', the very air became inspired, clairvoyant, animated, even human.[39] *My Sister, Life* (published in 1922) took nature as the key to 'all that is most unusual and elusive to be learned about Revolution'. Although a poet did nòt forge the Revolution 'with a hammer', he did have a role in absorbing it 'like a sponge'.[40] More than any other lyric poet, Pasternak acquired a reputation for aloofness.

It seemed as though he inhabited an inner world of private moods distinct from social experience, but this was misleading. Pasternak was not apolitical: he had as a boy shared the revolutionary enthusiasm of 1905 recorded later in his long poem *Lieutenant Schmidt*. Like the fictional Zhivago, he may have been attracted by the 'splendid surgery' of 1917. Lenin, whom he saw at the Ninth Congress of Soviets (in 1921)[41] made an indelible impression. As a leader with the audacity 'to act in the first person', he had 'allowed the sea to become stormy', and 'the hurricane to lash out with his blessing'. Yet Pasternak already feared that the cost might be high. 'From many consecutive generations someone steps forward/ a genius comes as the forerunner of privileges/ but takes revenge for his departure by oppression.' Pasternak, too, was conscious of the distinction between the Revolution itself as a great and exhilarating event, and the oppressive government that might issue from it.

A third group, the Futurists, saw themselves as the cultural counterpart to the political revolution. Their inspiration had come from pre-revolutionary theatre, of which Meyerhold was the greatest innovator. Discarding Stanislavsky's mimicry of life on stage,[42] he turned to pantomime, circus acrobatics and the dance as purely theatrical forms worth exploring for their own sake without any attempt at imitative realism. Theatre was treated as distinct from life and subject to its own laws. The purpose of a theatrical performance was to startle and astonish an audience. Thus his production *Columbine's Scarf* (1910) mingled pantomime and many *commedia dell'arte* devices with the chilling and grotesque drama, reminiscent of Hoffmann. When critics protested that his play *Don Juan*, which ran in the same season, was simply a 'spectacle for spectacle's sake' Meyerhold agreed. He termed it 'a fairground show, inspired by strolling players' and based upon 'the apotheosis of the mask, gesture and movement.'[43] Futurism took art, literally, onto the street. Its sensation-seeking tours, most notably one to Kharkov, the Crimea, Odessa and back through Belorussia, were timed to coincide with, and distract from the visit of the Italian futurist Marinetti to Moscow in 1913.[44] Their *modus operandi* was frankly agitational: scandals, colourful and absurd parades, and exhibitionism such as Mayakovsky's famous yellow jackets with a wooden spoon in the buttonhole. In their final fling before the First World War, the Futurists lambasted 'Roaring Parnassus' – the entire literary establishment – under the heading 'Go to Hell'. The Symbolists were singled out for special attack, and the Acmeists were 'a pack of Adams with partings in their hair' who 'tried to attach an Apollonian label to their tired songs about samovars from Tula and toy lions'.[45]

The Futurists' own poetry played havoc with convention. Their first document *Menagerie* (1909) was published on wallpaper. Its author, Khlebnikov, held that all language derives from a common root and maintained that his own contribution had been to dissolve Russian into 17 basic elements. He used the discovered 'roots' to form new words of his own, challenging conventional vocabulary, first through neologisms and later by the invention of a special trans-sense language (Zaum').[46] He also devoted himself to calculations based on the assumption that the world was directed by a central number 365 plus or minus 48 (in most cases 317). He signed 'A slap in the face of public taste' (1912), which proclaimed:

- The past is crowded.
- The Academy and Pushkin are more incomprehensible than hieroglyphics.
- Throw Pushkin, Dostoyevsky, Tolstoy etc. etc. overboard from the Ship of modernity.
- He who does not forget his *first* love will not recognise his last.
- But who is so gullible as to direct his last Love towards the perfumed lechery of Bal'mont? Does it reflect the virile soul of today?
- Who is so cowardly as to be afraid to strip the warrior Bryusov of the paper armour he wears over his black tuxedo? Is the dawn of an undiscovered beauty seen there?
- Wash your hands you who touch the filthy slime of the books written by those inumerable Leonid Andreyevs.
- All those Maxim Gorkys, Kuprins, Bloks, Sologubs, Remizovs, Averchenkos, Chornyis, Kuz'mins, Bunins, etc. etc. need only a dacha by the river. Fate rewards tailors in this way.
- We look down on their nothingness from the height of sky-scrapers.[47]

The Futurists seemed blithly unconcerned that their anti-art gestures, rejection of conventional syntax and vocabulary and affirmation of the right to innovate at all costs might be as incomprehensible to a public brought up on Pushkin as hieroglyphics. But despite all this, Futurism was gradually accepted. Its members were received in Petrograd salons from 1915 and their respectability was confirmed when Mayakovsky was brought out by a 'real' publishing house in October 1916.

Futurism greeted the October Revolution as its own. Mayakovsky put it:

> To accept or not to accept? There was no such problem for me or other Moscow Futurists. My Revolution! Went to Smolnyi and did what was necessary. Meetings began.[48]

An 'artistic October' was accordingly announced. Schemes were mooted to throw art 'like rainbows' from street to street. Mayakovsky prophesied that the Revolution would bring forth a new song whose 'never-ending thunderous music of volcanoes turned into flutes will resound from mountain ranges' and that 'ocean waves will be forced to play on chords stretched from Europe to America'. Half-anticipating Stalin's famous phrase, he declared that war and revolution had emptied Russian souls which now awaited their new engineers. In manifestoes signed jointly with Burliuk and Kamensky he declared that art was 'for the people.'[49] *Too early to rejoice* (December 1918) declared the need to incinerate museums and libraries and to execute Pushkin.[50]

Futurists quickly laid claim to places in the Fine Arts Section (IzO) of Lunacharsky's Commissariat. They were joined by Tatlin, Malevich and Kandinsky, which made it a stronghold of the *avant-garde*.[51] Mayakovsky and Brik asserted that since Futurism was the most advanced form of art and the proletariat the most advanced social class, then Futurism must be proletarian art. But the Bolsheviks were reluctant to endorse too many of their schemes. Lunacharsky, much needed in these debates as a modifier, commented impatiently at the end of 1918 'I have declared dozens of times that the Commissariat of Enlightenment must be impartial in its attitude towards the various trends in art'.[52] Given that Futurists were the authorities' most enthusiastic collaborators, so neutral an approach implied discouragement. True, Lunacharsky did visit the Poets' Café where Mayakovsky invited him to address the customers on 'the future of art, which no doubt belongs to Futurism'. His tactful reply, while praising Mayakovsky's verse and lively presentation, condemned Futurism for exhibitionism and for contempt of the bourgeoisie which it was in fact serving.[53]

Mayakovsky threw himself into mass agitation, writing propaganda texts for the telegraphic agency ROSTA during the Civil War. He found the atmosphere exhilarating: 'telegraphic news immediately translated into posters' and Party decrees rendered instantly in verse.

It gave him the sense of being at the battle-front. His contemporary rendering of Noah's flood *Mystery-Bouffe* (1918), showed the Revolution washing away the impure old world and its reconstruction according to the design of the simple worker (played by Mayakovsky) who comes to the proletarian pure walking Christ-like across as the waves. The Revolution's international significance is described in his poem *One Hundred and Fifty Million*. The giant peasant Ivan, whose heels are the size of the Steppes and arms the length of the Neva, wades the Atlantic to do mortal combat with Woodrow Wilson, portrayed as a bloated capitalist with a top hat the size of the Eiffel Tower.[54] But Lenin called this rendition 'hooligan communism' and proposed that the 'absurd, stupid, monstrously stupid and pretentious poem' should be printed in an edition of 'not more than one thousand five hundred for libraries and eccentrics'. Its sponsor, Lunacharsky, should be 'whipped for his futurism'. But the state publishing house went ahead and Lenin received an author's copy inscribed 'to Comrade Vladimir Ilich, with Com-fut greetings'.[55] Such insubordination would not happen under Stalin.

For Khlebnikov, October expressed the uprising of the poor peasantry – a return of Pugachev and Stenka Razin – against an unjust social order.[56] This is put mostly directly in *Ladomir* (1920) which Tynyanov called 'the sum total of all his poetry'. The name refers to an ideal city of the future, formed from two roots: *Lad* (harmony) and *Mir* (peace). We see the old regime swept away by a revolution from below and natural forces which send skyscrapers and palaces up in smoke. The tsars are not annihilated but allowed to propagate in a cage with monkeys. Technological advances establish a harmonious utopia whose symbol is a giant statue of Hiawatha on the peak of Mont Blanc.[57] Such fantasies recall the poet's *Cities of the Future* (1910–11). There, geometrically designed in glass to resemble a mammoth honeycomb, is a city whose buildings would have hair and whose streets would run with water nymphs, thus 'combining' modern architecture with romanticism.

For a moment the *avant-garde* flourished. In poignant contrast to the social and economic conditions around them, Cubists and Suprematists mounted exhibitions, Tatlin made his model for the Third International. Futurists painted themselves, the trees of the Kremlin and public buildings; dramatic moments from the Revolution, such as the storming of the Winter Palace, were re-enacted as mass-action spectacles involving the Red Army, the Fleet and casts of thousands.[58] But although the Futurist project was in some senses revolutionary, the general public found much of its work hard to follow. They shared the difficulty with many Bolshevik leaders. Nor was conservatism in art peculiar to Bolshevik politicians. Ilya Ehrenburg noted in 1920:

> In their concealed love for the old realists and for traditionalists of the Nekrasov type there is a touching agreement between the Bolsheviks, Mensheviks, Social-Revolutionaries and Anarchists. . . . Soviet newspapers, the state publishing house, perhaps without realising it, are preparing the restoration of the Academy. Their art is old, academic, with only thematic changes. [He added that] in the Moscow School of Art pupils are taught 'political literacy'. Alas, no-one has thought of giving a course on 'artistic literacy' to members of the government.[59]

Bolshevism had no literary policy before the Revolution, but historians have supplied one. In Soviet historiography, the policy is dated from an obscure article by Lenin of 1905.[60] This stress on continuity served the dual purpose of granting later policies the retrospective sanction of a 'Founding Father' while also circumventing awkward questions that could arise from any suggestion that policy was somehow interrupted by the Stalin era. Most Western historians have concurred, though with an opposite intention. They argue that Stalinism simply continued in the literary sphere the lines laid down for it by Lenin in 1905. How valid is this? Can Lenin's article be fairly taken to be the *locus classicus* of later interventionism, or was it simply a response to the special circumstances in which it was written? Quite apart from the difficulties involved in predating what was done in subsequent decades to statements made before the Revolution, and the assumption of basic continuity over three-quarters of a century, there is the problem of status. Did Lenin's article have universal applicability, or was it merely a product of the particular moment in which it appeared?

From what we know of Lenin's literary tastes, assiduously documented in numerous volumes, he fell short of furnishing any doctrine. The mammoth compendia of *Lenin on Literature and Art*[61] are probably as complete a record of Leniniana as will ever be published yet they reveal little more than a busy man with a fair grounding in Western European literature.[62] His statements on the cognitive value of the arts are drawn from the more utilitarian of the nineteenth-century critics, and also demonstrate an unconcealed distaste for experiment and elitism in art. Futurism, for instance, he did not understand, and its antics he abhorred. The absence of precise directives is striking, given Lenin's insistence on so many other matters in fifty-five volumes of *Collected Works*. It might lead us to the conclusion that Lenin had no doctrine of 'literary control'. That, though, is heresy, as witnessed by the response to one Soviet scholar who had the temerity to argue the proposition. An article published in 1956[63] argued that Lenin's article 'On Party Organisation and Party Literature' referred solely to the requirement that Party members should toe the line when writing in Party journals. Its key principle of party-mindedness (*partiinost'*) showed Lenin's determination to maintain unity in the face of new possibilities of expression opened up by the relaxation of Tsarist censorship in 1905. The expression 'Down with non-party writers', often quoted from it, had referred to opponents of the Bolsheviks within the social-democratic movement, Axel'rod, Trotsky, Parvus, Plekhanov and others, and not to non-party writers in general. Hence 'Party literature' meant political, theoretical and publicistic writing, and was to be under Party organisation and adhering to its programme, The rest, Lenin wrote, should be a 'really free and independent literature', serving the proletariat. This revision, however, received a very sharp rebuke from the custodians of cultural orthodoxy[64] and the above interpretation did not reappear in print. Instead, a milder version was put forward which went some way towards the heretical view.

According to the *Literary Encyclopedia*, published in the early 1960s, Lenin's article had a sociology of its own. In periods of 'growing tensions', such as 1905, war, Revolution and, most particularly, the first five-year plan, class considerations were uppermost. At such moments it would be natural for the Party to require all writers to adopt 'openly and consciously' the outlook of a particular class and Party. But in more normal times, in the aftermath of 1905, during the Twenties, and by implication in the Sixties when the new *Encyclopedia* appeared,[65] Lenin's injunction should be applied to Party members alone. His article thus becomes an index of alternating phases in Soviet literary policy, and the uses to which it was subsequently put reflected, rather than determined, what Party leaders of the time thought policy should be. Treated this way the history of the Lenin article seems to fit the course of literary policy quite well. However, almost all of Lenin's writings are replete with anti-intellectualism. When organising his separate Bolshevik faction after the Social Democratic split in 1903, Lenin attacked his opponents in terms such as 'the unstable mentality of the Intellectual', 'bourgeois intellectuals who fight shy of proletarian discipline and organisation', 'the flabbiness and instability of the intellectual . . . bourgeois individualism, spineless whining . . .'[66] At the height of the Civil War, he would complain to Gorky about 'accomplices of the bourgeoisie, lackies of capital who fancy themselves the nation's brain. In fact they are not the brain but the shit'.[67] But such intemperate outpourings could not disguise the practical problem of the reliance of the Bolsheviks upon skills that only the pre-revolutionary intellectuals were able to provide. How could the Revolution secure their services? The failure to articulate any clear view on the subject was part of the puzzling legacy from the 'founding fathers'.

When Lenin sat down to re-examine these inherited texts and prepared the pamphlet that has come down to us as *State and Revolution* (1918) he was able to find little more than the *Communist Manifesto*'s prediction that, 'a small section of the ruling class cuts loose and joins the revolutionary class'. Marx and Engels offered little indication as to ways in which a Revolution could utilise the remainder. In 'Will the Bolsheviks retain State power?' (September 1917) Lenin envisaged their subordination to workers' organisations. But how was this to work in practice? The culture and science of the past was that of the bourgeoisie: the proletariat had still to create a culture of its own. Old specialists re-employed by the Revolution, might begin to impose their own terms of reference upon it. There arose, therefore, the danger of contamination. As one Soviet historian put it: 'This form of class struggle was complicated, many-sided and not without its own dialectical contradictions'.[68]

The first authoritative prospectus of Bolshevik policies, the *ABC of Communism* (1919), devoted much space to education, which was given precedence over sections on agriculture and industry, but made no mention of literature beyond a passing reference to the need to reassemble private libraries in public collections.[69] Although written in haste and in crisis – at the height of the Civil War – this omission might seem surprising. The author of the cultural sections was Bukharin, later a prominent advocate of pluralism in literature and the arts. Yet the absence of a firm statement on this subject was not an oversight. It reflected the fact that, like so much in the new state, Soviet policy towards literature would have to be improvised.

In the early years after the Revolution, institutional supervision of the arts was left to the government through *Narkompros*. The distinction between Party and government was actual. As Commissar,

Lunacharsky always insisted that while the Party reserved the right to intervene on one side or another in high cultural debates, the state must stay neutral between competing views.[70] The state's cultural functions were conducted by: 'chief administrative organs' oversee-ing higher education, political education and science; an 'academic centre' with powers to direct 'theoretical, scientific and aesthetic work' in an overall policy-making sense but without executive authority, and finally an 'organisational centre' in charge of finance, supply and inter-departmental matters.[71] Those initially employed in government administration of the arts included the Symbolist V. Bryusov, the proletarian writer A. Serafimovich and very briefly Mayakovsky. But the Arts Sector of *Narkompros* did not survive the re-organisation of the whole Commissariat at the end of the Civil War. Lenin had proposed it be retained. He told Lunacharsky that *Narkompros* should 'leave the Arts Sector as a single section, ap-pointing "politicians" from amongst Communist Party members . . . in all leading aspects of this sector'. However, when this idea was put to a Party meeting, only members of the pre-existing sector sup-ported the proposal. They called for a separate Department, or at least a Chief Directorate of the Arts (*Glaviskusstvo*), but no-one else agreed. The meeting merely accepted the need for a *Glavkom* within the 'academic' centre whose functions were left undefined.[72] This body led a shadowy existence until 1928.

The first steps by the Party were preventive. A Decree on the Press was issued three days after the Revolution. The censorship was rapidly reconstituted. It dealt with 'counter-revolutionary activity', a vague but far from vacuous category until the end of Civil War. The statutes were made public the following year.[73] State control of publishing was still limited by private activity, re-established in the early twenties, and the use of Russian publishers abroad, to establish international copyright.[74] Initial policies towards libraries were har-sher. A circular of 1920 ordered the removal of 'anti-artistic and counter-revolutionary literature', including Plato, Kant, Schopen-hauer and V. Soloviev from public collections. 'The section on religion', it added 'must contain only anti-religious books'.[75] Treatment of the non-Bolshevik press was unremitting in its hostility. By the start of the Civil War in mid-1918, all opposition organs had been closed down. Some of these dictatorial measures reflected ideology; others arose from the exigencies of civil war and were justified by reference to them. However, the end of fighting was not accompanied by a dismantling of controls. Indeed, afterwards administrative measures became more formalised and authoritarian policies were still some-times enacted. There was, though, a distinction between those Bol-sheviks who accepted violence as normal, simply as routine, and others who were careful to check this growing habit and to articulate an opposite awareness that in culture, as in many spheres, coercion alone would be unsuccessful. The more sophisticated amongst them were well aware that the employment of too stringent measures against writers and artists was certain to be self-defeating.

In a famous essay, Gorky depicts rural Russia as cruel and insur-rectionist, reduced by lack of rights to 'zoological' individualism and condemned, by ignorance, to superstition.[76] Progressive classes – 'members of the educated stratum', 'producers of the bread of the spirit and workers, creators of the mechanism of urban culture' – were liable to be swallowed up by the backward masses. He feared that 'the whole store of intellectual energy' accumulated during the nineteenth century had been expended on the Revolution, and what remained would quickly be dispersed by the popular mass. The peasantry would quickly grasp the importance of technical improve-ments such as tractors, medicine and electricity but would take a long time to understand Shakespeare, Leonardo or relativity. 'A Garden of Eden cannot be grown in a rotten swamp'.[77] In April 1917 he wrote: "The Revolution has overthrown the monarchy, true! But maybe this has driven the disease deeper down inside the organism.' The malady he meant was not medical but cultural and included the nation's backwardness and bureaucracy, its censored art and re-stricted science policy. The remedy was intellectual: for the Revolu-tion to establish 'such conditions, institutions and organisations' as would rapidly develop the country's intellectual resources.[78] Without them, he predicted Bolshevism would dissolve into the ocean of old Russia 'like a grain of salt cast into a muddy pool'.

Gorky's first reaction to October had been hostile. His newspaper deplored the suppression of Kadet and Menshevik programmes and the arrest of former ministers, and compared Lenin and his followers with 'anarchists and conspirators of the Nechaev type'. He felt confident that the working class would 'come to its senses and remove the Bolshevik regime'.[79] But by the spring of 1918 he considered that the Bolsheviks had come to theirs. He now claimed publicly that the whole intelligentsia is 'able to work in conditions of greater freedom'. There was no evidence for this and his own newspaper was shut down shortly afterwards. Despite this set-back he held to his viewpoint.[80] The reasons for his *volte-face* are complex. It was partly inspired, and publicly explained, by his respect for Lenin, with whom he was reconciled following Fanny Kaplan's assassination attempt. A less honourable motive was his conception of the 'uplifting lie' (*vozvyshayushchii obman*). According to this dubious notion, unpleasant aspects of the present have to be concealed in order to hasten the arrival of a more elevated future. Perhaps most important was his desire to close the widening gaps on the one hand between the old intelligentsia and the Bolsheviks, and on the other between intelligentsia and 'the people'. He cast himself in the role of intermediary between the bearers of the old culture and the new regime.

During 'War Communism' (1918–20) Gorky became 'unofficial minister of culture'. He sought to alleviate the terrible privations of writers and artists by creating institutions and establishments that provided them with employment and housing.[81] One of his most important initiatives was a publishing venture formally instituted by *Narkompros* on 4 September 1918. This was a vast project to translate the classics of World Literature into Russian, each with annotation, illustrations and an introductory essay. Gorky envisaged a 'basic library' of 1,500 titles and a more 'popular' collection of 3,000–5,000 volumes. The editorial staff was to consist of 150 textual scholars and a team of 200 translators. The eventual output was more modest: two volumes appeared in the first nine months and a total of 59 by 1921.[82] For once, though, the official explanation – shortage of paper – did carry conviction. Gorky's other practical measures included the accommodation of writers in a House of Arts officially opened on Nevsky Prospekt in December 1919. So, too, was a House for Scholars brought into existence, and dining facilities provided by the Petrograd Union of Writers (founded in March 1918) chaired by Sologub with Gorky, Gumilev and Blok as prominent members. It lasted for a little over a year.[83] Undoubtedly, Gorky's initiatives saved many writers and artists from starvation.

In the spring of 1921, Lunacharsky sent the Politburo a request that Blok and Sologub be allowed to travel abroad for health reasons. The Politburo refused this petition. Lunacharsky responded with an impassioned protest, questioning the Politburo's judgement. The decision was reversed, but Blok had died in the interim.[84] A second blow soon struck the literary intelligentsia. In August 1921, Gumilev was arrested in Petrograd. Neither the collective pressures of an *ad hoc* commission, chaired by President of the Academy of Sciences, nor individual efforts, such as those of Pasternak who toured the prisons, were able to ascertain the charges. The press reported on 1

September that he had been shot together with sixty-one other 'monarchists' in connection with the 'Tagantsev conspiracy', evidence for which has never been revealed.[85] Gorky, who had intervened unavailingly in both cases, went abroad shortly afterwards. He remained there throughout the next – NEP – period.

2 NEP in Literature

> Here is work for whole decades . . . it cannot be carried out at the tempo, with the speed and in the conditions under which we carried out our military work.
>
> Lenin, 1922.

Origins of the New Economic Policy (NEP) lay in the society which confronted Bolshevism following its victory in the Civil War and the prospects that its leaders saw before them at this point. Schooled to see politics as the product of social forces, they expected social analysis to provide the key to the future of Russia and also – no lesser matter in those early years – to enable them to gauge the chances of their own political survival. But the classes which presented themselves were very different from the ones that theory had taught them to expect. Instead of taking power at the head of a strong industrial proletariat, as Marxism demanded, the Party inherited a ruined, largely peasant country. Other strata were absent, dispersed or, after seven years of world war, revolution and civil war, simply destroyed. As Moshe Lewin has pointed out, the Bolsheviks had always known that they might rule one day, but none had anticipated that they would do so in social isolation.[1] And Lenin quickly saw that in the absence of an advanced working class, a policy of immediate compromise with ideologically unreliable elements – the peasantry, small traders and intelligentsia groupings – was the indispensable order of the day. The last link was vital. First in the military, then in science and medicine and finally as the introduction of NEP deepened in education, literature and the arts, members of the old intelligentsia were encouraged to resume their former occupations.

Lenin's explanation for this *volte-face*, set out in his last articles ('On Cooperation' and others),[2] amounted to a call for collaboration between classes. For him this was perhaps merely an essential prelude to the final, violent, transformation of society into socialism. But as the twenties proceeded, that rider to his theoretical 'testament' receded and the possibility of an entirely peaceful transition came to the fore. These Leninist ideas, originally just a rationalisation for tactical surrenders, were elevated by other leaders to permanent status within the Party programme.[3] Such an extension could be legitimised by reference to Lenin's last writings where he argued that

21

'we are compelled to recognise a radical change in our whole view of socialism. Formerly we placed the emphasis on political struggle . . . now the stress must be shifted to peaceful organisational and cultural work'.[4] However, so radical a retreat from revolutionary commitment could not fail to bewilder some party leaders and many more in the rank-and-file. This section of opinion found it hard to see how Soviet Russia could ever reach a socialist millennium through a policy of permanent cooperation with 'bourgeois specialists'.[5] They continued to hold reservations about the compromise and the society which expediency was starting to engender. From its outset, therefore, NEP was controversial.

The starting-point of NEP in literature was the acceptance of heterodoxy amongst groups and trends. Under 'War Communism' pro letarian spokesmen in literature and the arts had advanced their claim to class exclusiveness and dominance. Post-revolutionary Russia, they asserted, contained a dichotomous social structure[6] based upon a clear distinction between the proletariat and the bourgeoisie. It could only be resolved by an antagonistic confrontation of 'two camps' in which the proletariat would prevail. Such a military analogy was naturally appropriate to times of crisis and would be heard again during the first Five Year Plan, but at more normal times, such as NEP, the party leadership took a more differentiated view of the society over which they ruled. Under this conception, the crucial boundaries, though not abandoned, were blurred so that it was difficult to state with certainty where the critical caesura came. This opened up the possibility of third parties, intermediate strata (the equivalent of 'middle' peasants) between the proletariat and the bourgeoisie. Such intermediaries in literature were christened by Trotsky 'fellow travellers' of the revolution:

> A majority of these writers are very young: in their twenties. They have no revolutionary past whatsoever and if they broke away from anything at all it was over trifles. In general their literary and spiritual outlook has been formed by the revolution or at least by that corner of it which caught their attention and they have all accepted the revolution, each in his own way.[7]

Fellow-travelling writers were thus an unstable product of immediate circumstances. A generation which 'came too late to prepare the revolution and too soon to be educated by it', they would not be able to grasp it 'intellectually', in its entirety. They would follow the revolution so far as they pleased but at a moment no-one could predict might break with it and 'change into the train going the other way'.[8] Despite this instability, however, they were to be nurtured, for upon them the future of literature would largely depend.

Trotsky's tolerant attitude towards the fellow-travellers arose partly from his rejection of the possibility of proletarian art. He pointed out that the great art of the past derived from decades of cultural continuity under the patronage of an educated bourgeoisie. 'Proletarian dictatorship', begun in 1917 in Russia, was purely transitional and, he argued, would provide too short a space of time for any specific cultural formation.[9] A future socialist art would not be based on class at all, nor could it be the product of proletarian cultural groupings. The second reason for his wager on the *poputchikè* (fellow-travellers) was more pragmatic. It simply reflected the circumstance that in the first years after the revolution an overwhelming majority of talented writers and artists were fellow-travellers. If art and literature were to continue, therefore, a tolerant policy towards them was unavoidable.

The first controversy to which this policy gave rise concerned the group of 'Serapion Brothers'[10] whose manifesto had been issued in Petrograd in February 1921. It openly opposed all orthodoxy. 'At a period of the greatest regimentation, registration and barracks style regulation, when everyone was given a single cast iron and boring principle, we have decided to gather without principles or chairmen, without elections. We consider that the shape of our future meetings will emerge by itself and we take an oath to remain ever true to the principle of the hermit Serapion'. The hermit was Hoffmann's and the principle was that art should be separated from politics. To repeated questions 'With whom are you? Pro-Communist or against? For the revolution or against it?', members replied 'with the hermit Serapion'. When asked if that meant 'with no-one? A quagmire of intellectual aesthetes? Without ideology, no convictions, an ivory tower?', their manifesto replied

No! Each of us has his own ideology, his own political convictions each paints his hut in his own colour. So it is in life. We stand for the reality of the work of literature whatever its colour. We believe that literary chimeras have a special reality and we do not want utilitarianism. We do not write to propaganda. Art is real, like life itself.[11]

Enlarging on the puzzling final comment, the manifesto declared literature to be 'organic, real and living its own special life'. Literature might reflect the epoch in which it was written, or it might not do so and be none the worse for that. All genres were equally acceptable: traditional realism had no greater merit than adventure stories, fantasies or Jules Verne.

To Trotsky 'such glorying in lack of principle'[12] seemed dangerous idiocy and childishness. No more than any other Marxist critic did Trotsky believe that an artist could avoid a distinct relationship to social life, even if only subconsciously. The Serapion theorist Lunts replied to this 'official critique': 'ideology is only one element of art. The more elements there are the better. I welcome a novel that would integrate and develop original convictions in politics, philosophy or – horrible dictu? – religion'.[13] Calls for 'Bolshevik tendentiousness' were rejected, and one member, Slonimsky, summarised their position as the determination to avoid 'being turned into some kind of society for Serapion Brothers under the Commissariat of Enlightenment (*Narkompros*)'.[14] The early stories of Serapion novelists are either politically non-committal or bipartisan. Characters fight, as had Vsevolod Ivanov, the most prominent Serapion, on both sides in the Civil War.

The principle of heterodoxy in literature was confirmed by an important political initiative in the literary field. A meeting between Lenin, Krupskaya (his wife), Gorky and the old Bolshevik A. K. Voronsky in the Kremlin resolved to re-constitute the traditional 'thick' journal as a Soviet genre.[15] First to appear was *Krasnaya nov'* under the general editorship of Voronsky. No literary group or method was favoured in its pages. Even the terminology 'proletarian' and 'fellow-traveller' was avoided, though the concern for quality tended to favour the latter. However, Voronsky did loosely differentiate between two categories of literary intelligentsia: 'remnants of the old' (A. Tolstoy, Ehrenburg and Gorky – who edited the literary section) and promising new writers (such as Vsevolod Ivanov). A more crucial distinction was drawn between those tolerated as 'contemporary' through their acceptance of the revolution, and those whose negative attitude was thought to render them anachronistic. Yet even this was flexible: Zamyatin's anti-utopian *We* was praised for its 'artistic excellence' despite Voronsky's recognition that its political devotion to 'malicious causes' might prove a damaging influence on younger writers.[16] Only one-fifth of the opening number (in June 1921) was devoted to *belles-lettres*. Voronsky's leading article explained that the editors 'attach great importance to questions of philosophy, physics, biology and other branches of science', and they undertook 'to attract contributions on as broad a basis as possible from representatives of scientific thought'.[17] Other sections covered political economy (Preobrazhensky and Varga), scientific and popular literature (Timiryazev) and 'from the foreign press' (Radek). Both Lenin and Krupskaya contributed to the first issue. A companion 'Journal of Criticism and Bibliography' *Pechat' i revolyutsiya* was launched, under the editorship of Vyacheslav Polonsky.[18] These two editors were principally responsible for the revival of intellectual life in Russia in the early 1920s. Under their auspices, 'Soviet literature' made its appearance.

A predominant theme of this new writing was the Revolution and Civil War. Ivanov's *Partisans* (1920) relates the exploits of guerilla leaders amongst a Siberian population of Khirgiz, Mongolians and Chinese. The characters in the conflict, nomadic peasants, god-searchers or atheists, are portrayed as exotic or cruel creatures rather than as political actors. Another Serapion novel, by Nikitin, describes an encounter between two armoured trains: a white 'Kornilov' and a red 'Bela Kun'. Both sides display their depravity: a white general mutters patriotic prayers in the bathroom while his wife makes love with a cynical young officer; the red commissar indulges himself with his American secretary. Superhuman commissars, a standard subject of the 1930s, are yet present. Progressive Bolsheviks, whom Pil'nyak dubbed 'leather jackets' in his novel *The Naked Year* (1921), are still shown in conflict with the dark and elemental forces of the Russian people. Pil'nyak portrays a running battle between tradition, superstition and commissars whose efforts at enlightenment are often unsuccessful.[19]

Related ideas were expressed abroad by the *Smena Vekh* movement of Russian emigre intellectuals based in Prague, Paris and Berlin[20] which saw the Soviet leadership as patriotic heirs to the Russian national tradition. The October Revolution was treated as a logical outcome of the intelligentsia tradition, with the added advantage that taking power had made those ideals realisable. The movement sought to reconcile Russians abroad to the Soviet regime and thus reconstitute the unity of the intelligentsia that emigration had broken down. NEP was treated as a hopeful sign of moderation, as one put it: of a trend 'from utopias to a healthy spirit'.[21] Smena Vekh encouraged emigres to return home and urged the 'civilised world' to recognise the new regime. But this prospect was not promoted by the wholesale deportation of Soviet citizens, principally of the non-Bolshevik intelligentsia, in 1922.[22]

In the spring of that year the Bolshevik leadership first explored the possibility of bringing 'Soviet writers' into a single association. The task was delegated to a Politburo commission consisting of Voronsky, Meshcheriakov (head of the state publishing house), Lebedev-Polyansky (head of the literary censorship) and Yakovlev of the party's *Agit-prop*.[23] Its report to the Politburo recommended the forming of a loose confederation to include the following:

1.   Older writers, who joined us in the first period of the revolution (Bryusov, Gorodetsky, Gorky)
2.   Proletarian writers, from the Petrograd and Moscow *Proletkul'ts*
3.   Futurists (Mayakovsky, Aseyev and others)
4.   Imaginists (Esenin and others)
5.   Serapion Brothers (V. Ivanov, Nikitin, Tikhonov and others)
6.   A group of hesitants, still politically immature, amongst talented young writers (Pil'nyak, Zoshchenko)
7.   *Smenovekhovtsy* (A. Tolstoy and others).[24]

As this list shows, the Party was already differentiating between a wide range of literary currents, and, proposing to admit a wide variety of them. At the same time, however, it introduced the outlines of political involvement. As can be seen, the groups were ranked in a rough order of political proximity to the Party. Moreover, the report stated that the society, while catholic in membership, should be given a 'secure profile'. In other words, in common with other Soviet institutions at the time, it was to include a ruling 'communist fraction': a procedure which was indeed followed a decade later when the remaining literary groups were brought into a single Writers' Union.

By mid-1922, therefore, the political problems of NEP in literature had received official recognition. Could institutions be devised which, while accepting heterodoxy and providing for differentiation and competition between literary groups and trends, would also give the Party some means of supervising what was going on? Was social and cultural pluralism, now tolerated, likely in the long run to be compatible with the Party's political monopoly, which had been fully established by 1921?[25] Did NEP literature have a transitory character arising from the peculiar circumstances in which the Party found itself following the Civil War or was there a real chance it could settle into some more stable pattern? The answer to these questions depended upon the third aspect of NEP in literature: the principle of the Party's non-intervention. Here, again, the original parameters were laid down by Trotsky.

In a detailed treatment of these issues for *Pravda* in the summers of 1922 and 1923, Trotsky designated three modes of Party intervention. In some fields it was Party policy to intervene directly and 'with authority'. In a second area the Party kept a watchful eye over broad generalities, without making detailed interventions. But in a third sphere, including in Trotsky's view culture, 'the party is not called on to command'. Should it be called on to intervene, the Party should limit its activity simply to 'taking its bearings'. For the policy of non-intervention in culture was predicated on a prescient understanding of the risk that the Party might run in being steadily drawn towards involvement. It could then find itself in the unenviable position of 'one circle struggling with another'[26] – an accurate prediction of the Party's later relationship with the Russian Association of Proletarian Writers (RAPP). Indeed, no sooner had the policy been defined, than its basic assumption was challenge by a new wave of proletarian militancy.

In the course of 1922–3, new factions entered the cultural arena. Amongst these were an Association of Artists of Revolutionary Russia (AKhRR)[27]: a Russian Association of Proletarian Musicians (RAPM), and an offshoot of the All Union Association of Proletarian Writers (VAPP), the new group of proletarian writers *Oktyabr'*.[28] Its leadership included several previously non-affiliated writers: Bezymensky, Libedinsky and Tarasov-Rodionov, and the critic G. Lelevich. They were later joined by the writers Furmanov, Serafimovich and Demyan Bedny, and an ambitious young Party politician just making his debut in literary criticism, Leopold Averbakh.[29] Although four-fifths of its leaders came from families of the pre-revolutionary intelligentsia, *Oktyabr'* pronounced itself 100 per cent proletarian. The manifesto published in their journal *Na postu* ('On Guard') declared that they stood 'on guard over a strong and clear communist ideology in proletarian literature'. Shortly afterwards, they called for the 'hegemony' of proletarian literature over 'all sorts and kinds of bourgeois and petty bourgeois literature'. Directly challenging Voronsky's policy for *Krasnaya nov'*, they declared 'we shall fight those "Manilovs" who attempt to build an aesthetic bridge between the past and the present, using the rotten fabric of the literary creations of fellow-travellers who distort and slander our revolution'.[30] This posed the problem of what official attitude to adopt towards the call for party intervention. In the aftermath Trotsky's original policy started to be supplanted as the Party, though not yet the state, began to adopt a more ambiguous attitude towards involvement.

The state's neutrality was jealously guarded by Lunacharsky as Commissar. While the overlap of state and party functions could in principle produce a difficult position, whereby a government official might (in that capacity) oppose policies which party discipline obliged him to accept, Lunacharsky was cheerfully aware of the dilemma. Members of the government, he wrote, however much they might personally favour proletarian and communist groups in literature and art (as he evidently did) could not allow themselves as officials 'any trace of discrimination' against those groups that were neither.[31] Nor would he tolerate any form of 'official opposition' to his policy from within *Narkompros*. When the head of the theatrical censorship (*Glavrepertkom*), Arvid Pel'she, proposed that *Narkompros* adopt a more discriminatory policy in favour of proletarian art, Lunacharsky sharply reminded him that *Glavrepertkom* was a subordinate department within his Commissariat and that its very existence was precarious since Zinoviev had recently placed a motion for its abolition before the Central Committee.[32]

While the government thus remained aloof, lower echelons of the party apparatus edged towards involvement. On *Agiprop*'s prompting, three proletarian literary groups amalgamated to form a new Moscow Association of Proletarian Writers (MAPP).[33] A further proletarian group, *Kuznitsa*, was reprimanded by *Agiprop* for continuing to ignore its instructions to enter MAPP.[34] Then 'with the approval of the press section of the Central Committee' MAPP called a congress of local branches from Leningrad, Rostov-on-Don, Kharkov, Kiev and other cities. The meeting was raised to all-union status and the label VAPP revived for the purpose.[35] A mass membership began to be recruited, mostly from young factory workers. In a memo to the Central Committee, the *Na postu* group advocated the use of 'literary cohorts' to enforce party policy, pointing out that 'the Central Committee already has such detachments in the organisation of proletarian writers. They are communist, disciplined and creatively growing'.[36] Faced with such insistence party leaders could no longer avoid involvement. In December 1923 the Central Committee press section agreed to convene a meeting of party writers, at which the proletarians would put their case. Before this could be held, however, the political arena was transformed by Lenin's death.

Though long anticipated on medical grounds, Lenin's departure was nonetheless a psychological shock to the Bolshevik party. His successors held a heated debate about the putative canonisation of their late leader. Stalin proposed to embalm the deceased and urged upon reluctant colleagues that 'Lenin is Russian and ought to be buried in accordance with that fact'.[37] He emphasised the benefits that would accrue to the party by tacitly endorsing the orthodox tradition that incorruptible remains were proof of sanctity. An alternative secular religion, first suggested by Trotsky in his writings on the culture of everyday life,[38] began to be constructed around the dead Lenin. The propagation of Lenin was set in motion rather (as Pasternak remarked in another context) like the propagation of potatoes under Catherine the Great. A huge industry of Leniniana started to saturate the public mind with an idealised image of the founding father.[39] His ideas began to be codified into 'Leninism', a simplified digest of often disparate utterances brought together to provide party education and justification for current policies.

Lenin's literary legacy was also re-examined. Ivan Maisky, editor of the Leningrad journal *Zvezda*, drew attention to the article 'On Party Organisation and Party Literature' of 1905 and announced it favoured proletarian culture.[40] Lenin had, it is true, distinguished in that article between the free and proletarian literature of the future, which would be socialist, with the present 'fettered' literature of the bourgeoisie. Lenin meant that writers could not be free under the free market. But Maisky's attempt to construe this as support for the *Oktyabr'* group was quite fantastic. Bukharin dismissed the claim out of hand[41] and an authoritative series of articles on 'Lenin and Literature' by Vyacheslav Polonsky disproved it in detail.[42] While conceding that Lenin had subscribed to a Marxian sociology of knowledge, according to which all writers and critics were class-bound and would remain so until the classless socialist society of the future, Polonsky showed that Lenin's article had referred to political, theoretical and popular writing in the party and not to *belles-lettres* with which it was deliberately juxtaposed. Indeed Lenin had called for a *belles-lettres* that was 'really free and independent'.

A second part of Lenin's scant legacy on literature, his rebuff to *Proletkul't*, was also scrutinised in the light of subsequent developments. The *Proletkul'ts* were proletarian cultural and educational organisations which sprang up in the summer of 1917. They eventually gathered some 80,000 potential artists of the working class into literary clubs, theatrical and musical studies, mostly in Petrograd and Moscow. According to their leader, Bogdanov, art was an expression of labour in its most developed and complex form, combining physical with intellectual work, and the most advanced technology.[43] The function of art, he taught, was thus to organise the social experience of labour in all its aspects and promote such qualities as the spirit of collectivism, hatred of exploitation, revolutionary struggle and proletarian internationalism. Just as the political aspirations of the working class were embodied in the Bolshevik party and its economic aspirations organised by trade unions, the *Proletkul't* was to be the institution through which the proletariat developed culture. The three spheres had to be autonomous. In particular, the *Proletkul't* should be separated from the Bolshevik party which, he implied, was rather less ideologically advanced since it contained and relied upon non-proletarians. To the call for subordination to the Bolshevik party, the main *Proletkul't* journal replied that this would make proletarian culture submit to representatives of peasants, cossacks and the petty bourgeoisie, offending the dignity of the working class and denying its right to cultural self-determination.[44]

Lenin had looked askance at this audacious experiment. Some of his suspicions stemmed from his pre-war philosophical dispute with Bogdanov, an old antagonist from the Capri school, but there were also more immediate considerations. Above all, Lenin rejected Bogdanov's contention that the proletariat could rapidly create a culture of its own. He told the Third Congress of Komsomol in October 1920 that proletarian culture could not be 'clutched out of thin air; it is not an invention of those who call themselves experts in proletarian culture. That is all nonsense'. Although the proletariat had long been preparing for and had now taken the political leadership of the country, its assumption of cultural leadership would only be possible after the proletariat had assimilated the lessons and inheritance of the past. 'Proletarian culture must be the logical development of the store of knowledge mankind has accumulated under the yoke of capitalist "landowner and bureaucratic society"'.[45] The proletariat had to master the inherited culture before proceeding to create a new one of its own. To argue for immediate proletarian exclusiveness was to be guilty of *komchvanstvo*: a conceited attitude to what communism in culture had already created. Lenin's famous 'Letter to the *Proletkul't*', issued in the name of the Central Committee on 1 December 1920, put paid to its separatist aspirations.[46] Thereafter, its studios were allowed to operate only under license from *Narkompros* and its theatres were transferred to the trade union organisation, itself, by now, subordinated to the state.[47] In his rebuff Lenin had expressed, with customary frankness, the dependence of the revolution upon the old intelligentsia. In the past, he had sometimes recognised that the proletariat lacked experience in 'the practical implementation of its dictatorship' and in the 'techniques of administration'. Now, in power, he knew the problems were even more fundamental. The proletarian party aspired to reorganise the entire economic and cultural life of the whole country on new scientific bases, yet it still lacked the elementary knowledge and ability with which to do so. It was, therefore, imperative for Bolshevism to win over the hostile intelligentsia at least to positive neutrality, and better still to active support of the new regime. The militancy of *Proletkul't* could do nothing to assist this process, and was accordingly restricted.

Despite this clear injunction, Lunacharsky declared in 1924 that while Lenin had feared *Proletkul't* as a potential source of 'philosophical, scientific and ultimately political deviation', he had not opposed its cultural principles. Lunacharsky thus disagreed with Trotsky, whose rejection of proletarian culture was, together with many of his other ideas, already coming to be considered heretical.[48] He suggested instead that Lenin's prime concern was to bring the activity of proletarian groups in literature and art, at least nominally, under the control of the party.[49] A new political combination was in the making. Rejection of Trotsky by the party and revision of Lenin by Lunacharsky, looked favourable to a proletarian cultural hegemony.

This prospect was sufficiently alarming to non-party writers to inspire a collective letter to the Press Department of the Central Committee. Its tactful preamble drew attention to the forthcoming conference on literary policy and expressed the belief that 'the course of modern Russian literature and consequently our course is tied to the course of pre-revolutionary Soviet Russia'. Yet, while literature had to reflect 'that new life which surrounds us, in which we live and work' the preservation of individuality was vital. The twin values of literature were talent and contemporaneity. The letter protested against 'groundless attacks on us. The tone of journals such as *Na postu* and those critics claiming to speak for the communist party as a whole is deliberately distorted and mendacious. We must point out that such an attitude is worthy neither of literature nor of revolution.'[50] The signatories included Mandelstam and Esenin, the

Serapions Vsevolod Ivanov and Nikitin, Pil'nyak, Zoshchenko and Alexei Tolstoy.

The debate opened in the Press Department on 8 May 1924. Voronsky spoke on behalf of the *status quo*. Current policies, under which a considerable and impressive literature had emerged, should be preserved. No group had obtained a monopoly of wisdom on literary questions, nor was it desirable that any one should do so. For art, like science, has its own laws which could not be laid down by party regulation. The party's policy should be to grant all literary tendencies, except counter-revolutionary ones, 'complete freedom'.[51] Replying for the proletarians, I. Vardin claimed that such a *laissez-faire* policy gave no guidance to editors of state publishing houses and journals, or to the staff and students of higher educational institutions such as workers' faculties. Formulation of a definite party line was essential to avoid confusion. Voronsky's failure to provide one proved he was 'not a Bolshevik critic' and lacked 'a Marxist approach to literary investigation'. He reminded one of a 'traditional *intelligent*: a critic from Belinsky's time'. Rather more damaging than this comparison was Vardin's claim that Voronsky's attitude toward the proletariat echoed that of the intelligentsia as a whole: 'ebbing, worn out, sceptical'. Still more seriously he implied that it mirrored Trotsky's negative attitude towards the building of socialism in one country.[52]

Trotsky retorted that Vardin's speech, and the *Na postu* journal, were monstrously arrogant in tone and miniscule in understanding. Vardin had tried to mask his total ignorance of Marxism behind insults, insinuation and 'juggling quotations'.[53] His grasp of art as a specific form of human endeavour was equally wanting. Trotsky restated his view that the creation of high culture was a lengthy process. During the transition to socialism, a relatively short period of perhaps fifty years, it would be far better to master the inherited classics than to impoverish and retard the socialist future by their iconoclastic overthrow. Besides, the future society would be classless, hence any attempt to create a specifically 'proletarian' culture was time-wasting and futile.

None of the leaders present spoke in favour of the proletarians, but this did not mean that anyone was eager to agree with Trotsky. Lunacharsky took a middle line. Vardin had erred in believing it possible to draw up a literary policy on the lines of a policy for trade or transport, thus failing to recognise that the artist was a person of special type. Trotsky had erred by denying that proletarian culture was possible. Why, Lunacharsky asked, should a proletarian state be unable to develop a proletarian art?[54] Bukharin offered an ambivalent oration which Vardin later claimed stood 'ninety-nine per cent for the proletarians'. This was an overestimate, though he too made concessions in their direction.[55] The meeting forwarded a non-committal declaration to the forthcoming party congress, which suggested that the party remain neutral on literary questions.[56]

Despite this setback, proletarian pressures continued. At the end of 1924 they obtained their first victory when Voronsky resigned from *Krasnaya nov'*. In a letter to Gorky he simply stated 'I have had to leave. The journal has gone over to the *Napostovtsi*. You know all about them and there is no need for me to elaborate'.[57] Gorky did know. He replied that the *Napostovtsi* were 'anti-revolutionary and anti-cultural' and would destroy the journal.[58] He too resigned, informing the new editor-in-chief, F. F. Raskol'nikov 'I cannot contribute to a journal in which you evidently will play the leading role'.[59] Perhaps as a result of these protests, Voronsky was reinstated. But the proletarians' campaign continued with such intensity that, by early 1925, the Politburo no longer felt able to avoid involvement. A commission was appointed to prepare the first statement of party policy on proletarian literature, which was soon generalised into a statement of the party's literary and artistic policies as a whole.

Formally speaking, the commission consisted of Bukharin, Kamenev, Tomsky, Frunze, Kuibyshev, Andreyev, Lunacharsky and Vareikis (now head of the Press Section of the Central Committee). But at the first session a sub-committee was established of Bukharin, Frunze and Lunacharsky with Vareikis in the chair.[60] The quartet heard evidence from a range of literary groups. Mayakovsky spoke on behalf of the Left Front of Art (LEF).[61] There were representations from the Union of Peasant Writers and from *Proletkul't*. The principal proletarian groups *Kuznitsa* and VAPP both made submissions, as did a number of individual writers and critics.[62] More important than these contributions was a major speech from the Chairman 'on Party policy towards *belles-lettres*': the first from a high official to talk explicitly of intervention. While rejecting both the mechanical transference of the methods of political life into the sphere of art as so 'ardently recommended' by the *Napostovtsi*, and Vardin's proposal that the party should establish a 'Bolshevik fraction' (composed of VAPP) in literature, on the grounds that such organisational 'monism' was a 'dangerous bureaucratic utopia' liable to ruin the genre, he also stated that the Party could no longer stand aside. It had already secured 'nine-tenths of the leadership of litera- ture' through editorial policy, party criticism, 'through the press monopoly of the working class' and censorship. The Party should support the proletarian writers materially and morally, to secure the rest.[63]

Some of the implications for the fellow-travellers were discussed by Lunacharsky at a subsequent session. Rather than treating them as a single entity, he proposed internal differentiation. Although his own account was largely analytical,[64] distinguishing such categories as the Serapions, the *LEFovtsi* and the *Smenovekhovtsi*, this provided a new tactic that the proletarian critics would be able to use more polemically later on. Bukharin, however, modified his earlier stance. While still accepting the 'possibility of proletarian culture' (a blow at Trotsky) he also spoke in favour of cultural diversity: 'let there be one thousand organisations or two thousand, let there be alongside MAPP and VAPP as many groups and organisations as you please'.[65]

The Commission's draft findings were reported to the Politburo on 18 June 1925. Trotsky protested and submitted a counter-- memorandum,[66] but Bukharin and Lunacharsky, together with a member of VAPP, Lelevich, were designated to edit the final resolu- tion. Far from enshrining neutrality, as sometimes suggested, their text makes much more sense when interpreted as a step towards intervention. According to Lunacharsky's notes taken during the work of the commission, but not published until the 1960s,[67] it contained two main principles. The first task of the party in the literary sphere was 'development of proletarian literature and critic- ism'. Proletarian hegemony was admissible, but should be achieved by 'peaceful means'. Second, proletarian writers must maintain 'care- ful relations' with the fellow-travellers.[68] Thus the resolution did not outlaw the proletarian cause but only certain of its methods.

NEP permitted considerable freedom to Russia's brilliant elites, which led the world in many areas of intellectual endeavour. Through their pioneering work, new disciplines appeared: developmental economics, peasant studies, the sociology of law, and new branches of educational psychology.[69] Institutes such as the Communist Academy and its numerous publications[70] built up a body of original thought whose implications are not yet exhausted in our day. Leo- nard Schapiro once called this 'the golden age of Marxist thought in the USSR'.[71] Cultural experiment was equally exuberant – constructivism, suprematism, utopian architecture and innovative theatre[72] – offering an artistic counterpart to the political revolution. But the position of the intelligentsia as a whole was uncertain. On the one hand, it was officially encouraged as an essential agency on the path to socialism. In the short or medium run, the intelligentsia was regarded as a necessary 'bearer of culture' while the remainder of society attained its level of skill and education. On the other hand, the party held over it the threat, implicit at first, but becoming more overt as the decade proceeded, of eventual dispossession. The length of their reprieve could not be predicted, but perhaps the non-Party intelligentsia was already living on borrowed time and incurring a fatal debt to be called in once the party had used them to train their more reliable replacements? This predicament provided a rich source of literary inspiration.

A major theme of the 1920s was the new social order's impact upon ordinary individuals, often 'old intellectuals' who try to adjust to unfamiliar surroundings. The hero of Fedin's *Cities and Years* (1924)[73] is forced to choose between two moralities: the traditional, represented by the debt owed to a German count who had helped him escape from prison during the World War; and the new, found in his political duty to denounce the same man who is now a counter-revolutionary. As a member of the Russian intelligentsia, he selects the former and is condemned to death by a loyal communist, once his closest friend. Though overly reliant on coincidences, and seemingly banal in its political message, Fedin's novel manages to suggest that, on closer inspection, the choices to be made are not so simple. The novels of Leonov seem equally authentic. They investigate the changes recently brought about by 'revolutionary history' well before these had been codified into an 'authorised' version. *The End of a Petty Man* (1924) describes the efforts of an old professor to finish a definitive catalogue of mesozoic fossils in the starving Petrograd of 1919. While realising that his own undertaking is irrelevant to the new world, he also doubts the ability of the revolution to create a new culture. The novel concludes with a Dostoyevskian dialogue between the old *intelligent* and a demonic double, following which he destroys the manuscript and prepares for death. Unlike the tendentious prose of the later 1930s, such conflicts over cultural or moral discontinuities seem genuine and their resolution causes real torment, accurately reflecting dilemmas faced by the intelligentsia as a whole.

A second feature of novels during NEP is their treatment of the peasantry. There is little effort to disguise the negative potential of the 'awkward class'. Leonov's *The Badgers* describes peasant partisans – mostly deserters from the Red Army – who have burrowed their way into a wooded hideout from whence to attack Bolshevik food requisitioning vans. Using a literary device typical of the period, the author makes the opposing leaders brothers. What distinguishes Leonov, however, is his neutrality between the contesting parties. The decisive battle is left unfought. Instead, the brothers discuss the separate paths they have chosen: peasant instincts versus rational communism. Leonov's own attitude might be surmised from seemingly incidental passages, such as the anti-utopian tale, related by a badger, of King Kalaphat who tries, through collective labour and foreign conquest, to build a tower up to the sky. But he cannot climb it: for every step mounted, the tower sinks further into the ground. This recalled Pil'nyak's suggestion that the party's victory in the countryside was by no certain. The revolution could peter out amidst the vast spaces of rural Russia. Although Bolshevism had come to stay, its final content remained undetermined: the question 'who (beats) whom?' had not yet been decided.

The third element of NEP in literature is its undercurrent of social criticism, often none too hidden. NEP society had its seamy side and spawned a lively literature of little men. Swindlers and racketeers, profiteers and speculators, hoarders, tax evaders and tricksters are presented in a vast rogues' gallery by Grin's *Golden Chain* (1925); Kaverin's *End of the Gang* (1926); V. Katayev's *Embezzlers* (1927); Leonov's *Thief* (1927) and *The Twelve Chairs* (1928) by Ilf and Petrov. In Leonov's story, a Red Army instructor and former revolutionary turns criminal. The author blames his downfall on NEP society rather than on the individual thief who, for all his apparent degeneracy, remains loyal to the ideals of the revolution now, in his view, betrayed. This came under immediate criticism, followed by a complete ban on the book in 1936.[74] Sharper still was Zabolotsky's *The Scrolls*, written between 1926 and 1928. Its characters, in certain ways reminiscent of Blok's poem, are the whores and beggars of the Leningrad demi-monde. A typical setting is the low tavern 'the bottle paradise' – where 'people fell downstairs cracking their cardboard shirts' and in the text slang and folk jingles abound. This was regarded as overtly anti-NEP and the whole edition was seized in 1929.[75] Of this new fiction, none could match Isaac Babel's magnificent creation: Benya Krik, king of the Odessan criminal underworld. In the first tale, Krik forestalls a police raid, timed to coincide with his sister's wedding feast, by setting fire to the police station. 'How it was done in Odessa' shows Krik's first assignment: a holdup which goes wrong and results in the accidental death of a bystander. Krik makes a spectacular appearance at the funeral, in a car whose wheels cast thunderbolts and plays 'laugh, clown, laugh' from *Pagliacci* on its horn.

Such histrionic writing contrasts greatly with that of another Odessan, Olesha, whose short novel *Envy* was acclaimed as a masterpiece on its appearance in 1927. Utterly unlike Babel, he wrote not of 'real life in the raw' but of inner emotions expressed through brilliant metaphors.[76] His hero is a hopeless dreamer who attempts to found a 'conspiracy of feelings' against the contemporary world. This character, so counter to the official self-image of the age, anticipates the coming epoch with 'the envy of old age'. He is hopelessly at odds with the revolution and regards its intended future, to be based on a mechanical society, as empty and philistine. From such quixotic individualism it was a small step to despair. Noting this, Communist critics could contrast Olesha's gloomy preoccupation with the private life and inner 'feelings' of his outmoded hero, with the public optimism and iron self-determination of the 'new man', such as the war leader in Fadeyev's *The Rout* (1927).[77] Fellow-travelling writers such as Olesha did help, probably unwittingly, to prepare a context in which individual dissent seemed doomed, and non-conformity irrelevant or merely anachronistic.

Such themes of displacement in the modern world were also prominent in poetry. Esenin felt increasingly outcast, like, as he put it, 'a poor pony in the age of steam'. In *Soviet Russia* (1924) he returned to his native village, where a band of Komsomols descend the hillside 'bawling furiously to the accordian and singing Bedny's agit-verse'. He recognises that 'my poetry is not needed here and I myself am perhaps unwanted too'. Like Olesha's hero, he raged against the cult of modernity, the destruction of the countryside by machinery, and referred favourably to Pugachev and Nestor Makhno, leaders of peasant revolts against the autocratic state. *Homeless Rus'* (1924) bemoaned the waste of vagrant children who might have become great leaders such as Trotsky, Bukharin or Zinoviev (Stalin was not mentioned) or even poets of the stature of Pushkin and Esenin.

In correspondence, Esenin showed acute anxiety about the course of literary politics. He wrote of Voronsky towards the end of 1924 'it will be terribly unpleasant for me if the *Na postu* people swallow him up. It will mean then "beat the drum and open up the shop". It is impossible to write according to a given line. That would bore everyone to tears'.[78] He added that the *Na postu* leader Vardin was 'kind and considerate towards me' and active in literature from the motives of an honest communist: 'the only trouble is he loves communism more than literature'.[79] Towards Voronsky himself, Esenin was cautious: 'we will work together and be friends but bear in mind I know you are a communist. I also favour Soviet power. But I love *Rus'*, in my own manner. I will not allow myself to be muzzled and will not dance to anybody's tune'.[80] Much of his final verse had self-destructive premonitions. One contemporary noted 'he foretold his own end in every theme, cried it out in every line: one merely needed ears to hear him, but we did not hear'.[81] In 1925, one month after a psychiatric clinic had diagnosed 'delirium tremens and hallucinations', Esenin hanged himself from a hotel ceiling. Trotsky ended his emotional obituary in *Pravda* with the rousing phrase 'the poet is dead, long live poetry'.[82] But his poetry fell under a cloud almost immediately, and a wave of suicides led to a campaign against 'Eseninshchina'[83] amongst Soviet youth.

Mandelstam was already regarded as an anachronism. Now aged thirty-two, he was invited to prepare an autobiographical essay on the 'old world', perhaps in the hope of reconciling him to the new. But the commissioning editor rejected his 'Noise of Time' as 'untimely' and his protector Bukharin warned that he would only be allowed to publish translations.[84] While it is sometimes thought that silence descended on Russian writers only in the 1930s, Mandelstam fell silent in 1925. He turned to prose, but an essay on the previous generation of poets served to underline his isolation. Blok alone was found to be a contemporary to 'the marrow of his bones' in the sense that 'his age will perish and be forgotten but he will remain a contemporary of his time in the consciousness of future generations'. Since Blok, he had found himself without 'contemporaries'. Even Akhmatova was sharply derided, in passages the author removed from a later edition of his prose.[85] Not until 1929 did he regain his lucidity. He found Stalin's political victory had cleared the air, ending much of the moral ambiguity of the period which preceded it. He returned to writing poetry after a self-imposed silence of five years.

Akhmatova was also living under some secret injunction. She prepared prose studies of Pushkin which examined his difficulties with the political authorities and especially its censorship.[86] An offer was made to publish a two-volume edition of her poetry with a

preface by the versifier Demyan Bedny but she 'categorically declined this honour'.[87] None of her poetry was printed between 1925
and 1940. As Nadezhda Mandelstam observes 'the state pensioned
her off with a pittance' in her early thirties.[88] In a social or political
crisis, such as a revolution, an intelligentsia is forced back to its
cultural roots. For Akhmatova, these consisted of the parks and
palaces of Tsarskoye Selo, the imperial summer residence where she
had spent her childhood. This regal aspect never left her and became
the subject of constant ridicule. The *Literary Encyclopaedia* of the
late 1920s described her as 'a poetess of the aristocracy' who had 'lost
her role in feudal society without finding it in the capitalist [*sic*]'.[89] *Na
postu* had once attacked her poetry as 'a small and beautiful fragment
of our aristocratic culture . . . The range of emotions open to the
poetess is exceptionally limited. She has responded to the social
upheavals, basically the most important phenomena of our times, in a
feeble and hostile manner'.[90] Mayakovsky anticipated official attitudes quite accurately when he referred to Akhmatova and the
Symbolist Vyacheslav Ivanov as 'literary landmarks, last remnants of
a crumbling order. They will find their place in the pages of histories
of literature, but for us, in our age, they are pointless, pathetic and
comic anachronisms'.[91]

Futurist poetry was itself in crisis. Kruchenykh conceded 'one
often hears questions: why does LEF no longer organise literary
evenings? Why does it not publish its periodical and in general why
does it not roar and fulminate as it used to in 1922/23? Is this not
exhaustion? Decline?' In mitigation he mentioned that 'Mayakovsky
is now engaged in LEFist agitation abroad particularly in America'.[92]
Indeed, Mayakovsky had consciously turned from poetry to political journalism, giving recitals in dozens of cities, reviving what he
called 'the interrupted tradition of troubadours and minstrels'. But
hectic activity could not conceal the loss of vitality amongst the
avant-garde.

The Futurist poets Aseyev and Sel'vinsky, accompanied by Pasternak and Osip Brik, visited Trotsky in March 1926 to complain that
their experimental works were no longer published. Trotsky then
held a meeting with four editors thought likely to be favourable to
such an approach.[93] When, however, the Futurist journal *Novyi LEF*
appeared in January 1927, it received a withering riposte 'LEF or
Bluff?' from one of them, Vyacheslav Polonsky. He declared the
bankruptcy of Futurism: 'When we turn from LEFist proclamations
and promises to its practical achievements, we see that LEF has

nothing new to offer. LEF is frozen, arrested in its development'. Its claims to the leadership of communist culture were derided as 'boundless pretensions and overblown ambitions'. Futurism he declared 'is dead!'. It was 'revolutionary art without anything new to say'.[94] Criticised on all sides, *Novyi LEF* collapsed after seven issues. Mayakovsky abandoned the association shortly afterwards.

In literary criticism, the ground was being laid for a politically unequal contest between Marxism and Formalism. The quarrel had been brewing for some time. Trotsky had recognised Formalism as a pioneering mode of literary criticism with its own technical accomplishments and distinctive field of study. He accepted that art was governed by aesthetic laws, distinct from laws of historical materialism.[95] In 1924, however, Lunacharsky rejected this distinction: 'real art is always ideological'. Formalism, he added, was the 'last refuge of the unreconstructed intelligentsia, looking furtively towards bourgeois Europe'.[96] To such accusations,[97] the Formalist critic Eikhenbaum replied that Formalism and Marxism were separate disciplines. While Marxist sociology examines the mechanisms of social change, Formalist criticism is restricted to the analysis of literature's evolution.[98] Historical materialism, he implied, was of little relevance to literature and literary criticism. His own work made minimal concessions to the Marxist school, interpreting its economic determinism very narrowly and literally in a study of the economics of book publishing in the Pushkin era. Other Formalists, including Jakobson and Tynyanov, evaded sheer empiricism by claiming to discern distinctive 'series' in literary history. These, they argued, could be identified and contrasted with contingent 'series' in other spheres of culture.[99] Tynyanov also turned to historical fiction. Shklovsky's response, however, was rather different.

In *Zoo or Letters Not about Love*, written during his post-revolutionary exile, Shklovsky had symbolically surrendered the 'times' unto the powers that be. On his return to Russia, he seemed to repeat the device and to surrender again. He remarked 'we are not Marxists, but if we should need this utensil . . . we will not eat with our fingers out of spite'.[100] He explained later that he wanted to 'capitulate to the time, not only capitulate but take my troops over to the other side. I wanted to speak with my time, to understand its voice'.[101] His autobiographical *Third Factory* (1926) refers to three schools of the author's life. He had enjoyed freedom in the first, childhood, and in the second, association with the avant-garde group *Opoyaz*. Now, in the 'third factory' of the present day, freedom was lost. Yet 'time cannot be guilty'. It was impossible to maintain that 'the whole company is out of step, one ensign is in step'. He rejected withdrawal into the silence of artistic integrity on the rather questionable grounds that integrity is 'useless if not used'. Usage meant 'nursing one's work and oneself, changing oneself, cultivating one's material, changing once more, cultivating the material, reworking the whole thing and then there will be literature'.[102] The literature to which he referred was now reportage, high journalism or not so high, derived from the ideas of Osip Brik on 'social command' and from literary constructivism. One commentator has argued that Shklovsky's surrender was only ostensible and that between the lines one can find in the *Third Factory* a passionate defence of Formalism.[103] But a contemporary, Kaverin, in his novel *Skandalist* (1929) compared Shklovsky to an acrobat and implies that his adjustment was too hasty and ill-judged.[104]

Voronsky, too, attempted to adjust. He elaborated a new aesthetic system which combined materialist aesthetics with the intuitionism of Freud, in order to demonstrate the interconnection between external reality and the artist's inner and subconscious faculties. He explored ideas of cognition and made much of the 'unveiling' principle of Tolstoy.[105] The nineteenth-century classics were regarded as realistic rather than naturalistic: Soviet writers did not imitate them slavishly but innovatively. They were 'neo-realists', a category broad enough to accommodate Pil'nyak, the Serapions and some proletarian writers of *Kuznitsa*. Voronsky's new system, even if not always argued satisfactorily, served the vital purpose of keeping open a broad mainstream in Soviet literature at a time when this was starting to be narrowed by political exclusiveness. Although outlawed before it could be developed more fully, it may be safely predicted that Voronsky's 'neo-realism', unjustly derided by his proletarian critics as 'Bergsonian idealism', would have permitted a much wider range of writing than later admitted by their own 'psychologism' and socialist realism. But this possibility was precluded by an extraordinary event which greatly embarassed the principal proponents of NEP in literature.

The War Commissar, M. V. Frunze, who had succeeded Trotsky in January 1925, having earlier been considered by Lenin as the replacement for Stalin as General-Secretary, underwent surgery for an ulcer on Politburo instructions. He died on the operating table. No ulcer had been found and medical reports of the cause of death were contradictory. Further uncertainties surrounded visits of Stalin and

Molotov to the hospital.[106] As rumours multiplied, *Novyi Mir* (May 1926) published a story by Pil'nyak which virtually accused Stalin of engineering Frunze's death. Pil'nyak prefaced this bizarre tale by the disingenuous disclaimer that he had hardly known Frunze personally and remained ignorant of the 'real circumstances' of the case. 'Reportage of the death of the people's commissar' was not the purpose of the story. Yet there followed a tale of compelling detail: even the time of year (the first snowfall) coincided with the season of Frunze's demise. To make matters plainer still, the operation is ordered by the bureaucratic Number One of a ruling troika with many of Stalin's characteristics: a face 'lost in the shadows', taciturn, ominous and insomniac. The whole issue was hurriedly withdrawn. Subscribers received a substitute in which the Pil'nyak story was replaced by another of identical length from a certain A. Sytin. A note from the editor Vyacheslav Polonsky admitted that publication of Pil'nyak's tale had been a 'gross error'.[107]

Pil'nyak's story had been dedicated 'to Voronsky in friendship'. The dedicatee described this, in the next issue, as 'in high degree insulting to me as a communist' and likely to damage his party reputation.[108] Yet the connections were difficult to disavow. Frunze had been his prison comrade before the revolution, a fellow party worker in Ivanovo-Voznesensk, and a life-long friend who used to attend his Moscow literary evenings. Moreover, we know from Gladkov, that Pil'nyak had read his story to Voronsky 'who approved of it'.[109] He indeed recommended it to *Novyi Mir* which, given the current shortage of good material, probably accepted it without further consideration. In the immediate aftermath of publication, Voronsky's own position at *Krasnaya nov'* looked hopeless. As he admitted to Gorky 'my relations with those in high places have become rather strained. I am accused of inspiring Pil'nyak. Admittedly he did learn a little from me but I am not principally to blame'.[110] Gorky tactfully replied 'I cannot understand the story of you and Pil'nyak. What is it about? My own attitude to Pil'nyak is negative, he is a poor writer'.[111] For the moment Voronsky escaped with a reprimand.

However, proletarian critics were soon to press home their advantage. They revived the argument that both Voronsky and Polonsky were neglecting to publish proletarian writers. This familiar complaint seemed to have more substance now that with the appearance of Gladkov's *Cement* (1925), Fadeyev's *The Rout* (1927) and the early stories of Sholokhov there were at last some proletarian writers to neglect. Yet there were counter-arguments. For instance, *Cement* had been first published in *Krasnaya nov'*. Voronsky's journal printed a wide variety of literary tendencies such as LEF (Maya- kovsky, Aseyev), Literary Constructivists (Sel'vinsky) and the Ser- apion Brothers, and certain peasant writers and poets.[112] It could be said that proletarian writers were 'under-represented' largely on account of their poor quality. Voronsky's response to criticism was summed up in a satire 'thunderous applause'[113], a parody of the proletarian 'hero' which did nothing to mollify his opponents.

By the spring of 1927, Voronsky's dismissal was widely anticipated. Gladkov reported to Gorky 'the decision it seems is final'.[114] His position was expected to be taken by a new troika: Kerzhentsev, a former *Proletkul'tist*, and later a major figure in Stalin's cultural policy; the critic Ermilov from *Molodaya gvardiya*; and Gusev, head of the Central Committee Press Department. Gorky wrote to Voronsky:

> If this is true it is most deplorable . . . you have created the best journal possible to have in these difficult conditions . . . I do not think that replacing you by Kerzhentsev will help *Krasnaya nov'*. I know of Kerzhentsev only as the author of political tracts and a book on theatre.[115] His opinions on literature are unknown to me. I have long valued you as the journal's editor-in-chief.[116]

But this time Gorky's testimonial proved unavailing. Voronsky was summoned before a large and hostile meeting at the Press Section of the Central Committee on 18 April. His speech for the defence, 'Mister Britling Drinks his Cup to the Dregs'[117] proved his swan song. The meeting forwarded a resolution to the Central Committee ac- cusing Voronsky of 'irresponsible tactics' and Gusev labelled him a 'Trotskyite' in *Pravda*.[118] His resignation was made public later in the year.

In accounting for Voronsky's dismissal, the charge of Trotskyism is hard to judge. He had signed the 'platform of the 46', an important oppositional document of 1923, reiterating Trotsky's criticism of party policy.[119] Yet his association with Trotsky was no closer than that of his chief accuser, Averbakh, for whose first book Trotsky had provided a preface in the same year.[120] Potentially more serious was the charge that Voronsky shared Trotsky's rejection of 'proletarian culture' and had deliberately denied proletarian writers access to *Krasnaya nov'*. To this Voronsky replied that he had always been willing to publish proletarian writing of quality, such as that of

Furmanov and Gladkov. Probably the most serious charge was that he preferred a non-interventionist cultural policy. With the political decline of Trotsky, this *laissez-faire* view was increasingly difficult to sustain.

Determined to prompt party intervention, Averbakh summoned representatives of proletarian associations in art, cinematography, music and the stage, to a grand meeting on the tenth anniversary of the revolution. There the proletarian writer Kirshon called for a consolidation of proletarian forces: 'Our front – the revolutionary front in art – must be strengthened, must be united'.[121] Lunacharsky was more restrained. He warned against communist conceit and specialist-baiting. The old intelligentsia needed to be attracted by the force of argument rather than by the argument of force. He reminded his audience that the Party's policy was to win over the old intelligentsia by peaceful means.[122] But this notion of NEP was becoming increasingly untenable. The idea that the intelligentsia would 'grow into socialism' was coming to be regarded as tantamount to defeatism.

Following the meeting, Averbakh drove home the argument in an article on 'The Opposition Bloc and Questions of Culture'.[123] He alleged that, besides Trotsky himself, the 'Bloc' consisted of Preobrazhensky, Vaganyan (author of a 'scandalous book *On National Culture*'), Voronsky and various Zinovievites forming a 'left' in VAPP (Lelevich, Vardin). Their common feature was to deny the possibility of a proletarian cultural hegemony. Thus by skilfully combining politics and literature, Averbakh was able to discredit existing policies. For beneath the charges and counter-charges lay a proposition that was hard to deny: that the proponents of NEP in literature lacked a sense of 'class militancy' at a point in Soviet politics when this once more became ascendant.

Following the left's defeat in December 1927, Stalin adopted much of its platform. He espoused rapid industrialisation and central planning, and also drew from this policy certain conclusions that Trotsky had not drawn, above all the necessity of using force against the peasantry.[124] A diversion was created to conceal this abrupt shift. Stalin's previously 'centrist' position, articulated most clearly by Bukharin, was now portrayed as a 'right deviation'.[125] The view that socialism could be reached by evolution, a continuation and deepening of NEP, was dismissed as 'Menshevik'. Such 'capitulationism' began to be contrasted with Stalin's insistence that 'there are no fortresses which Bolshevism cannot storm'. In a frenzied atmosphere not known since the civil war, Stalin exhorted the party leadership and its rank and file to launch a 'third revolution'.[126] Formerly differentiated views of the social structure began to become polarised. All strata of society were forced to take sides. Every area of policy formation was transformed into a contest between 'theirs' and 'ours'. No aspect was neglected: in policy towards literature, too, the 'neutral' notions of NEP began to be replaced by their opposites: the fostering of competition between cultural groups and trends gave way to their gradual elimination; the acceptance of heterodox views on literature and art was gradually withdrawn; government neutrality was steadily supplanted by an active Party policy of intervention in the arts. During this transition, the hitherto separate spheres of literary policy and high politics began to converge. As they did so, a fourth aspect of policy-formation, notably absent during the earlier NEP period, made its appearance: the political intervention in literature 'from above' by Stalin.

Although he had not expressed a public attitude against NEP in literature, Stalin had taken care to cultivate the proletarian cause. In a letter of 1924 he advised the proletarian poet Demyan Bedny to travel south for inspiration: 'if you have not yet seen a forest of oil derricks, then you've seen nothing. I'm sure Baku will provide you with a wealth of material'.[127] Similarly, Gladkov's construction novel *Cement* (1925) received his enthusiastic approval, and according to the author, he personally sanctioned its publication in a mass edition.[128] While unassociated with the Central Committee's Commission on literature of 1925, he did privately receive a delegation of proletarian writers during its deliberations.[129] This established a convention, according to which Stalin withheld public approval from proletarian literary groupings while in private giving its leadership a sympathetic ear. But such high connections could only develop with time. Initially, the focus of proletarian pressures was on lower levels of the Party apparatus.

The Party had no *Kul't-prop* department in the 1920s and the rubric of its sections overseeing culture was rather narrowly defined. The Central Committee's press section, which had held the 1924 'Conversation', normally confined itself to supervising the Party's periodicals and other publications. It did reorganise the proletarian writers' journal *Oktyabr'* in the autumn of 1926, when Serafimovich was appointed general editor to 'strengthen proletarian forces',[130] but no other guidelines were laid down. In 1927, it removed Voronsky from *Krasnaya nov'* as we have seen, appointing one of its own members in his place.[131] This trend toward intervention continued. The scope of *Agit-prop* was similarly extended. Prior to 1927, it had been restricted largely to the supervision of Party schools and preparation of Party cadres through higher education. Thereafter, partly on the prompting of proletarian literary groups, it enlarged its interests and called a conference to discuss the theatre. This heard severe criticism of *Narkompros* from VAPP, from second- ary officials within *Agit-prop* and from the theatrical censorship (*Glavrepertkom*).[132] But Lunacharsky retorted that censorship criteria were already too stringent: '*Repertkom* needs to relax its requirements, the theatres themselves should be responsible for their choice of plays', adding that it was easier for a camel to pass through the eye of a needle than for a play to pass *Glavrepertkom*.[133] His defence of NEP in culture was echoed by the head of *Agit-prop*, Knorin.[134] Although Averbakh claimed that Lunacharsky and Buk- harin were supporters of his '*Napostovtsi*' line, this was an obvious overstatement. Even he admitted that 'it is still too early to talk about a proletarian hegemony'.[135]

A second conference discussed Party policy towards the cinema. It heard an unequivocal call by Krinitsky, now head of *Agit-prop*, for political involvement. 'Cinema of all the arts may not be apolitical': it was a 'weapon of the proletariat in its struggle for hegemony'.[136] Speakers criticised both Party and government officials for their neglect of this genre. While the line laid down for literature in 1925 was still regarded as 'basically applicable' to all the arts, the final resolution condemned the failure to consider the 'peculiarities' of cinematography, and in particular 'the need for proletarian cadres'.[137] Such stress on proletarian exclusiveness, seemingly stronger than the ritual reference to the 1925 resolution, showed the proletarian cause was gaining respectability.

Under these pressures in the Party, Lunacharsky made a belated effort to restore governmental authority. *Narkompros* established a central arts administration (*Glaviskusstvo*).[138] It included depart- ments for literature, theatre and music (headed by P. I. Novitsky) cinema, painting and amateur art and the circus. But, as Sheila Fitzpatrick has pointed out, *Glaviskusstvo* was really a theatrical administration: the other departments led only a shadowy exist- ence.[139] Lunacharsky hoped that this new body would prevent leftist influence from spreading through cultural policy too fast. But it was regarded, from the outset, as 'rightist' and thus provided a new target for the proletarians.

Attacks on the 'right' provided the central focus for a first All-

Union Congress of Proletarian Writers (30 April–8 May 1928) at which the Russian Association of Proletarian Writers (RAPP) was formed. This group, which was to dominate literary politics during the first Five Year Plan, was headed by the critic Averbakh. It consisted principally of ambitious young Party activists, whose chosen sphere just happened to be literature. Only a minority of the leadership were actually writers, two of whom, Fadeyev and Libedinsky, addressed the Congress.[140]

In contrast to the Party's earlier aloofness, Krinitsky, the new head of *Agit-prop*, attended the Congress and delivered the opening address. He expressed regret that over the past three years (evidently since the 1925 Resolution) proletarian writers had 'not yet established their hegemony over Soviet literature'. The first priority for RAPP, he stated, was to bring all proletarian literary groups together. To this end the Congress constituted an All-Union Association of Proletarian Writers (VOAPP) in which RAPP predominated. Yet Krinitsky still insisted that this consolidation of proletarian literary groups and trends must not be detrimental to the fellow-travellers, with whom 'correct and necessary relations' should be maintained.[141] In other words, proletarian hegemony should be obtained by peaceful means. This was reiterated by Lunacharsky. His speech to the Congress, 'On Marxist Criticism', made obeisance to 'class struggle, in the shape of struggle for building a new way of life' (a very weak formulation) and described 'the weapons of art – particularly literature – [as] extremely important at the present time'. But the thrust of his argument was aimed against impermissable police measures and 'what almost amounts to informing'. In particular he condemned 'intemperate accusations against fellow-travellers: anger is not the best guide to criticism and often means that the critic is wrong'.[142] In retrospect, the Congress may be seen as a turning-point in literary politics, leading towards a unitary and exclusive party line. Yet its resolutions echoed the main speakers' insistence upon tolerance.

At this point, however, Stalin emerged as an autonomous political actor. Faced with a shortfall in grain collection, which may well have resulted from the party's own stringent pricing policy,[143] Stalin took to the countryside. Grain was requisitioned at gunpoint from reluctant peasants and the immediate threat of starvation in the towns averted. But this first use of force made further violence inevitable. Any peasantry from which 'surplus' has been forcibly extracted will revert to subsistence farming, making further shortfalls certain. In the Soviet context this meant that the centre would need to escalate its 'extreme measures'. Anticipating this danger, Stalin's colleagues in the Politburo called him to account. After reprimanding him for exceeding his powers, they demanded assurances that there would be no repetition of his 'Urals-Siberian method'.[144] Such guarantees were insincerely given. Stalin declared that

> talk to the effect that we are abolishing NEP, that we are introducing a surplus-appropriation system, de-kulakisation, etc., is counter-revolutionary chatter that must be most vigorously contested. NEP is the basis of our economic policy and will remain so for a long historical period.[145]

He also declared: 'it is stupid to say that NEP is being abolished'.[146] Yet Stalin's rejection of the principles of NEP was soon extended to old specialists, and that in turn was to have profound repercussions for the intelligentsia as a whole.

On 18 May 1928, proceedings began in Moscow against a number of old engineers and specialists from the Shakhty mining region of the Donbas, on charges of industrial sabotage and treachery. Massive publicity was given to this first major 'show trial' of the Stalin era. Presided over by Vyshinsky, it resulted in a guilty verdict and the execution of five defendants.[147] Few now dispute that Stalin fabricated the whole affair. Just as the grain shortfall, in January, was presented as 'the first serious action under NEP of the capitalist elements in the countryside against the Soviet government', so now the Shakhty affair was 'economic counter-revolution plotted by a section of the bourgeois experts, former coal owners now living abroad and from counter-revolutionary, anti-Soviet capitalist organisations in the west'.[148] These traitors 'at home and abroad' were mutually dependent. To defeat them, a new relationship was needed between rulers and the ruled. Soviet leaders, Stalin said, were in danger of losing touch with the masses. This could result in their becoming conceited, considering themselves above criticism or even regarding themselves as infallible. By contrast, Stalin had recently stated 'I have never regarded myself as infallible'.[149] He now called for a vigorous attack on 'shortcomings in our work' by 'hundreds of thousands and millions of Soviet people from below'. Their vigilance could prevent such 'surprises' as the grain shortfall and the Shakhty sabotage. 'The chief task now', he added in May, 'is to start a broad tide of criticism from below'.[150]

A second and more sinister implication of the Shakhty affair was not yet made explicit. 'Bourgeois experts' might all be suspect. Shakhty might prove that NEP itself, based on collaboration with bourgeois specialists, put the revolution in peril. Increased participation 'from below' could mitigate this problem but not resolve it. In the long run, Stalin asserted, 'the working class cannot be the real master of the country if it does not succeed in overcoming its lack of culture, if it does not succeed in creating its own intelligentsia, if it does not master science and learn to administer the economy on a scientific basis. We need hundreds and thousands of new Bolshevik cadres capable of mastering the most diverse branches of knowledge.'[151]

This analysis struck at the heart of NEP. As Rykov, President of *Sovnarkom*, rightly saw, the whole affair was a deliberate challenge to his conduct of the government. To Stalin's socio-political interpretation he counterposed his own: Shakhty was the consequence of economic mismanagement. 'The root of these evils', he stated, 'lies in the general shortcomings of our methods of work as a whole . . . by party, trade union and economic organisations'. He reiterated Lenin's argument that industrialisation could not be carried out without bourgeois specialists, who would therefore need to be attracted by higher wages. 'Wrecking' explained nothing.[152] Tomsky, head of the trade union apparatus, concurred.[153] For the time being, they prevailed in the Politburo.

The Politburo rejected a proposal by Stalin that higher technical education be transferred from *Narkompros* to the Supreme Council of the National Economy (*Vesenkha*). According to the only available report, Rykov's motion obtained two-thirds of the vote, while only one-quarter or fewer of those present voted with Stalin.[154] Rykov successfully argued that the major obstacles to economic progress were technical and cultural backwardness. This could not be eliminated overnight. A major educational advance would take years of careful planning, a point that Lunacharsky had often made as Commissar. But Stalin retorted: 'facts have shown that *Narkompros* has not been able to cope with this task [of educating a new technical intelligentsia]. We have no reason to suppose that *Narkompros*, left to itself and with few ties to production, with its inertness and conservatism, will be able to manage it in the foreseeable future'.[155] Thus cultural policy became a major target of Stalin's growing campaign against the 'right'.

Lessons from Shakhty were spelled out by Krinitsky at a special session of *Agit-prop* (30 May–3 June 1928). He claimed that 'bour-geois elements, supported by remnants and survivals of the influence, traditions and customs of the old society', had mounted an offensive upon the cultural front. They were 'struggling to increase their share, fighting for their own school, their own art, their own theatre and cinema, and trying to use the state apparatus for that purpose'. *Narkompros* under Lunacharsky had failed to recognise the threat. Disarmed by their 'anti-revolutionary, opportunist conception of cultural revolution as a peaceful, classless raising of cultural stan-dards – a conception which does not distinguish between bourgeois and proletarian elements of culture', they had failed to recognise the 'fierce struggle of the proletariat against the class enemy in everyday life, the school, art, science and so on'. In an apparent reference to Bukharin's warning of 1925 against 'inflaming class war in culture',[156] Krinitsky commented 'some comrades may perhaps reproach me: have I not talked too much about the revival of class war?' But was it 'fanning the class war' to rebuff 'the attempts at a bourgeois counter-attack against the triumphant march of the proletariat?'[157] Institu-tional consequences of the assumed negative answer were soon apparent.

Agit-prop brought its various cultural sections together to form a single department 'for agitation, propaganda and the press'. This contained a new section for 'creative literature and the arts'.[158] It then issued a call for greater party intervention in the arts. In theatre, it was necessary to 'oust enemy ideology'; in cinema, the party should 'secure a clear proletarian line'; in literature, there should be 'a more active policy' which differentiated between the fellow-travellers. Their 'left flank' should be attracted towards the proletariat, while all efforts by 'right reactionary writers to revive bourgeois ideology should be smashed'. The basic party task was 'strengthening party influence', through 'greater proletarian control over our organisa-tions' and 'Marxist, communist criticism'.[159] The resolution added that the proletarian literary and artistic associations would find useful allies in the communist schools of higher education: the Institute of Red Professors, the Social Science Research Institutes (RANION), and the Communist Academy. These, too, came to constitute a source of opposition to NEP in literature.

The Communist Academy greatly expanded its cultural activities. It announced a 'first Marxist *Literary Encyclopedia*' to be edited by Lunacharsky, Lebedev-Polyansky (head of *Glavlit*), and three lead-ing critics of the day: Pereverzev, Friche and Nusinov.[160] To help them, the Communist Academy decided to recruit 'a good number, if not all, at least a determinable proportion, of the communists working on literary questions'. 'Unfortunately', a report for 1928–9 added, 'on art we have still not started and have hardly any workers'.[161] However, the sub-section for 'communist criticism' had 'fulfilled various undertakings for the Central Committee' and held joint meetings with Moscow and Leningrad party activists'; with various (unnamed) literary groupings, and with the literary departments of the Institute of Red Professors, RANION and Moscow University. Sub-sections were established for Marxist theatre studies (under Novitsky and Pletnev): materialist linguistics (under Marr): and fine arts. Cinema and music were given separate sub-sections in 1929.[162] In short, a communist cultural policy was being worked out for the first time.

Simultaneously the Institute of Red Professors overcame its 'deviations' of the previous five years. As L. Mekhlis noted afterwards, 'a large group of graduates, comprising an ideological nucleus of Trotskyites' had been expelled from the party.[163] The new intake, however, had become devoted acolytes of Bukharin, around whom had emerged an influential 'school' of pupils.[164] But in May 1928, Stalin boldly entered 'Bukharin's bailiwick', the Institute of Red Professors,[165] and poured scorn on would-be 'liberals' who – as he was to say of Bukharin later on – 'shrank from extreme measures like the Devil from holy water'. Following his address, Stalin was introduced to a number of ambitious young graduates, who were secretly enrolled in 'theory brigades' whose task was to discredit Bukharinite ideas in culture and the social sciences.[166]

Only now did Bukharin feel compelled to intervene. A note to the Politburo in May had declared his disagreement with radical policies towards industrialisation and agriculture, commenting 'if all salvation lies in *kolkhozes*, where are they to obtain their financing and machinery?'[167] A second note, addressed to Stalin personally, deplored policy divisions: 'we have no agreed line or consensus'.[168] At the July plenum of 1928 Bukharin put the issue of grain procurements into a wider perspective. The problem of agriculture was at root political: the failure to stimulate 'cooperative initiative'. The resort to force would create a 'hypercentralised bureaucratic apparatus'. By taking on enormous new responsibilities, the state would become a swollen entity, or as he put it earlier, a 'new Leviathan'.[169] But Stalin responded on 9 July with a new analysis of the state. 'The more we advance, the greater will be the resistance of capitalist elements and the sharper the class struggle'. Far from withering away, therefore, the state would have to be strengthened as socialism approached.[170]

To any orthodox Marxist this theoretical revision was absurd. Meeting Kamenev unexpectedly, Bukharin called it 'idiotic illiteracy'. To the astonishment of his interlocutor, Bukharin proposed a 'bloc' to restore Kamenev and Zinoviev to the Politburo and remove Stalin. He now saw Stalin, his former ally against the left, as a 'Genghis Khan' who would drown the revolution in a sea of blood. Thus Stalin had demanded death sentences for the Shakhty defendants: 'we [that is, Bukharin, Rykov and Tomsky] voted against it' in the Politburo. Concluding this semi-hysterical outburst, Bukharin explained that his telephone was tapped and his movements monitored by the GPU.[171] Indeed they were: Stalin soon learnt of the whole episode and Bukharin's rash breach of party discipline in contacting the 'illegal opposition' provided fresh ammunition against him.

A great debate had now been joined about the future of NEP and therefore, of the Revolution. For about a year from the early summer of 1928, Bukharin and his allies in the Politburo, initially with major supporters in the government and trade union apparatus, the Moscow party and the central press,[172] argued strongly for NEP's continuation. They faithfully reiterated its central principles: conciliation between classes and non-violence towards the peasantry; a balanced and proportionate approach towards industrial development, favouring light industry first in order to supply the peasantry with consumer goods that would make them willing providers of foodstuffs for the towns; and retention of the services of non-party specialists. Accordingly, the latter became Stalin's next target.

On 13 July 1928 he outlined a new policy towards the old intelligentsia. Employment of old experts 'who are not Soviet-minded or not communists, but are willing to cooperate with the Soviet government', was not to be terminated as such. But the number of such old experts who were 'prepared to work hand in hand with the Soviet government' had been steadily reduced. The lesson of Shakhty, Stalin asserted, was that 'we must speed up the formation and training of a new technical intelligentsia'. It was 'absolutely necessary to have new forces of younger experts to succeed them'. These new specialists should be recruited solely from the working class: 'class is class comrades, there is no getting away from it'.[173] This meant the abolition of NEP. The compromise with those educated under the old regime was to be withdrawn, and the positions they had occupied, together with the numerous new posts that would arise from rapid industrial development, were to be filled by proletarian cadres, technically trained through higher education.[174]

In retrospect, therefore, the Shakhty affair was seminal in the moulding of Stalinism. In the aftermath, enormous pressure was put on the government apparatus to abandon its tolerant policy towards 'bourgeois specialists'. Before long, proletarian and party activists found a 'Shakhty' equivalent in culture. Indeed, a convenient victim was readily at hand. A former deputy Commissar of Agriculture, Svidersky, who has been described as a whole-hearted supporter of the classic NEP model, had been appointed to head the Central Arts Administration in *Narkompros*.[175] It did not require great ingenuity to suggest that a committed 'rightist' on the economy, who was unmoved by the supposed threat to party policy from the *kulaks*, had brought with him similar short-sightedness towards *kulak* equivalents – bourgeois specialists – in culture.

Pretexts for their attack were conveniently provided by two theatrical scandals, one of which arose from Svidersky's incautious designation of two plays by 'rightists' as the best of the 1928 season. That this might merely indicate the poverty of the remaining repertoire was overlooked in the ensuing uproar. Svidersky's 'gaffe' was seized upon by his proletarian opponents as evidence for the 'capitulationism' of his line and his kow-towing before bourgeois specialists.[176] Although one of the plays, Zamyatin's *Atilla*, was passed for performance by the local censorship and was supported by Gorky, rehearsals were abruptly cancelled on order of the Central Literary Censorship *Glavlit*.[177] As Zamyatin put it subsequently, in his letter to Stalin, 'the death of my tragedy *Atilla* was a genuine tragedy for me too and made entirely clear the futility of any attempt to alter my situation'.[178]

Svidersky's other favourite was Bulgakov's *Flight*, a Civil War play portraying the decision of several citizens to emigrate rather than remain under Bolshevik rule. At first, the play had powerful support. Vyacheslav Polonsky declared that *Flight* was one of the most talented plays of recent times and that its author should be given the chance to become a Soviet playwright. Svidersky was even more liberal: 'Polonsky stated that the play is not Soviet. If a play is artistically successful, then we as Marxists should treat it as Soviet. We can do without such terms as "Soviet" or "anti-Soviet" plays'. Gorky was warmest of all: 'a wonderful comedy. I read it three times and read it again to A. I. Rykov and other comrades. It is a play with a profound, cleverly concealed satirical content'.[179] As a result of these recommendations rehearsals began, but the play's opponents continued to protest behind the scenes.[180] Lunacharsky strongly supported the play within *Narkompros* and Svidersky defended the play at a meeting of the Art Workers' Association,[181] but the 'left' prevailed. *Komsomol'skaya pravda* accused Bulgakov of patronising the 'white guard' movement so sympathetically depicted in the play.[182] On 24 October, *Pravda* announced that *Glavrepertkom* had banned the play.

Despite this injunction, rehearsals continued. The leaders of RAPP Averbakh and Kirshon responded with outrage. They excoriated the playwright's 'ultra-liberal' defenders at a further meeting of the censorship.[183] The arguments became more heated still over Bulgakov's next play *Crimson Island*, whose main theme is censorship. Its opening night, at the Kamerny Theatre on 11 December, caused a sensation. Proletarian attacks upon Bulgakov redoubled. It was ordered that the play would be banned on 30 January 1929 unless the author was willing to make fundamental changes. Bulgakov refused.[184]

Finally, Stalin intervened. He took the view that *Flight* could be put on if the author agreed to alterations:

> In its present form *Flight* is an anti-soviet phenomenon. However, I have nothing against the staging of *Flight*, if to his eight dreams Bulgakov were to add one or two others, where he depicted the inner social mainsprings of the civil war in the USSR, so that the audience might understand that although these seraphims and all sorts of university lecturers, were 'honest' in their own way, they were ejected from Russia not by the caprice of the Bolsheviks, but because (in spite of their 'honesty') they were sitting on the necks of the people, that, in expelling these 'honest' supporters of exploitation, the Bolsheviks were carrying out the will of the workers and peasants and were therefore acting quite rightly.[185]

In a cautious rebuff to 'left' critics he stated 'of course it is very easy to criticise and demand the banning of non-proletarian literature. But what is easiest must not be considered the best. It is not a matter of banning but of step-by-step ousting of old and new non-proletarian trash from the stage by competing against it, by creating genuine, interesting, artistic Soviet plays capable of replacing it'.[186] As to the factional dispute between differing branches of *Narkompros*, Stalin declared his neutrality. 'It is true that Comrade Svidersky very often commits the most incredible mistakes and distortions. But it is also true that *Glavrepertkom* in its work commits at least as many mistakes, though of an opposite nature. Recall *Crimson Island, Conspiracy of Equals*, and similar trash that for some reason or other is so readily sanctioned for the really bourgeois Kamerny Theatre. As to rumours about "liberalism" let us not talk about that – leave rumours to the gossiping wives of Moscow traders.[187]

A second theatrical scandal concerned Meyerhold. His theatre was greatly in debt: box-office takings had fallen off, largely due to the lack of new repertoire. So serious was the dearth of new plays, that the theatre had offered no new work to mark the tenth anniversary of the revolution. Promised works from Mayakovsky, Erdman and the poet Sel'vinsky, had not materialised.[188] Meyerhold, therefore, decided to cancel the season and in late July 1928 went on holiday to France. A month later his close friend Mikhail Chekhov, artistic director of the second Moscow Art Theatre, emigrated. Dismayed by rumours circulating in Moscow that Meyerhold planned to do likewise, *Komsomol'skaya pravda* published an open letter begging him not to desert his post on the 'cultural front'. The financial plight of his theatre was blamed on Svidersky, whose treatment of Meyerhold was described as shabby and 'rightist'.[189]

In response, *Narkompros* set up a commission to investigate his theatre, with the intention of providing a short-term grant to overcome the crisis. Meyerhold misinterpreted this as a threat of closure. His anguished telegram from Paris, denying any intention to emigrate, was published in *Pravda* on 20 September. A further telegram, to Rykov on 27 September, begged the head of the government to 'halt the action of the liquidation commission. Do not allow the ruin of the theatre and my annihilation as an artist'.[190] Meyerhold now perceived a conspiracy against his theatre, while Lunacharsky and Svidersky more accurately saw a plot to discredit their government. Further confusion was provided by the proletarian playwright Bill'-Belotserkovsky, who entered the debate with an 'ultra-left' statement: 'Frankly speaking in class terms, I welcome the departure of M. Chekhov and Meyerhold abroad. The working class has nothing to lose from this journey. Rather than saying of Chekhov and Meyerhold that they have left, Soviet society might reply conversely that we have left them'. In his view, the parlous state of their theatres showed that the modern stage could not succeed unless it 'held to the course of contemporary spectators and presented the plays of Soviet dramatists'. Only the blind or the reactionary could fail to see this.[191] He implied that all those 'protecting the fellow-travellers' came in this category.

The row continued at the First Plenum of RAPP held in Moscow (1–4 October 1928). While a few speakers attacked Meyerhold from the 'left' and called for his dismissal, leading members of RAPP took his side. Averbakh came straight to the point: 'We must defend such a theatre against Svidersky'.[192] Others derided the 'agronomist', a reference to his previous appointment in agriculture. Support for Meyerhold had already been expressed in *Pravda*.[193] Under such pressures, *Narkompros* backed down. It agreed to pay off the debts incurred by Meyerhold's theatre and to extend its state subsidy for a further two months.[194] No sooner had this expired, than Meyerhold returned home to stage a play long promised by Mayakovsky, *Klop*, with sets by Rodchenko and Shostakovich's score. It opened to huge popular acclaim six weeks later.

Averbakh then launched a bitter personal attack on Bill'-Belotserkovsky, whose article was described as not the voice of the working class but 'wailing of déclassé lumpen elements'. His statement welcoming M. Chekhov and Meyerhold's departure was 'stupid, ignorant repetition of an assertion by the émigré press'. The author was 'objectively a class enemy'.[195] Stung by this rebuke, Bill'-Belotserkovsky and several colleagues protested to Stalin. Stalin reprimanded Averbakh, and that, in turn, led a group of 'communist writers from RAPP' to ask Stalin for clarification. His reply is here published for the first time.

To the Writer- Communists from RAPP:[196]

Dear Comrades,

1. You are displeased that I defended Bill'-Belotserkovsky in conversation with Averbakh, against the attack of *Na litpostu*. I did indeed defend him. I defended him to the extent that the attack on him in *Na litpostu* was incorrect in principle and inadmissible. Let *Na litpostu* seek simpletons where it will – serious readers will never believe that comrade Bill'-Belotserkovsky, author of *The Storm* and *Voices from the Womb*, represents 'déclassé lumpen' elements, that his statement on Meyerhold and Chekhov 'repeats the assertion of the émigré press' and that he is 'objectively (?!) a class enemy'. Criticism must above all be truthful. The whole

trouble is that the criticism of *Na litpostu* was incorrect and unjust in principle.

2.   Was Bill'-Belotserkovsky mistaken in his statement about Meyerhold and M. Chekhov? Yes, he did make some mistakes. On Meyerhold he was more or less correct – not because Meyerhold is a communist (though few amongst communist people are 'worthless'), but because he, that is Meyerhold, as an activist in the theatre, despite certain negative attributes (affectation, eccentricity, unexpected and damaging excursions from real life into the 'classical past'), is undoubtedly part of our Soviet society and cannot be numbered with 'aliens'. But, as is evident from materials appended to your letter, Bill'-Belotserkovsky had admitted his mistakes about Meyerhold two months before criticism of them appeared in *Na litpostu*. As for Chekhov, it must be said that Bill'-Belotserkovsky is right in principle, even though it is rather exaggerated. There can be no doubt that Chekhov went abroad not from love of Russian society and formed his opinions there, from which it does not follow, however, that all of M. Chekhov must be wrong. Can we, on the basis of his extremism, granted that Bill'-Belotserkovsky had already rectified it, classify him as a 'class enemy'? Clearly not. Moreover, to classify him in this way means to admit the worst of all possible extremes. In this way people of the Soviet camp will never be united, but rather scattered and confused, to the delight of 'class enemies'.

3.   'But is it possible that you (namely I) object to the sharp tone?', you ask. No, the question is not of the sharp tone, although this is not without significance. The question is, first, that the critique by *Na litpostu* of Bill'-Belotserkovsky was inadmissible and incorrect in principle (it was correct only in part). Second, that RAPP is evidently unable to construct the literary front, so disposing of its forces on the front as to be certain of winning the battle, and winning the war against 'class enemies'. It is a poor commander who cannot find the proper place on his front for both storm-troopers and the lighter divisions, for cavalry and artillery, for the regular forces and partisans. The commander who does not take into account the particularities of all these diverse parts and uses them *diversely* in the interest of a *single and undivided front* – I ask you: what kind of commander is that? I am afraid that RAPP sometimes seems to me a commander of this sort. Judge for yourselves: your general line is correct; you have strength enough,

since there is a whole quantity of apparatus and publishing facilities at your disposal. As workers you are ingenious and unusual people, willing to lead – more than willing – yet all the forces you dispose of on the front, and the front itself, are so drawn up that instead of harmony there is strident discord, instead of success: shortcomings. You write of 'cautious relations with fellow-travellers', of 'communist re-education of them under comradely conditions'. At the same time, you are ready to annihilate Bill'-Belotserkovsky and a whole group of revolutionary writers over trifles! Where is the logic, the proportion, or the consistency in this? Do you have many such revolutionary dramatists amongst you as Bill'-Belotserkovsky? Take, for instance, a fellow-traveller such as Pil'nyak. It is well-known how skilled this fellow-traveller is at seeing and describing the seamy side of our revolution.[197] Is it not strange that you used the word 'cautious' in relations with such fellow-travellers, but not for Bill'-Belotserkovsky? Is it not strange that in abusing Bill'-Belotserkovsky as a 'class enemy' and defending Meyerhold and Chekhov from him, *Na litpostu* could not find a single word of criticism in its arsenal either for Meyerhold (he needs criticism!) or, especially, for Chekhov? Is this the way to reconstruct the front? Is this the way to dispose of forces on the front? Is this the way to wage war with 'class enemies' in literature? The question is evidently not one of the sharp tone, but one of the leadership of the complex front of Soviet literature. But for the leadership of this front, you, and only you, with your 'Russian Association of Proletarian Writers' are qualified. You forget that to whom much is given, even more is expected of in return. It is comical to complain and whimper: 'they are criticising us'; 'they are baiting us'. Who is to do the criticising and 'scolding' if not you?

4.   Was comrade Kerzhentsev[198] right to come to the defence of Bill'-Belotserkovsky from the attack of *Na litpostu*? Kerzhentsev was right. You stress the formal point: 'The Central Committee has not passed a formal resolution'. But you can be in no doubt that the Central Committee does not support the attempt of *Na litpostu* to annihilate Bill'-Belotserkovsky. What do you think the Central Committee is for? Maybe it is possible to take issue with the Central Committee's view? I advise you, amicably, not to press the matter: it is inappropriate and will certainly fail.

5.   Amongst the questions in your letter is one which for some

reason you do not want to state directly, though it comes through
in every line of your letter. I mean the question of my corresponding with Bill'-Belotserkovsky in person. You seem to think that my
corresponding with him was not accidental, that it marks a change
in my relationship with RAPP. Not true. I wrote to him in response
to a collective request from various revolutionary writers, headed
by him. At the time of writing, I had no inkling of the dispute
between RAPP and *Proletarskii teatr*,[199] nor even of the latter's
separate existence. I will continue to reply to every comrade
directly or indirectly related to our proletarian literature, if I have
time. It is necessary. It is useful. Finally, it is my duty. It seems to
me that your differences with proletarian writers of the Bill'-
Belotserkovsky type do not have, and cannot have, an essential
character. You can and must find a common language with them,
despite certain organisational 'differences'. This can and must be
done because the differences between you are, in the last analysis,
microscopic. Who needs such 'polemics' now, which only amount
to empty bickering? Obviously no-one needs such 'polemics'. As to
my relations with RAPP, they remain as close and friendly as
before. But that is not to say that I will refrain from criticising its
mistakes, as I understand them.

With comradely greetings,

J. Stalin

Despite the final warning, this letter endorsed RAPP's role in
literature. But it urged a reversal of priorities. Instead of quarrelling
amongst themselves, proletarian writers were redirected against the
fellow-travellers. A leading representative, Pil'nyak, had been
singled out as a suitable target. Before the assault on NEP in
literature could be launched in earnest, however, high political
business had still to be done. RAPP could not be openly unleashed[200]
until Stalin's political opponents had been removed from the party
leadership.

In autumn 1928, the Moscow party apparatus, previously a 'right'
stronghold, was won by Stalin.[201] Other party organisations across
the country drew the logical conclusion that further resistance was
futile. Realising how rapidly the 'right' was being out-manoeuvred,
Bukharin responded with an ultimatum. It opened with a call for the
re-establishment of genuinely free discussion between party leaders:

1.   All Politburo members must guarantee that contentious and complex questions of economic policy and policy in general are discussed beforehand, collectively, and with an appropriate degree of tolerance. This particularly applies to Monday meetings of the Politburo.

2.   To ensure by means of a Central Committee directive to all Central Committees of the national republics, oblast', krai and guberniya party organisations that the Central Committee circular 'On Self-criticism' is carried out in full, including that point in the circular which condemns the labelling of deviations and speaks in favour of the comradely character of debate etc.

3.   To publish a critique in *Pravda* of the incorrect methods of conducting the campaign of struggle against the right danger (the mistakes of *Komsomol'skaya pravda*, resolutions of local party organisations published in *Pravda* number 262, etc) or by inserting similar articles in the central party organ. To conduct a decisive struggle against groundless speculation about political disagreements in the Politburo.

4.   To instruct the press through the *Agit-prop* department of the Central Committee that it must not confine itself simply to recording adopted resolutions, but must guarantee observance of the norms mentioned in point 2 above, and guarantee business-like discussions, without attaching labels, of all complex questions of the country's economic, political and cultural life.

5.   In the course of decisive and serious ideological work on overcoming right deviations, and conciliatory attitudes towards them, to cease drawing 'organisational conclusions' in the Moscow party and to stop the hounding of Uglanov and other comrades.

The remainder of the seventeen-point 'ultimatum'[202] showed the extent to which Stalin's power over appointments had depleted the right. Much of its potential support in the cultural sphere had been removed in this way. Sapozhnikov had been sacked from the board of *Revolyutsiya i kul'tura* and dispatched to Voronezh as rector of the university. Bukharin's editorship of *Pravda* was constrained by Stalin's watchdogs (Krumin and Saveliev):[203] Bukharin sought their replacement by two of his supporters (Meshcheriakov and Zaitsev).

For the moment, Stalin proved willing to compromise on minor items in the 'ultimatum' in order to keep Bukharin and his colleagues

Rykov and Tomsky in the Politburo. He thus averted a public split for which the party, and the country as a whole, was unprepared. Thereafter, the great debate about the country's future took place behind closed doors. With hindsight, it is clear that by agreeing to confine discussion to the 'absurdly restricted private forum of the Politburo'[204] Bukharin and his colleagues sealed their fate. Yet they undoubtedly expected at the time that they could win the inner-party argument. This was not inherently implausible: party leaders were not yet obedient appointees of Stalin. The several dozen top oligarchs of the Party were Old Bolsheviks of standing, persons of independent mind.

Addressing the November plenum of 1928, Rykov stated that the main danger to the revolution was Trotskyism, with its exaggerated tempos for industrial development. The right tendency, he stated, 'barely exists'.[205] Bukharin as usual took the argument further and accused the Stalinists of 'an ideological capitulation to Trotskyism'.[206] In an article for *Pravda* on the fifth anniversary of Lenin's death (24 January)[207] and in further statements to the Politburo of 30 January and 9 February, he predicted the shape of Stalinism as a vast and unaccountable bureaucracy, building 'barracks socialism' on the basis of 'military-feudal exploitation of the peasantry'.[208] Yet Stalin weathered the storm. The great majority of the party's top officials, including all those previously neutral, came over to his side. By April 1929, Stalin felt confident enough to inform the Central Committee that the Party had harboured a 'right deviation'.[209] Its rout (*razgrom*) was celebrated at a special party conference.[210]

The reasons for Stalin's victory have been amply discussed in the western literature and may be summarised under three heads. First, of course, was his manipulation of the Party through its apparatus, enabling him to promote supporters, such as delegates to the Congresses which then elected him. It also gave him the power to relegate opponents to insignificant positions, as the Bukharin 'school' discovered during its enforced diaspora of 1928/29.[211] The second reason for his victory was the appeal to 'revolutionary' aspirations that NEP frustrated. Since 1921, the party's policy had been retreat: a mixed economy and private peasantry, compromise between classes, reliance upon 'bourgeois specialists' and a project for socialism that – as Lenin had admitted – would take 'years and years'. The 'great break' of 1929 promised advance at last. The fortress-storming spirit that made the revolution and won the civil war seemed relevant again. For younger party members more than historical re-enactment was involved here. The campaign to collectivise was their own civil war, the one against the peasantry.[212] Finally, there was a more mundane aspect: the career prospects that Stalinism could open up. A vast expansion of state activity would require the recruitment of new cadres in huge numbers. Those upwardly mobile would take for granted the proposition that further promotion depended on utter loyalty to the General-Secretary.

The onset of Stalinism was a turning-point in Soviet intellectual development. A measure of pluralism had been permitted under NEP on the assumption that Marxism would eventually prevail in free debate. This was most passionately believed by Bukharin, an intellectual *par excellence*, the last Old Bolshevik of this type.[213] None has been seen in the Politburo since his day. Long noted as a patron and protector of the non-party intelligentsia, the defeated Bukharin was no longer so easily able to perform this function. This was clear to Mandelstam: 'Until 1928 he would shout "Idiots!" and pick up the phone, but after 1930 he just frowned and said: "we must think whom to approach".'[214] The consequences of his defeat for cultural policy were immediately apparent.

Voronsky had already been arrested in a roundup of 'Trotskyites' in the first days of 1929. He was sentenced to internal exile although its terms do not seem to have been too onerous. One writer who met him there described him, though ill, as in good spirits and 'in love with literature as before'.[215] A few months later, Voronsky renounced his 'Trotskyism' and was restored to the Party. He returned to Moscow as an editor of the state publishing house where, despite private forebodings, 'partly on account of continual reductions in the supply of paper, partly on account of the overwhelming mass of worrisome trifles which one can't avoid', he was still able to publish an autobiography, and some fiction.[216] He began to prepare a critical study of Gogol, which was confiscated at the time of his arrest in 1937.[217]

A second defender of NEP in literature, Vyacheslav Polonsky, was replaced in February 1929.[218] His journal appeared under a new board dominated by the Communist Academy, which also included Kerzhentsev and acknowledged 'greater assistance' from the Institute of Red Professors and from RANION. The transfer of editorial duties was quite gentlemanly, as shown by the correspondence between Polonsky and Friche in archives.[219] This left only Lunacharsky of the senior defendants of NEP in literature. He too appears to have resigned in February 1929, although the circumstances of his departure remain obscure. Only part of his resignation letter has been published, a section dealing with educational discrimination.[220] The maligned 'rightist' Svidersky seems to have resigned with him, although neither change of office was made public until the autumn.

Their protectors gone, attention turned to the fellow-travellers. On 1 April 1929, the RAPP Secretariat deplored the 'strengthening of reactionary elements' within the fellow-travellers' association. Libedinsky perceived a 'process of deformation' amongst them: fellow-travellers now tended to adopt a 'right' posture, or retreat into 'apoliticism'.[221] Averbakh suggested that acceleration of this 'deformation process' was the 'basic task of literary politics'.[222] Taking their cue from Stalin's letter, they singled out Pil'nyak as especially reactionary. According to their resolution he was 'actively recruiting new forces, especially amongst the young', and attempting to undermine RAPP's dominance of the Writers' Federation (FOSP).[223]

In May, Averbakh accused *Literaturnaya gazeta* (the newly established newspaper of the Writers' Federation) of promoting the politics of Pil'nyak.[224] RAPP wrote a memorandum to the Central Committee Secretariat, demanding that the newspaper be reorganised and placed under its own auspices. But this was refused.[225] Until the party struggle against the 'right' had been made public, such attempts to force the literary issues ahead of those in politics were discouraged. For instance, the next issue of *Literaturnaya gazeta* attacked Mandelstam for plagiarism. The author of this accusation, D. Zaslavsky,[226] thus began a long career as literary provocateur which culminated in his infamous attack on Pasternak in 1958. Mandelstam, however, could reply in print that 'publication of intentionally false, incomplete, inaccurate or garbled information, and similar publication of any derogatory unfounded statements in the press is called slander'.[227] A collective letter of defence describing Mandelstam as 'an outstanding poet, one of the most highly qualified of translators, and a literary master craftsman (master of the written word)', was signed by Pasternak, Pil'nyak, Valentin Katayev, Fedin, Olesha, Zoshchenko and Leonov.[228]

A further impediment to proletarian ambitions was Gorky. He had stated earlier 'I am personally not interested in the critics' debate about who is a "proletarian" writer and who is not. Such terminology no longer corresponds to the real position of the working masses of the Soviet Union'.[229] Averbakh replied, with characteristic audacity, that Gorky was not 'one hundred per cent on the side of the proletariat'.[230] *Pravda* then declared that 'we must defend Gorky from such obviously hypocritical and illiterate "criticism"'.[231] Averbakh sent in his resignation to *Agit-prop* and asked to be transferred to other party work. He was posted to Azerbaidjan.[232] Hectic lobbying from other members of the RAPP Secretariat was needed to persuade the Central Committee Secretariat to rescind their decision.[233]

Gorky's first homecoming, in 1928, had been a national festival. Met at the Belorussian Station by high functionaries of party and state, that evening they had been joined by Stalin in the Bolshoi Theatre. There followed a triumphant procession around the country. This included a visit to his birthplace, Nizhni-Novgorod, where he met the local Party Secretary, one Andre Zhdanov, and the local *Agit-prop* Secretary Shcherbakov, later Secretary of the Writers' Union.[234] His second return in 1929 was much less triumphant. His only public appearance was at the Second Congress of Atheists.[235] After a brief visit to Leningrad, where he talked to the writers Libedinsky and Chumandrin and met the Party Secretary Kirov, he was sent south for a long sojourn.[236] In his absence, the literary scene was rapidly transformed.

The change was signalled by Stalin's letter to Feliks Kon.[237] This explained the General-Secretary's decision to contribute the preface to an 'insignificant brochure written by a person unknown in the literary world' as a blow for equality.

> I am decisively against providing prefaces to books and brochures only by literary 'grandees', literary 'big names', *'coryphaei'*[238] etc. I think that it's time we dropped this *aristocratic* habit of promoting only literary 'grandees', whose 'greatness' is holding back young writers, the country's 'unknown and downtrodden literary forces'.[239]

Stalin stated that there were thousands of talented young writers struggling to rise upwards, but whose advancement was being blocked by 'well-known literary names, the bureaucracy and callousness, some of our organisations'.[240] Such charges fitted perfectly with the anti-NEPian assault upon 'bourgeois specialists' and held before rank-and-file writers, or even complete beginners, the chance of rising rapidly in a new establishment.

Few could resist this prospect, but for once Averbakh did not lead the field. The initiative was taken by a certain Kurs, his counterpart and caricature in Siberia. As a Soviet historian points out,[241] in common with all caricatures, Kurs demonstrated many features of the original. Thus, addressing the Siberian *Agit-prop* on 12 August, this local demagogue attacked a number of prominent writers as class enemies. Furthermore his contempt for RAPP appeared to be total: 'I do not know with which ignominious words to describe this leadership'.[242] His journal accused Gorky of defending 'the rightist "Pil'nyakism" in all its manifestations, not only on the literary front'.[243] Although Kurs' own career was cut short (his organisation was the subject of a special Central Committee resolution, and he was expelled from the party)[244] the charges he had made in Siberia were soon reiterated in Moscow. On 21 August, *Pravda* announced the dismissal of Bukharin from Comintern, and three days later the general public was finally informed that Bukharin had headed a 'right deviation' in politics.

The next *Literaturnaya gazeta* declared that Pil'nyak and Zamyatin led a similar 'rightist' tendency in literature. The source of this assertion was Boris Volin, who wrote the original article.[245] He addressed the RAPP Secretariat on the day of publication. From the minutes we can see its intention was to single out two leading fellow-travellers, as a prelude to purging their entire organisation. The proposed technique was 'to split the fellow-travellers' associations, discredit its former leadership, dissolve its literary circles, revise its socio-political programme and wean young members away from older teachers'.[246] Thus the purge would be extended to the whole literary community. As with the later campaigns against Shostakovich and others in 1936, Akhmatova and Zoshchenko in 1946 and Sinyavsky and Daniel' in 1965, an attack on well-known figures was meant to signal a change of policy towards the whole cultural intelligentsia. Denunciation of the famous on trivial or trumped-up charges, was intended to be followed by pressure on their colleagues to join in a swelling chorus of 'public indignation'. In the relatively mild atmosphere of the late 1920s however, there were undercurrents of resistance from the literary community.

Astonishingly, Pil'nyak managed to refute the main charge against him. According to Volin, he had sent his short novel *Mahogany* abroad to avoid the censorship. But Pil'nyak pointed out that this had been done legally, through the normal channel of the Society for Cultural Relations Abroad (VOKS), as was standard practice for a Russian writer to establish international copyright. Moreover, he cited his Berlin publishers' catalogue which stated that they also printed Fedin, Alexei Tolstoy and Kaverin and, most recently, Sholokhov's

Quiet Don. Pil'nyak explained that he had not protested at their publication of *Mahogany* to save embarrassment to these Soviet writers, adding that he had spoken out, immediately, when emigrés tried to use his story 'for anti-Soviet purposes'. They, rather than his publishers, were the 'white guards' of the affair. This detailed rejoinder was published by *Literaturnaya gazeta*,[247] and the point went home. The attack now shifted from the act of publishing abroad to the more sinister charge of the allegedly 'alien' content of the work in question.

RAPP asked how the Moscow fellow-travellers' association could tolerate as chairman Pil'nyak who sent 'anti-Soviet' publications abroad. *Kuznitsa* condemned Pil'nyak's 'political double-dealing', and the Literary Constructivists declared that 'Soviet society' considered the act 'unjustifiable'.[248] *Literaturnaya gazeta* reported that 'the literary community unitedly rejects the anti-Soviet deed of B. Pil'nyak. The union of writers to be reorganised'.[249] Eighty members of the fellow-travellers were expelled on various pretexts including 'hostility to socialist construction', and a further 160 (of a total membership of 570) were removed to a 'translators' union'. A new programme was adopted and by way of summary, the explanatory epithet 'Soviet' was added to the association's name.[250]

The Leningrad campaign was less successful. Zamyatin stood firm and accused his accusers of adopting a procedure unknown to jurisprudence: 'first the guilty verdict, then the investigation'. He demonstrated Volin's charge that he had arranged publication of his novel *We* abroad to be a fabrication.[251] Slander was thus shown to lie at the root of the campaign. In these circumstances, the Leningrad association of fellow-travellers was reluctant to pursue the case and when a conference was called to review Zamyatin's publication, several colleagues came to his defence. One even remarked that despatch of manuscripts abroad was an unavoidable necessity for writers living under censorship.[252] The Moscow press retorted that 'the Leningrad branch of the Union of Writers needs a thorough purge'.[253] This was eventually done, resulting in some sixty-five dismissals. Anticipating this outcome, Zamyatin had resigned, announcing in *Literaturnaya gazeta* 'I cannot remain in an organisation which takes part, even indirectly, in the persecution of a fellow member'.[254]

Conclusions were drawn by *Literaturnaya gazeta*. An unsigned editorial stated that the campaign posed 'concretely rather than academically' the questions of how authors should write and how they should behave at home and abroad. It had demonstrated that 'the concept of a Soviet writer is social and not geographical. Only he who binds himself and his work to socialist construction – the present period in which the proletariat attacks the remnants of capitalism and encounters frenzied resistance from class enemies of socialism – can call himself a Soviet writer'.[255] But Gorky, who had returned to Moscow on 12 September, demurred. He wrote that the punishment of Pil'nyak was 'far too severe'. The whole campaign reminded him of the lynching of pickpockets in 1917. He saw in it an indication of mob rule: the envy of little men who 'throw themselves onto someone who has made a mistake in order to take his place'. It was evidence of a foolish inclination to 'raise people into high places only to cast them down into the mud'.[256] This was a remarkable prophecy of cultural policy under Stalinism.

3 Proletarian Hegemony

'Ally or Enemy?'

RAPP, 1931

A third revolution now began. Millions of peasant households were driven into collective farms; building sites began to cover the vast countryside with towns and factories; and the repressive organs stretched outwards in a growing *GULag* empire of concentration camps, forced labour colonies and transit prisons. Simultaneously, the social structure was transformed. Peasants became workers, migrating to the towns in search of work or food, until halted by the restoration of internal passports in 1933. Workers poured into offices, swelling the ranks of lower administration, and into the Party, whose membership had trebled before recruitment was stopped in January 1933. The upper echelons expanded mightily, coming to form an amorphous and privileged elite, misleadingly entitled the 'Soviet intelligentsia'. This included in its ranks the 'old' or 'bourgeois' intelligentsia, educated before the Revolution; 'new' or 'Red' official-dom trained during the 1920s; and a third element, newer still, of 'proletarian' cohorts, seeking to wrest intellectual leadership from the other two.

The proletarians called this striving for 'hegemony'.[1] They challenged the older intelligentsia head-on. Adopting military methods and terminology – such as 'light cavalry' and 'raiding parties' – from 'War Communism', they started to transform all areas of Soviet life from grain procurement[2] to the social sciences, into struggle with 'class enemies' on the particular front. Little was exempt from their iconoclastic interventions. Traditional schooling was supposed to be swept away in favour of the 'brigade method' and pupil self-management.[3] Academic requirements for higher education were similarly rejected in favour of class quotas, making entrance examinations irrelevant. Workers' faculties were greatly expanded amidst the virtual suspension of other university teaching, and their products pushed up by the *vydvizhenchestvo*[4] system of promoting workers to responsible positions. Social legislation was proposed to supplant the bourgeois family and end the thralldom of women. The solitary household was to be replaced by 'commune settlements', purpose-built by utopian architects[5] whose revolutionary designs would render obsolete the traditional cities, retaining only a handful of the more interesting anachronisms, like Moscow, as museum-pieces. Even the calendar was to be reformed and given new names for its five-day week.

Yet three years later, the militants of 'class war' in culture whose agitation had pitted pupils against masters and challenged orthodoxies were themselves condemned by a Politburo decision. Those groups once favoured, the proletarian associations in literature, art, architecture and music, were swept away at a stroke.[6] Previously encouraged to persecute older specialists, to disorient and demoralise non-Party professionals and to bring fellow-travelling to an end, the proletarians were abruptly rejected by an ungrateful Party leadership and by a strengthened state which – far from withering away – moved swiftly to extinguish their radical intentions. Cultural policies of the five-year plan were thus transitional between the quasi-pluralism of NEP and the incipient monopolies of Stalinism.

Leadership of the 'left' in literature was claimed by RAPP at a 'widened' Plenum (20–29 September 1929).[7] Averbakh launched a new slogan 'For the Bolshevization of Proletarian Literature', designed to unify proletarian writers on the basis of 'class struggle, of understanding the bourgeois danger'.[8] He called for the amalgamation of 'all Marxist forces under one writers' organisation, making a united front', and anticipated RAPP's becoming the expression of that unity. But the theoretical standpoint for such a consolidation was not made clear: literary theory was not Averbakh's *forte*. Instead he merely offered the model of Friche, a recently deceased literary critic, who 'devoted his scientific work to the needs of the working class' and had posed questions 'like a Bolshevik, not cutting off his literary studies from politics'.[9] As the conference proceeded it became apparent that there were substantial differences between the representatives of competing proletarian groups.

Fadeyev raised the question of theories 'harmful to the Bolshevization of proletarian literature'. He attacked those who rejected class criteria in literary criticism, and suggested several tests by which one could determine whether a given writer was proletarian. He also talked with some sophistication about the process of writing.[10] In the hands of its main theoreticians, Fadeyev and Libedinsky, RAPP's outlook was far less crude than its politics would lead one to expect. As Libedinsky put it: 'Before attempting to write my *Commissars*, I sat down and re-read *War and Peace* and some of Turgenev. Fadeyev did the same before writing *The Rout*. Tolstoy is particularly valuable for his excellent development of character. He teaches us how to do this ourselves'.[11] To the charge that they neglected the nineteenth-century radical democrats (such as Chernyshevsky), whom Lenin had approved, RAPP retorted that Lenin had also praised Tolstoy. Indeed, their call to 'Learn from the Classics' was quite comprehensive, including the great nineteenth-century realists Flaubert and Balzac, Stendhal and Zola. However, their slogan 'Down with Schiller', derided idealism, romanticism and varnishing reality.[12]

A number of those present criticised RAPP for 'psychologism'; dwelling overly upon the inner experience of characters – such as the hero of Fadeyev's *The Rout* – rather than the objective historical circumstances. The most radical of these, Osip Brik, made a witty little speech explaining reasons for the split in *Novyi LEF* the preceeding autumn.[13] LEF rejected 'psychologism' and sought a 'literature of fact' or documentary genres. It favoured 'social command', an idea coined by Brik and adopted by the Literary Constructivists whose first album had been *Gosplan literatury* (1924). This gave primacy to the present, and indeed to the future. Condemning the Slavophile tradition, with its 'idealising the poverty, filth, running noses and hooliganism of old Russia', they espoused technical and economic development as practiced in the west. Their rejection of psychological realism and call for a technological revolution led them quite close to a later formulation that writers were to be 'engineers of human souls'. Essentially, they were arguing for useful art, and anticipated that its producers would be 'a technological intelligentsia of engineers, architects and practical men, free from the *Chekhovian mood*'.[14] At the outset of the five-year plan, fortified particularly by Stalin's insistence that 'Russian sweep' should be accompanied by 'American efficiency', their prospects for official approval looked promising.

As the debate deepened, the irrepressible Averbakh defended the need for 'psychologism'. He reminded his audience that it had originated in RAPP's dispute with *Kuznitsa*, whose principles had been too abstract and remote from ordinary experience. Now, he remarked, '*Kuznitsa* does not want to join a united front of proletarian literature. It even refuses to take part in our plenary sessions or meetings. It has many petty-bourgeois elements within it'.[15] Similar scorn was directed at another absent group: *Pereval*, who were equally reluctant to consider merger. Averbakh contented himself with describing its membership as 'very miscellaneous'. Outright assault was reserved for a subsequent occasion.

The only sign of movement towards RAPP came from a quite unexpected quarter. Mayakovsky declared that Averbakh's speech had been excellent and he accepted its main points. Moreover, on behalf of colleagues in LEF's successor REF, he announced 'We consider RAPP to be the organisation with which we are in agreement on most questions'.[16] He continued his rapprochement after the Plenum had concluded.

Strictly speaking, Soviet policy on literature remained that laid down five years earlier: the Resolution of 1925 had never been rescinded. Yet its NEPian assumptions were now anachronistic. The Party apparatus, therefore, began to consider what new statement there should be. The Central Committee's Orgburo instructed RAPP to provide reports on its own work (prepared by Kirshon) and on Soviet literature (by Fadeyev) and provide a draft resolution (delegated to Averbakh and Libedinsky).[17] Wider consultations were also set in motion. *Agit-prop* sent out a circular to all its provincial bodies seeking contributions and comments on such a resolution, promising 'wide public discussion' of their responses.[18] The press noted with some impatience that the 'proletarian hegemony' in literature expected 'sooner or later' by the 1925 Resolution had yet to be established. It was high time, one editorial stated, to translate this 'algebraic formula' into 'mathematical fact'.[19] Despite these promptings, public discussion did not ensue. As in 1925, the problem was delegated to a party commission. Unlike its predecessor, however, this was not filled with senior politicians, but by a new type of government and Party official. The Chairman was A. I. Stetsky[20] who became the founding head of *Kul't-prop* (in January 1930) and an *Agit-prop* official, P. M. Kerzhentsev,[21] was appointed to draft the Resolution.

His draft is preserved in archives. It opens with a polemical assault on both 'left' and 'right'. He rejects as the 'leftist' theory of 'Trotskyism' (and its followers 'Voronsky and others') that socialism could not be built in one country and their arguments against the possibility of proletarian culture. Similarly the 'rightist' theory of Bukharin on the transition period had greatly underestimated the potentialities of proletarian culture, while relying too heavily on the fellow-travellers. But the era of class conciliation was now closed. Previous policies of class differentiation were now redundant. In place of complex strata and tendencies,[22] Kerzhentsev advocated a simple bi-polarity. Fellow-travellers could vacillate no longer: either they would reveal themselves to be revolutionary writers aligned with the proletariat, or they would pass irredeemably into the camp of class enemies. There was 'no third way for the fellow-travellers'. Looking to the future, he called for 'a clear Party line in *belles-lettres*'. Echoing the military vocabulary of Stalin's letter to RAPP, he called for a 'proper deployment of literary forces'. In particular, it was necessary 'on the basis of wide self-criticism to write all literary forces into a single organisation (for instance RAPP in the RSFSR) as a genuine consolidation of forces strengthening VAPP'. It concluded, emphatically: *'Our hopes for the future of literature rest on the proletarian associations'.*[23]

At first glance, this appeared to offer RAPP the recognition by the Party that it had long sought. Yet its leadership fought shy of this particular resolution. Stetsky complained in a letter to Stalin:

> I decided to form a drafting committee, consisting of representatives from the main writers' organisation – comrades Kirshon and Sutyrin of RAPP – Kerzhentsev and myself. We met twice to consider the draft Kerzhentsev had drawn up. Comrades Sutyrin and Kirshon declared it pointless to work on the draft presented. I therefore asked them to re-draft it, or to produce one of their own. They agreed, but have done neither, though a month has gone by, despite repeated promptings.
>
> Moreover, comrades Kirshon and Sutyrin have spent the past fortnight in trying to avoid me. My efforts to reach them have been unavailing. The last time I phoned RAPP's offices, the secretary told me both comrades were out of Moscow, even though Sutyrin was here for a literary meeting that very day. I thus concluded that they are deliberately shirking collective work preparing the Central Committee resolution. Such behaviour in relation to the Central Committee is inadmissable for responsible communists.[24]

The reasons for RAPP's prevarication are not entirely apparent. One obstacle was Kerzhentsev himself, a former *Proletkul'tist* and long-standing antagonist of RAPP, who considered RAPP to be 'rightist' and had recently so described them in his journal.[25] He was unlikely to use his senior position in the Party apparatus to their advantage. This was demonstrated by the draft Resolution which offered RAPP cautious approval as a unifying association only at the price of self-criticism. Public apologia was not Averbakh's style. RAPP often argued that such self-criticism would confuse their younger members, a serious consideration for a mass organisation with eighty or so local branches scattered across the RSFSR. Since peripheral organisations had an uncanny tendency to reproduce the style of the centre, as did Kurs of the Siberian APP, the local demogogue and caricature of Averbakh,[26] we may assume resistance went all down the line. Finally, RAPP may have calculated that its hegemony would be more easily established *de facto* than through a somewhat double-edged resolution which was presented to the Central Committee but never published.

By now, RAPP had other guidelines to rely upon. Two major contributions on literature appeared in *Pravda* – now securely in Stalin's hands[27] – in quick succession. First came a partial critique of RAPP's leadership for its slowness in grasping the need for 'struggle of the Party against semi-Trotskyite tendencies, of Shatskin, Sten etc'.[28] Even so, RAPP was expected to have an especially responsible role in the future amalgamation of literary groups. According to a second authoritative analysis, 'despite the growth of proletarian literary groups (VOAPP and RAPP) and of comrades (Institute of Red Professors, RANION, the Communist Academy)' certain abnormal positions still obtained. There continued to be squabbling between proletarian journals. All of them were responsible for the perpetuation of harmful tendencies in literature such as sectarianism and communist conceit (*komchvanstvo*).[29]

To replace them, *Pravda* called 'For the Consolidation of Communist Forces of Proletarian Literature'[30] which should consist of 'the maximum coming together of communist forces in *belles-lettres* . . . not as an eclectic unification of diverse viewpoints but based on a Marxist-Leninist line towards basic questions of the theory of art, literary science and literary policy'. Further guidance was offered by Stalin in his first major theoretical speech, made to the Society of Marxian Agronomists on 27 December 1929.

'Theoretical thought', Stalin told his audience, 'is not keeping pace with our practical work'. 'Theory, if it is genuine theory, gives practical workers the power of orientation, clarity of perspective, confidence in their work and faith in the ultimate victory of our cause. All this has – it cannot fail to have – colossal significance for our socialist construction'. The trouble was, he declared, that theory had 'lagged behind life', thus failing to fulfil its function of 'arming our practical workers in their struggle for Socialism'.[31] The present imperative for the intelligentsia was to reconsider 'bourgeois and petty-bourgeois theories' (above all those of Bukharin and the 'right deviation') in the light of 'new conditions'. Until this was done, the heads of practical workers would remain 'clogged-up with rubbish. These theories should have been eradicated and discarded long ago'. To illustrate his thesis, Stalin subsequently criticised the 'Rubin School' in economics. Their disputations were 'largely scholastic and far-fetched', degenerated into 'talmudic abstractions', and time-wasting work on abstract themes without relevance to reality'.[32] Following Stalin's lead, these new guidelines were applied across the entire theoretical 'Front'.

According to the Moscow dissertation of B. T. Ermakov, Stalin's remarks were taken up within the philosophy section of the Institute of Red Professors where the predominant school of Deborin was obliged to offer some self-criticism. This, we learn, was 'not accepted' by a group of younger philosophers which insisted on a sterner recantation in line with Stalin's statements. When this was not forthcoming, these youthful vigilantes put their case before the Party committee at the Institute, but were outvoted. Self-criticism was again blunted.[33] At this point, they found an ally in *Pravda* which allowed their leaders Mitin and Yudin to publish a denunciation of Deborin.[34] When the Deborinite majority boycotted a lecture by Mitin to the Institute, he warned that sanction 'from above' would soon be sought for an about-turn (*povorot*) on the 'philosophical front'. Shortly afterwards, the militant faction did indeed meet Stalin who emphasised, Ermakov reports, both the 'anti-scientific' character of Menshevik idealism and its 'anti-Party character'. This dictum sufficed to end Deborin's domination. Resolutions were rapidly pushed through the Institute of Red Professors and Communist Academy displacing the old majority, and the Central Committee subsequently confirmed Mitin and Yudin as new leaders of the Institute (from which they had graduated eighteen months earlier) and editors of its journals.[35]

New intellectual leaderships appeared in many fields.[36] The Soviet Academy of Sciences, untouched since the Revolution, was subjected to planning, production techniques and political nomination. After initial hesitations, the old academicians acted prudently and agreed to take a greater part in 'socialist construction'.[37] The enlarged Communist Academy, which had now absorbed the Institute of Red Professors, deplored the fact that many disciplines were still taught by those who 'fail to understand Leninism or even dialectices' and declared an assault across the board from biology to psychology and aesthetics.[38] These political campaigns, and the theoretical changes associated with them, did not take long to reach literature, where the views of Professor Pereverzev were suddenly discovered to be 'deviations'.

Pereverzev was the doyen of Marxist literary criticism, whose classic studies of Dostoyevsky (1912) and Gogol (1914) were regularly re-issued up to 1929. His literary Marxism had two tenets. First, all works of art must be analysed according to the 'relations of production' prevalent at the given time, this is from man's material circumstances as a working person. 'Subjective factors', such as thought, consciousness or emotion, contribute nothing to the literary process. As he put it: 'I'm not prepared to search the works of Dostoyevsky to find his *Weltancshauung* since asking this is like asking a cook to make a pair of boots'.[39] Pereverzev considered it impossible for any writer to transcend his class: no bourgeois writer could produce a proletarian character, nor *vice versa*. He thus denied that Gorky could be a proletarian writer.[40] But since expecting proletarian literature from non-proletarian writers was futile, it followed that literary policy had only two choices 'to order those who can to sing the necessary songs and to order those who cannot to be silent'.[41] *Partiinost'* – party-mindedness – could not be imposed from outside. Hence all efforts at political re-education of bourgeois (or proletarian) writers was pointless. Clearly, such doctrines were incompatible with the social and pedagogic purposes of the Five Year Plan.

Debate on Pereverzev's opinions was begun by the Communist Academy in the winter of 1929–30.[42] At the first meeting, the Professor gave a summary of his views, which were received politely and with applause. Then his official 'opponent' delivered a paper contrasting Pereverzev's view of literature and art with the more didactic purposes favoured by Plekhanov.[43] But the contrast was mildly made and his presentation reminded a later speaker of a 'student essay read out in the presence of his master'. It took RAPP to bring rancour to the debate. Averbakh condemned his 'revision of Marxism': his distinction between the reflective and the real world led him 'to deny the active role of consciousness' in social transformation.[44] Kirshon declared that such quietist views disarmed the proletariat in its ideological struggles and denied the proletarian dictatorship in literature and art by allowing writers to be 'apolitical or neutral'.[45] Sutyrin added that it 'donned the mask of objectivity' in order 'to remain oblivious to class struggle'. Pereverzev and his followers – 'the predominant Marxist tendency in many higher schools, Party schools and research institutions' – were 'internal enemies' to be torn out 'root and branch'.[46]

Despite this rhetoric, indicative of the deteriorating intellectual atmosphere and misuse of language which RAPP fostered, it was still possible for loyal pupils to spring to Pereverzev's defence. Having carefully taken cognisance of the need for ideological commitment (*ideinost'*) in art, as one put it 'of the needs of the moment', they counter-attacked. Bespalov called RAPP's journal 'eclectic' and an organ of 'vulgar publicism': writing 'one thing today, the opposite tomorrow'. Nusinov pointed out that Pereverzev's early works were pioneering at a time when the victory of Marxism in literary criticism was far from assured. Gel'fand enquired why RAPP had remained silent on allegedly 'grievous errors' until 1929.[47] *Pravda* published a long statement by pupils in Pereverzev's defence.[48] Evidently, the definition of *partiinost'* which RAPP preferred still had authoritative opponents. Despite this brave rearguard, the limits of legitimate discourse were being steadily eroded. It is difficult to disagree with Ermakov's comment that this debate marked a turning-point from '*a-political* literary theory to *partiinost'* in literature',[49] though what final shape that policy would take had still to be determined.

Despite the Party's call for consolidation, the fragmentation of proletarian literature was its most constant characteristic. Unlike politics, where inner opposition had been ended by the ban on factions in 1921, and subsequent disagreements had been conducted within a context of inner-party unity rather than diversity, splits and splinters of proletarian literature continued throughout the twenties. Thus the original secession of *Kuznitsa* from *Proletkul't* led to their parallel organisation down to 1930. VAPP also split on several occasions, with the fundamental break occurring in 1926 when the old 'left' was displaced by the ambitious Averbakh. The further disagreements this caused, however, were given sudden pause in early 1930.

In a dramatic gesture, Mayakovsky applied for membership of RAPP. His *zayavleniye* stated 'I have not and never have had any disagreements with the literary political line of the Party, being carried out by RAPP. Stylistic and methodological differences can best be resolved within the association'. He added 'all active members of REF' should reach the same conclusion which followed 'from our whole previous history'.[50] But the remnants of Futurism found this unilateral decision bewildering. Even Brik rejected it. Protesting that RAPP, far from being proletarian, was a clique of ruling bureaucrats, he took Lili off on holiday to England.[51] Other former colleagues joined an official boycott of Mayakovsky's exhibition

'Twenty Years of Work'. He put on a brave face at the opening ceremony 'there are no writers here? Excellent: I am delighted that those first-rate spit-soiled aesthetes did not come'. To a chance acquaintance he perhaps revealed his deeper feelings: 'I have no friends. I am joining RAPP. We shall see who (beats) whom. It's ridiculous to be a fellow-traveller when one feels like a revolutionary'.[52]

For their part, RAPP trembled at the prospect of Mayakovsky joining their organisation. As Libedinsky put it, they were afraid that their slender vessel would sink under the weight of such an elephant.[53] They prevaricated. Receiving no reply for some weeks, the poet precipitated the issue. He appeared unannounced at a MAPP conference and strode onto the platform from which he recited his new poem *In Full Voice*:

I'm fed up with *agit-prop*. I used to sing the praises of lofty feelings and have income and recognition. But year after year I suppressed my song, I trod on its throat for all I was worth. Listen, comrade descendants, to the rabble-rouser at the mass meeting. Drowning the semi-tones of lyric poetry, I will leap through its stream, volume after volume, speaking living to the living. I will come to you in the communist fairway, not like Esenin bard of the lands of song. My poem will reach over the backs of ages, over the heads of poets and governments.[54]

After this pronouncement, RAPP admitted him with stringent conditions. In its view Mayakovsky could only become a proletarian writer after extensive re-training. Fadeyev explained 'Mayakovsky is suitable material for RAPP and has proved the affinity of his political views with the proletariat but this does not mean we are admitting him with all his theoretical presuppositions. We will accept him to the extent that he disposes of them'.[55] Libedinsky later admitted that the tutoring was conducted in a 'petty and pedantic' manner.[56] This is confirmed by Shklovsky. In his book on Mayakovsky, he recalls a procession of leading bureaucrats passing into the House of Writers in Moscow. 'They carried briefcases. They were on important business. A short bald man passed by, pale skin stretched over his skull, carrying a large shiny leather portfolio. He was in a tearing hurry: on his way to re-educate Mayakovsky'.[57]

The progress of consolidation was discussed by Fadeyev in February 1930. He defined a struggle on two fronts. One was against the 'right deviation in literature' as represented by Bukharin's followers Slepkov and Astrov, and the more familiar targets Voronsky and Vyacheslav Polonsky. The other struggle, against 'leftist' tendencies, was more complex. They included both *Proletkul'tist* elements manifested in its largest offshoot *Kuznitsa*, and LEFist tendencies (though these were treated as Leftist in inverted commas) of the Literary Constructivists. It was RAPP's task to lead such recalcitrant elements into proletarian literary organisations. It was clear, however, that, in all cases, consolidation would be on RAPP's terms.[58] When conditions of entry were discussed with *Kuznitsa*, its negotiators attempted to set limits to the amalgamation.[59] But RAPP replied with an open letter to all members of *Kuznitsa* demanding its dissolution.[60] RAPP also bargained with the Literary Constructivists, who described themselves in a six-page declaration as 'a literary social group, a left intelligentsia'.[61] On 4 April 1930 it held a joint session with the RAPP Secretariat at which Kornely Zelinsky was the constructivist spokesman. The essence of his argument, that the constructivists could accede only as a 'creative fraction' within RAPP, was rejected by all members of RAPP who spoke.[62] The meeting ended in deadlock.

In the meantime, Mayakovsky's relationship with RAPP deteriorated. The focus of contention was his new play *Banya* which was just entering production. Whereas his previous play *Klop* had poked fun at NEP with its racketeers, big-wigs and 'proletarian philistines', transposed in Act 2 to a communist millennium, this one was devoted to the present. He called it 'a drama of our country with circus and fireworks' most of which were, characteristically, verbal. His title referred to 'a bath-house to wash bureaucrats'. The RAPP critic Ermilov protested against the forthcoming production and implied that its anti-bureaucratic sallies were Trotskyite.[63] Meyerhold, the producer, retorted that critics should never deliver judgement on the basis of a fragment. To do so showed 'complete ignorance of what happens to a script when it receives theatrical form'.[64] When the play did open, Mayakovsky displayed a placard in the auditorium: 'It's not easy to clean out the army of bureaucrats. There aren't baths enough nor soap. And these bureaucrats are helped and comforted by critics like Ermilov'. A scandalised press had this removed and took the line that *Banya* was 'unintelligible' to audiences.[65]

At his retrospective, Mayakovsky observed that his twenty years of literary work had 'mainly been a literary battering of heads, not literally, but in the best sense of the word: at every point I had to defend literary views and fight for them against the fossilisation that occurs in our thirteen-year old republic'.[66] He perhaps envisaged one last battle. Encountering the film director Dovzhenko in the *Aleksandrovskii sad*, he raged against the 'unbearable, impossible, literary regime of the cannibals, scoundrels and hacks of RAPP'. He invited Dovzhenko, to whom he was drawn by the savage attacks on his latest production *Earth*, to visit him later to inaugurate a small group for the defence of art from the RAPP regime.[67] But no such meeting materialised: Mayakovsky shot himself next morning. According to official sources, the suicide was unconnected with his literary work. This 'secretarial verdict', as Trotsky put it, cannot be substantiated.[68] No doubt affairs of the heart, with Lili Brik absent and refusal of a passport to revisit Paris, were background factors. But the main reason was the hopelessness of the cultural situation. As E. J. Brown justly comments, Mayakovsky felt a 'cloud of disapproval' hanging over him which he had hoped to dispell by joining RAPP, but paradoxically this had led him to even greater isolation.[69] His suicide note contained a word of mock consolation to his 'comrades of RAPP'. 'Don't think me a coward – nothing could be done. Tell Ermilov he needn't have had the slogan taken down: we could have argued it out'.[70] Yet RAPP remained unrepentant. Their Secretariat called in the *Pravda* obituarist Zonin to condemn his 'incorrect line' in having called Mayakovsky a proletarian poet. They then passed a resolution reprimanding *Pravda*, the Party's main organ, for its 'political mistake'.[71] Such insubordination was unparalleled. Numerous protests ensued: prominent proletarian writers such as Serafimovich and Bezymensky spoke in the sharpest terms to the RAPP Secretariat. Lunacharsky did the same in public. Communist Academy colleagues of the reprimanded Zonin came to his defence.[72] Even so, it was almost a month before RAPP finally admitted that their line had been mistaken.[73] It was an error they would not be allowed to forget.

RAPP now turned to *Pereval*, whose name denotes a mountain pass. Social perhaps rather than geographic, it expressed their aspiration to mediate between the fellow-travelling writers and the proletarian *Oktyabr'* from which they had disaffiliated in 1924. Accepting the view of Voronsky (from whose writings their name was taken) that art is the cognition of reality, they rejected the RAPP opinion that the purpose of art is to change it. Their writings emphasised the importance of intuition, sincerity, and cultivation of an artistic personality, summarised in their slogan, 'being like Mozart' (*Motsartianstvo*). In the context of the five-year plan this attitude could easily be misconstrued as passive contemplation. Their wish to mediate scandalised one critic into declaring that it amounted to putting reactionary writers such as Bulgakov and Zamyatin on a par with Furmanov and Fadeyev.[74] So long as members concentrated on cosmic themes, as did Gorbov quite literally in his collection *In Search of Galatea* (1929), *Pereval* could still hope for toleration. But any treatment of the contemporary world, above all of collectivisation, could expect a sharp response indeed. Thus Ivan Katayev's story *Milk* (1929) was sharply denounced for its sympathetic portrayal of the kulak's dilemma in a time of terror.[75] Moreover, rather than showing that poor peasants had noble motivations for the expropriation of kulaks 'as a class', Ivan Katayev showed them to be inspired by baser qualities such as envy.

Most controversial of the *Pereval* writers was Platonov. His *Kotlovan* (1930), first published in the Soviet Union in 1987,[76] records the effort to industrialise through the image of a pit. Enormous efforts are made to excavate a clearing but nothing arises on its foundations, a metaphor echoing the parable of Leonov's 'Tower'. The hero of *Kotlovan* is dismissed because he interrupts the burning tempo of production with his 'increasing enfeeblement and thoughtfulness'. Platonov adds: 'contemplation means educating yourself by the unfamiliar events around you. Let people study the realities of nature as long as possible so that they can begin to act late but not erroneously, solidly with the instruments of experience in their hands. All sense of society arises from bright young men interfering with it. If only history could be left alone for fifty years everybody would achieve an effortless well-being'.[77] A second novel, *Chevengur* (1928–29), of which one chapter appeared in Russia under a separate title, takes the theme of collectivisation. Here Platonov's semi-literate poor peasants expel the kulaks and then settle down in their new commune to await a communism that never comes: 'The communism of *Chevengur* was defenceless in those dark days on the steppes because people overcame their tiredness from daily life through sleep and forgot what it was they believed in'. Movement there may be, but Platonov does not confuse this with direction. 'Where are you going?' an old peasant is asked, 'Who? Us?' is the reply: 'We'll go anywhere so long as we're not stopped. Turn us around and we'll go in the opposite direction.'[78] This form of fatalism is blended with rough peasant wisdom and Party slogans to produce many verbal surprises. Discouraged by publishers who regarded his text as 'counter-revolutionary', he sent the manuscript to Gorky who conceded that the book was 'extremely interesting', but doubted its chances of publication. He thought its ironical treatment of collectivisation, its plethora of negative characters and shortage of resolved revolutionaries, would not endear it to the censorship.[79] This remained the case until 1988.[80] A subsequent story, *Vprok: A poor peasant's chronicle*, did appear. It offered a far from flattering description of Party policy in the countryside, not shying away from the repressive aspects of collectivisation.[81] Platonov's editor, Fadeyev, was sharply censured for permitting this publication.[82] He recanted in a subsequent issue of his journal, accusing Platonov of being a 'kulak agent' in literature and stating that his story was 'counter-revolutionary' in content.[83] Platonov appears to have come under a ban for the next three years.[84]

Pereval replied to RAPP's insinuations with a brave open letter 'Against slander'.[85] A special session held at the Communist Academy to try the case accused *Pereval* of being 'merely a motley collection' of petit-bourgeois writers who had hoped that NEP would lead to a more 'liberal' regime. Their literary programme was alleged to be 'objectively hostile to Marxism', rejecting such basic elements as class struggle and even adhering to humanism. Their most rancorous opponents, Kirshon and other leading lights of RAPP, insisted upon their immediate dissolution.[86] In his reply, the *Pereval* spokesman A. Lezhnev admitted that their earlier programme had been open to the charge of 'passive contemplation'. But, he contended, this was true only of the past. They had now adopted a new slogan 'the dynamic principle of literary presentation' which enabled them to keep pace with current developments. RAPP, he added, had been shameless plagiarists of their earlier ideas: 'without doubt between 1926 and 1930, Fadeyev, Libedinsky, Ermilov and Averbakh have borrowed many slogans such as "psychologism" and "for the living man" from us'. To point this out was not to protect a patent but simply to show RAPP's ingratitude, and to indicate the spuriousness of their claim that a great chasm lay between *Pereval* and the proletarians.[87] The chairman saved RAPP further embarrassment by closing discussion at this point.

Pereval managed – unlike other groups – to preserve some measure of its independence until the end of 1932. A further volume of their fiction was issued;[88] Voronsky, now partially rehabilitated, became Chairman of the critics section. Although its objective treatment of collectivisation was prohibited, some principles of *Pereval* were preserved. Ideas they favoured such as rejection of the rigid tenets of a literary 'dialectical materialism', encouragement of writers to work as individual personalities rather than class entities, and a high regard for Gorky, especially in early works such as *Mother*, were all incorporated into the later doctrine of socialist realism.[89] When RAPP was eventually removed there were thus some elements of an alternative aesthetic in the making.

In the late spring of 1930, a new left arose in literature. This militant tendency first appeared in Leningrad, at grassroots level, with an anti-RAPP petition from sixteen literary circles. Attached to it, as members of a 'shock brigade' visiting the various factories, were the names of Prokofiev, Vishnevsky, and other well-known writers.[90] This evidently-inspired call was taken up by *Leningradskaya pravda*, which published a fierce declaration against the RAPP majority.[91] Their principal complaint was that RAPP's rule was repressive. In their view, Soviet literature was being run by a narrow clique of conceited bureaucrats. Evidence for their next manoeuvre comes from the archive of another RAPP antagonist, Bezymensky. His papers include a 'declaration of the literary group *Krasnaya zvezda*", also drawn up in Leningrad, which may mark the starting-point of the new campaign. The document further demanded that the forthcoming conference of the Leningrad Proletarian Writers' Association (LAPP) should undertake new tasks in line with the reconstruction period. It criticised RAPP's espousal of classic novelists such as Tolstoy to the neglect of revolutionary classics such as Saltykov-Shchedrin and Gleb Uspensky. Above all, RAPP had overstated the importance of psychological novels to the neglect of other genres: production and scientific novels, topical and agitational verse, pamphlets and songs. It argued that the conference should adopt a new slogan: 'topical themes, expressing the gigantic scale of socialist construction' and '*militant politically directed art*'.[92]

The conference, which convened in Leningrad in May 1930, marked the public appearance of an anti-RAPP coalition. The founders called themselves *Litfront*. In addition to appealing to military methods and terminology, as the name implied, its leaders attacked the 'theoretical errors' of the RAPP leadership. The Communist Academician Gel'fand condemned their adoption of the slogan 'for the living man', together with those of 'psychological realism' and 'immediate impressions'. He condemned the purely psychological exploration of individual motivation and argued instead for a clear characterisation of class and class conflict. It was social psychology that determined the individual and not conversely: 'we proceed from the class to the individual'.[93] The conference concluded that while RAPP's basic line 'for the Bolshevisation of proletarian literature' laid down at its September Plenum should be pursued more energetically on the basis of self-criticism, RAPP was prone to the 'Right danger'. It still clung to bourgeois tendencies in literature: an uncritical attitude towards the classics, elements of idealism and formalism, a neglect of contemporaneity and underestimation of working-class themes. Accompanying criticism of 'left deviations' was much more routine. RAPP's leadership was singled out for Communist conceit, narrowness and cliquishness, complacency and facile optimism and a tendency towards bureaucratisation, charges that the Party leadership itself made when abolishing RAPP two years later.

The defending delegate, Kirshon, responded that RAPP had been correct in its struggle against the Pereverzev school and other deviations in literature. The 'RAPP leadership working under the leadership of the Party' had pursued a generally correct literary-political line. He rehearsed victories of RAPP including that over the so-called 'left minority' including Bezymensky.[94] Of the literary issues raised by *Litfront* he made no mention at all. Reporting back to the RAPP Secretariat on 19 June, Kirshon adopted the same tactic, as several speakers pointed out. But a further effort by Bespalov to pursue the *Litfront* platform was rebuffed:

Bespalov: Our view is that there now exists in RAPP a monopolistic and single creative group. This monopoly, as with all monopolies, leads to petrification, inability to take a critical approach towards creative work. We consider it necessary to bring about a creative discussion, a creative search within proletarian literature. This is our demand.

Kirshon: We now have a frontal attack on us on literary questions by groups with mechanistic, anti-Marxist and Pereverzevist views (*noise*). The main editorial task of *Na literaturnom postu* is once again to unmask an anti-Communist, anti-proletarian tendency (*noise*).

Bespalov: 'Anti-communist, anti-proletarian'. In such statements you condemn yourselves not us . . . (*laughter, noise, exclamations*).

Kirshon: I repeat, an anti-communist, anti-proletarian tendency on literary questions. This is what we have here. It is undeniable for every deviation from Marxism is anti-communist (*noise*).[95]

The sitting was suspended. RAPP sent a circular to its local branches warning them *Litfront* was an 'anti-proletarian tendency'.[96] But this attempt to suppress discussion proved inadequate in an atmosphere heightened by the approaching Party Congress.

Support for *Litfront* widened to include *Komsomol*'s leader Taras Kostrov and the editor of *Literaturnaya gazeta*, B. O'lkhovy. It was joined by the former left opposition in VAPP (Vardin, Lelevich and Semyon Rodov), and the pupils of Pereverzev, Gel'fand and Bespalov.[97] But the playwright and versifier Bezymensky was the real animator. His private feud with RAPP was of long-standing. He had been part of the 'left opposition' in RAPP since 1926. Utterly unlike their penchant for 'psychologism', was his preference for aphorism, epigram, wit and satire. His rapid, journalistic doggerel, a style derived from Mayakovsky but much inferior to its model, proved a ready vehicle for publicising the Party policies of the Five Year plan. Prior to *Litfront* he had written a play, *The Shot*, which had immense success for which Stalin was partly responsible. Shortly before the *Litfront* controversy, Stalin wrote:

Comrade Bezymensky,

I am somewhat late in replying.

I am not an expert on literature, and certainly not a critic. Nevertheless, since you insist, I can give you my personal opinion.

I have read both *The Shot* and *A Day in Our Life*.[98] There is nothing 'petty-bourgeois' or 'anti-party' in these works. Both, and especially *The Shot*, may, for our time, be considered models of revolutionary proletarian art.

True, they contain certain vestiges of Komsomol vanguardism. Reading these works, the unsophisticated reader might even get the impression that it is not the Party that corrects the mistakes of youth, but the other way round. But this defect is not the main feature of these works, nor the message they convey. Their message lies in concentration on the shortcomings of our apparatus and in their profound belief that these shortcomings can be corrected. That is also their principal merit. And this merit more than compensates for and altogether overshadows what, it seems to me, are minor defects dating back to the past.

With communist greetings,

J. Stalin

March 19, 1930[99]

Since RAPP had also criticised *The Shot* for its satire on careerism, bureaucratisation and toadying,[100] a warning to them may also have been intended.

More was to follow. It was a sign of how militant Soviet politics had become that *Litfront* rather than RAPP should have found favour with the sixteenth Party Congress. Kirshon began his report by boasting that RAPP was Leninism in literature and launched a series of attacks on easy targets: Pil'nyak, Pereverzev and overly-liberal censorship. But the tone was defensive. Far from steady progress towards consolidation of literary forces, he had to report that RAPP was threatened from within by a group 'which challenges our whole programme and our literary slogans'. To justify RAPP's record he produced a long list of proletarian literary productions.[101] Congress was unimpressed. A voice from the hall declared them too little and, by implication, too late. By contrast, the spokesman for *Litfront*, Bezymensky, received an ovation. His report consisted mainly of a satirical poem which ridiculed RAPP's programme and poked fun at such leaders as Libedinsky and Sutyrin. It concluded on a *Litfront* note:

Congress Comrades!
I am a worker of RAPP
But I am first of all a Bolshevik
A Bolshevik
   does not beat about the bush
Therefore
   my short report
   will be as sharp
   as a bayonet.

RAPP is not a club! It is an army of words.
For the country
   is on the offensive,
And during battle
The Bolshevik campaign needs words.
   So members
   of this army
Must be given their
   marching orders.[102]

This recital was frequently interrupted by laughter and followed by thunderous applause. No doubt that response was principally spontaneous, expressing a welcome relief from the tedious recital of achievements of the Five Year Plan. But such criticism of RAPP could not have been made without political approval. *Litfront* was evidently influential in the upper party echelons.

Following this setback, RAPP attempted to restore its authority. The editor of *Literaturnaya gazeta* was summoned by its Secretariat to account for his extensive publicity for *Litfront*. At first he failed to attend, pleading business with the Party Congress. His note of absence commented that 'the abnormal situation in RAPP gives no guarantee of an objective discussion'.[103] He eventually appeared to argue that *Literaturnaya gazeta* – as an organ of the Writers' Federation (FOSP) – had to take an even-handed approach to literary disputes. RAPP retorted that the newspaper must be 'a militant weapon of the Party in its struggle for pure Marxist-Leninist theory and for proletarian literary groupings'.[104] In short, it should be an organ of RAPP. But the editor refused to be brow-beaten and continued to carry statements from *Litfront*.[105] RAPP responded with a six-point resolution, expressing insincere surprise at the existence of *Litfront*, whose formation they had learned of only two days earlier 'from the newspapers'. Its creation was held to be incompatible with the Party policy of consolidating 'communist forces within RAPP'. The statement ended by expressing the hope that *Litfront* would shortly rejoin the 'Averbakh group within RAPP'.[106]

Institutional conflict was now extended to the Communist Academy. The critics Bespalov, Gel'fand and Zonin, and RAPP's recent ridiculer Bezymensky, announced the formation of a Society for Marxist Literary Scholars, without RAPP's participation. RAPP appealed to *Kul't-prop* to prohibit this rival centre of Marxism in literature, pointing out that its initiators included members of the discredited Pereverzev school and also Kerzhentsev (now Vice-President of the Communist Academy) who had been waging a fierce campaign against RAPP in his journals.[107]. But *Kul't-prop* was unmoved. The Praesidium of the Communist Academy sent a slighting reply which confirmed the statute of the new society. They added mischievously that the proposed inclusion of Fadeyev from RAPP placed it in a more privileged position than unrepresented literary groups such as the Writers' Federation (FOSP), the Peasant Association (VOKP) and *Kuznitsa*.[108]

These developments were damaging RAPP's political standing. Their position worsened when *Pravda* published a long article by Bespalov on the 'new tasks of proletarian literature', which argued that the methods of *Na literaturnom postu* had had their day.[109] Clearly relishing the role of provocateur, Bezymensky then made a scene in the RAPP offices, banging the table, accusing them of being 'bureaucrats, *kulak* sympathisers, and rabble not Bolsheviks'.[110] Finally a *Pravda* editorial accused the RAPP critic Ermilov of 'right opportunism'.[111]

RAPP's Secretariat met in a crisis session on 29 September. For once Averbakh seemed at a loss. He confined himself to noting that Bespalov's article had been 'quite inadmissible', and that he should be called on to recant his views.[112] But this reticence was short-lived. Shortly afterwards, the RAPP leaders took the extraordinary step of sending a note to Stalin, in effect demanding that he stop meddling in literature:

Comrade Stalin!

To characterise the relationship between RAPP and *Pravda* we enclose our comments on the article which you propose to publish. This not only fails to state that the editors of *Pravda* 'fundamentally' agree with our reply and withdraw the charge of 'right deviation' against Ermilov, but on the contrary they confirm the original article.

We also find it necessary to forward an affidavit given us by Comrade Litvinov board member of the journal *Pechat 'i revolyutsiya*. This states that when *Pechat' i revolyutsiya* was waging its aggressive campaign against RAPP, he protested about this to the editor Kerzhentsev. Comrade Kerzhentsev however told him to 'bear in mind' that the line their journal adopted towards RAPP had been dictated to him by Comrades Stalin and Ordzhonikidze.

With communist greetings,

Averbakh, Panfyorov, Fadeyev, Kirshon.[113]

The obvious implication was that a similar line had been dictated to Stalin's protégé Mekhlis, editor of *Pravda*. A more succinct ultimatum to the party secretariat on the same affair stated 'either silence *Pravda* or change the leadership of RAPP'.[114]

Despite such defiant gestures, the initiative in literary debate still lay with the accusers. Their utilitarian approach was more attuned to current party needs, and the claim to speak with authority on Marxism was much more convincing than the efforts of RAPP, who

had neither the facility nor the training to do so. Yet taking this
dispute into politics, as Bespalov had done, proved a fatal blunder.
No-one was more adept than Averbakh at using political means to
discredit an opponent. The rash charge of 'right opportunism' allowed RAPP to regain the ascendancy.

Averbakh's major speech on the inner party situation of
30 October informed the RAPP party fraction that the recent past
had indeed been characterised by 'right opportunist' activity. The
agronomists Kondratiev and Chayanov, and economists Groman,
Sukhanov and Ramzin, as revealed in the recent trials – the Menshevik Trial, the Industrial Party Trial, that of the Toiling Peasants Party
and others[115] – had still hoped to realise their 'right deviation'
in politics. The new stage of such unprincipled activity had been the
expedient coalition with 'left deviators' to form a 'left-right bloc':

> The evolution of counter-revolutionary Trotskyism from super-
> industrialising adventurism, which he defended in the reconstruc-
> tion period, to struggle against the Bolshevik tempos of industrial-
> isation in defence of minimum ones, again revealed the disbelief of
> both right and left opportunists in the possibility of building social-
> ism in one country.[116]

Exclusion of 'right opportunist dealers' from the party, such as
Ryutin, and Slepkov and Maretsky (of the 'Bukharin school') was
welcome; more so would be their condemnation by the main leaders
– Bukharin, Tomsky and Rykov – of the 'right deviation'. A struggle
on 'two fronts' was needed: 'against double-dealers Nusinov and
Kavralsky, the leaders of liberal bureaucrats, right capitulators'; and
against 'left deviators of the type of Lominadze, Shatskin and Sten'.

Even though Stalin had probably invented the 'left-right' bloc in
politics,[117] the allegation did have a certain plausibility. An irony of
the party struggles of the 1920s was the retrospective realisation by
the defeated parties that their mutual differences were minor in
comparison to the divergence between their views and those of
Stalinism. By contrast to the five-year plan embarked upon, their
proposals had indeed been similar and their strictures on the lack of
inner party democracy, which they had hitherto expended every
effort to deny each other, identical. This does not prove, however,
that such a 'bloc' existed. All we do know is that some conversations
did take place between Syrtsov, a high government official from the
'right', and Lominadze. It was Averbakh who likened these to issues

of literature. *Litfront*, he alleged, had contacted Lominadze, through the Trans-Caucasian proletarian writers' association (ZAPP), where he was party Secretary. Similarly three members (Zonin, Rodov and Sayanov) had made contact with Syrtsov of the RSFSR, on one occasion travelling to Novgorod for discussion with him. The purpose of the meetings was to involve these politicians with the *Litfront* groups, but it had misfired.

> It is not a law, naturally, that literary discussions precede party ones, but there are a number of causes in which literary discussions did begin first, the sense of them only being fully understood *after* the party discussion had taken place. The 'left-right' bloc is such a case.[118]

No greater piece of fortune for Averbakh and the embattled leadership of RAPP could have been imagined. Accession of the former leadership of VAPP, the so-called 'left Mensheviks', had given *Litfront* an adverse political complexion: but there was little glory in a further routing of the old minority. By making *Litfront* the equivalent to opposition to Stalin in politics, however, RAPP scored a double victory. For Averbakh personally, it was the moment of his greatest triumph. He alone had 'made the connection' between the disparate spheres. However slender the actual evidence, his weaving together of the threads of politics with literary 'deviation' had been a *tour de force* of which his colleagues would not have been capable. It was no wonder that Mandelstam now listened with fascination to Averbakh's 'hempen speeches'.[119]

Under such accusations, *Litfront* disbanded. Bespalov and Bezymensky were expelled from RAPP. The rank-and-file of the movement announced their repentance in *Literaturnaya gazeta* on 15 November. For once RAPP celebrated a 'victory' justly and other proletarian groups finally acknowledged its 'ascendancy'. The largest of these, *Kuznitsa*, terminated its protracted negotiation over terms of entry and was admitted to RAPP on conditions which allowed of no further independence.[120] Thus by the end of 1930 the consolidation of communist and proletarian groups in literature had been achieved. It remained only to extend this hegemony to the writers who adhered to neither.

During the Five Year Plan, the 'gradation scheme' of differentiated class analysis was replaced by a simple dichotomy: for or against the Revolution. To be an ally it was no longer sufficient merely not to oppose: now Party policy required a positive commitment. As Kirshon put it to the 1930 Party Congress:

> Fellow-travellers and those of them who are becoming our allies, should understand we cannot consider as allies those who are not inspired by the fight and work which the Party leads, because in what could our association consist? The whole purpose of our activity and work lies in the fight for the building of socialism and its construction.[121]

It was now essential that they 'break more decisively with old traditions, cast off aloofness, and intelligentsia individualism'. For, he suggested, echoing Stalin, literature had lagged behind life. 'Reality surpasses our creative imagination.' The fellow-travelling writers had largely failed thus far to reflect this present reality in their literary output. Their civic duty was clear. Writers must 'throw themselves into the thick of the building programme, must go to the village and to the construction sites, abandon their urban studies and literary clubs so as to gain material for creative work with and amongst the proletarians and so re-educate themselves'.[122]

As Stalinism started on its frantic race to industrialise the country, writers' brigades were formed for collective journeys to observe and report what was going on.[123] The Plan, an unprecedented and exhilarating event, had considerable impact on many writers. Vyacheslav Polonsky noted in his pamphlet on *Magnitostroi* how a new city sprang up almost out of thin air where 'eighteen months previously there was only wind playing across the steppe'. He considered that 'not only the mountain and the steppe are being rebuilt but also man himself' and rashly predicted that 'with the building of the Magnitogorsk and Kuznetsk plants we shall overtake in the near future the largest most powerful capitalist countries'.[124] Before long, such publicistic writings, sketches and notebooks, began to be supplemented by more substantial genre. Production novels appeared, the best of which fully recognised the difficulties encountered in remote areas when attempting to fulfil a centrally determined plan.

The theme of overcoming obstacles, material and psychological, is presented by Valentin Katayev's *Time, Forward!* (1932). This describes a single day at a chemical combine in Magnitogorsk on which the hero-organiser strives to set a new world record for concrete mixing, confirmation of which arrives in the last line of the novel. His personality is entirely positive: only through his heroism, altruism and selflessness is the record reached. During the day he does not pause for a single instant to reveal any doubt or hesitation to his fellow workers. Naturally this behaviour is contrasted with that of reactionaries, drunkards and foreign engineers. Distinguishing his outlook from that of the more pragmatic American engineer, the hero becomes Promethean:

> You lack imagination. We shall conquer nature. We shall bring back its lost paradise to humanity. We shall surround the continents with warm streams. We shall force the Arctic Oceans to generate billions of kilowatts of electricity. We shall grow pine trees there – a kilometre high.[125]

The landscape changes so rapidly that the engineer has to follow a new route to work every day; building sites have sprung up where there had been only muddy tracks before. As the title indicates, time rushes too. For the hero, time is not an abstract concept but rather refers to the precisely calculated period required to complete a given process: 'there was no real disagreement between him and time: they moved together like two runners'. Thus the novel accurately reflects the hectic first stage of Stalinist construction in which target and tempo, rather than 'technique', were treated as decisive.

Production themes became banal, but it is worth recalling the context in which they first appeared. However fatal an artistic precedent, such early novels authentically recorded many of the problems facing central planning at its outset. Katayev's engineer, a hero of his time, was not intended as a hero for all time. Of course, we cannot be sure whether this genre contained the potential for further development. So much of the fiction that followed was merely an imitation of established 'classics', such as Katayev's. Writers were obliged to follow accepted models long after the context in which they were written had gone. For this extension, pioneers of the production novels were not responsible.

The muddle, shortages and bureaucratic bungling of the Five Year Plan are given full rein in Leonov's construction novel *Sot'* (1930), about the building of a paper mill on the northern river from which the book takes its name. This too was successfully realised, although Gorky perhaps overstated the case in his preface, putting the novel on a par with 'the greatest of our old literature, Lermontov and Tolstoy'.[126] Leonov's novel shows the new world with its shock brigades and socialist competition pitted against the forces of nature, which must be harnessed to give water power, and of reaction, epitomised by a mysterious monk, the leader of a local sabotage attempt. Although the protagonist appears the essence of proletarian purity, carrying socialism to the backwoods irrespective of obstacles, the difficulties he encounters are not minimised. Indeed the reader is left with the suspicion, echoing that of Leonov's *Badgers*, that the future for which the Party leadership was extracting so many sacrifices is distant and may never come.

The conflict between old and new recurs in heightened form in Leonov's next novel, *Skutarevsky* (1932), concerning the career of an old *intelligent* who had been praised by Lenin, promoted and put in charge of an Institute engaged in scientific research of top priority. The novel, though, is set much later: after the Shakhty trial of old specialists and against the background of further arrests and executions in the Five Year Plan. Professor Skutarevsky tries to ignore these goings-on but is forced to face them by the involvement in sabotage of his son. He responds by rejecting family ties and moving towards the Party, which he eventually joins. A parallel evolution is undergone by his brother, an artist who had lost his bearings during the immediate post-Revolutionary period but regains them as a production artist, painting factory murals, for the Five Year Plan. Despite its predictable outcome, the novel well illustrates the power of patriotism above that of family loyalty, to which the Party appealed in order to attract non-Party specialists to assist the Plan.

The psychological consequences are discussed in Ehrenburg's *Second Day* (1932). This describes the dilemma of the young 'hereditary' intellectual attempting to retain a hold on his cultural past while also endeavouring to be an exemplary member of a production team and Komsomol. In heated debates he defends Dostoyevsky but eventually gives up the effort and, accusing his accusers of being 'not Komsomols but cowards', commits suicide. At a deeper level, Ehrenburg is concerned with the 'superfluous' men of nineteenth-century fiction, alienated from society, who had lost their way in the world. Before the Revolution, such figures still enjoyed a certain independence and were at least able to offer criticisms of the *status quo* or even solutions, however powerless they were to bring any to effect. But now such outsiders were derided. Those whose practical skills could have earned them a comfortable living in the new society at the cost of intellectual integrity, and chose not to do so, were regarded as outcasts. Ehrenburg calls them *izgoi*. An *izgoy* is defined from the dictionary as 'one struck off the list, an illiterate son of a priest, a prince without a kingdom, a ruined foreign merchant, a bankrupt'.[127] The image here is that of 'losing' one's place in society. Just as earlier landowners and merchants had lost their possessions in the Revolution, now he implied the intelligentsia had been dispossessed.

One of the first fellow-travelling writers to conform to the new regime was Pil'nyak. The editor of *Izvestiya*, I. M. Gronsky, despatched him as a special correspondent to Central Asia. He produced a series of reports, *Tadzhikistan: Seventh Soviet*, on the latest autonomous republic. Through such journalistic forays, Pil'nyak's editor probably intended him to make restitution for his previous 'crimes' and thus rehabilitate himself before Soviet society. The author's willingness to do so extended to substantial re-working and enlargement of his story *Mahogany*, which had caused such offence in 1929, into a novel of the Five Year Plan. According to Victor Serge, he was assisted by Yezhov in this exercise.[128] The outcome, *The Volga falls into the Caspian Sea* (1930), is an interesting example of both censorship and self-censorship. The major additions are a construction setting in which the original village is due to be flooded under a vast hydro-electric system. The local opposition, represented by the village elder Shudrin, is no longer a typical Pil'nyakian remnant of feudal Russia but an active saboteur of the new order who conspires with the engineer Poltorak to blow up the 'monolith'.[129] There follows a litany of denunciation and the unmasking of wreckers.

'Wrecking' had become a central theme of public life. At the end of 1930, a major show trial was held of 'saboteurs', with strongly anti-intelligentsia overtones. It was alleged in court that an 'Industrial Party' had been created for the purpose of converting the Soviet Union into a technocracy by conspiracy with foreign statesmen such as Poincarré, aimed allegedly at restoring capitalism in the Soviet Union and its partition between the western powers.[130] The press was used to arouse public anger against the accused, enabling citizens to express or sublimate their rage against the actual shortcomings of the Soviet economy. Pressure was put on writers to join the chorus. Many did so. A typical statement read: 'We, Soviet writers and dramatists, heartily acclaim that true sentinel of the Revolution the OGPU and petition the government to award it the Order of Lenin'.[131] *Pravda* recorded demands from writers under the headline 'Shoot the wreckers'. Pil'nyak reported on the trial for *Izvestiya*. Although his piece 'Listen to the footfalls of history'[132] contained an equivocal section contrasting the Tsarist practice of jurisprudence through defence counsels with the Soviet system of judgement 'by the people', he nevertheless gave full support to the prosecution. In fact, the seven men condemned, solely on the basis of their own confessions, were all reprieved, and the alleged ringleader Professor Ramzin was re-employed on government work and even decorated. This may indicate how seriously the authorities treated the evidence of treason. Judicial review aimed at annulment of such trials was set in motion some fifty-five years later.

Olesha also attempted to adjust. An article 'The need to reconstruct myself is clear' stated that he would do so soon, but in his own way, for 'nothing is more important to an artist than his own ways'.[133] His chosen path, however, proved self-destructive. As Arkady Belinkov superbly demonstrates in his study of Olesha, a steady deformation of his work takes place during the Five Year Plan.[134] This he openly conceded during a later speech:

> I could have gone to a construction site, lived amongst factory workers, described them in an essay, even in a novel. But this was not part of my blood, part of my breath. With such a theme I would not have been a real artist. I would have lied, fabricated: I would have lacked what is called inspiration. It is hard for me to understand this type of worker, this type of revolutionary hero. I cannot become one. This is beyond my strength, beyond my understanding. So I didn't write about it. I became afraid and started to think that no-one needed me.[135]

Olesha could no more comprehend a worker-hero than become one. While rejecting the theme of heroic labour, he retained his obsession with the role of the artist in society, but found himself with neither the material nor the means with which to communicate this to his readers. As his conceptions narrowed, so the subject matter ceased to supply the brilliant metaphors on which basis alone his literature was able to survive.[136]

Kaverin, too, rejected given themes. As he put it, 'It is impermissible to set a subject prematurely. A writer must discover it for himself.' His *Prologue* (1930) deliberately avoided 'canonised material', and politics, on the grounds that both were 'inert from the literary point of view'. He argued that economic construction was a prelude (prologue) to a much more significant transformation of human nature in which the new man would emerge with correspondingly advanced moral qualities. In the same way, the literature of the future needed not only ideology but new forms.[137] Yet with the virtual collapse of the Formalist school and the extinction of the *avant-garde*, symbolised by Mayakovsky's suicide, he saw this prospect as betrayed. The theme is developed in *'Artist: Unknown'* (1931) whose hero Arkhimedov boldly assails Marxian precepts, above all its confidence in the materialist future, expressed in the novel by a technical specialist. These two characters quarrel over technology, construction techniques, history, morality and the meaning of art. When challenged, the technician concedes: 'Morality? I have no time to consider the word, I am busy building socialism. But if I had to choose between morality and a pair of trousers I would choose the trousers'. By contrast, Arkhimedov (whose name itself symbolises discovery) is a rebel, in constant search of innovation. Like Olesha's hero Kavalerov (on whom he may be modelled) he spurns the world of expediency and hypocrisy, and dreams of a new universe in which 'the language of people true to their word will differ from the words used by deceivers'. Although his hero dies defeated, Kaverin has the last word. He comments that the artist's last painting could only be produced by a man with 'the freedom of unfettered genius'. He adds that the 'precaution and dishonesty of contemporary art, which is so remote from people, could not have achieved such a work'.

In an autobiographical fragment, Kaverin reflects on the collapse of fellow-travelling now visible around him. He notes wistfully that whereas the Serapion Brothers had once searched each other's work and commented on it seriously, they were now reluctant to read each other's books. They had 'aged, grown stout, become more careful, pensive and polite'. More ominous still, they were no longer able to distinguish literary disagreements from personal ones. Their distractions, he noted, were several: indifference, self-absorption, fear of speaking a solecism, hypocrisy and philandering. Although he did not intend a funeral oration, still less a 'civil burial', Kaverin declared that the Serapions would 'look back on their lost youth as though it had passed with the beating of a drum'.[138] Much later, Katayev recalled fellow-travellers as having had a double identity or a shadow following one pace behind. They were 'a rare cross between a man and a woodpecker, a heavily-built swine, a real animal, a buffoon, a time-server, an arch-racketeer, an informer, a bootlicker, an extortioner and a bribe-taker. A monstrous product of those far-off days.' His sharpest observation is put in the mouth of Osip Mandelstam: 'It's phenomenal! To be a pigmy and look like a giant! Let us hope this historical paradox will soon be relegated to eternity.'[139]

To Mandelstam himself the ending of the 1920s was almost a relief. The era of ambiguity was over and Stalin's political victory seemed, paradoxically, to clear the air. Mandelstam no longer felt himself to be 'the sick son of the age' and returned to poetry after a break of almost five years.[140] Further evidence of his restored lucidity was *Fourth Prose* (1929–31)[141] which cast off the 'fur coat of official literature' that he had momentarily donned and called down curses upon the literary establishment. Even without the first section, a philipic on socialism which the poet destroyed at a dangerous moment in the later 1930s the text remained unpublishable in the Soviet Union for fifty years.

Its early passages deplore the lust for violence of mob rule; its lynchings of a shop assistant who gave short weight, of a cashier whose accounts came out a kopeck short, of a director who signed some document in error, or of a peasant who had hidden rye in his barn. This hoodlum justice dispensed by Komsomol meant that 'animal fear taps at the typewriters, proofreads gibberish written on lavatory paper, scribbles denunciations, hits those that are down and demands the shooting of prisoners'. It reminded him of small boys 'drowning a kitten in the Moskva river before a crowd of onlookers'. A later theme is the division of world literature into works written with or without permission. The first are rubbish: 'I spit in the face of every writer who seeks prior permission. I want to beat them over the head with a stick. . . . I would prohibit such writers from marriage and procreation. How can they have children? Children must continue our work, carry out what is most important to us, yet their fathers have sold out to the pock-marked devil for three generations to come. Now there's a "literary" page!'. His recent persecutor Gornfel'd was characterised as a 'would-be murderer' of Russian poets, who, 'preaching morality and state authority' carried out the orders of a regime completely alien to himself yet accepting them 'as he would a mild attack of indigestion'. To die at his hands would be as pointless as being run over by a bicycle or poisoned by a parrot's bite: 'but even a parrot can be a literary murderer'. It can imitate the sense or language of night, yet 'knows no age or day from night. If it should bore the master, it'll be covered over with a black cloth which for literature is the surrogate of night'. In conclusion, Mandelstam noticed his colleagues, 'the masters' dogs staring at me with eyes of canine tenderness, imploring: drop dead!' The only evidence of humane authority he now saw was Bukharin who indeed managed to win him a temporary respite.[142]

On Bukharin's prompting, the Central Committee press section sent Mandelstam on a journey to Armenia. Here his poetic inspiration miraculously returned. But any official expectation that the trip would reconcile Mandelstam to socialism was disappointed. Instead, he rediscovered his roots in the traditional cultures of the Mediterranean and Christianity, which Armenia had adopted in the fourth century. He also found in the Armenians' fullness of life a message for the present. 'Their rough tenderness, their noble inclination for hard work, their inexplicable aversion to metaphysics of any kind and their splendid intimacy with the world of real things – all this told me: you are awake, do not be afraid of your own time'. For all its ominous episodes, which included meeting Beria, the journey restored Mandelstam to health. However, it also brought him a sixth, 'Ararat' sense: one of foreboding. His account of *The Journey to Armenia*[143] ends with King Arshak imprisoned by the Assyrians in a pitchblack dungeon from which no escape is possible. He wishes the conquered king one additional day of freedom, full of hearing, taste and smell. His editor was dismissed for publishing this parable in defiance of the censors.[144]

In contrast to Mandelstam, Pasternak continued to be courted by the literary establishment and to maintain relations with them. This apparent cordiality led Mandelstam, probably on the basis of misreading, to accuse him of seeking a privileged poet's place: 'a seat by the columns'.[145] For Pasternak, the events of 1929, as of 1917, were initially inspiring and may momentarily have seemed attractive before the costs in human life became fully known. As Mrs Mandelstam points out, the two poets were antipodes: different poles that may nonetheless be connected by the line between them.[146] Pasternak also travelled south in the early 1930s, but whereas Mandelstam had marvelled at the remnants of its ancient and remote culture, Pasternak was overcome by a sense of wonder at its present. He found Georgia unfamiliar and amazing: 'the huge dark stormy mountains looming' at the end of every Tbilisi street. The great military highway, grandly celebrated in Pushkin and Lermontov, is described as tapering off in its lower slopes 'like crumpled bedclothes'.[147] To the poet this surprising, homely analogy provided a panorama of what a socialist future might be.

Pasternak's *Second Birth* (1931) offers a remarkable poetic tribute to Mayakovsky, published on the first anniversary of his suicide. Asking whether the poet should 'take measure from the Five Year Plan', falling and rising with it, he appears to answer in the negative.

Pasternak declares: 'it is unfortunate that during days of great decisions, when preference is given to a higher passion, the post of poet
is retained: it is dangerous, if not vacant'.[148] He does not make a clear
whether this vacancy referred to the spiritual emptiness of actual
occupants such as the versifier Demyan Bedny or Bezymensky (even
Mayakovsky in his most propagandist mode), or to the physical
absence of a poet worthy of the Five Year Plan. That poetry could be
dangerous, however, seemed not in doubt. An angry rebuttal by
Selivanovsky, a leading RAPPist, confirmed official touchiness upon
this subject.[149] Pasternak now fully appreciate the enormity of suffering that Stalinism produced. His memoirs recall the unmitigated
tragedy it brought to the countryside:

> In the early thirties it was fashionable for writers to visit collective
> farms and gather material about the new ways of rural life. I
> wanted to be like the rest and set out on such a trip with the
> intention of writing such a book. But there are no words to
> describe what I saw. There was such inhuman misery, such fright-
> ful poverty, that it began to take on an almost abstract quality, as if
> it were beyond what the conscious mind could absorb. I fell ill and
> could write nothing for a whole year.[150]

In order to gain capital for industry, to recruit a labour force and
feed it, together with the swelling industrial populations and new
towns, the peasantry was forcibly incorporated by the state. Bukharin's peaceable alliance (*smychka*) was rejected and the non-violent
mode of 'growing into' socialism left unexplored. The Stalinists
seized upon the *kolkhoz* as the only possible solution and without
prior experiment on a smaller scale ordered its imposition across the
whole country. Stalin's explanation for doing so was fulfilment of
Lenin's 'cooperative plan'. But collectivisation was in fact a police
operation. The Smolensk Archive contains numerous OGPU reports
on 'dekulakisation'.[151] Central direction of the first stages was provided by top secret Series 'V' telegrams, nine of which are from Stalin
personally.[152]

The policy was disastrous for the peasantry. Vasil' Bykov has
recently published his reminiscence of childhood in a poor Belorussian village during collectivisation:

> In our area, we had no *kulaks* whatsoever. But it was demanded
> we "dispossess the *kulaks*". It wasn't possible to identify 'blood-

suckers' by land-holdings – no-one had such land. Even so, 3 people in the village, poor folk like the rest, were 'dispossessed'. The *aktiv* met in all-night session, wracking their brains and not knowing whom to single out. But then they discovered that some-one had not a single cow but one and a half cows – a cow and a heifer – and they put him on the list. Another was to be dis-possessed because of a hired helper during harvest time, a distant female relative helped him. A third was singled out for some reason such as that his mare had a foal. [He describes how mill-stones were broken to prevent hidden grain being ground into flour and the social consequences of such an act.] After all, the people committing these arbitrary acts were not some strangers from outside but our own fellow villagers. . . . Discord arose amongst people who had lived in the same village for centuries and inter-married. Suddenly, everything fell apart.[153]

Party leaders acted in vital haste as though they were running out of history. Yet the harder they tried to change rural Russia, the more they pressed, bullied, cajoled or destroyed, the more they tended to reinforce the old.[154] A peasant put into a *kholkhoz* overnight without warning or preparation, simply stripped of his belongings or forcibly contributing them to a common pool, could not fail to harden in his attitudes and cling to what still remained of his confiscated life. He took into the collective farm his former family relations, his old attitudes to authority, his prejudices, resentments and superstitions.

The great assault upon religion is a good example of the Party leadership's wilful and superficial attitude towards the peasantry. An outburst of militant atheism – attacks on churches and exiling of priests – accompanied the Plan, but the peasant household continued its simple ceremonies without them. This was tacitly acknowledged later when atheist propaganda was greatly reduced and the journals and the national newspaper devoted to it were closed down.[155] Even cultural campaigning in the countryside was received poorly. Would-be bringers of literacy, often young Party members or Kom-somols, were indistinguishable in the peasant mind from urban political agitators. Violent and even murderous attacks on 'enlighten-ers' were a regular occurence from 1929.[156] Indeed, the Party drew the logical conclusion by placing cultural work in the countryside under the auspices of the much hated Political Departments which ran the security aspects of *kholkhoz* life. Yet this response was entirely predictable: faced with the prospect of losing everything the peasant

was bound to resist his new masters by every means he had. Active
and passive resistance took place on a massive scale, leaving Soviet
agriculture backward to this day.

Collectivisation has yet to receive full scholarly treatment in the
USSR, but important glimpses are left to us by contemporary writers.
Babel described some of the consequences in a series of stories
planned on the lines of *Cavalry Army*. The two that have survived,
both written in the spring of 1930, show this could have been a
magnificent book. The first describes the slaughter of livestock by
peasants due to be dispossessed:

There was a harnessed horse standing in Ivan's yard. The red reins
were thrown over some sacks of wheat. In the middle of the yard,
near a crooked lime tree, there was a stump with an axe stuck in it.
Ivan touched his cap with his hand, pushed it back and sat down.
The mare came up to him dragging a sledge behind her. She put
out her tongue and curled it up. She was in full foal and her belly
was very distended. Playfully she caught her master by the shoulder of his padded coat and nuzzled at it. Ivan was looking down at
his feet. The trampled snow around the stump dazzled him. With
hunched shoulders he jerked out the axe, held it up in the air for a
moment and struck the horse on the head. One of its ears jerked
back, the other twitched and then lay flat. The mare groaned and
bolted. The sledge turned over and wheat scattered in curved lines
over the snow. The horse reared up with its forelegs in the air and
its head thrown back. Beside one of the sheds it got caught up in
the teeth of a harrow. Its eyes appeared from under a veil of
pouring blood and it whinnied plaintively. The foal stirred inside it
and a vein swelled up in its belly. 'I didn't mean it', Ivan said,
stretching out his hand towards her 'I didn't mean it, little one'.
The palm of his hand was open. The horse's ear was limp, its eyes
were rolling and there were bloody rings around them. Its neck
formed a straight line with its head. Its upper lip was curled up in
despair. It pulled on the harness and moved forward again, dragging the harrow behind it. Ivan drew back his hand with the axe
behind his back, he hit the mare right between the eyes . . . Ivan
wandered round the yard, went up to a shed and dragged out a
seeding machine. He smashed it with long slow blows and twisted
the axe in the delicate mesh of the wheels and in the drum. His wife
appeared on the steps of the house in her long gown. 'Mother',
Ivan heard his wife's voice in the distance, 'Mother, he's wrecking
everything.'[157]

The second story is equally laconic. It shows how one village was collectivised in a single day: 'the judge had nine *kulaks* jailed and next morning they were to be packed off to Sakhalin Island. And when they came back in the morning to take them away what did they find but the nine swaying under the rafters on their belts.'[158] However, transportations did take place in hundreds of thousands. A British Embassy official in Moscow observed a trainload of *kulaks* being dispatched by cattletruck to Siberia.[159]

Stalin evidently decided that the whole process did merit one literary account. Sholokhov, while still working on *The Quiet Don*, was summoned to him. Collectivisation was discussed and he later claimed 'the conversation was very profitable for me and encouraged me to put into practice new artistic ideas'.[160] He worked on the new topic at speed and dispatched a book-length text to *Novyi Mir* at the end of 1931. Initially the response was negative: the editors wished deletions and changed the original title *With Blood and Sweat* to *Virgin Soil Upturned*. Again Stalin intervened, expressing the view that 'we were not afraid to dispossess the *kulaks* – why should we be afraid to write about it now? The novel should be published'.[161] It appeared during 1932 and remains unsurpassed as a documentary record of collectivisation.

The action is confined to early 1930 and the emotional climax is reached in March with Stalin's article 'Dizzy from Success'.[162] This arrangement implied, as Stalin's article had said explicitly, that the 'excesses' of collectivisation were the fault of local subordinates. A major character in the novel, Borodin, though a former Red Guard with impeccable credentials, is shown to lack the qualities necessary for Stalin's 'rural revolution'. The 'de-kulakisation' he carried out is portrayed as a heartless and arbitrary exercise, arousing great popular resistance rather than the glorious crusade of a fearless revolutionary. By contrast, the local party secretary is seen to be an efficient organiser who has not lost the human touch. Most positive of all is a Leningrad metal worker mobilised for collectivisation by the Party 'Thousands',[163] Davydov, who is shown to be adept at gaining the cooperation of ordinary people. These characters are presented as capable Stalinist *praktikanty* coping well in a hostile environment, peasant Russia, which provides many violent episodes. Both Davydov and the party secretary are murdered during an orgy of destruction near the end. The reader is not spared details of terrified children, families in despair and the working of the terror apparatus. Since the 'excesses' of both sides are fully noted in the novel, the author's vindication of his main argument that the overall policy was justified is quite a *tour de force*. Sholokhov shows a genuine conflict in which the future of the countryside is actually at stake and the eventual outcome by no means predetermined. Throughout his novel, the clash of opposites is mediated by the presence of the *srednyaki* or middle peasantry. Recognition of such strata necessarily brought the author closer to the real peasant world than did *ex-cathedra* pronouncements on class polarisation by the Kremlin. For *kulak* was not an objective category: in the poorest village the only peasant to own a cow could be designated a *kulak*.[164] While showing that the policy was based on the expropriation of 'rich' kulaks, Sholokhov also demonstrates that its central objective was mass enrolment of peasants in the *kholkhoz* irrespective of wealth. Peasant psychology is made a major theme and an understanding of it shown to be at least as valuable to activists as a willingness to use force. One may ask, therefore, as Soviet scholars did in the 1960s, whether Sholokhov fully subscribed to Stalin's theory that class struggle intensifies as socialism approaches.[165] The construction of the story itself, with its emphasis on middle strata and the use of 'Dizzy with Success' rather than the simple incitement of 'class against class', seems to suggest that he had doubts.

The book was received in adulatory terms. Contemporary reviewers referred to the work as an artistic textbook for the countryside, virtually a handbook on 'how to collectivise'.[166] Some local officials took this literally. For instance, the party organisation in Podol'sk (Moscow Oblast') wrote:

> We request you to visit us for comradely discussion of *Virgin Soil Upturned* which has been scrutinised by all members of our party bureau and some of the *aktiv*. A number of questions arise from it which we wish to resolve in personal discussion with you. On behalf of the Party Committee I hope you will visit us without delay.[167]

Other critics emphasised its 'epic' qualities but this was premature. The prospects of embarking upon a second volume were diminished by the consequences of policies described in the first. As resistance to the campaign grew, the Party returned to a policy of mass terror which could not be expressed in a publishable novel. Yet restricting the plot to 1931 or even to the second half of 1930 would leave it inconclusive. As Sholokhov himself put it: 'frankly, there's little room in it for characters to prove themselves. It would be nice to place them in 1932, when their personalities could be made to blossom. But, as things are, I foresee the second volume will be more boring than the first.'[168] Several announcements of a sequel came to nothing, as did the author's intention of completing the story in some different genre, such as a play, or as a separate novel. No second volume appeared in Stalin's lifetime, and considerable re-writing of the first was required. A sequel, devoted solely to the summer months of 1930, appeared in 1960.

Although Sholokhov's work was unequalled in its frank treatment of collectivisation, other writers took up the theme. Panfyorov became the best known and most popular. The action of his multi-volume novel *Bruski* takes place on a Volga estate from which the novel takes its name. It opens with Leninist 'committees of village poor' seizing control of the locality in 1917. This limited act is contrasted with the 'great turn' of 1929–30. As in Sholokhov, class divisions of the countryside are carefully portrayed, making its documentary value quite considerable. For instance, one scene (somewhat reminiscent of Dovzhenko's *Earth*) describes the first appearance of a tractor:

> A loud rumbling sound came from the street. He started, thinking that the bell tower had fallen down. But when he saw the peasant men and women, boys and girls, running along the street he called out 'What's that noise. What is it?' 'The devil alone knows. It's dragging something along. It runs and there are ploughs behind it and on the ploughs there are boards and on the boards there's Stepan Agneyev.' The peasants crowded into Agneyev's yard just as dealers crowd around a goodlooking horse at the annual fair. One man ran round the tractor several times slapping the steel flanks. Wiping the sweat from his face he announced, 'No, it won't go, it's bad enough with horses in our fields, but look at these huge wheels, they'll sink right into the earth'.[169]

The book was well received by contemporary critics[170] but came under fire later on for its colloquialisms in a campaign by Gorky to raise literary standards.[171] Its rather racy sexual interludes were toned down in subsequent editions.

For writers who were themselves peasants the position was already perilous. Critics began to put their writing into 'positive' or 'counter-revolutionary' categories. Anticipating this danger, the Peasant Writers' Union (VOKP) had revised its statute to state that 'not all those writing about the peasantry are fully peasant writers'. The latter included 'only those who on the basis of proletarian ideology, though with the help of peasant imagery of their own, use their creative works to organise feelings and awareness of the toiling peasants . . . for collective agriculture'. 'Exploiting *kulaks*', it stated, was utterly repudiated.[172] A further resolution restricted the definition to 'writing which reflects the interests of the basic mass of peasants on its path to socialism'. 'Revolutionary peasant literature' had nothing in common with 'patriarchal tendencies' representing *kulak* and bourgeois literature.[173] All such efforts to prevaricate were regarded as reactionary and a 'right opportunist effort' to gloss over class differences in the name of an 'alleged unity of proletarian literature'. The programme was put through under a new leadership dedicated to pursuing class struggle in the countryside.[174]

Careers could be made by identifying and castigating '*kulak* literature' and its 'defenders'. The author of an encyclopaedia entry in 1931[175] alleged that '*kulak* literature' provided an idealistic picture of old Russia, juxtaposing its traditions, hierarchical establishment and 'soul' with the 'soulless USSR'. He deplored in it an anti-urbanism, seeing the towns as the source of all evil, threatening the purity of the countryside. He found there a rejection of science (including the dialectic in Marxist-Leninism) and a deification of nature, partly religious but also pantheist and mystical. He complained that in such writing portrayal of *kulak*s, *bednyaks* and exploitation was absent. He rejected its assumed rural solidarity between hardworking and labour-loving peasants as antithetical to the principles of collectivisation. His main target was 'the father of modern *kulak* literature', Nikolai Klyuev. Forbidden to publish after 1928, he continued to write 'for the drawer' and supported himself by giving poetry recitals at dinner parties and soirées. Following one of these he was arrested for reciting unpublished works and after a spell in the Lubyanka was sent to Siberia. Upon the intercession of Gorky and others, he was transferred to the city of Tomsk where he lived as a deportee from October 1934 until August 1937.[176] A second target was Sergei Klychkov[177] who had been under criticism as a '*kulak*' since 1925 and thereafter turned to prose. The same encyclopaedia refers to him as 'one of the most blatant representatives of modern *kulak* literature', noting that he was a faithful disciple of Klyuev. Despite this, he was not silenced and made several brave and controversial interventions in literary debates during 1932.[178]

During collectivisation a gigantic series of crimes was committed that could not be concealed from society. Rather than admit to them, however, the Stalinist leadership attempted to silence all cultural and intellectual dissent. As Pasternak commented later through *Doctor Zhivago*:

> I think that collectivisation was both a mistake and a failure and because that could not be conceded every means of intimidation had to be used to make people forget how to think and judge for themselves, to force them to see what was not there, and to maintain the opposite of what their eyes told them.[179]

Paradoxically, this great deception was accompanied by a radical reversal of the Party's policy towards the older intelligentsia. Previously negative appraisals were discouraged and proletarian exclusiveness ended. The 'show trials' of former specialists and bourgeois 'wreckers' were halted and remained in abeyance for most of the next quinquennium. The non-Party specialists were rehabilitated. Stalin gave the signal for this *volte-face* in a speech of June 1931.[180] Previous measures of repression against the intelligentsia, he explained, had been necessitated by circumstances. 'About two years ago the highly skilled sector of the old technical intelligentsia was infested by the disease of wrecking'. This had been a fashionable activity. 'Some engaged in wrecking, others shielded the wreckers, yet others washed their hands of what was going on and remained neutral, while still others vacillated between the Soviet regime and the wreckers.' In such conditions, Soviet policy had to concentrate on unmasking active wreckers, differentiating the neutrals and enlisting those who were loyal. But an entirely new situation had now arisen. Capitalism had been routed in both town and countryside. The Moscow trials had served to discredit the notion of wrecking, and the hopes of foreign intervention had been dashed. The rejection of non-party specialists was now 'stupid and reactionary'. Stalin added hypocritically 'we have always regarded specialist-baiting as a harmful and disgraceful phenomenon'.[181]

This new analysis of the intelligentsia had three practical corollaries. Firstly, it replaced class with functional criteria for political assessment. Proletarian commissars, christened by Pil'nyak 'leather jackets', gave way to professionals and experts who had to be loyal, but did not have to be party members. Thus class exclusiveness, which was not revived in Stalin's lifetime, can be seen as characteristic only of the first, though most dynamic and fluctuating, stage of the Stalin epoch. From mid-1931, non-Party specialists were promoted in many fields. Stalin criticised the policy of 'pushing aside non-party comrades who possess ability and initiative' and promoting party members 'although they may be less capable and show no initiative'. This was a form of neo-NEP, in a more stringent guise, and developed in the mid-1930s under the aegis of Gorky and Bukharin into a potentially more tolerant regime.

Secondly, the new policy deliberately fostered economic inequalities to differentiate the mass of the population from its burgeoning elite. A privileged lifestyle began to be instituted through special access to education, scarce goods, books, travel, social provision and entertainment. Approval of this tendency was given by Stalin's denunciation of equality as 'bourgeois levelling'. Thus ended an important Bolshevik objective. Stalinism recognised that rhetorical appeals for support, and bullying pressures for conformity, had failed to produce an adequate response. Now the state sought voluntary cooperation and was willing to offer material rewards to those who offered their services to 'socialist construction'.[182] It led eventually to 'middle-brow' values – *meshchanstvo*' – which flourished in the late 1940s, but whose roots were clearly being laid here.[183] Finally, there is a growing desire for political guarantees against any repetition of the transitional convulsions of the Five Year Plan. The new 'haves' began to look askance at the 'have-nots' and to seek protection for themselves from the state. This new system settled down much sooner than anyone had anticipated, and began to articulate classic conservative demands for regularity and order.

The shaping of Stalinism took place over the next three years. A new political order began to be instituted, based upon a mass Party, Stalin's private Secretariat and the 'cult', and an overbearing police state. A new economic order was consolidated on the basis of collective agriculture and the absolute priority for heavy industry. The social order was increasingly divided between those situated 'above' and the great majority 'below'. A new intellectual order was fashioned, as we have outlined elsewhere.[184] Finally, a new literary order emerged with institutions and doctrines distinctively its own.

Stalin played a decisive role in this last transformation. His relationship with RAPP turned full circle between the private letter of support to its leaders in February 1929, and his abolition of their association three years later. One could argue that Stalin had intended this outcome all along, and merely concealed it, using RAPP in the meantime, in a Machiavellian exercise of political duplicity. But the reality is less complex. Stalin's endorsement of RAPP's activity, so eagerly sought, was withheld. He left open the option of discarding them later on.

Far from being constant master of the situation, as often assumed, Averbakh was in trouble time and again. In 1928, he was only saved from exile to Azerbaidjan by colleagues' intervention.[185] On the eve of the Five Year Plan, he was again under suspicion for sympathy with Shatskin's 'Komsomol deviation'. This did lead to punishment, and he was transferred to Smolensk 'for political mistakes'.[186] There he remained, despite numerous appeals to the local Party to 'spare him more time for literary work', and occasional forays to meetings in Moscow, until reinstated with RAPP, on Stalin's authority, in August 1930.[187] As Averbakh's fortunes indicated, the party leadership had more than a passing interest in the politics of literature at this stage. At the height of collectivisation, and the accompanying threat its 'dizzy' pace produced for his political position, Stalin found time to defend Bezymensky, allegedly on the basis of personal reading. He deliberately denied RAPP the public sanction for which it was pressing, thereby allowing other writers to vie for his ear.

But if Stalin could play political games then RAPP could too. Archives show their frequent manoeuvrings between party institutions. At first they hoped for sympathy from *Kul't-prop*, established in January 1930. When this was not forthcoming, they turned to other organs: the party Secretariat, its Orgburo, even Stalin, in search of satisfaction.[188] Yet the central apparatus had no determinate 'line' on literature. Party leaders used this period experimentally, to extend and test some of the individuals and instruments through which literary policy might be conducted once RAPP had gone.

In his pioneering study of the RAPP group, E. J. Brown raises the intriguing possibility that they were driven by Stalin's own attitude into joining one of the political combinations against him. As he points out:

> The communist party of the Soviet Union was engaged throughout this period in a struggle – sometimes open, more often concealed – with an opposition to Stalin's policies which included a large part of the Bolshevik leaders who had participated in the revolution and the civil war. The leadership of RAPP was undoubtedly a part of the concealed opposition.[189]

However, the author notes in an adjoining passage that RAPP was 'considered useful to the party in these years (1928–1932) chiefly as the scourge of certain opposition groups in politics and literature'.[190] If it was both in opposition, and acting as the scourge of opposition, RAPP's activity would seem self-defeating. Moreover, the connec-

tion between party opposition to Stalin's policies and the oppositional activity of literary groupings (such, allegedly, as RAPP) is
not explained. It seems more likely that RAPP would have wanted to
continue an intimate relationship with Stalin in the hope of ultimately
obtaining recognition as the party's organisation in literature. Which
other leader would have been more likely to offer this recognition,
Brown does not say. In what follows we shall try to put forward an
explanation for the fall of RAPP without recourse to undocumented
notions of 'opposition' to Stalin.

It is commonly assumed that RAPP was a single entity, and thus to
treat the course of literary policy in this period as that of Averbakh's
group alone. Yet closer examination of its inner workings reveals
undercurrents of resistance to the formal leadership. By early 1931, a
significant minority of the hierarchy were expressing reservations
about Averbakh's demagogic conduct. His character stimulated such
considerations. For while having powerful friends, such as Yagoda,
his brother-in-law, he had also, as Lunacharsky once remarked, an
unrivalled capacity for making enemies. Thus, following a devastating review in *Na literaturnom postu* accusing him of right opportunism and wrecking,[191] Gladkov, a new recruit to RAPP, wrote to
Averbakh for an explanation. 'What do you want? I ask you as the
editor of what purports to be a serious journal of Marxist criticism.
You evidently want to finish me off as a writer.' A substantial portion
of his letter[192] dealt with his disappointment at his recent accession to
RAPP:

> I entered RAPP with the fervent hope of finding a comradely
> atmosphere conducive to cooperative work. *Kuznitsa* was stifling
> and sickening: I felt nothing but enmity and hypocrisy both open
> and concealed. Surely, I thought, I would be able to work well with
> you, Fadeyev and Libedinsky in close friendship and harmony. But
> no such comradely atmosphere exists. It's awful. Many in RAPP
> are saying the same.
>   There is a tiny self-centred clique, constantly blowing its own
> trumpet, attracting the least talented writers. Those outside this
> group are beaten, lynched and tormented with unsparing energy.
> How can this lead to a development and perfecting of proletarian
> literature? Will this help create a 'great art of Bolshevism'? It is a
> difficult almost unbearable atmosphere in which to work . . .
>   We need to consolidate forces and rule them wisely. That is our
> party task . . . but it is very difficult to collect cultural forces of

writers, to train them, strengthen their enthusiasms and belief in their own abilities. This requires a great love of literature, a broad knowledge of culture with class sense. Enemies must be dealt with mercilessly but we must treat comrades-in-arms carefully and respectfully. We do live in war-like times, that's true, but military tactics against enemies must not turn into the method of treating comrades.[193]

Averbakh's semi-literate rejoinder, a furious philippic of fourteen pages, ignored the call for improved conditions for literary work. It concentrated solely on political aspects of literary debates and assailed Gladkov with fresh charges.[194]

Although Averbakh appeared impervious to arguments about literary standards, other members of the RAPP Secretariat showed greater awareness of the problem. Fadeyev expressed his reservations privately, conceding that he had often considered resigning from the RAPP Secretariat whose 'constant inner struggles' left no time for literary work. He stayed on 'in order not to encourage class enemies'.[195] Less altruistic motives became apparent later when Fadeyev became the first of RAPP's leadership to break ranks after its abolition. Others were more forthright. Panfyorov and a small number of followers withdrew from the RAPP mainstream. In the course of a stormy plenary session, mutual anathemas were pronounced. Panfyorov's group argued, as had *Litfront* before them, that RAPPist novels of Fadeyev and Libedinsky indulged too much in character exploration and 'psychologism', at the expense of contributing to the 'revolutionary transformation of the countryside'. The RAPP majority replied by castigating the Panfyorov group for naturalism, colloquialism and careless composition.[196] To refute Panfyorov's 'slanders' about 'passive contemplation' and their lack of contemporaneity, RAPP coined a new slogan: 'for the enrolment of shock-workers in literature'. *Udarniki* were declared the 'central figures of the proletarian literary movement'. Their recruitment, Averbakh announced with characteristic hyperbole, would be a fact of 'gigantic importance in the history of our movement' and mark the 'end of RAPP's pre-history and the beginning of its real existence'.[197] Indeed, within a matter of months, RAPP's rank-and-file grew from 4,000 to 10,000, for the first time justifying its claim to be a mass organisation of proletarian writers.[198] These fresh cadres were ordered to 'face production' and dispatched on fact-finding visits to construction sites across the country, an exercise that RAPP theorists had previously derided as 'mere empiricism'.

Reporting to the *Kul't-prop* Secretariat on the current literary debate, RAPP admitted the emergence of a dissident group headed by Panfyorov, which criticised the 'abnormal conditions' within the association.[199] The Panfyorov group sent the Party Secretariat a sharp critique of RAPPist practices.[200] Both sides were then summoned to put their case before a panel of party officials, chaired by Yaroslavsky. Panfyorov and his followers Il'yenkov and Isbakh (whose memoirs are our only record of this meeting) presented themselves as a 'parliamentary opposition' within RAPP. Averbakh made a haughty speech which recapitulated all his former services and achievements. Panfyorov replied with a catalogue of Averbakh's administrative high-handedness and 'suppression of self-criticism'.[201] It is not clear who won the argument but it does seem that Panfyorov's grouping felt gratified that their case had been heard. As Isbakh noted, it was the first time that their group had been called into the Party Secretariat, whereas Averbakh, Kirshon and Libedinsky were often in the Kremlin, 'being, so to speak, its own people'.[202] Panfyorov was confirmed as chief editor of *Oktyabr'*; the board included many of his supporters.[203] Nevertheless, had opposition to RAPP been confined within its ranks, Averbakh's clique could perhaps have staved off a reform of literature. But once that criticism was taken up by other sections of the communist establishment their position became far less secure.

The first external challenge to RAPP's sovereignty over literary affairs came in the autumn of 1931 from Komsomol. Kosarev, its first secretary, admitted 'it may be, as RAPP alleges, that we in Komsomol have little grasp of literary questions', but it was also true that 'RAPP considers no-one apart from itself capable of understanding literary affairs'. RAPP treated as 'superfluous' the self-criticism called for by *Pravda*, and, even more seriously, effectively denied the Party's right to be the ultimate arbiter of literary questions.[204] Such 'RAPPist arrogance', together with its 'unprincipled and damaging sectarianism', began to be assailed in *Komsomol'skaya pravda*. Typical of these editorials, which the paper did later admit were on a rather low level, was an *ad hominem* critique of Fadeyev as a 'petit-bourgeois subjectivist'.[205] RAPP replied in kind, asking why Komsomol had remained silent during the previous months in which RAPP had routed 'bourgeois-*kulak* agents in literature'.[206] RAPP's Secretariat sent them a stream of vituperative memoranda, claiming an exclusive right to determine party literary policy and insisting that 'dualism' was inadmissible.[207]

Battle was joined at a meeting on 5 November 1931. Averbakh reported on RAPP's correspondence with *Komsomol'skaya pravda* about its many mistakes and maintained that *Litfront* was still active there. Komsomol had ignored these warnings and impudently replied with a whole range of completely new positions 'or rather old ones with new arguments which are once more directed against the RAPP leadership'. Moreover, one of their leaders had 'completely officially announced that *Komsomol'skaya pravda* is oriented towards the Panfyorov group and considers its line to be correct'. Kirshon accused the newspaper of disorienting both Komsomol and members of RAPP by propounding views 'alien to Marxism' and alien to a Bolshevik line in literature. The opposition replied with a general critique of RAPP for neglecting self-criticism and *partiinost'*, and for trying to present the attack on mistakes of certain leaders as a campaign against its whole organisation. They called for open discussion of its mistakes. Isbakh declared that the critique by *Komsomol'skaya pravda* was basically correct and its unrepentant editor defended his line, adding that his newspaper could not remain neutral in literary debates.[208]

This critique now received official endorsement. A *Pravda* correspondent, Vasil'kovsky, reviewing RAPP's conduct over recent months, regretted the persistence of many errors on the part of its leadership. Ermilov's criticism contained 'a whole crop of subjective and idealistic mistakes'; Averbakh and others had committed 'Deborinite' errors. The question of the party leadership in literature would be best answered, the article added, by the Communist Academicians who had dealt with Deborin so successfully.[209] RAPP, now seriously alarmed, summoned Vasil'kovsky to a session of its Secretariat, but did not let him speak. The editor of *Pravda*, Mekhlis, ignored his invitation to attend. An unseemly row developed about the *Pravda* article, revealing deep divisions amongst the RAPP leadership.[210] A week later the Communist Academicians did enter the literary arena. Mekhlis published an article by Mitin and Yudin, the displacers of Deborin, on 'proletarian literature at a higher stage'. It announced that, since the summer, the Communist Academy had engaged in a joint project with RAPP to investigate the views of Plekhanov on art. Yudin insinuated that further research into 'the Leninist theory of cultural revolution', as opposed to Plekhanov's, might reveal serious mistakes in RAPP's theoretical position.[211]

In the meantime, Soviet intellectual life was thrown into disarray by Stalin's 'Letter to the editors' of the historical journal *Proletarskaya revolyutsiya*. Perhaps at the suggestion of the Press Department

of the Central Committee, he criticised an article on the Bolsheviks'
role in the Second International as 'rotten liberalism'. Stalin's concern was not with raising standards of historical research: 'who,
except hopeless bureaucrats, can rely on written documents alone?
Who except archive rats does not understand that a party and its
leaders must be tested primarily by their deeds.' His real objective
was 'to rebut the attempts of certain *writers* and *historians* to
smuggle disguised Trotskyist rubbish into our literature. We cannot
permit a literary discussion with these Trotskyist smugglers . . . even
Comrade Yaroslavsky's work contains a number of errors in matters
of principle and history'.[212]

Thus prompted, the Communist Academy praesidium declared
that Stalin's letter applied not merely to historiography but to the
entire 'theoretical front'.[213] Stormy investigations of supposed con-
trabandists were set in motion.[214] For once RAPP was not in the
vanguard. One may assume that Averbakh, himself a former Trotskyite, was none too eager to discuss this particular credential. Instead,
on 19 December, the Literature and Language section of the Institute
of Red Professors took up the challenge. It identified: 'rotten liberalism' (criticism of Lunacharsky and Lebedev-Polyansky); 'serious
mistakes' (Nusinov, Gel'fand and others); agents of the second
international in literature (Voronsky and Gorbov) and those subject
to bourgeois and *kulak* influence (Polonsky). The Communist
Academy heard a speech from Sergei Dinamov on 'militant tasks of
Marxist criticism'[215] which stated that Stalin's letter had colossal
significance for 'all theoretical fronts, including the literary front'. He
regretted that the literary front had been particularly laggardly in this
regard; 'rotten liberalism' had appeared in *Krasnaya nov'* (Platonov's
story *Vprok*) and in *Zvezda* (Kaverin's *Artist: Unknown*); 'Mistaken
thoughts' were found in the writings of Averbakh.[216] Stavsky discovered 'contraband' in a handful of novels by Gorbatov, Ovalov and
Isbakh of the Panfyorov school.[217] But the consequences for these
authors were not severe and the entire campaign soon subsided
following Postyshev's warning against 'misinterpreting Stalin's letter'
in early 1932.[218]

An outward calm returned to literary politics. That, however,
concealed an interlocking series of manoeuvres behind the scenes.
For RAPP's opponents now coalesced. Together they appealed to
the Party Secretariat for a change of leadership in literature. This *ad
hoc* coalition gave Stalin the opportunity to make a decisive intervention.

Doyen of the anti-RAPP coalition was the veteran proletarian writer Serafimovich. He had served on the RAPP journal *Oktyabr'* until June 1930. Although his note of resignation does not give reasons,[219] his private misgivings become explicit later on. He had a lively exchange with Averbakh at sessions of the RAPP secretariat in late 1931, at which his support for the Panfyorov group became clear.[220] In January 1932 he wrote a protest letter to the Central Committee Secretariat. This characterised the Averbakh group as: 'intolerant, arrogant, unparalleled in its rudeness, lies, intrigues, hypocrisy, inexhaustible in its hatred of those who dare to point out the leadership's mistakes.'[221] He also prepared, but did not publish, a devasting exposé of RAPP's leadership for *Komsomol'skaya pravda*. He sent the draft to Stalin with a covering letter asking 'when will all this end?'[222] Stavsky also detached himself from the RAPP leadership at the last moment. He too wrote to Stalin. Declaring that internecine conflict was endemic to RAPP and that all efforts to end it had been unavailing, he too begged for personal intervention: 'Comrade Stalin, further delay would be inadmissible'.[223] Such appeals may have helped to convince Stalin that he would, following RAPP's demise, have more compliant cadres for the rule of literature. Its abolition was announced shortly afterwards.

That same day, all literary Moscow celebrated the event. Serafimovich played host to the largest gathering.[224] His guests included prominent writers within RAPP who had formed its inner opposition, Panfyorov, Gladkov and Bill'-Belotserkovsky, and representatives of party institutions who had joined the anti-RAPP coalition: most notable amongst them were Kosarev of Komsomol, Galin, a senior journalist on *Pravda* and the philosopher Yudin of the Communist Academy. Yudin had only the previous day provided the theoretical background to the Party's resolution.[225] In the expectation that the new party policy would bring about a literary conciliation, Serafimovich proposed a forgiving toast: 'let bygones be bygones'.[226] But it fell to an altogether more sinister figure, the prominent writer Pavlenko, discovered drinking at the Herzen House, to make a more. accurate prediction: 'The war in literature is only just beginning'.[227]

4 The New Order

Stalin dove and shattered in one blow this mighty organisation.

Max Eastman, 1934[1]

Most commentators regard the abolition of RAPP as sudden and unexpected. Gleb Struve sees it simply as a 'bolt from the blue'.[2] Max Hayward, while considering the decision explicable 'in terms of Stalin's temperament' notes that 'having used RAPP as an instrument to bludgeon non-Party intellectuals into conformity, he now abruptly got rid of them'.[3] This is confirmed by Soviet reminiscences. Isaac Babel stated that 'For a fortnight, Stalin called in Averbakh and the like and gave them severe reprimands. He then realised he could do nothing with such people'.[4] We also have the report of Kaganovich to the next Party Congress. 'When the question of literature came up' – he did not explain how it arose – 'various solutions were considered by the Politburo'. These included a radical reform of RAPP or a long declaration 'on the tasks of communists in literature'.[5] But Stalin had seen that half-measures would be ineffective. He opted instead for an 'organisational' solution: 'That is how the idea of abolishing RAPP and setting up a single Writer's Union was born'.[6] Despite the hagiography, designed to demonstrate Stalin's genius in every sphere, this account has the mark of authenticity. It was characteristic of Stalin to treat problems of any sort as amenable to administrative solutions. The ability to reduce all matters to bureaucratic management had been perhaps his most salient feature as a politician.

The text of the Central Committee Resolution 'On the Reformation of Literary-Artistic Organisations', issued on 23 April 1932,[7] was curt and to the point:

Some years ago, when alien elements still exerted some significant influence in literature, most actively in the first years of NEP, while proletarian literary cadres still remained weak, the Party did its utmost to assist the creation and strengthening of basic proletarian organisations in literature and art, in order to strengthen the position of proletarian writers and art workers. But now, when proletarian cadres in literature and art have grown up, bringing on new writers and artists from work places, factories and collective

114

farms, the existing structure of proletarian literary-artistic groups (VOAPP, RAPP, RAPM etc.)[8] is too narrow and forms an obstacle to the serious development of artistic work. There is the danger in this situation that organisations may be transformed from a mighty means of mobilisation of Soviet writers and artists around the tasks of socialist construction into a means of cultivating cliques, cut off from contemporary political tasks and from a considerable number of writers and artists sympathetic towards socialist construction. It follows that a corresponding reorganisation of literary-artistic organisations is required to widen the basis of their work. It has therefore been decided to abolish the associations of proletarian writers (VOAPP, RAPP) and to unite those writers who support the platform of Soviet power and aspire to participate in socialist construction in a single Union of Soviet Writers with a communist fraction in it. Parallel changes are to be enacted in other spheres of art.[9]

In retrospect, it is apparent that this is the moment at which Soviet writers are ordered to become 'artists in uniform'.[10] The system of 'command-management' which Bukharin had anticipated now begins to be installed. This was not solely of literary concern: the Resolution was directed at the arts as a whole, and was – despite the slipshod phrasing of the final sentence – to be a guiding directive throughout the cultural spheres. Yet its totalitarian intention was not immediately apparent to contemporaries. On the contrary, in juxtaposition with the preceding proletarian period, it looked almost liberal. Its replacement of class criteria, such as 'proletarian' or 'peasant' origin, by the broader label 'Soviet writer' seemed less exclusive; likewise, the extension of membership to all those supporting the platform of Soviet power and aspiring 'to participate in socialist construction' did not appear unduly restrictive. Even the provision for a communist fraction within the incipient Union was not a novelty. This had been a common practice since the Revolution through which 'bourgeois specialists' could be re-employed alongside Party watchdogs within Soviet institutions. It did not automatically imply political manipulation of the Union from within. In all these senses, the Resolution could plausibly be presented as an act of reconciliation with non-Party writers after the traumas and persecution of the RAPP era. Its closure of that period, and abolition of the proletarian associations was quite explicit, while the arrangements that would follow remained studiously vague.

Several years were to pass before the full import of the Resolution became clear. There is a curious interlude in literary politics, during which contesting attitudes and aspirations can still be heard. These should not be overlooked. They present alternatives to an incipient Stalinist order which were not easily silenced. It took time for the system of bureaucratic management and intervention 'from above' to end dissent and establish a single and incontestable interpretation.

On 26 April 1932, the Moscow fellow-travellers' association gave the Party Resolution a cautious welcome. However, no-one agreed with Seyfullina that a new literary era had already dawned. The peasant writer Klychkov caused astonishment by referring to the Resolution as a 'return to NEP in literature' and by announcing that RAPP had been a 'reactionary organisation'. The press reported the general attitude to be 'temporising and vacillating'.[11] Shortly afterwards, thirty-one non-party writers stated in a letter to the Central Committee that while RAPP remained in existence they would not join the new Union.[12] Indeed, from the outset, RAPP engaged in resistance to the Party's Resolution. Reporting on this to Stalin, Panfyorov stated:

> Over the last few days Averbakh has extended his agitations. Announcing to all and sundry that he and his young friends had been longing for such a resolution for their whole lives, they are trying to turn this wise document to their own account. Averbakh has arranged everything so that he will once again occupy the top post in the Writers' Union, going behind Gorky's back and overcoming the opposition (he is past master at that).[13]

According to Panfyorov, Averbakh had named a 'new leadership of literature'. On his list Gorky was titular head while the real executive authority was exercised by himself. Yet he pointed out, were this permitted, writers would find no real difference between the RAPP regime and the new Union. He called for Stalin to take sterner measures to eliminate the heresy of *Averbakhovshchina*.[14]

Averbakh himself informed a session of RAPP's Secretariat on 3 May, 'it is well known that when the Central Committee held a meeting to discuss the draft resolution I took part as a leader of RAPP and spoke in its favour'. Some people were trying to portray the Resolution as a 'blow against RAPP', but on the contrary, it was clear beyond question that the creation 'according to Party policy' of particularist proletarian associations had been correct and remained so. Hence the Resolution should be understood as 'a new stage of the struggle for proletarian literary hegemony'. Admittedly, existing organisational arrangements had become too narrow for the new stage, leading to the shortcomings that the Resolution had indicated. RAPP now needed to work harmoniously with 'those cadres who have been transferred from RAPP to the single Writers' Union'. The fact that the Central Committee had passed a resolution showed how closely the Party leadership attended to literature and to its leadership. Equally, 'it is obvious that we are the organisation which the Party in its Resolution called the communist fraction within the Writers' Union'. Although RAPP was not yet ready to 'take responsibility for the whole of literature' they had a duty to make clear to non-party writers that 'we are not talking about cessation of class struggle in literature but rather of carrying it out under new conditions'. He concluded that 'the Central Committee decision is to be used to increase the fight against class alien influence and not to extinguish class struggle in literature'.[15]

Makar'yev enlarged upon this militant theme. 'We are not here discussing portfolios – the leadership of the Writers' Union – though that is an important question. For us workers in proletarian literature it is no small matter whether the leadership will be in the hands of unprincipled people, former *Litfrontists*, or in the hands of those who will carry out the Party line'. He too argued that to regard the Resolution as a blow against RAPP was 'to misunderstand the Party line in literature. We hear that Bezymensky has coined the slogan "Smash the RAPPist leadership". That is a highly original understanding of the Central Committee resolution'.[16] Neither he nor Averbakh had mentioned RAPP's abolition.

Only Stavsky disagreed. He told the meeting that discussions about a new leadership for literature had already begun. Gorky, who returned to Russia on 24 April, had 'written down 25 names over dinner but then tired of it and stopped'. Stavsky had heard this from 'the communist Pavlenko' and from various non-Party writers including Alexei Tolstoy and Nikolai Tikhonov. They had travelled from Leningrad for the occasion. So too had Slonimsky who recalled the joyful feeling of many writers present that space was opening up for creative freedom within an overall consensus on 'ideological unity'.[17] Stavsky stated bluntly that RAPP had only itself to blame for its exclusion. When for instance in December 1931 'a group of comrades had visited Stalin', such access had been wasted since the remainder of the association 'were not even told what took place'. More culpable still had been concealment of Stalin's 'historic letter of great significance' – the unpublished answer to 'Writer-Communists of RAPP' in February 1929 – 'from which many new comrades here could have learned much'. Makar'yev retorted that the decision not to publicise its contents had been made while Stavsky was the responsible Secretary of RAPP. Averbakh expressed his regret that Stavsky had not acquainted colleagues with the contents of his own recent letter to Stalin, which Averbakh claimed nonetheless to know. The session degenerated into heckling and recrimination.[18]

Faced with such recalcitrance, the Party attempted to enforce its decision. *Pravda* printed a long editorial on literary policy intended to elaborate and define the somewhat cryptic Resolution. Its starting-point was the new trend amongst the intelligentsia which Stalin had first identified in June 1931. Allegedly, 'a majority of the old technical intelligentsia', impressed by the achievements of the socialist economy, had 'crossed over' to the Soviet side. An about-turn (*povorot*) had already taken place in the Academy of Sciences whose members now directed their energies towards current tasks of socialist construction. There had been a similar move in literature where 'numerous writers' cadres', such as Leonov, Tikhonov and Marietta Shaginyan, now accepted Soviet power and were actively assisting socialist construction. Simultaneously there had been a colossal development of the new proletarian intelligentsia. Therefore, existing organisations in literature, above all RAPP, had become too narrow and a barrier to literary development. Their attack on fellow-travellers had been 'a great political mistake'. The crude dichotomies of *Na literaturnom postu*, summarised in the slogan 'not fellow-traveller but ally or enemy' were inadmissible. Averbakh was singled out for his 'schematisation and vulgarisation of the Party line towards the intelligentsia'. RAPP's concentration on individual psychology was rejected: of Libedinsky's 'Birth of the Hero' *Pravda* stated 'such Robinson Crusoes have nothing in common with Marxism'.

In its place, the editorial offered the first authoritative statement of the literary objectives of the new union. There now stood before writers the 'tremendously important task of creating a highly artistic literature, socialist in content'. They must assist 'the principal task of the second Five Year Plan to liquidate capitalist elements and classes in general', a process that writers should illustrate 'in its concreteness and in its contradictions'. Soviet writers and artists were to show 'the creative role of the Communist party in socialist construction, to depict heroes of the distant past, the civil war and present day: shock workers, collective farmers, komsomols and communist activists'.[19] Here, in embryo, was socialist realism. Nevertheless, RAPP responded with further resistance.

RAPP's *Na literaturnom postu* appeared on 10 May without reprinting the Resolution. Its claim to have gone to press before its publication was indignantly exposed by a further *Pravda* article. RAPP also made a detailed reply to Yudin's article of 23 April disputing its findings and condemning his method of 'false quotations'.[20] Privately, the RAPPists sent two protest letters to the Central Committee Secretariat outlining their reasons for refusing to accept RAPP's dissolution. One was signed collectively by Fadeyev, Kirshon, Makar'yev, Sholokhov and Béla Illyés (the Hungarian author): Averbakh wrote on his own account.[21] These protests necessitated further action by the top Party leadership to clarify and enforce its Resolution. A Commission of the Politburo was formed with Stalin as the main spokesman, and Kaganovich, Stetsky (*Kul't-prop* Secretary) and Gronsky (editor of *Izvestiya*) as ordinary members. Postyshev took the chair.

Although its term of reference was to call on a 'wide representation' of literary groups to give evidence, it seems that only proletarian writers were summoned: Kirshon and Afinogenov (for RAPP), and Illyés (for the International Organisation of Revolutionary Writers (MORP)). Averbakh was evidently excluded. RAPP's militancy was now tempered by more prudent consideration. While recognising that there would have to be a Writers' Union, they requested special status as a 'autonomous section for proletarian literature' within it. But even this more modest formulation was clearly contrary to the Resolution's call for unification of all writers within a single Union. It was quickly dismissed. A second proposition, however, concerning literary theory, was more tenable and discussion of it lasted several hours. RAPP defended its 'dialectical-materialist method' (*dia-mat*) drawn up for theatre by Afinogenov during 1931,[22] which it now sought to extend to all genres as the 'literary platform of the union'. This plea was more easily defensible than the first: while institutional autonomy had been precluded by the Resolution, RAPP's putative orthodoxy was not. No minutes of the meeting are available, but we do know that a compromise was eventually proposed. Theoretical problems were to be delegated to a further commission, which would, at some unspecified date, formulate a literary method for the Union.[23]

With this, RAPP capitulated. A collective letter to the Party Secretariat from Fadeyev, Averbakh, Kirshon, Makar'yev and Sholokhov apologised for their opposition in abject tones. They conceded that their protests had been misconceived and their refusal to accept the Resolution had been 'undeniable sectarianism' which they now repudiated.[24] Illyés and others later wrote in similar terms.[25] A public statement of RAPP's abolition, signed by each member of the Secretariat, appeared in *Pravda* on 15 May. Commentary was left to Komsomol. Concluding its long campaign, *Komsomol'skaya pravda* noted that RAPP's incorrect reaction to the Resolution reflected the persistent errors of the 'Averbakh faction'. RAPP had been removed for 'mistakes of individuals in its leadership'. In future, the Writers' Union would be 'the Party's agency on the literary front'.[26]

A new stage of literary consolidation now began. Whereas the first was directed solely towards Party writers, seeking their amalgamation in a single communist association, the second reached out towards the former fellow-travellers, with the aim of achieving their voluntary affiliation in the Writers' Union. Since obligation and bullying were unlikely to achieve this objective, positive inducements had to be found. The process took far longer than anyone had anticipated. Initially, the Party leadership expected the Union to be inaugurated by the end of 1932. During 1933, it reluctantly agreed to several postponements. The Union eventually came into being after the First Congress of Soviet Writers in September 1934.

During this interval of more than two years, the conduct of literary policy was entrusted to a new body. On the day of RAPP's public demise, an *Orgkomitet* (Organising Committee) was established to set up the Writers' Union. It forms the central focus of literary politics for this whole period. Hence its initial composition was a matter of immediate interest. It struck a balance between the previously warring groups and factions. Its first President was I. M. Gronsky[27] and V. Kirpotin[28] became the inaugural Secretary. Neither had connections with RAPP or with the anti-RAPP coalition. Eight of the former fellow-travelling writers were included (V. Ivanov, Leonov, Malyshkin, Pavlenko, Seyfullina, Slonimsky, Tikhonov and Fedin) and these were balanced by an equal number from the proletarian side (Afinogenov, Bezymensky, Kirshon, Panfyorov, Serafimovich, Stavsky, Fadeyev and Chumandrin). A smaller number of individuals were coopted from other literary groups and Bill'-Belotserkovsky and the veteran Berezovsky were included on their own account. In all, twenty-four members attended the first meeting of the *Orgkomitet* on 19 May 1932.[29] This was clearly too large a committee for smooth administration. It therefore decided to delegate everyday decision-making to a seven-man Praesidium. Sharply differentiating the new leadership of literature from the old, Averbakh's faction was excluded. Indeed, both Kirshon and Stavsky were sent on leave.[30] In addition to Gronsky and Kirpotin (*ex-officio*), the Praesidium consisted of Leonov, Tikhonov, Malyshkin, Panfyorov and Fadeyev, with Pavlenko and Aseyev as candidates. It got down to work a week later.

The first priority of the Praesidium was to take control of the main literary newspaper: *Literaturnaya gazeta*. This paper had, as *Pravda* pointed out, 'blurred the importance and significance of the Central Committee Resolution' and eventually acknowledged the liquidation of RAPP 'only through clenched teeth'.[31] Its RAPPist editor, Selivanovsky, was removed, but agreeing a replacement took time, during which Kirpotin ran the paper through an editorial collective. Some praesidium members favoured a non-sectarian appointment (such as Kirpotin himself): others preferred an editor from the Communist Academy (such as Ral'tsevich) in order to hasten a radical critique of RAPP. Eventually, a former editor, Dinamov, was reappointed after promising the Praesidium a 'systematic critique of all the mistakes of RAPP'.[32] Much of this materialised, but as a colleague commented in the autumn, 'despite numerous editorials on the mistakes of the RAPP leadership we have yet to hear a single word of self-criticism from Dinamov – a former member of the left wing of RAPP'.[33] Similar steps were taken to remove RAPP's influence over journals. The Communist Academy argued, successfully, that publications on which it had collaborated with RAPP, such as *Literaturnoye nasledstvo*, should henceforth be edited by the Communist Academy alone.[34] It also made a bid for control over RAPP's journal *Na literaturnom postu*, but here the Praesidium was more reluctant. After some delay, during which the journal made an abject apology for previously resisting the Resolution,[35] it was abolished. With the demise of other proletarian journals,[36] this left no major vehicle for literary criticism. The Praesidium therefore decided to launch a new journal: *Literaturnyi kritik*.[37] This appeared a year later under the editorship of Communist Academician Yudin and established itself as a leading literary journal of the later 1930s.

With the press and journals secured, the *Orgkomitet* turned its attention to the structure of the future Writers' Union. A commission on 'apparatus', chaired by Kirpotin, was to draft a statute setting out conditions for membership. Another was to formulate 'methods of preparation' for the inaugural congress at which the Union would be brought into being. A third was given the task of organising the 'creative life of the Writers' Union', somewhat nebulous terms of reference, on which the *Orgkomitet* as a whole was also to be consulted.[38] No deadlines were fixed for accomplishing these tasks, although it was assumed that this could be done within a matter of months. Such expectations were unduly optimistic.

One of the organisational complexities became apparent at the subsequent meeting of the *Orgkomitet*. On 21 June the anomalous continuing existence of the literary association of the Red Army and Fleet (LOKAF) was reviewed. Its spokesman, Subotsky, (who subsequently became an *Orgkomitet* member) argued for its retention as an autonomous organisation. Another member advanced the claim that 'having fulfilled the Party line in relation to the Soviet intelligentsia', unlike any other literary or artistic organisation, LOKAF need not be abolished. A second possibility, canvassed by Stavsky and others, was to transform LOKAF into an organisational cell or section of the incipient Writers' Union. But summing up, Kirpotin declared 'the Soviet Writers' Union is not going to be constructed as a federation of the old autonomous literary organisations, such as LOKAF'.[39] Underlying this discussion was the problem of amalgamating previously disparate groupings within a single Union to be based upon a common programme. Within this, nothing proved more difficult than the incorporation of the former RAPP grouping.

As a former member has pointed out, RAPP's leaders found it hard to adjust to the Central Committee edict. He recalls: 'The *Na literaturnom postu* group was cemented by many years of personal relationships, and immediately after the abolition of RAPP, all of us wanted to preserve it above all as a creative grouping'. It was difficult to discard remnants of this collective psychology, even though he conceded that the group had long since left literary inspiration behind and degenerated into a bureaucratic and sectarian clique. The single exception was Fadeyev, who, following the Resolution, had 'radically altered his relationship with communist writers' and said when meeting Panfyorov, Bezymensky, Stavsky or others 'now we are together again'.[40] His conciliatory attitude contrasted sharply with that of the majority in the Averbakh faction. The co-option of Averbakh, Makar'yev and Ermilov onto the *Orgkomitet* in August, supposedly to allow them to 'overcome their sectarianism',[41] had, in fact, the opposite effect. The Averbakh group maintained its cohesion and obstructed the Orgkomitet's activity by every means it could. The consequent confusion was described by Fadeyev in a letter to Gorky: 'literary affairs are in a shocking state. The most shocking is not that the *Orgkomitet* is doing nothing, has no programme, is sunk in squabbles and scandals, and awaiting a "re-working" (a dreadful word adopted from ideological struggles) of the former RAPP – all this is fully to be expected and "natural" – but the most shocking is the conduct of many former RAPPists, my associates'. This applied, he explained, not to those members who really were writers such as Sholokhov, Libedinsky and Afinogenov but to the 'whole critical and organisational flank' which now revealed themselves to be 'philistines and literary bankrupts (Selivanovsky, Serebryansky, Makar'yev and many others)'. Such critics who regarded themselves in their day as 'the Central Committee's cell in literature' and pontificated 'to left and right', now 'revelled in their inactivity'.[42]

In an effort to overcome this inertia, the Communist Academy held a series of lectures during the summer months. Although their ostensible purpose was to discuss literary theory, the real function was to discredit RAPP. Yudin, opening the series, took the view that Averbakh had 'slid into Trotskyist positions'. RAPP had made numerous mistakes in literary theory, such as the 'living man' slogan, and other expressions of an 'idealist' position.[43] Ye. F. Usievich, author of a scurrilous book on RAPP to which Yudin contributed the preface,[44] made further political accusations. RAPP's slogan, 'ally or enemy', stemmed 'irrefutably from Trotskyite opinions'. Averbakh's views, she asserted, were derived from an indiscriminate reading of Plekhanov, Deborin and Bukharin. Since these three had been discredited during the Five Year Plan this was a serious charge, the more so since Averbakh allegedly 'mistook their writings for Marxist opinions'.[45] Such charges would be reiterated in 1937 when the terror swept away a majority of RAPP's leadership. In the milder climate of 1932, however, Fadeyev was allowed to answer them.

His cycle of articles was intended 'if only in part to begin the serious work of giving a thorough account of exactly what from the old shows a positive way forward, and what is found to be mistaken and to be rejected'.[46] The first, 'Ally or enemy and where the chief danger lies', concentrated attention on the RAPPist experience. Its slogans had to be considered in their historical context. Thus 'Ally or enemy' had been coined in the period of crash collectivisation and liquidation of the *kulaks* as a class. At that time it was not 'leftist' but corresponded to the Party line. For instance Kuibyshev had remarked in a speech to engineers and technicians that 'those not with us are against us'.[47] The second elaborated on the lessons to be learned from the RAPP episode. Its critical jargon should be avoided in favour of a practical discussion of mistakes, which should be spelled out in precise terms. 'It is high time to translate the whole of our literary criticism from the level of quotational scholasticism, polemicising with each other, into concrete ideological and educational work with writers'. The 'quotational' method was illustrated by damning reference to Yudin. Prior to the April resolution Yudin (with Mitin and Ral'tsevich) had referred to RAPP in *Pravda* as 'correct in its literary political line', while afterwards he described RAPP as 'fundamentally anti-Leninist'. Moreover his *Bol'shevik* article had accused RAPP, simultaneously, of Bukharinism, Bogdanovism, Deborinism, Stenism, right opportunism, left vulgarisation and Tolstoyism. This catalogue, Fadeyev wrote, demonstrated Yudin's total lack of principle. The other articles looked ahead to future tasks of literary criticism in its 'struggle for socialist culture'. Class struggle in culture had not 'ended with the liquidation of RAPP' but needed to be pursued amongst the broad mass of writers in the light of new conditions.[48]

Such exhortation was a constant theme of literary editorials. One declared 'at no time in any place have artists had before such material, such background, such an epoch, such people . . . down to work!'. Another admitted 'working out forms and methods of work for the new writers' union, especially creativity and various problems associated with it – none of these will take place without writers. This is necessary even during the summer months'. A third noted 'the end of the summer is approaching and in the near future writers will come back from holiday. The Soviet Writers' Union must be an ideological, not simply an organisational, centre of Soviet literature'.[49] Writers themselves showed little enthusiasm for this task. In this apathetic context, the *Orgkomitet* sought out a non-controversial means by which writers could be brought together. Before the *Orgkomitet* had itself achieved practical results, a way was found to demonstrate movement towards unanimity. Though there was as yet no common highest factor, there might at least be a common denominator.

In September, the decision was taken to adopt Gorky as such a symbol. A high-level commission presided over by Postyshev, and including Yenukidze, Stetsky (*Kul't-prop* Secretary) and Gronsky and Kirpotin of the *Orgkomitet*,[50] began the process of installing him as a pillar of the Soviet establishment. His name was bestowed upon his birth-place, Nizhnii-Novgorod; Moscow was given both a Gorky Street and a Gorky Park; Gorky himself was invested with an Order of Lenin. The Gorky Literary Institute (IMLI) was founded in his honour.[51] A lavish *Collected Works* was ordered with portraits, to include one with Stalin. Gorky's personality was to be projected on the widest possible scale, in newspapers and journals, radio, film and postage stamps.

The public climax of these celebrations was reached on 25 September – the fortieth anniversary of his first publication – at a special meeting in the Bolshoi Theatre, attended by Stalin and the Politburo, official representatives of culture and science and foreign guests. They heard an opening speech by Stetsky, which addressed the 'dominant motif' of Gorky's work. This had prompted Lenin to describe Gorky as the greatest exponent of proletarian art. It was that, though a master of human psychology, Gorky did not confine his analysis to individual life in some enclosed circle but rather demonstrated typical characters in relation to social conditions. 'The closer Gorky comes to the workers' movement the more vividly appears his basic method of realism.' 'He doesn't amass trivia, pile up detail for its own sake. No, he lets real life pass through his creative laboratory.' His writing thus became 'revolutionary realism'.[52] A later speaker, Bubnov, described Gorky's lifelong committment to struggle with the conservative, backward and decadent mentality of the Russian bourgeois intelligentsia. It was to be demonstrated that evening at the Vakhtangov Theatre with the performance of Gorky's new play *Yegor Bulichev and Others* which in a 'scourging and dazzlingly comic form presents the *fin-de-siècle* of the Russian bourgeoisie'.[53] There followed greetings on behalf of the incipient Writers' Union (by Vsevolod Ivanov); from the French left-wing intelligentsia (transmitted by Henri Barbusse); and announcements of honours (made by Postyshev and Bulganin).

Gorky replied that old age precluded any show of modesty, but, of course, his value had been overestimated. His brief remarks reiterated a familiar injunction to fellow writers: get to know the country, its past and prospects from firsthand experience: 'The maxim is simple: study!'[54] Yet his political reservations about Stalinism, though carefully hidden, may have found expression in an earlier letter to Stalin which had protested against the practice of 'self-criticism', a favourite technique of Stalinist politics. It argued that negative material published in the Soviet press was reproduced by western correspondents, thus damaging the image of the Soviet

Union abroad. He called for more objective presentation: 'we must give much more serious attention to the cultural and political development of young people. Above all, we must give a more objective picture of current affairs, balancing the negative facts now published in our press with more positive ones . . . we cannot permit the facts of slovenliness, laziness, drunkeness, pilfering and hooliganism to predominate over the facts that are fostering revolution and culture: the construction of housing, factories, bakeries and palaces of culture, and schools . . .'[55] In place of self-criticism, he proposed that space be allocated in daily newspapers for the celebration of economic and cultural achievements, and that a number of new journals be launched for the same purpose. As in his jubilee address, Gorky placed great emphasis upon the need to study reality, while also making clear that the circumstances to be observed were progressive ones: leading the country on the path to socialism.

Stalin's reply alleged that Gorky was opposed to all forms of criticism. He read the writer a sharp lecture; 'We cannot do without self-criticism, we simply cannot, Alexei Maximovich. Without it, stagnation, corruption of the apparatus, growth of bureaucracy, sapping of the creative initiatives of the working class are inevitable'. Of course, Soviet self-criticism could provide material for adverse reportage abroad, but this risk was well worth taking. As for Gorky's example of 'grumbling youth', a certain Zenin, he considered them 'an insignificant by-product of successful revolution which inevitably produced a minority of diverse deserters to the enemy camp'. 'These are unavoidable overhead costs of revolution.' However, Gorky's positive suggestion was accepted with enthusiasm. Stalin agreed to commission a collective *History of the Civil War* by participants, assisted by Alexei Tolstoy and other writers, though not under the editorship proposed. 'It will be safer to entrust these undertakings to politically staunch comrades than to invite Radek and his friends as collaborators. That will be safer.' An anti-war journal, to be edited by Voronsky, was vetoed on the grounds that 'Voronsky's line in wanting to launch a campaign against the "horrors" of war differs very little from the line of the bourgeois pacifists'.[56] Indeed, Stalin's personal interest in literature was expressed at two special gatherings in Gorky's Moscow home during 1931. At the first, Stalin conducted a long conversation with Sholokhov on the third volume of *The Quiet Don*.[57] On the second occasion, Stalin accompanied by Molotov and Voroshilov, visited Gorky to discuss the *History of Factories* project, which had just been announced.[58]

This collective venture was intended to portray the history of industrial production 'from the forms and methods of old exploiters to the revolutionary techniques of the present day'. Such new forms as shock-working, socialist competition and production surges (*pod"emy*) would receive especial attention.[59] The editorial board, headed by Gorky and established writers such as Libedinsky, Chumandrin and Seyfullina, also formally included Kaganovich, Postyshev, Yenukidze and Bukharin.[60] According to an instruction issued in 1931, RAPP would have a 'prominent place' on the editorial collegium.[61] Gorky was enthusiastic about Averbakh's participation: 'a talented young man and fine organiser, although in a tearing hurry to reach conclusions. He is educable'. However, he concurred with Panfyorov and Serafimovich in criticising the mistakes of the RAPP leadership,[62] and looked forward to the consolidation of literary groups around a common programme. Such a view was expressed in a letter to the Party Central Committee, in early 1932, setting out some ideas which the Resolution later embodied. Though none of this important letter has ever been published, the editor-in-chief of Gorky's *Collected Works* informed the present author[63] that it will appear in the forthcoming second edition.

Gorky's developing role as intermediary between Stalin and the literary intelligentsia, one which he had earlier performed under Lenin, was consecrated after the jubilee in a further special evening at Gorky's town house. This gathering took place on 26 October 1932. Writers were summoned at short notice; many were invited on the day. There was no time to contact Leningrad, let alone those living further afield. Some forty-five had assembled by 9 p.m. when they were suddenly joined by Stalin, Molotov, Voroshilov and Kaganovich.[64]

Welcoming the leaders, Gorky referred to the improved atmosphere and quality of literature since the April Resolution. Much previous writing had been shoddy and made cruder still by RAPPist 'methods of education', but RAPP had now acknowledged its mistakes, thus removing the main obstacle to the development of the new literature. This would depict the gigantic changes now taking place in the economic structure of the country. The non-party writers V. Ivanov, Leonov and Nikitin spoke in the same vein. Only Seyfullina struck a dissentient note. Sharply disagreeing with Gorky's statement about the genuineness of RAPP's repentance, she declared that its former leadership, Averbakh amongst them, were simply biding their time and would later make a bid for leadership of the

Writers' Union. Although she was called to stop by protestors from the floor, Stalin allowed her to finish.[65]

An interval was then called. Drinks were served in an antechamber, over which writers took turns to converse with the leader. One enquired about his recent interviews with Emil Ludwig and Bernard Shaw.[66] Another asked about his assessment of *The Quiet Don*. From Stalin's detailed comments, such as those on the portrayal of Gregor Melekhov, it 'became apparent that he knew the works of many writers better than other participants in the conversation'. Dinner was then served during which Stalin preserved a 'serious demeanour'. He proposed a toast to Lenin: 'to the great man'. All stood. Malyshkin replied with one to Stalin. Eventually all the courtesies and preliminaries were dispensed with, and Stalin could address the gathering. His remarks were taken by all present as the first authoritative statement of Stalin's policy towards *belles-lettres*. Yet they were never made public. His statement is published here, from archives, for the first time.

> What is the essence of today's meeting? Its essence lies in the relationship between party and non-party writers. This is the nub of the problem. To begin with we gathered the Party writers. It is a habit of us Bolsheviks to do that. It is our custom. First we gather the Party people and talk to them heart-to-heart. We check up on one another. Then, when we see that we have reached agreement, we stand up for each other. We stand up for each other once we have resolved what the party view is. It is a good way. We check up on all our work. So you see, comrade Seyfullina, we first collect the party people together and we check up amongst our number – it would be good if this measure were applied to the RAPPists in the *Orgkomitet*. And now we are discussing this with you, discussing all our work. What did Il'ich teach us? He always said that non-party people should check up on party work. And *vice-versa*: the party checks up on non-party people. How strong is our party? It is as strong as the backing it has from the broad mass of non-party people. Maybe we don't know that amongst party members are scoundrels and time-servers. We expel them from our midst. We expel them in individual instances and in purges. From time to time we purge our party. It is a big event in party life. And we invite non-party people to the purges. Lenin always said that the nub of the problem is that the party must always carry non-party people with it. Because it means that non-party people will work with us for the victory of socialism? It means that amongst

them some do not want something that they still don't understand. It means we must enlighten them. The party is small, but non-party people are very numerous. How would it be if the mass of Bolshevik workers did not support the party? It is easy to discard sympathisers – I don't speak here of enemies, we are not discussing them today – it is easy to push them aside, but to gain their trust is difficult. Discarding people is easy, but winning them to one's side is difficult.

Why did we liquidate RAPP? Because RAPP was cut off from non-party writers, because it ceased serious party work in literature. This is why we decided to liquidate all groups in literature. Sectarianism created an unhealthy atmosphere, not conducive to trust. We disbanded all groups and removed the biggest group – RAPP – which was responsible for sectarianism. Now we will demand that all party writers follow this policy.

How then will we organise the Writers' Union? In the centre will be a strong nucleus of Communists and around them a wide strata of non-party writers. There, in the fraction, you can have any amount of people. Peace is found only in the grave-yard (*Laughter*). But the communist fraction must be united. Communists must bring writers with them.

When Seyfullina spoke here, she complained that she did not trust the leadership of RAPP. The leadership complain that Seyfullina is not alone in this. I know that others think the same, but were afraid to say so. They claimed that she is a coward. But it turned out the other way round. She spoke a 'home truth', one that everyone was thinking. We must take non-party writers into account. They are not party members, but they know life and know how to portray it. They also do serious work. Writers are a lot more numerous than you think. There are now thousands, and tens of thousands of new writers, young people, learning . . . and this is our good fortune. A majority will be non-party. You must learn to work with them. That is the task of the future Writers' Union. It must create working-conditions for every Soviet writer, accepting the platform of Soviet power and taking part in Communist construction.

And still on that, there is more I want to say. Still about two things (three in all). About what should you write? Poetry is fine. Novels are even better. But plays are now best of all. Plays are easy to understand. Our workers are busy. They spend eight hours in the factory. They come home to the family, to their children. Where can they sit to read a long novel? Comrades, how many

volumes are there in your novels. Three volumes. When is the
worker going to read them? Certainly, this doesn't mean that you
should stop writing novels. I don't mean that. But plays are the art
form that we now need most of all. Workers can watch plays easily.
From plays they can easily get our idea of parody, instilling it in
people. It is no accident that the bourgeois class, at its outset,
produced some of its greatest geniuses in drama: Shakespeare,
Molière. The bourgeoisie . . . was then more popular in contrast
to feudalism, to the nobility. We in our republic are now a more
popular republic in contrast to the bourgeoisie. And plays are now
the largest-scale art form in literature. We must make our own plays.
That is why you should write plays. But only good plays, artistically
done, if you please. (*Animation. Voice*: 'We'll do our best.')

Finally, the last question: the material funding of the future
Writers' Union. We must do everything to secure conditions for
work. For this reason we are setting-up a Literary Institute –
named after you Alexei Maximovich. In it we will train the young
people about which I spoke, the new cadres. (*Questioner*: 'With
paper likewise?')

Paper will be provided. It's all up to the *Orgkomitet*. The
Orgkomitet or Writers' Union will look after everything. There is
no need to refer everything to the government or Central Committee. It was said here that the Writers' Union is not a professional Union. Why not? Why can't it look after the material affairs
of its members? It must look after all of them, all sides of the lives
of its members. That's all I wanted to say.[67]

That was the extent of Stalin's contribution. Yet, despite its clumsy
and repetitive formulation, the major outline of his literary policy
shows through. Its essence, as indicated earlier by the April Resolution, was organisational. The previous stage, uniting Party writers,
was a precondition for bringing non-Party writers into a unified
association. Tact was needed and the RAPP approach was implicitly
rejected. However, the purpose of the new policy was, as RAPP's
had been, monopolistic. This was made clear in the explicitly political
composition of the incipient Writers' Union. 'In the centre will be a
strong nucleus of Communists and around them a wide stratum of
non-party writers'.

The most obvious shortcoming of Stalin's statement was any guidance about the literary method for the new Union. Stalin did add an
afterthought:

I forgot to talk about what you are 'producing'. There are various forms of production: artillery, automobiles, lorries. You also produce 'commodities', 'works', 'products'. Such things are highly necessary. Engineering things. For people's souls. 'Products' are highly necessary too. 'Products' are very important for people's souls. You are engineers of human souls. Your work is in vain if the souls in them are rotten. No, 'production' of souls is a most important task.

The whole production of the country is linked to your 'production'. And that, in its turn, is not entrusted without the understanding that people enter life when they take part in the production of socialism. As someone here rightly said, the writer cannot sit still, he must get to know the life of the country. Rightly said. Men are transforming life. That is why I propose a toast 'To Engineers of Human Souls'.[68]

But this famous phrase, which Stalin later denied uttering[69], was hardly a substitute for a defined literary method. Nevertheless, socialist realism was subsequently attributed to the 'supreme leader' whose 'simplicity of genius', as Fadeyev once put it, had enabled him alone to find the appropriate formulation. Although such an ascription seems politically plausible – who else in Stalin's Russia would have had the authority to make so significant an innovation? – it is not supported by any evidence. On the occasion of his alleged definition, the above meeting, the term is not mentioned at all in the main body of his talk and only referred to briefly in the question period. A former RAPP activist enquired:

– Comrade Stalin, how do you see the role of world-view in art?
– You talk and talk about dialectical materialism, not in the least understanding what it is you talk about.
– Does that mean a poet need not be a dialectician?
– No, he may be, it is well and good if he will be a dialectical-materialist. But I wanted to say that he will then not want to write poetry (*Laughter*). I'm joking, of course, but, speaking seriously, you mustn't stuff an artist's head with abstract theses. He must know the theories of Marx and Lenin. He must know life. An artist must above all portray life truthfully. And if he shows our life truthfully, on its way to socialism, that will be socialist art, that will be socialist realism.[70]

This casual aside was later constructed into a mammoth edifice, and attribution of the act of definition to Stalin was obligatory for twenty years.

Later, other 'authors' of the doctrine came forward. Kirpotin claimed he had first mentioned the term in print.[71] Reference to that text, however, an editorial in *Literaturnaya gazeta* of 29 May 1932, somewhat diminishes the force of his assertion. The term socialist realism is there qualified by a number of adjectives: 'sincere, truthful, revolutionary, socialist, realism'. In any case, it was not the first published reference: Gronsky had referred to socialist realism in the same paper a week earlier. Subsequently, Gronsky advanced his own claim to authorship in two interviews. He told the Soviet scholar Sheshukov in the late 1960s that the Politburo Commission convened to enforce RAPP's dissolution had delegated the problem of literary method for the incipient Union to a 'formulating commission on the method of socialist realism'.[72] He amplified this claim to the present author in 1974, stating that when the Politburo Commission had discussed literary method, he had suggested the new term. According to his version, Gronsky had proposed 'proletarian, socialist realism' and Stalin approved, adding that it would be even better without the 'proletarian'. Since no other participant was living, and none left memoirs, it is impossible to confirm this reminiscence. Gronsky explained the lack of a protocol from the meeting thus: 'Stalin did not like putting things down on paper'.[73] Perhaps Gronsky did find the 'correct formulation', even though he says elsewhere he proposed 'communist realism' and had written in the first published reference of 'revolutionary, socialist realism'. He was on good terms with Stalin until his arrest in 1937, though in later years he tended to exaggerate the connection.[74] However, the *Orgkomitet* did put its decisions on paper and these indicate that the problem was not taken up in earnest until early 1933. The last months of 1932 were taken up with further demonstration of Soviet writers' new-found 'unanimity'.

The principal forum in which this was to be demonstrated was a First Plenum of the *Orgkomitet*, opened by Gronsky three days after the meeting with Stalin. He claimed that the gathering confirmed the 'coming over' of the great majority of the old literary intelligentsia to the Soviet side. RAPP's fundamental error had been to overlook and hinder this process, for which it had been liquidated. However, three of their former leadership had been included in the communist fraction of the *Orgkomitet* to give 'these comrades the chance to correct their mistakes'.[75] The critic Subotsky agreed that the new

situation in literature had thus far provided preconditions for liquidating 'sectarianism' but thought much still had to be done. The
literary world had been 'radically refreshed', but for the attainment
of unity there needed to be 'continuous, thorough, systematic criticism of all the mistakes of the RAPPist leadership. Without such
criticism of its errors there will *not* be created guarantees against the
re-appearance of sectarianism'.[76] Fadeyev's contribution to the reconciliation process was praised, though not without reservation.
From the discussion that followed, it was clear that many non-party
writers required to be persuaded that a new era in literary organisation had really dawned. Klychkov, while disclaiming any revanchist
attitude, continued to insist that RAPP had played a reactionary role
and that Averbakh in particular had no understanding of art.[77] This
was dismissed as 'nonsense' in Subotsky's closing speech.[78] A more
reserved position was taken by *Pereval* whose spokesman Ivan Katayev
made a cautious restatement of their theoretical position.[79] Even this
mild utterance caused uproar. Libedinsky protested that it presented
'a whole row of idealistic and reactionary prejudices in aesthetics
carried over into the sphere of literary politics. If our (RAPP) group
was harmful, how much more is this one. Such a group as *Pereval*
must make a radical review of its programme. For truly the Central
Committee decision concerned not RAPP alone, but all'.[80] After this
assault *Pereval* was obliged to circulate a statement announcing the
group's liquidation.[81]

A more ambivalent attitude was adopted by the majority of
fellow-travellers. In successive speeches, Slonimsky, Vera Inber and
Tikhonov avoided political issues altogether and dwelt rather on
problems of writers' self-definition and the inner essence of the
literary process.[82] Their modest statements indicated the return of
Soviet literature to self-reflectiveness within the calmer atmosphere
restored by the April 1932 Resolution. This was confirmed by several
members from the old intelligentsia appearing on an official platform
for the first time since the Revolution. Prishvin declared his satisfaction with the new regime and asserted that he re-experienced youth
every time he began a new book and 'now I am young again because I
have just started a fresh one'.[83] Though such 'veterans' had hardly
'come over to the side of Soviet power' in any active sense, they did
manage to find some grounds of enthusiasm for the literature of the
Soviet period, especially works of Gorky. Bely even asserted that
Averbakh's review of his *Moskva* had 'seemed to me very interesting
and was accepted by me as a guide'.[84]

Amongst the 500 delegates were many non-Russian writers, making this the first All-Union literary occasion. Their reports indicated that the April Resolution had been enforced with difficulty in many regions. Proletarian resistance had not been confined to the RSFSR. Those in Belorussia had remained intransigent, leading the well known non-party writers Kupata and Kotas to refuse to join the *Orgkomitet*, giving it the character rather of a widened APP than of a newly-unified organisation. Kirpotin's dispatch from Moscow had been required to achieve the reform of literature.[85] The Ukrainian position, greatly complicated by current nationalist repression, required repeated local Party resolutions.[86] In Georgia, the local party established a special committee to enforce the April Resolution.[87] The Kazakh Communist Party Committee issued a special resolution on literature.[88] Only after such measures had it been possible to form an All-Union *Orgkomitet*, half of whose fifty members came from non-Russian republics.[89] Non-Russian delegates to the Plenum noted that Gronsky had referred to national literatures as 'the literature of the people of the Soviet Union', but work on this question was delegated to a commission. The problem of translation was left unresolved.

The Plenum also heard speeches from former RAPPist leaders. Most of them looked back on their period of rule with a mixture of pride and regret. The Leningrad member Chumandrin, who had been most militant in his opposition to the Resolution, now raised the question 'what does hindering the realisation of the Central Committee decision signify?' Did it mean sitting idly and passively resisting the Resolution or active struggle with it? 'Such a struggle none of us engaged in nor called for.' But he did admit that the proletarian leadership had tried to maintain their previous forms of work and perpetuate a lordly attitude toward non-party writers. Such 'old habits and forms of work' had now been overcome. He called his post-April opposition 'a *Magnitostroi* of Cliquishness' and withdrew his assertion that 'the creative grouping of *Na literaturnom postu* was, will and must be'.[90] Libedinsky was less repentant. He offered a series of remarks concerning Averbakh. 'How should we evaluate him? It should be said right away that Averbakh who sees broad trends, often makes mistakes in matters of detail.' 'Therefore', Gronsky interrupted, 'he missed the reorganisation.' A little later, answering an interpolation by Averbakh, Libedinsky retorted, 'you do not understand everything that is going on at this Plenum'.[91]

A third RAPPist, Kirshon, stayed stubbornly defiant. While he did admit some mistakes in relations with non-party writers, he remained full of praise for RAPP's 'positive achievements'.[92] Makar'yev, too, proceeded to catalogue the 'successes of proletarian literature'. As evidence that his group had fulfilled the Resolution, he noted that RAPP's leaders had not coordinated their speeches to the Plenum in advance, which proved there was 'no longer a strong, monolithic, robust and authoritative RAPPist group'.[93] Averbakh was least contrite of all. In a speech which contained no word of self-criticism (though Gronsky interrupted several times to call for it), he referred to RAPP as 'a fine organisation which has trained many thousands of young proletarian writers' and to which he personally was 'proud to have belonged'.[94] One member of the audience complained 'we had come expecting a speech of self-criticism from Averbakh' but had heard none.[95] Only Chumandrin's full account of his errors was treated by the *Orgkomitet* as exemplary. No other RAPPist had repented.

The principal reason for calling the Plenum had been to hear public self-criticism from RAPP. Since this did not materialise there was little to justify the claim that Soviet literature had reached a 'new stage'. Instead, Gronsky concluded the proceedings with the thought that, apart from Klychkov, 'the unity of the whole body of writers from Chumandrin to Andrei Bely' had been demonstrated. The abolition of *Pereval* and LOKAF during the proceedings gave substance to his claim that disparate groups in Soviet literature no longer existed. But little constructive work had been done. Organisation of the future Union was delegated to a series of sub-committees: on structure and membership, the statute, and literary and critical methods.[96] However, perhaps the most important point about the First Plenum is that it took place. As Kirpotin stated: 'for the first time in fifteen years of Soviet power there were assembled in the same hall writers of the most diverse backgrounds from the old schools as well as party writers'.[97]

The atmosphere in which the literary intelligentsia now worked was demonstrated by an extraordinary episode six days after the Plenum. Stalin's wife died suddenly aged thirty-one. The official announcement gave no cause of death, which was ascribed by officially-inspired rumour to appendicitis, but it was almost certainly suicide. Her daughter believes there was a note addressed to Stalin but this has never been substantiated.[98] Since it was now mandatory for public bodies to express their sorrow, Soviet writers were obliged to express their grief. Condolences from members of the literary establishment, stated:

> Dear Comrade Stalin. It is hard to find words of condolence to express adequately our sense of loss. Accept our grief at the death of N. A. Alliluyeva, who devoted all her strength to the cause of the liberation of the millions of oppressed humanity, a cause which is headed by you and for which we are ready to sacrifice our lives in confirmation of its unconquerable lifegiving force.[99]

Pasternak evidently refused to sign this banal statement. Instead, he appended a terse message of his own:

> I share the feelings of the Comrades. The day before (the announcement of Alliluyeva's death) I thought deeply and intensively about Stalin: as a writer – for the first time. Next morning I read the news. I felt shaken as though I had been there living by his side and had seen it. Boris Pasternak.

His laconic message, in such stark contrast with the sycophantic and hackneyed language of the collective letter, gives almost a feeling of compassion.[100] But why had Stalin been thought of 'as a writer' only now for the first time? What did the premonition of Alliluyeva's death betoken? Was this the attempt to initiate a private dialogue – Ivinskaya calls it a silent duel[101] – between the poet and the Party leader? In many respects this seems fanciful. Yet, almost uniquely amongst Soviet writers of the first rank, Pasternak was not touched. Were the police files of his numerous indiscretions and misdemeanors marked with a special indication that a case was not to be brought without the approval of the highest political authority? Did Stalin perhaps somehow perceive the signal Pasternak was sending and respond by sparing him?

Alliluyeva's death seems to have affected Stalin quite profoundly. He was evidently shocked by the loss of perhaps the last person he really trusted. His morbid suspiciousness of others, no doubt already present, was given impetus and the OGPU took charge of his personal households.[102] But his reaction was not purely paranoid. In the years immediately following his attainment of political preeminence, several protests were made against him.

In 1930, as we have seen, a conversation between two Central Committee members, Syrtsov and Lominadze, about the possibility of a change in the party leadership was alleged by Stalin to have constituted a 'left-right bloc', though the existence of an actual organisation seems lacking.[103] While the outcome of collectivisation remained uncertain, Stalin was able to play on the threat of anarchy, or even civil war, which would, he alleged, have ensued from his removal from the supreme position. However, opposition to Stalin continued.

The 'Ryutin platform', an oppositional document, circulated in the upper Party echelons over the summer of 1932 blamed Stalin's policy for the upheavals of collectivisation and, after an exhaustive catalogue of his personal characteristics, concluded that he was not the person to preside over a change of course. But without his replacement no recovery of harmony within the party would be possible.[104] Stalin's response to the Ryutin document was sharp indeed. He demanded the death penalty for its author but this was denied him – no doubt on grounds of self-preservation – by the Politburo.[105] However, repression against Party or former Party members was stepped up and 1932 ended with the uncovering of an Eismont and Smirnov 'group' and widescale arrests of oppositionists. Stalin confronted critics of such police measures at the Party plenum of January 1933.

Forced collectivisation, he declared, had been an absolute necessity. Having launched the policy it would have been impossible to stop half way 'although certain excesses were committed'. It was essential to take 'organisational' steps to make sure that 'collective farms have come to stay'. Many Party members had become complacent, ignoring the fact that the defeated hostile classes were worming their way back into farms, offices and factories: 'Some of them even managed to creep back into the Party'. Everywhere, they engaged in sabotage and undermining: 'They set fire to warehouses, and break machinery . . . some of them, amongst whom are certain professors, go so far as to inject the germs of bubonic plague and anthrax into cattle and help to spread meningitis amongst horses'. Blind to all this wrecking, some members of the Party had espoused the 'counter-revolutionary theory' that state authority would diminish as socialism was approaching. Stalin declared that, on the contrary, the abolition of classes is not achieved by damping down the class struggle but by intensifying it. 'The state will die out not by weakening state authority but by strengthening it to the utmost necessity'.[106] *Pravda* pointed out in 1956 that this 'erroneous thesis' provided the theoretical basis for mass repression.[107]

By now, the great famine was in progress. There is little reason to doubt that the Politburo knew its scale and proportions. Both Molotov and Kaganovich had toured the starving countryside and Khrushchev reports 'we knew . . . that people were dying in enormous numbers'.[108] Stalin was directly informed by the Party First Secretary in Kharkov who requested immediate grain to save the population. His reply was published in 1964: 'It seems you are a good story-teller. You've concocted a story about famine, thinking to frighten us. But it won't work. Wouldn't it be better for you to leave your Party post and the Ukrainian Central Committee and join the Writers' Union? Then you can write your fables and fools will read them.'[109] It seems likely that this was not an isolated protest, but a concerted attempt on behalf of Ukrainian Party leaders to influence the January 1933 Plenum. Estimates of the extent of famine vary greatly but all serious investigations indicate that tens of millions were directly involved. A recent Soviet source suggests that 77 million people were affected, of whom some 30 million lived in the Ukraine.[110] The mortality rate is unknown, but western estimates, supported by demographic evidence, suggest several million deaths to be the minimum figures.[111] Scholars differ fundamentally over attributing responsibility, some suggest deliberate genocide, others that the tragedy followed from major economic mistakes.[112] However, few deny that this was a catastrophe of huge dimensions.

One writer to take this up with the political authorities was Sholokhov, himself a Party member from November 1932. He sent a protest letter to Stalin. It reported that 'disgusting methods' were being used for forced requisitioning from starving peasants including beatings and torture. These were not merely local 'excesses': in his own region, the Don,

> They are the 'Method' of procuring grain that has been decreed for the whole *raion*. I have heard these facts from communists or from collective farmers themselves who have personally experienced these "methods" and afterwards come asking me to write about them in the newspaper. Do you remember, Iosif Vissarionovich, Korolenko's story *In the Pacified Village* (1911)? Now the disappearing act has been performed, not on three peasants suspected of stealing from a *kulak* but on tens of thousands of collective farmers. As you can see, it is being done with more refinement and more advanced techniques.[113]

The letter called for the dispatch of emergency food supplies to the Upper Don and for 'genuine communists' to carry out an impartial investigation of 'not only those who employed the loathsome "methods" of torture, beating and abuse against collective farmers, but also those who inspired them.' Physical suffering of the peasantry was also reported, probably in the same letter: 'they lie down in the ploughed fields like exhausted oxen. The half-dead are transported to the village'.[114] But despite his frankness, the writer appears to have left the growing mountain of corpses unmentioned.

Stalin replied by telegram: 'Thank you for the information. We shall do everything that is needed. Give the figures'. Sholokhov supplied this information and Stalin sent him a second telegram giving details about extra grain supplies. He also wrote Sholokhov a letter which admitted that Party officials did occasionally abuse their powers inadvertently and lapsed into sadism for which they should be punished. But the main purpose of the letter was to give Sholokhov a political reprimand for overlooking the fact that a silent war was being waged by 'esteemed grain growers' against Soviet power which threatened to leave the Red Army and working class without bread.[115] However, some grain relief was sent to the Upper Don, helping to promote Stalin's image as a 'great protector'. Sholokhov's intervention thus saved thousands of peasants' lives. As his western biographer adds: 'It would be interesting to know if any other Soviet writer acted in the way Sholokhov did.'[116]

It is difficult to imagine the mentality of those who imposed mass starvation on the peasantry. One of the handful to have left an honest account is Lev Kopelev:

With the rest of my generation I firmly believed that the ends justified the means. Our great goal was the universal triumph of Communism, and for the sake of that goal everything was permissible – to lie, to steal, to destroy hundreds of thousands and even millions of people, all those who were hindering our work or could hinder it, everyone who stood in the way. And to hesitate or doubt about all this was to give in to 'intellectual squeamishness' and 'stupid liberalism', the attribute of people who 'could not see the forest for the trees'.

That was how I had reasoned, and everyone like me, even when . . . I saw what 'total collectivization' meant – how they 'kulakized' and 'dekulakized', how they mercilessly stripped the peasants in the winter of 1932–3. I took part in this myself, scouring the countryside, searching for hidden grain, testing the earth with an iron rod for loose spots that might lead to buried grain. With the others, I emptied out the old folks' storage chests, stopping my ears to the children's crying and the women's wails. For I was convinced that I was accomplishing the great and necessary transformation of the countryside; that in the days to come the people who lived there would be better off for it; that their distress and suffering were a result of their own ignorance or the machinations of the class enemy; that those who sent me – and I myself – knew better than the peasants how they should live, what they should sow and when they should plough.

In the terrible spring of 1933 I saw people dying from hunger. I saw women and children with distended bellies, turning blue, still breathing but with vacant, lifeless eyes. And corpses – corpses in ragged sheepskin coats and cheap felt boots; corpses in peasant huts, in the melting snow of old Vologda, under the bridges of Kharkov . . . I saw all this and did not go out of my mind or commit suicide. Nor did I curse those who had sent me out to take away the peasants' grain in the winter, and in the spring to persuade the barely walking, skeleton-thin or sickly-swollen people to go into the fields in order to 'fulfil the Bolshevik sowing plan in shock-worker style'.

Nor did I lose my faith. As before, I believed because I wanted to believe.[117]

Such brutal candour remains a rarity. The response of most participants was and long remained more cynical: denying that a famine was raging, or attempting to pass it off as a purely local phenomenon. Just such instructions were delivered to writers by Usievich, who insisted that temporary 'food shortages'[118] were not worthy of becoming a literary theme.

The treatment of Zabolotsky's *Triumph of Agriculture* was a sharp warning against making the famine a subject for literature. A second part of this long poem was published in *Zvezda* (Feb/March 1933) but the entire issue was immediately withdrawn. It was resubmitted to the censorship which made numerous cuts and alterations.[119] Although the poet had attempted 'to show the absolute, proprietal structure of the old countryside and its struggle with the new'[120] the work was officially regarded as a lampoon. A press campaign was whipped up by Beskin, continuing his role as peasant vigilante. Ermilov in *Pravda* called it 'ludicrous in Poetry' and Usievich 'unmasked' it in *Literaturnyi kritik*.[121]

Collectivisation re-appeared as a literary theme only in the 1960s evidently after the 22nd Party Congress had enjoined historians to research into this episode. There were then published the stories *Na Irtyshe* by Sergei Zalygin (now editor of *Novyi Mir*) which showed the policy to have been a national catastrophe, and Stadnyuk's *Lyudi ne angely* which, while vindicating the policy as such, gives a horrifying description of the resulting famine. Permission was shortlived. Under Brezhnev, there took place what Afanas'yev calls 'the campaign to damp down on scholarly initiative in historical science, led by S. P. Trapeznikov'.[122] The topic, once again, became taboo. *Literaturnaya gazeta* stated recently that 'the famine of the early 1930s, which carried off many hundreds (*sic*) of people . . . was hardly mentioned in the artistic literature of this time'.[123] This has now begun to be remedied. A multi-volume study commissioned from a team of experienced historians, all earlier victims of Trapeznikov's purge, is due for publication in the early 1990s. When it appears, Soviet readers will, after almost sixty years, receive their first history of this dreadful calamity.

5 Socialist Realism

> An artist must above all portray life truthfully.
>
> J. V. Stalin, 1932[1]

Stalin's political ascendancy was accompanied by major changes on the 'theoretical front'. The ideas of Bukharin on social science were publicly repudiated;[2] Deborin's philosophers were 'exposed' as 'mechanists' and 'menshevising idealists',[3] T. D. Lysenko and other charlatans began meteoric careers in the natural sciences.[4] One common feature of this changing landscape was the introduction of new orthodoxies by individuals or cliques with open support from the political authorities. But whereas Party officials were appointed to formulate an approved 'line' in intellectual life, cultural activity tended to be re-organised around non-party 'authorities'.[5] Stanislavsky's system began to be canonised after *Pravda*'s announcement of a high award to its creator on 13 January 1933. Makarenko was to be appointed a pedagogic authority, as we shall see in Chapter Eight. Marr's teachings held sway in linguistics until abruptly replaced by Stalin's in 1950.[6] The prototype of these 'cultural authorities' was Gorky, whose authorship of a new literary theory is regularly maintained. Indeed, much of Soviet literary historiography is concerned with presentation of socialist realism, through Gorky's early writing, as the natural heir to the 'critical' realist tradition in Russia of the nineteenth century.[7] A difficulty with this argument is to accommodate the interim, notably in the first quarter of this century, when much writing was in reaction to the dominant realism, above all in prose. An ingenious solution is to argue that socialist realism already existed in all but name. Indeed, many parallel formulae had already been suggested: proletarian realism; dynamic, organic and dialectical realism; monumental realism (Alexei Tolstoy); tendentious realism (Mayakovsky) and even proletarian realism (Gladkov and others). Failure to coin the phrase 'socialist realism' before the 1930s is passed off as incidental. However, the origins of socialist realism were considerably more complicated than this picture of continuity suggests. Socialist realism became the subject of intense debate, occupying the *Orgkomitet* both in public and private throughout 1933, with the return of Gorky to Russia in May of that year a crucial turning-point.

Discussion began at the second Plenum of the *Orgkomitet* (12–19

142

February 1933).[8] Lunacharsky's opening speech, on Soviet theatre, marks the first sustained attempt to apply the principles of socialist realism to that genre. He took it for granted that dramatists regarded reality as their proper subject-matter. But straightforward presentation of this 'raw material' would not suffice: reality needed to be interpreted in a progressive manner. This would distinguish a Soviet realist from his western counterpart. Social conditions in capitalist countries were so frightful as to induce a passive contemplation of reality, a wringing of hands in helpless indignation. By contrast, the Soviet writer was a conscious and active agent furthering history in its 'revolutionary development'. Thus when describing a house being built, a bourgeois realist could only record that it as yet lacked a roof: Soviet writers could report 'a magnificent palace in the making'. Socialist realism does not accept reality as it now is, but anticipates and depicts what it will be. Hence it follows that 'the socialist realist is not obliged to stick to the limits of realism in the sense of verisimilitude'. This opened the way for a realistic 'romanticism', and even for 'the creation of the image of a proletarian Prometheus', as the 'artistic embodiment of infinite resources'. Lunacharsky defended bold fantasy: 'A communist who cannot dream is a bad communist. The communist dream is not a flight from the earthly but a flight into the future.'[9] In conclusion, he echoed Stalin's strictures on dialectical materialism in literature. Membership of the future Writer's Union could not be restricted 'to the minority of writers who have mastered Marxism – if there is one'. A special study of philosophical principles could be recommended 'only to the few writers who show special aptitude for it, and these will not necessarily be the best writers'. It would be absurd to prohibit an impassioned piece of writing on the grounds that it was 'insufficiently philosophical' to give a 'rounded interpretation'.[10]

This last point met a surprising rejoinder. Far from welcoming socialist realism, the dramatist Afinogenov loyally re-affirmed the dialectical materialist method. In his view the RAPP 'theatrical document' of 1931 which enshrined *dia-mat*[11] retained its relevance and 'defines the divisions in literature today'. Naturally this doctrine should not be used to 'intimidate other writers'. To uphold it was simply to recognise that 'we are communist dramatists actively building a socialist society'. He did admit that the April Resolution had been a serious shock to RAPP and precipitated a prolonged 'methodological crisis' within its ranks. Self-scrutiny had revealed serious errors in their position. That exercise, however, taken with their long experience in leadership, put RAPP in 'a stronger position than before to guide literature to its next stage'.[12] This speech caused uproar. During the sharp conflict of opinion that followed it was asked whether the abolition of RAPP had or had not ushered in a new stage of literary policy.

Kirshon took this 'passionate course of discussion' as the cue to restate the RAPP position. The Plenum was 'not a gathering of aesthetes somewhere in the Pen Club to discuss the sense of this or that line from this or that unknown author'. They were 'creating a militant class literature in conditions of struggle' and knew full well that 'abstract aesthetic viewpoints can be used to hide the conflict of differing class positions'. Unequivocal statements should therefore be made to clarify debate: 'with nothing omitted or left unsaid'. Taking his own advice, Kirshon addressed socialist realism. The new term was 'on every tongue, speakers orate on it, critics criticise with it'. Authors were setting down to write according to it, yet no-one had so far produced a clear definition. In his view, socialist realism was simply 'the method of the proletariat' in art. The method was proletarian because this was the only class which while existing in the present, also belonged to the future. By showing the most essential relations – those of class – between characters in a book or play, a socialist realist would also promote consciousness of classless relations to come. Romanticism was irrelevant to this process and Lunacharsky had been wrong to advocate it for Soviet writers, though it remained necessary for the bourgeois writer who was obliged to 'falsify reality'.[13] He too reiterated the RAPPist theatrical programme, differentiating it from the competing 'left' contention.

The 'left', represented by Vishnevsky and Pogodin at the Plenum, expressed their theatrical credo in the slogan 'New Means of Reality demand New Means of Artistic Depiction'.[14] Richly dramatic moments of Soviet history such as the Revolution and Civil War could only be reconstructed or re-enacted on a gigantic scale. Likewise, celebration of shock-workers, collectivisers and socialist heroes required a monumental scale of mass action spectacle. To 'traditionalists' such as Afinogenov and Kirshon their 'innovation' was hopelessly superficial. Kirshon considered it could capture 'simply the moment when the great Revolution was taking place'. Its extravagant, 'arithmetical method', piling up casts of thousands, precluded the psychological portrayal essential to profound theatre. The characters in a drama should not consist of typical heroes or supreme individualists but composites of 'social experience', located clearly in one class or another while retaining sufficient individuality to present a credible interpretation.[15] The debate showed there was still diversity to be found within Soviet dramaturgy. Introduction of socialist realism did not preclude, but rather tended to enhance, its disagreements.[16]

The Plenum ended on an optimistic note. *Orgkomitet* officials stated that RAPP's 'Theatrical Document' was mistaken, without bothering to point out the corrections it needed. Lunacharsky's conciliatory 'concluding word' rejected the call of many writers for the prohibition of *dia-mat*. *Dia-mat* was the 'basic aesthetic direction' towards which Soviet drama was moving, but RAPP had been wrong to insist on it as an obligatory point 'from which all writers must allegedly start out'. Socialist realism would permit a broad variety of styles. From the high vantage point of the future socialist art, contemporary differences, such as those between traditionalists and innovators, would seem insignificant.[17] However, no final resolution was passed at the end of five days' discussion, and the unusual procedure was adopted of naming a group to work out such a statement 'on the basis of materials' provided by the Plenum.[18] Summing up, Gronsky explained that RAPP's recidivism was 'now restricted to a handful of individuals'. There was no longer a 'strong monolithic unit bound by internal discipline for future struggle against the *Orgkomitet*'. He considered that substantial progress towards the unification of writers had taken place since the previous Plenum.[19]

But the Party leadership did not share this sanguine assessment. Their first act after the Plenum was to remove Gronsky from the *Orgkomitet*.[20] While retaining the editorships of *Novyi mir* and *Izvestiya*, he took no further part in the reorganisation of literature. He was not even a delegate to the first Writers' Congress. A new triumvirate was given charge of literature. The first advanced was Fadeyev who had already indicated his willingness for such work. In a letter to *Kul't-prop*, he reported 'serious deficiencies in the "communist fraction"' of the *Orgkomitet*: it met rarely and failed to formulate 'matters of literary principle' in advance of wider discussions. Fadeyev insisted it should work out a 'really united line for communist writers' and make 'literary communists' answerable to it for their work.[21] This strategy was similar to Stalin's, outlined at the October meeting: first attain unity amongst communist writers, then bring non-party writers into line.

The second to be elevated was Stavsky, who became secretary of the *Orgkomitet* Praesidium. These were important promotions for two former RAPP leaders, both of whom had jettisoned their association at just the right moment. Both were rewarded with the office of First Secretary of the Writer's Union.

Kirpotin completed the new troika. He took charge of an *Orgkomitet* brigade, established at last, to discuss socialist realism.[22] This was restricted to party members with former RAPPists, such as Averbakh, Makar'yev and Afinogenov, co-opted to 'widen the debate'.[23] At the first session Kirpotin proposed that socialist realism be defined as 'a synthetic artistic style' rather than as a creative method. Being a synthesis, it could accommodate both realism and romanticism on the grounds that 'for the proletariat the socialist goal and reality are indistinguishable'.[24]

A series of Party critics, Serebryansky, Nusinov, and Ermilov, elaborated, but their speeches aroused little enthusiasm. The press complained 'most writers are simply not interested in this discussion'.[25] It noted that a second meeting, at which non-party writers were allowed to speak, 'was again far from full'.[26] Only a handful had been willing to offer an opinion as to what socialist realism might mean. The brigade drew two conclusions. Their effort to involve non-party writers in discussion was abandoned, as was the public mode. They decided that formulation would now proceed *in camera*.

These decisions were challenged by Gorky, who returned to Russia on 17 May. At once he declared his dissatisfaction with Kirpotin's analysis of socialist realism, it was too 'abstract' and his contribution on the subject to *Literaturnaya ucheba*, a journal Gorky edited, was rejected as 'vague and incomprehensible'.[27] He considered that the *Orgkomitet* brigade had failed to formulate socialist realism in a 'sufficiently practical form' for writers' use.[28] And yet the Writers' Congress was due to open in a month's time.

An accompanying editorial also noted that it had 'not yet seized a sufficiently warlike tempo'. Writers were reminded that the 'first and chief task of preparing the Congress is creative discussion, creative competition, the slogan socialist realism including as a part of it the slogan of revolutionary romanticism'.[29] Spurred into action, the Praesidium despatched an angry letter to local *Orgkomitets* and also to 180 literary circles, urging haste in completing this 'responsible and important task'.[30] The Praesidium noted that vital preparatory discussions on socialist realism 'have not given the results we expected. Writers have not shown much interest in them'. It therefore decided to postpone the Congress until September, ostensibly in response to the request of certain provincial *Orgkomitets* for a deferment. But the real reason was writers' apathy; Fadeyev noted that 'writers must use the summer for study visits to construction sites and *kolkhozes*. If we receive new work from them this will be the best form of preparation for the Congress'.[31]

Fadeyev was now in charge of the *Orgkomitet*. He chaired its meetings and oversaw the work of non-Russian *Orgkomitets*. Stavsky had similar responsibilities within the RSFSR and for overseeing literary circles. Kirpotin assumed two new functions: setting-up an autonomous section for dramatists within the *Orgkomitet* and 'coming to an agreement with the Central Committee of the Party' concerning the statute for the Writers' Union. All three wished to streamline literary policy-making. They therefore set up a 'working part' of the Praesidium, consisting solely of themselves. It was to meet eight times in a month, while the full gatherings were fortnightly.[32]

Gorky played no direct part in the Praesidium. Fadeyev attempted to involve him more actively. For instance, on 5 July 1932 he reported back to the Praesidium on a conversation at Gorky's dacha and then wrote requesting his attendance at its next full session to meet 'the new leadership of literature'.[33] But Gorky kept his distance. He often made known his irritation at the energies Fadeyev expended on administrative work and on preparing the cycle of articles 'Old and New' the previous autumn. 'Better if he were writing a novel' was Gorky's crisp observation.[34] His dealings with Fadeyev at this stage had a 'purely businesslike and official character'. However, he did eventually agree to address the Praesidium.

His speech proposed a radically enlarged agenda for the Congress. It should open with a major account of Soviet literature which both traced its historical antecedents and set out the 'tasks' before it in the present day. Second, in view of the 'great resonance' the Congress was having amongst revolutionary writers abroad, there should follow an address on 'Soviet literature and the contemporary state of world literature'. It was necessary to approach 'the Central Committee or Comintern' to provide a speaker.[35] This theme was soon adopted by an all-Union meeting of *Orgkomitet* presidents,[36] which emphasised the immense political and international significance of the Congress of Writers. It was 'not a narrow literary affair'. Finally, Gorky proposed the remainder of the Congress be given over to a wide-ranging discussion of Soviet literature amongst party and non-party writers themselves.[37] He insisted that 'unity and understanding socialist realism' were preconditions of calling the Congress. Delegates must arrive with a clear understanding of the new method already established. Yet numerous articles and lectures had thus far failed to give it 'sufficiently profound expression'.[38] He therefore proposed the Congress date again be put back. This was accepted, although the postponement was once more attributed to an alleged request from non-Russian writers for more time to prepare their reports. The opening was now set for May 1934, by which time the Party would have held its own Congress, Gorky hoped to use the interim to popularise his own understanding of socialist realism. He now saw this as the key both to the future of Soviet literature and to its organisation. Most current definitions amounted to little more than rhetoric: 'based on the methods of socialist realism, based on an accurate living expression of new socialist relations of the mighty new epoch in human history, the future role of Soviet literature in world literature will be secured'.[39] However, Gorky's own conception was not dissimilar. He was determined to put literature in touch with 'the gigantic processes of socialist construction'. As he put it in a preface to *The People of the Stalingrad Tractor Factory*, first of *The History of Factories* series, while altering the physical geography of the country, the Soviet Union was 'reconstructing reality itself'.[40] Such assumptions were bound to bring literature closer to fulfilling political tasks of the moment. To promote the Plan was simultaneously to further the Stalinist state. Gorky's apparent readiness to assist in both is sometimes explained as part of a tacit arrangement with Stalin according to which he was rewarded for glorifying such policies with licence to install his own ideas in literature. But their relationship was much more complex. In any case, such a bargain would have been impossible: Stalin had no intention of allowing Gorky sole responsibility for the reorganisation of literature.

In August 1933 the *Orgkomitet* elected Gorky its president, formally relieving Gronsky of his duties on health grounds. But this was accompanied by an institutional innovation: the establishment of a Secretariat to conduct the day-to-day business of the *Orgkomitet*. This seemingly innocuous proposal had great long-term significance. The Central Committee's candidate for the new post was Yudin, advocated to them by Stetsky as 'a true Bolshevik, whose baptism of fire was in the Red Army, a philosopher in the vanguard of the struggle for Marxist-Leninist theory'.[41] He was the founder editor of *Literaturnyi kritik*, which had just appeared. We know that Yudin had enjoyed Stalin's patronage since 1928.[42] His appointment to be Secretary within the incipient Union was reminiscent of Stalin's rise in the Party.

The initial effect of Yudin's secondment to literadure was a diminution of Gorky's personal authority. While the new Secretariat also included Stavsky, Fadeyev, Kirpotin, Mikitenko (of the Ukrainian *Orgkomitet*), Tikhonov and V. Ivanov, only the last two were on close terms with Gorky. Their personal contacts opened coolly with Gorky impressing his priorities on the new Secretary: the need to foster literatures of the national republics and to improve preparations for the Congress.[43] Complaining to Makar'yev on 23 September about the inertia in literary affairs, Gorky noted that organisational work was largely in the hands of Yudin, Averbakh and himself.[44] Their relations soon deteriorated. In the following spring Gorky sent Yudin a furious epistle: 'you have disorganised the communist fraction, driven off non-party writers and generally done great damage to literary affairs'. He was 'dishonest and a poor communist'.[45] When asked by Stalin to explain this outburst, Stetsky put the blame on Averbakh for surrounding Gorky with a 'web of conspirators and squabblers' and 'using all means to isolate Gorky from the *Orgkomitet*. There is no doubt about it'.[46] No doubt Averbakh still believed that with Gorky's help, he could displace Yudin as Secretary of the future Union, but this should not disguise the substance of Gorky's complaint: the conduct of Yudin himself.

The second purpose of Yudin's promotion was to bring Party discipline into literary management. While Gorky encouraged non-party writers to accede voluntarily to the incipient Union, Yudin presented the element of intimidation. Shortly after his appointment, Yudin told a widened session of the Praesidium that steps were needed to 'improve the situation' politically. It was essential 'to remove all individual and anarchistic elements in our organisation' in order to establish the Writers' Union as 'an authoritative organisation' in the near future. In terminology typical of the time, he declared that writers must be brought to see that the serious responsibility placed on them by the country and its working class could not be discharged without organised and disciplined work. As overseers of this process, Yudin called for recruitment of a reliable nucleus of communists within the future Union and for the expulsion of recalcitrant sectarians.[47] The Party purge, first announced in the spring of 1932,[48] thus reached literature. Its goals were set out in an editorial: 'The Party cell of writers cannot be detached from general party life'. This pointed out that communist cell and individual writer-communists were active participants in socialist construction under the Party's general line. However, some writers, including Party ones, had underestimated the part played by the communist fraction and had even questioned its reason for existence. It was therefore essential for enhanced Bolshevik vigilance 'to strengthen the Party's position in the sphere of literature'. This would be done through 'purging its ranks of class alien elements, double-dealers, transgressors of the Party's iron discipline, defeatists, careerists, self-seekers, idle bureaucrats and moral bankrupts'.[49]

Despite this long catalogue, the Party purge in literature was not severe. Few 'agents' of 'counter-revolution' were actually discovered. A majority of those expelled were not 'class alien elements who had wormed their way back into the Party through deception' but smaller fry who had 'violated the Party's iron discipline'. The literary press did find 'slanderous anti-Party elements' in the novels of Parfyonov and 'Trotskyist contraband' (a phrase from Stalin's letter to the editors of *Proletarskaya Revolyutsiya*) in the criticism of Tarasov-Rodionov.[50] But the main focus was on rank-and-file Party writers, many of whom were required to account for the tiniest details of their 'revolutionary biography'. The hearings were comparatively good-tempered, with some arraigned, such as the Moscow critic B. Levin, defended by others present as 'a good Communist, modest, thoughtful and serious'.[51] Those questioned had the right of reply and generally escaped expulsion from the Party by contrition or self-criticism. Summing up the Moscow writers' meeting, the old Bolshevik Magidov, who headed the Purge Commission, declared that the Party cell had 'failed to make sufficient efforts to see its decisions realised' or 'to assist the *Orgkomitet* in its literary work'.[52] Such reproof was mild enough.

A partial exception was the theatre. The Purge Commission discovered a serious deviation amongst members of the former *VseRoss-KomDram*. This body, set up in 1931 to serve the material and professional interests of theatre people, also included sections for composers and screen writers, and had some 3,000 members. Afinogenov was the Secretary and its staff consisted principally of leading members of the RAPP theatrical establishment. It had been criticised after the Second Plenum for 'failing to correct the RAPPist tendency' in its work,[53] and later abolished. Some eighty members were expelled from the Party, mostly from the rural theatre section. Magidov reminded those who remained of Stalin's dictum about the importance of their genre.[54] As in the Party purge, the main leaders

Afinogenov, Amaglobely and Rossovsky were untouched. In its place, the *Orgkomitet* set up an Autonomous Section for dramaturgy headed by Kirpotin which published several symposia and may have contributed something towards the new spirit of unanimity that was supposed to prevail amongst Soviet dramatists. But its contribution to defining socialist realism was unimpressive. A collection issued later in 1933[55] referred to the 'vulgarisation of the dialectical-materialist method' as too abstract and not permitting full exploration of the 'viewpoint of the working class and the interests of socialism'. It was asserted that this could be done through socialist realism, but the method was left unexplained.

Resolution of this problem was the final reason for Yudin's promotion. Archives show a Secretariat session on 27 August 1933 at which only six persons were present: Gorky, Yudin, the troika (Fadeyev, Stavsky, Kirpotin), and Vsevolod Ivanov. The minutes reveal that they decided the new doctrine should be formulated by committee. To list the names of those participating in this enterprise is to call the role of the Stalinist establishment: Yudin, Mitin and Usievich (from the Communist Academy); Lifshits and Shiller (from the Marx-Engels Institute); former RAPPists Averbakh and Makar'yev; a number of editors and critics: Lebedev-Polyansky, Luppol, M. Rozental', Serebryansky, Troshchenko and K. Zelinsky.[56] Gorky himself was not a participant, nor were any writers included. Thus the most central question remaining in the inauguration of Stalinism in Soviet literature had been delegated to a sizeable contingent of philosophers, ideologists and critics, headed and epitomised by Yudin.

The existence of this Commission has never been admitted. No secondary source has even hinted at its existence. The researcher must therefore proceed by inference. Maybe, in common with committees generally, it began work on determining the origins of socialist realism by agreeing a division of labour amongst its members? If so, we may expect one or more of its number to have begun the search with a re-examination of texts by the founding fathers.

There is a great disparity between Marx's vast knowledge of world literature[57] and his miscellaneous and often fragmentary commentary on the subject. An early project with Bruno Bauer to criticise Hegel's doctrines of religion and art was abandoned;[58] an entry on aesthetics for an American encyclopaedia is incomplete. He left in draft an analysis of Balzac's *La Comédie Humaine*.[59] Though brilliantly expressed, such *obiter dicta* fall far short of a theory of literature. This was demonstrated by Petr Struve, who devoted an article to them at the turn of the century.[60] Moreover, any attempt to codify these sporadic utterances was bound to be contested, as shown by the number of competing interpreters in post-revolutionary Russia who attempted to appropriate Marx for their own programme.

Significant scholarship on Marxism in literature and art can be dated from the rediscovery of his *Economic and Philosophical Manuscripts* (1844), and *The German Ideology* (1845), the first publication of which took place, in Russia, in 1932. Whereas the determinism of the later Marx, crudely applied, would reduce art and literature to non-aesthetic (that is to say social and economic) criteria, his early writings show a 'young Marx' concerned with voluntarism. The origin of aesthetic experience is not merely located in given circumstances. Art is seen as a specific form of human activity through which the being discovers his essence. Unlike other species, Marx writes in the 1844 *Manuscripts*, the human being acts according to perceptions of beauty inherent in the natural object: he 'truly produces only in freedom'. The opposite condition, that prevailing in all civilisations of Marx's day, was 'alienation': the separation of the producer from his work, from fulfilment through work, and ultimately of the human being from his essence.[60] *The German Ideology* envisages that the distinction between work and play would one day disappear: work would become increasingly aesthetic and unspecialised. Every person would become capable of artistic achievement.[61] The relevance of this radical, young Marx to Stalin's industrialisation programme was not immediately apparent. Accordingly, the Commission member charged with examining these early writings was cautious about actual applications.

M. Lifshits, in his Preface to *Towards Questions of the opinions of Marx on Art* (1933), refers to the work simply as a 'collection of materials' on whose basis something more methodical might eventually be devised.[62] Even so, an unavoidable impression is given of Marx as a staunch defender of literary freedom. Lifshits mentions Marx's famous *Commentary on the Prussian Censorship* (1842). This fulminated against the 'absurdity of hoping to bring about an improvement of the tone and content of the press in future by removing its present rights and possibilities'. The fate of his newspaper, closed down by the Prussian censorship,[63] reminded Marx of Sancho Panza: 'the court physician removed all food from his sight in order that no stomach upset should render him incapable of discharging the duties put upon him'. Political censorship masqueraded as a censorship of style, it 'retarded the development of the German mind and spirit in a disastrous and irresponsible way' and left the writer only one honourable course: silence. Lifshits admitted that 'the censor was Marx's principal opponent' but distinguished this from the position of the Soviet writer engaged upon a 'Party struggle in literature'.[64] The contrast was not entirely convincing.

While Lifshits was investigating Marx, his colleague at the Marx-Engels Institute in Moscow, and co-member of the Commission, studied Engels. This was F. Shiller, whose biographical note states that he had worked on the manuscripts of Marx and Engels since 1922, concentrating in the early 1930s on their opinions on literature.[65] The outcome was his *Engels as Literary Critic* (1933), the first work on the subject. Among several similarities with Lifshits' volume are the prefatorial disclaimer that he was offering the first word on the subject rather than the last and the obvious fact that Engels' views on literature were wide-ranging and unsystematic. However, a small number of texts were taken to be canonical and indeed synonymous with the views of Marx himself. This was a defensible procedure, in that Engels spent the latter part of his life filling in gaps that Marx had left behind and correcting misunderstandings of the master, though some would say that by inventing Marxism Engels created something distinctively his own. He made two main contributions to the later theory of socialist realism.

The first is found in Engels' account of Lassalle:

In drama, realistic portrayal should not be neglected in favour of the intellectual elements, nor Shakespeare in favour of Schiller. Had Lassalle introduced the wonderfully variegated plebeian social sphere of the time, it would have lent entirely new material which would have enlivened and provided an indispensible background. What wonderfully distinctive character portraits are to be found during this period of the breakdown of feudalism – penniless ruined kings, impoverished hireling soldiers and adventurers of all sorts – a Falstaffian background that, in a historical play of this type, could be much more effective than in Shakespeare![66]

There is an uncanny echo of this advocacy of historical materialism in Marx's correspondence with Lassalle. He stated that the playwright had missed the opportunity to show 'the representatives of the peasants (these especially!) and of revolutionary elements in the town'. To have done so he noted 'would have compelled you to Shakespearize more, while I now see Schillerizing, the transformation of individuals until they are mouthpieces for the spirit of the time. That is your greatest fault'.[67]

The second contribution to socialist realist theory was his idea of tendentiousness in art. Here Engels' correspondence with Minna Kautsky provided some potentially promising material. A letter of 1883 stressed that tendentiousness must arise 'in the action itself, without explicit attention called to it: the writer is not obliged to offer to the reader the future historical solution to the social conflict he depicts'. In Engels' view a 'socialist tendentious novel' could best achieve its purpose by demystifying bourgeois illusions, without directly offering a solution to them.[68] Moreover, he added later 'the more the opinions of an author remain hidden, the better for the work of art'. Balzac, for instance, 'was compelled to go against his own class sympathies and political prejudices' and this was 'one of the greatest triumphs of realism'.[69] For Engels, great literature could transcend a dominant class through its aesthetic dimension which is classless, reaching out to a universal, unalienated humanity. Thus art has the power to break the monopoly of an established reality. Soviet writers were invited to adopt his terminology without, however, its transcendent dimension.

Principal investigator of the second source of socialist realism, the Russian radical democrats of the mid-nineteenth century, was the Commission member Lebedev-Polyansky,[70] who supervised editions of their collective works. The theme and characteristic they had in common was rage against social conditions of their time. First came the 'furious Vissarion' – Belinsky – whose earliest literary criticism outraged convention by introducing taboo subjects such as the topical, the vulgar, and the grotesque. He discovered in Gogol' 'the banality, all the ugliness of this bestial, misshapen and ridiculous existence – you have such a realised conception of the actors in this stupid comedy that you can see their whole life so clearly'. Later he adopted Hegelianism, referring to the 'rational reality behind the facade of appearance' leading him briefly to political conservatism. Statements such as 'unconditional submission to Tsarist authority is not only useful and necessary for us but is the highest poetry of our times' are not dwelt upon by Soviet historians today. They rely upon Belinsky's third phase whose motto was 'struggle against the actual'. The purpose of literature was now to protest. He favoured a 'poetry of negation' and saw art generally as a weapon and a teacher.[71] This, however, was not merely a reductive utilitarianism.

As Isaiah Berlin points out, Belinsky did not believe it to be an artist's duty to 'prophesy or preach, to serve society directly by telling it what to do, by providing slogans'.[72] On the contrary, the artist should preserve his independence of both society and the state. This led him to offer an early definition of the literary intelligentsia. He argued that 'only in our literature, despite its Tartar censorship, is there any life or progress left'. In a curious anticipation of Solzhenitsyn, who saw a great writer as a second government, Belinsky asserted that the public regards Russian writers as its only leaders. It could thus forgive a bad book but never a pernicious one. Even Pushkin, he maintained, had 'quickly lost his popularity' once he abandoned his integrity and decided 'sincerely or otherwise' to serve the state. And the public was right. For the Russian writers were its only defenders against the 'black night' of an autocratic state. His statement of such values in the *Letter to Gogol* (1844) was regarded by Herzen as a masterpiece. Dostoyevsky was sent into exile for reading it to a public meeting.

Belinsky's writings had a permanent influence upon the radical intelligentsia. If anything, his standing grew after his death. Lebedev-Polyansky recalled:

Our generation born in the 80s read Belinsky with delight as his contemporaries had done, and perhaps the great critic's ideas were closer to us than to them . . . [especially] his passion, moral force, exceptional sincerity and the idea that literature, while continuing to be art, must also serve the goals of social struggle, maintaining precise ideas, passing judgements on current affairs and being the harbinger of the future.[73]

Trotsky took this a stage further. 'With Belinsky', he wrote, 'literary criticism took the place of politics and was a preparation for it'. Answering an imaginary critic of the 1920s, he suggested a suitable response to the complaint 'there are no Belinskys today' might be 'were Belinsky now alive he would probably be a member of the Politburo'.[74]

A second radical democrat taken up by the Commission was Saltykov-Shchedrin. Two volumes of his unpublished work were sent to press. A preface by Averbakh, the 'responsible editor', remarked that Shchedrin was 'not a philosopher nor a social theorist nor a political activist in the narrow sense of these words. He was above all an artist, a great artist'.[75] Averbakh's 'completely mistaken view' was overturned by a second preface two months later. This new version proclaimed him a radical democrat who had played a 'huge revolutionary role': in differentiating amongst the peasantry and in castigating the 'liberal bourgeois apparatus of the Tsarist dictatorship'. Leading Bolsheviks confirmed his political credentials. Lenin noted in a letter of 1912: 'it would be useful, from time to time, to recall and explain in *Pravda* Shchedrin and other writers of the "old" Narodnik democratic movement'.[76] Under the Commission's auspices, Saltykov was given wide publicity. Kirpotin undertook a popular biography[77] and edited, with Lebedev-Polyansky, his twenty-volume *Collected Works* (1933–41).[78]

There is a distinction to be drawn between the first generation of radicals and those that followed: 'men of far duller and cruder minds'.[79] The onset of utilitarianism, which Belinsky prefigured but to which he did not succumb, soon took written form. This can be seen in the critic Dobrolyubov whom the Commission extensively republished and popularised.[80] For instance, reviewing Saltykov, he asserted: 'literature always served as the first mouthpiece of public aspirations, clarifying them, and moderating them by strict and thoughtful thorough discussion'. Sharply deriding earlier writers, Dobrolyubov declared the new-found maturity of a literature which had 'cast off its swaddling clothes for ever'. He insisted that 'come what may, neither footmen's congratulations on high and solemn festivals nor valets' odes to gentlemen on their promotion' could recapture literature:[81] a far from accurate premonition of writing under Stalinism. However, Dobrolyubov admitted that art could only articulate the values and conceptions of an educated minority, populated largely by the 'superfluous men' of contemporary fiction. Yet their apathy, as Goncharov had demonstrated so brilliantly in *Oblomov*, seemed almost insuperable. The only possibility of salvation lay in the emergence of a new type of personality: 'men of action not of argument'.[82]

Such a man soon appeared. Enraged by the slowness of social reform, Chernyshevsky espoused partisanship in art.[83] Art, he taught, was educational. Though aware of the pitfalls of didacticism, he insisted that artists were an intellectual elite pointing the way to progress. Neutral literature cannot exist; all writing serves somebody's interest, though not necessarily a progressive one. His thesis was illustrated in the famous *What is to be done?* (1862). The hackneyed qualities of this novel have often been remarked upon: fiction was not his genre. However, the story caused an immediate sensation and it had a lasting impact on Russian literature and politics. Lenin commented of its hero, the rational ascetic Rakhmetov, 'under his influence, hundreds of people became revolutionaries'.[84] Later still, in the mid-1930s, the Bulgarian communist Georgi Dimitrov noted: 'I set myself the goal of being as firm, as self-possessed, to temper my will and character in the struggle with difficulties and disappointments, to subordinate my personal life to the service of the great cause of the working class – in short to be like this irreproachable hero'.[85] Lenin's interest in Chernyshevsky is described in Krupskaya's memoire. 'In the early stages of his revolutionary career, Vladimir Il'ich did not pay much attention to Chernyshevsky's philosophical ideas, though he had read Plekhanov's book *On Chernyshevsky*, where particular attention is given to this aspect.[86] She adds that in the philosophical dispute of 1908 Lenin re-read Chernyshevsky and referred to him as 'a great Russian Hegelian and a great historical materialist'. We learn that Lenin kept his works, alongside those of Marx, Engels and Plekhanov, in the Kremlin. 'In his spare moments he used to read Chernyshevsky over and over again.' This was not merely entertainment: 'Vladimir Il'ich liked books which vividly reflected social ideas and he chose his fiction accordingly'.[87]

Examination of Lenin's legacy on literature was undertaken by a *Literaturnyi kritik* group, four of whom including the editor (Yudin) and his deputy (Rozental'), were members of the socialist realism commission. Their characteristic findings appeared in such editorial statements as 'socialist realism, the new slogan, gives a clear and articulate presentation of the method and form of the Marxist-Leninist reconstruction of *belles-lettres*'.[88] Beyond this bold assertion, obscurity prevails. Rozental' attempted to cast more light on Lenin's attitude to literature through an account of his *Philosophical Notebooks*.[89] A miscellany of hagiographic articles explored both language and style in Lenin's writings and his portrayal in *belles-lettres*.[90] The only sustained attempt to systematise Lenin's scattered utterances on literature came from the Communist Academy's volume published in time for the Party Congress.

Following a cursory glance at the founding fathers and radical democrats, Yudin raised a new point: 'Analysis of Lenin's opinions on *belles-lettres* and criticism shows that the question of political tendency, of Party tendentiousness in literature is of the utmost importance'.[91] The article of 1905 was brought forward to prove the need for *partiinost'* in literature or at least to establish an intimate connection between the two. Lenin had said: 'Down with non-partisan writers! Down with literary supermen! Literature must become part of the common cause of the proletariat . . . Literature must become a component of organised, planned and integrated social democratic Party work'. The Leninist notion of Party control was that 'newspapers become organs of the various party organisations and their writers must by all means become members of these organisations'. Therefore publishers, bookshops, reading rooms, libraries and the like must all be under Party control. Otherwise, the proletariat would 'remain prisoners of bourgeois shopkeeper literary relations', and writing dominated by greed for profit and careerism. Lenin recognised, though, that 'hysterical intellectuals' and others might protest that turning literature into 'a cog' in a great Party machine could 'degrade, deaden, or "bureaucratize" the free battle of ideas, freedom of criticism, freedom of literary creation, etc. etc'. He replied that such fears were groundless. 'There is no question that literature is least of all subject to mechanical adjustment or levelling, to the rule of the majority over the minority. There is no question either that greater scope must undoubtedly be allowed for personal initiative, individual inclination, thought and fantasy, form and content.' In contrast to the hypocritical freedom of bourgeois property relations, socialist literature would be 'a really free one, openly linked to the proletariat'.[92]

This lofty vision is quoted in full. Yet it is clear from a paragraph not cited by Yudin that Lenin was writing about Party literature (political, theoretical and publicistic), which is quite specifically juxtaposed with *belles-lettres* in the article. While the former was to be under Party control and serving its programme, the latter was to be 'really free and open', serving the proletariat. Of course Lenin might not have minded its subsequent extension to literature of every kind, but this seems improbable for two main reasons. Firstly, literary policy in his lifetime included outright discouragement of proletarian literature, and under NEP opened up long perspectives for fellow-travelling. Second and more important is the distinction he made between Party and class literature. *Klassovost'*, as defined in 1905, simply expressed the inevitable circumstance that a writer in a class society, that is any society except the classless socialist society of the future, would necessarily occupy some social position. In non-Marxian terms this means that all writers can be evaluated from a socio-political angle: liberal, progressive, conservative and so on. As Lenin's article put it, 'one cannot live in a society and be free from society'. In the early 1930s, however, it began to be suggested that Lenin's article had much wider application. In his contribution to the *Literary Encyclopaedia* (1932), Lunarcharsky argued that while Lenin had been writing on political literature within the Party, 'the objective significance' of his article had 'gone further and could well apply to *belles-lettres*, that is to literature of every kind'. 'Although written almost four decades ago' the article had 'lost none of its significance for the present day'. It remained a 'guiding directive (*rukovodyashcheye ukazaniye*) of Party literary policy especially widely developed since Lenin's death'.[93] This was a vital extension. The second *Literary Encyclopaedia* (of the 1960s) gave Lunarcharsky the credit for 'making the connection' between Lenin's view of Party literature and his understanding of its class essence for the first time.[94]

The final source of the theory of socialist realism was said to be Stalin. A pocket-sized series of pieces entitled *Writers to the XVII Party Congress* was dedicated to delegates on 2 February 1934. There were sixty-seven authors, in alphabetical order. Yudin's preface stated 'the Party in the person of Comrade Stalin formulated the basic creative political and theoretical slogan of Soviet *belles-lettres* – the slogan of socialist realism'.[95] Yudin's other initiatives designed to demonstrate the intimacy of politics and literature remained un-fulfilled. The literary tribute 'On Lenin' which he told the Party fraction of the Secretariat would include 'everything that exists in literature on Stalin' did not materialise.[96] Nor did Soviet writers ever collaborate on a publicly-announced 'literary work' on the 1933 Party Purge.[97] However, Yudin was to be the principal rapporteur on literary questions to the Congress which, he warned the Party frac-tion in December 1933, would consider 'the undoubted successes of Soviet literature alongside a thorough Bolshevik self-criticism of all its shortcomings'.[98]

In August 1933, 120 writers sailed through the White Sea–Baltic canal. About one-third of them thereafter agreed to collaborate on a volume describing its construction.[99] It was to be written and pub-lished at high speed in time for the Party Congress. The editors included Averbakh, who evidently saw this as a way back into the leadership of literature, and S. G. Firin, a police chief later decorated with Yagoda for his 'services on the canal'. We cannot learn from this book, nor any subsequent Soviet source, the total number of workers and prisoners who perished under forced labour at the canal, an economically worthless undertaking. Nor can we discover why many prominent writers agreed to cooperate in this 'literary' enterprise. Was it already necessary to ensure professional survival by making obeisance to Stalin, after whom the Canal was named? Can it be said they did not know the full human costs of the project they depicted? No doubt on their brief visits to gather materials these writers met only a handful of specially prepared 'prisoners'. Pressures of time and ignorance may have helped to overcome their scruples. The method of 'collective authorship' may also have defused their moral senses. Indeed, the only signed chapter did note a moment of equivocation. Zoshchenko admitted to having held doubts about corrective labour prior to his first visit but claimed that these had been allayed at the Canal.[100] Whatever their reasons, publication of this work was the first major submission of Soviet literature to Stalinism.

Gorky was instrumental both as co-editor and in its publication. He wrote to Stetsky at the end of 1933 (in a letter published by L. M. Zak in 1959) that 'there is no need for me to emphasise the great social and artistic significance that this book could have: not only in the Soviet Union but beyond its borders'. Such lofty themes as the Canal and 'corrective labour' demanded a high standard of presentation. He asked Stetsky promptly to requisition 'the finest possible materials, if only for a limited edition'[101] so that the volume could be ready for the Party Congress. Stetsky apparently complied. A handsome edition appeared on 20 January 1934, less than a week before the Congress. Its title page stated 'the *Orgkomitet* of the Soviet Writers' Union, on behalf of the collective authorship and the *Histories of Factories*, dedicate this book to the XVIIth Congress of the Bolshevik Party'. A further note attributed the book's literary merit to the study and application of the 'artistic productive teachings of Lenin-Stalin'.[102] Such a dedication did not bode well for a non-restrictive formulation of the new doctrine.

6 Debate on Doctrine

> The problem of quality should be decisive on all fronts – in science, in economics, in the sphere of leadership and of ideas.
>
> Bukharin, 1934.

A distinct relaxation took place in Soviet politics early in 1934. It was the prevalent assumption of the 17th Party Congress, self-styled the 'Congress of Victors', that, terrible though the struggle against the peasantry had been, the worst was now over. The tone of innumerable speeches was self-congratulatory. There was no dissent from the public platform. Yet careful analysis of Kirov's speeches over the period 1933–4 reveal two interrelated propositions. Domestically, the need for 'legality' was emphasised, particularly in the countryside, where Kirov called for a cessation of punitive expulsion from *kolkhozy* which condemned many peasants to starvation. As 1934 proceeded, Kirov began to use the term more widely to cover the defence of citizens' rights against infringements by the state. A second preoccupation was international: concern with growing 'obscurantism' in western countries, and the consequent need for maximum differentiation between them and the cultural and scientific situation in the USSR. A whole passage on this subject in Kirov's Leningrad Party Conference speech of January 1934 was taken from one by Gorky some days earlier.[1] Bukharin became one of the first to recognise the threat posed by Hitler's accession and raised this danger in his speech to the Party congress. He tried to warn of the menace of German fascism by numerous quotations from *Mein Kampf*. Nazism was such a challenge to civilisation, he argued, that the USSR should take the lead in championing cultural values, science and human dignity. Shortly afterwards, he was appointed editor of *Izvestiya* and wrote a series of articles 'on the crisis of capitalist culture and cultural problems of the USSR'.[2] His designation as one of the Party spokesmen at the forthcoming Writers' Congress would provide an occasion to comment further on domestic policy.

In its first version, 'The Letter of an Old Bolshevik' (based on conversations between Bukharin and Boris Nicolaevsky), suggested a fierce political struggle between differing tendencies vying for Stalin's ear. In the weeks preceding the Congress of Writers Stalin is said to have been influenced by Gorky's position, summarised under the slogan 'Proletarian Humanism', a cultural programme closely associated with Kirov's alleged plans for reform.[3] The campaign for a restoration of legality appears to reach a climax in early July. This was reflected in a *Pravda* column '*Korotkiye signaly*' which began to publish regular complaints from ordinary citizens about low-level administrative incompetence or judicial abuse, often accompanied by the announcement of judicial intervention on behalf of the offended parties.[4] This column disappeared abruptly after Kirov's death. Most significant of all was the reform of the OGPU, replacing it by the NKVD on 11 July 1934, with markedly restricted powers, largely confined to primary investigations and seemingly depriving it of its former judicial role.[5] At the same time, however, it could hardly have escaped the attention of any participant that a genuine system of judicial independence would not be possible without drastically reducing the principal source of arbitrariness: the actions of Stalin. According to 'an Old Bolshevik', the policy of relaxation was forced upon Stalin by an oppositional trend within the Party. We do know that there were rumblings against Stalin in the Congress corridors and that several hundred delegates voted against his re-election to the Central Committee. Far fewer voted against Kirov.[6] However, the existence of a 'Kirov tendency' has never been proven. We have later testimony of a Congress delegate that, even though the opportunity to oppose Stalin was discussed behind the scenes, Kirov insisted publicly that the Party leadership was united. According to this source, a vital chance to prevent subsequent purges was thereby missed.[7] But there is only circumstantial evidence that the new trend in Soviet policy was not to Stalin's liking.

Debates in the spring and summer months of 1934 show greater intellectual vitality and diversity of opinion than had been possible at any time since the end of NEP. No Party spokesmen officially opposed the trend. The relaxation had important implications for culture, where greater leniency was exercised towards writers previously excluded. A concern for quality in literature and art was brought to the forefront of public debates.

On the day Bukharin addressed the Party Congress, Gorky launched a debate on quality in literature. He declared that despite 'certain successes', in the recent past, the level of most contemporary writing remained terribly low. It had possibly declined. Even so, literary critics greeted 'inferior works' with great enthusiasm. The reception of Panfyorov's novel *Bruski*[8] was an overt case of overestimation. This multi-volume epic of collectivisation had been widely welcomed by literary journals such as *Oktyabr'*[9] (still staffed by proletarian writers) and indeed even in the Party's theoretical journal *Bol'shevik*.[10] Panfyorov claimed to write in the 'language of millions' but this was totally misleading. A serious writer, according to Gorky's teaching, would sift and select from the 'mass of colloquialisms', the most capacious and sonorous vocabulary. Ungrammatical language would not do. Panfyorov could not be a model for other writers.[11]

His target was timely and must have been so chosen. Panfyorov was a delegate to the Party Congress and could thus reply to Gorky from the Congress platform. He countered with the assertion that 'a high standard of Soviet literature is already in existence'. This achievement was attributed to the highest authority: 'Comrade Stalin set us on the creative road'. The leader exerted an 'enormous influence on the literary front' and was said to have 'repeatedly in conversations given us instructions'. During his most recent talk with writers, Stalin had said so simply and wisely: 'let the writer learn from life. If he reflects the truth of life in a high artistic form, then he is unfailingly drawn to Marxism'.[12] Panfyorov did not however define, or even mention, socialist realism.[13] He devoted the remainder of his speech to a discussion of literary 'themes' and ended with a rhetorical flourish connecting Gorky with Stalin. This was his eleventh reference to the Party leader. Marx and Kaganovich had received one reference each. Lenin was not mentioned at all.

Panfyorov's joint rapporteur to the Congress on literary questions, Yudin, began by emphasising that he was 'not a writer'. He explained that it was the Central Committee of the Party which had appointed him as 'a Party worker in literature' and he made his report in this capacity. It began with literature's shortcomings. Unlike Gorky, however, his references to the need for quality were rather perfunctory, the problem of the choice of language being dealt with in a brief section. Echoing a familiar theme from Stalin's speech of three years earlier, Yudin complained that literature was 'lagging behind' life. Socialist construction, 'as so well demonstrated in the speeches of Stalin, Molotov, Kuibyshev and Kaganovich, should become literature's principal theme'. Writers should portray heroes of industry, such as shock-workers, of agriculture and of scientific work. He then turned to literature's achievements. Here he singled out organisational matters, particularly the role of Stalin and Kaganovich in providing 'systematic instructions and directives' to communists working in literature and 'organisational, political and theoretical direction for literature as a whole'. *Belles-lettres* had moved decisively in the direction of the Party and had now constituted 'an army of writers' dedicated to its cause. In a now predictable peroration, he emphasised the great proletarian writer Gorky's close links with the leader of the world proletariat, *vozhd'* Stalin.[14]

These rather mundane reports contrasted with the lively 'campaign for quality' developing offstage. On 14 February Gorky returned to the attack. He protested against the 'canonisation' of Panfyorov by Serafimovich and other defendants. Setting him up as a model for younger writers could only lead to a lowering of the quality of literature. Against their defence of colloquialisms and semi-literate speech Gorky enquired how such 'idiotic language could portray the heroism and romanticism of the USSR?'[15] He followed this with an article 'on glibness' in *Pravda*. This asserted 'literature is a militant revolutionary business. Its task is the struggle against remnants of the past and affirmation of socialist achievements of the present as a step towards the socialist future'. It therefore needed an equally elevated vocabulary: 'rich, simple, clear, firm'. As further illustration, he criticised Vishnevsky and his 'innovative school' of dramaturgy for disregarding the classics.[16] Yet for all Gorky's prompting, most writers remained reticent, perhaps waiting for some high-level political statement that this debate was legitimate.

Such sanction was provided by the *Kul't-prop* Secretary on 3 March. Stetsky's authoritative address to a literary meeting on 'The Seventeenth Party Congress and the Tasks of Writers' began by stressing the political importance of literature. Its major role was to assist Party and popular education by the publication of mass works. Thus Stetsky pointed out that since 1929 works by Gorky had appeared in almost 19 million copies, those of Sholokhov in 2.1 million, those of Gladkov and Panfyorov between one and two million and those of V. Ivanov, Kaverin, Leonov, Fedin and A. Tolstoy in hundreds of thousands. However, he agreed with Gorky that the qualitative achievements of Soviet literature were not so great. This was partly the fault of literary critics who had become too complacent or 'sugary' of late and neglected their role of 'teaching, assisting and controlling'. Stetsky welcomed Gorky's initiative in raising the question of literary quality, particularly his recent *Pravda* article. Writers had become careless, descending to mere empiricism or journalism, defined simply as 'writing down instantaneous reactions to events'. Moreover there were cases of writers (that of Panfyorov was evidently in mind), who 'having enjoyed one or two successes and entered a wider social arena had become presumptuous and lowered their literary standards'. A voice from the audience interjected 'there are far too many such cases'. Stetsky replied 'it is the responsibility of writers to react sharply to them'. They should do so collectively by bringing 'their social pressure to bear'.[17]

Pressure from the literary community had not been mentioned in preceding discussions. Did it promise greater influence for rank-and-file writers vis-à-vis the leadership and a corresponding reduction of secretarial control? Stetsky thought so:

> The *Orgkomitet* gives too little attention to creative questions. It is overly concerned with immediate economic and organisational matters. Reconstruction of its methods of work in the light of the Seventeenth Party Congress decisions must be based on a reduction of official rigmarole. Writers do not need endless meetings (*prolonged applause*).[18]

Stetsky singled out as most redundant the 'creative sections' of the *Orgkomitet* established by Stavsky and Yudin in 1933. These 'sections' later developed into an organ of higher censorship within the Writers' Union to which writers were expected to present and discuss their work before submitting it for publication. In 1934, however, they received Stetsky's criticisms:

> Comradely, mutual help should not be organised only on the initiative of the secretarial members of the *Orgkomitet*. Young writers, and not just the young ones, can greatly benefit from such consultation, but not from meetings with official consultants who hand down advice and prepare protocols. Writers should discuss their works in small groups amongst themselves and on their own initiative . . . Only if the *Orgkomitet* takes this line, the line of discussing creative works in specific terms, will it assist writers and thus fulfill its proper function.[19]

He ended on an anti-bureaucratic note: 'the *Orgkomitet* must reconstruct its work. The basic rule is: Down with official rigmarole: For greater creative work'. It is worth recalling that Stetsky had been a member of Bukharin's 'school' until the spring of 1929 when, almost alone of that group, he had defected to Stalin.[20] In the changing atmosphere of early 1934 he appears to have shifted back.

The holding of a Third Plenum of the *Orgkomitet* would offer the first opportunity to test these principles in practice. Before this met,, however, Yudin delivered a stern lecture, lasting two and a half hours, on the Party's close attention to literature. As evidence for this 'serious and profound' concern he mentioned 'the fact that the fundamental theoretical positions were recently formulated by Comrade Stalin, in particular the position on socialist realism'. No definition was offered, suggesting that his Commission had yet to provide results that could be put before the public. Only then did he reach Gorky's initiative. The campaign for quality was referred to solely as a 'signal' to which critics and writers should respond.[21]

Three poets took the opportunity at the Third Plenum of the *Orgkomitet*. Aseyev opposed demands for 'simplicity' as such on the grounds that a requirement of accessibility to all meant 'semi-literacy'.[22] Kirsanov protested against the 'profound dilettantism' prevalent in literary criticism. He singled out the former RAPPist Selivanovsky who had not a good word for anyone but simply sloganised and entirely omitted the specifics of literary craft.[23] Utkin was willing to concede that poetry 'lags behind life' but less so than other genres: 'a treasury of socialist literature' already existed in the work of Aseyev, Utkin and others, although this had been overlooked by the critics, who 'remain utterly ignorant of the poetic arts'. He broadened his attack to include *Orgkomitet* officials who opposed the existence of different 'creative groupings'.[24]

Surkov retorted that such speeches were on an 'extremely low theoretical and principal level'. He deplored their 'arrogant' attitude to questions of education and their brushing aside of much-needed self-criticism.[25] Fadeyev maintained that 'creative groupings' had lost their significance even before their formal abolition in the April Resolution. Debates amongst the 'old LEFovtsi, such as Aseyev and Brik' were of no contemporary interest. Only two serious 'tendencies' still existed: that of progressive writers seeking to move forward and remnants of the old world who were still struggling to turn the clock back. He stated bluntly: 'we do not need various groups'. Nor could communists constitute one particular 'tendency' and non-Party writers a quite different one. 'No, Soviet literature must not develop in the form of groups but of comradely creative discussion in the heart of a single Union of Soviet Writers'. He concluded: 'the Union of Writers should not become a Department of Literary Affairs but rather be a vast, creative, writers' club'.[26]

This speech was ill-received. Some writers thought it foreshadowed precisely the form of regimentation associated with a Department of Literary Affairs. As at the previous Plenum, Kirshon was most outspoken in rebutting the official position. After denying any 'RAPPist recidivism' and applauding the fact that groups such as LEF and *Pereval* had been abolished, he pointed out that all this was 'self-evident'. It rendered Fadeyev's speech 'at best, superfluous', at worst as calling for additional forms of 'unification'. If Fadeyev had meant the removal of all 'stylistic differences' between writers then his notion was nonsensical. Kirpotin interrupted with a statement that 'various styles and tendencies are permissible' within the ranks of the Writers' Union.[27] But Kirshon continued by charging Fadeyev with making a 'mistaken analogy' between literature and politics. Fadeyev's 'new theory' revived the RAPPist heresy of assuming in literary, as in party organisations, the necessity for a single line, deviation from which was inadmissible. But inner-Party terminology had no application to literary organisation. Fadeyev had referred to the creation of a 'single tendency' in Soviet literature: was this to encompass Panfyorov, Zamyatin and Zabolotsky? How could a 'single tendency' describe the 'genre, circumstances, methods, positions and individualities' of Soviet literature? Instead, he argued that plurality of creative tendencies was 'absolutely admissible within the boundary lines which the Party draws on literary questions'.[28]

Although not published for some weeks and then only in part, Kirshon's speech was not his last in the formation of the Writers' Union. One may assume that his analysis was not viewed as heretical. It was Fadeyev, rather, who suffered an eclipse.[29] However, the licence to differ, though present at the Third Plenum, had limits which were set by Bezymensky at the end of the debate. He declared that the dissentient poets had been 'absolutely correct' to raise the question of quality in literature. Much current poetry was 'stylistic and somewhat schematic': in the case of Surkov it betrayed 'a rhythmic emptiness'. It was also right to have raised problems of criticism. Critics 'had the power to do great damage especially to young writers, amongst whom there have been many personal tragedies'. But this could not be blamed on individuals such as Selivanovsky. The problems of standards and of criticism should be resolved within the *Orgkomitet*.[30] Bezymensky rightly implied the area of actual disagreement was not wide. This was to be demonstrated later at the First Writers' Congress, where Aseyev, Surkov and Bezymensky found themselves on the same side against a much wider definition of poetic quality espoused by Bukharin.[31]

On 18 March, the editor of *Pravda*, long known as a close associate of Stalin, joined the campaign. Mekhlis's statement noted: 'The Party, government and whole country demand the resolution of all cultural questions from Gorky's standpoint of the struggle for quality'. He confirmed that '*Pravda* fully supports A. M. Gorky in this struggle for quality of literary language and for a higher development of Soviet literature'. This testimonial was published alongside a further broadside from Gorky on current literary standards.[32] A wide range of writers now took Gorky's side. The non-Party writers V. Ivanov, Slonimsky and Leonov expressed agreement with his initiative.[33] Sholokhov, previously associated with the approval of *Bruski* (as a board member of *Oktyabr'*), now condemned Panfyorov's treatment of collectivisation.[34] The most outspoken of all, Alexei Tolstoy, declared that the entire achievement of Soviet literature over the fifteen years of its existence amounted to little more than 'the hastily noted reflections of a great epoch'.[35] Many of these contributions seemed authentic. Unlike the 'anti-formalist' campaign of 1936, the 'campaign for quality' is notable for the sincerity of those who took part. Many writers viewed the future Soviet literature with genuine enthusiasm, taking the campaign as a signal of greater freedom of expression to come. This improved literary atmosphere seemed quite propitious for the draft statutes of the Union which were at last ready for publication.

The statutes of the Writers' Union were supposed to fulfil two functions. The first was to set out the principles governing admission to this new association. When an early draft was being drawn up, in 1932, certain non-Party writers expressed the anxiety that proletarian 'hegemony' might be replaced by some other system of political exclusiveness. Aseyev insisted that 'actual literary merit as recognised by all' should be the sole criterion for admission. Indeed, a number of proletarian writers did attempt to introduce restrictive clauses, including Bezymensky who proposed to open the union to educable new cadres. Aseyev retorted that the Union could not be used as a training-ground for promising young writers. To do so would restrict it to 'youth alone' and in such a case it would hardly have the character of a professional organisation to which non-party writers were accustomed to belong.[36] Thereafter, the problem was delegated to V. Kirpotin, confirming the fact noted earlier that he had the responsibility of 'agreeing with the Central Committee on the subject of the statutes'. His first draft kept closely to the wording of the April Resolution. The Writers' Union would be open 'to all those who subscribed to the platform of Soviet power and are willing to take an active part in socialist construction'.[37] This was widely criticised as too capacious. The legal consultant to the *Orgkomitet* pronounced it 'insufficiently clear to govern admission to a professional organisation'.[38] He also found other ambiguities. Those he discerned in the division of duties between the Union's leading institutions were to have important consequences later on.[39]

The second purpose of the statutes was to define socialist realism. The Commission's lengthy deliberations now came to fruition. A proposal was put to the Central Committee and immediately afterwards made public.[40] This amounted to the first authoritative statement of the new doctrine. According to the statutes, socialist realism demanded from the writer a 'truthful and historically specific depiction of reality'. Traditional realism was supplemented by the requirement of 'ideologically moulding and educating working people in the spirit of socialism'. The 'engineer of human souls' was to portray reality 'in its revolutionary development'.[41] Thus, the present was not to be described simply as it is, but as it is becoming according to a teleological imperative. As Sinyavsky shows, this assumes a universe governed by purpose (*tsel'*). It raises, but does not answer, the question of how an as yet unachieved future may be accurately expressed through verisimilitude.[42]

The theory of socialist realism attempts to combine three disparate elements. The first and least controversial was popular appeal or comprehensibility for the new Soviet readership produced by recent literacy campaigns. These had developed a mass audience for literary works in Russia for the first time. As we saw in analysing Lenin's response to Futurism, the call for simplicity of form and clarity of expression was one which the Bolshevik leadership had often made.[43] Socialist realism added the didactic purpose of 'moulding and education of working people in the spirit of socialism'. An explanatory article, by Yudin and Fadeyev, announced that writers did not have to be professional philosophers but did need to 'rise to the level of contemporary culture' of which Marxism-Leninism was the highest expression.[44] While recognising that this would make art tendentious, the authors insisted, with Engels, that 'tendentiousness must spring from a situation in the action itself, without explicit attention being called to it'. They omitted the remainder of Engels' sentence 'the writer is not obliged to offer to the reader the future historical solution to the social conflict he depicts'. On the contrary, the socialist realist was expected to depict 'contemporary events in their revolutionary development'.[45] While taking reality as source material, he should show 'the present day giving birth to the morrow'. These 'principles of artistic creativity' expressed in the new doctrine were to become 'the basic method of Soviet *belles-lettres* and literary criticism'.[46]

In further exegesis, Yudin explained that the term 'method' was used deliberately to put an end to rumours and futile discussions about whether socialist realism 'is one style or tendency (*napravleniye*)' within Soviet literature. Method, intended 'in the Marxist sense', meant a guide to action, not merely a set of abstractions. This echoed the April Resolution's requirement that Soviet writers should 'actively participate in their artistic work in socialist construction'. Soviet writers were to create a celebratory literature 'really worthy of the great epoch of socialism'. As the statutes explained, the main task of the Union of Writers consisted in 'active participation through artistic work in socialist construction, defence of the interest of the working class and strengthening of the Soviet Union'.[47] Yudin's commentary described acceptance of this as a *sine qua non* for any successful application. He noted that membership would be voluntary but that none of those wishing to join would be allowed to do so unless they fulfilled these 'necessary political demands'.[48]

The third element required socialist realists to display 'Party-mindedness', possibly regarded as the summation of the other two. *Partiinost'* was a pre-Bolshevik term, used by Chekhov amongst others, to mean simply partisanship. It was used perjoratively by the early Lenin in debate with Petr Struve to mean the opposite of objectivism.[49] In a letter to Gorky of 1908 (first published in 1934) Lenin rejoiced that petit-bourgeois intelligentsia were fleeing the party – 'good riddance!'. Their departure provided an opportunity to change literary criticism: 'there is nothing good about all those long articles of literary criticism scattered through various semi-party and non-party periodicals. We should try to take a step away from this old intellectualist stuffed shirt, that is we should link literary criticism more closely with party work, with party leadership'.[50] Lenin's letter was used to argue the need for *partiinost'*, already introduced in philosophy and social science, in literary criticism.

Despite this, the statutes gave those who joined the Writers' Union special reassurance that 'socialist realism guarantees excellent opportunities for the display of creative initiative and choice amongst its various forms, styles and genres'. Yet another leading article by Yudin, 'The Criterion of Quality', insisted that artistic achievement would be the principal requirement for admission.[51] It seems reasonable to conclude, therefore, that the statutes were carefully formulated to sustain a dual interpretation. Restrictive use could emphasise *partiinost'* and Party goals; wider interpretation could point to the guarantee of a wide margin of creative possibilities within the overall rubric of socialist realism. The original Resolution had ordered the establishment of a single Union whose membership was to be broadly based around a nucleus of communist writers. To accommodate both party and non-party members within the 'Union of Soviet Writers', required a wide platform. This the new doctrine purported to provide.

Soon afterwards, a commission on Union membership was named, with Yudin as President and six ordinary members: V. Ivanov, Pavlenko, Fedin, Aseyev, Gladkov and Afinogenov.[52] Applicants had to supply information on their social position, Party status and level of education. They then reached question 6 on the length of their literary experience (*stazh*).[53] At its first meeting, a dozen writers were accepted and rather more rejected as 'not satisfying the requirements of the statutes'. By the end of May, over 200 writers had been admitted to the Union, with a roughly equivalent number of rejections.[54] Although he had received membership card Number One, on 10 May, Gorky's role was restricted for the next few weeks to a couple of short articles.[55] This must partly be attributed to the sudden death of his son from pneumonia.[56] A letter of condolence from Soviet writers was published the following day.[57]

As already noted, the statutes failed to specify in detail who or what would constitute political leadership within the Union.[58] The amount of work would be too great for *Kul't-prop* secretary Stetsky,[59] although he remained the general overseer of party organisation of culture. 'Party worker in literature' Yudin seemed unacceptable to Gorky and probably to many other writers. One would-be organiser who also had significant literary credentials, was Fadeyev. But officials considered Fadeyev had failed either to unite the party 'fraction' of the *Orgkomitet* – and hence make party members such as Kirshon conform to it – or to establish much authority over non-party writers.[60] It was probably at this time that the Party leadership resolved on two new appointments to literary administration. One of them, A. S. Shcherbakov, a member of the Central Committee *Agit-prop*, was to be brought in as First Secretary of the Writers' Union.[61] The second nomination was of the Party Secretary Andrei Zhdanov, to open the Congress. To a later generation, his name conjures up the spectre of *zhdanovshchina*, a byword for cultural repression.[62] That he was to introduce socialist realism in his speech might seem an ill-omen for the Congress. But other preparations indicate that Gorky at least intended the opposite.

A preparatory commission for the Congress had been set up on 17 March. It convened a series of hearings to review draft speeches for the Congress on different genres including dramaturgy (Kirpotin, Kirshon, Pogodin and Alexei Tolstoy) and poetry (Bolotnikov, Tikhonov and Usievich).[63] Gorky took an active part in the vetting. He found Usievich's contribution much too narrow and sectarian, failing to recognise the great variety amongst Moscow poetry.[64] It was not delivered at the Congress. He rejected first drafts by Kirpotin ('not a speech but an article') and by Stavsky on 'young writers', ('semiliterate') although both were eventually re-written to his satisfaction.[65] Kirshon escaped with substantial redrafting of his speech 'Socialist Realism in Dramaturgy' following Gorky's appraisal ('not a speech but an attempt to derive a theory of Soviet drama') and criticism of his polemical debate with Vishnevsky on dramatic form rather than reconciling the differences of opinion between them. He noted that Kirshon's statement 'needs to agree with the speech by N. Bukharin'.[66]

Bukharin's speech was rehearsed before the editorial board of *The People of the Five Year Plan* on 9 July 1934.[67] He used the occasion to raise 'questions of deep principle' later elaborated at the Writers' Congress. Perhaps for this reason no verbatim account was published. Nevertheless, certain key themes may be identified. His fundamental criticism was that contemporary literature still failed to portray current Soviet achievements in their variety and complexity. Much writing remained hackneyed, vulgarised, provincial and superficial. The old RAPPist notion of 'social demand'[68] had been misunderstood. He ridiculed those writers who relied largely upon 'the brigade method' of literary production with its vastly exaggerated expectation that 'if organisational' aspects of literature were correct, all would be well. This seemed a blow at the *People of the Five Year Plan* collective project. He called instead for an enlargement of 'cultural horizons' to replace the perspective of the 'seminarist' so regularly encountered in Soviet literature.[69] Used to being given mundane tasks, Bukharin's audience was astounded to hear its efforts measured against the pinnacles of international achievement. As Alexei Tolstoy said, they were unaccustomed to such alpinism. For Bukharin insisted that competition with capitalism had a cultural component. Soviet literature could not rise to a world level without mastering the classics. It must emulate 'the profundity of Goethe and the breadth of Shakespeare'.[70] He applauded the campaign for higher quality of literary language and tried to awaken writers from what Alexei Tolstoy called the somnolence that had descended on literary circles[71] by insisting that the cultural needs and demands of Soviet readers had increased enormously since the first Five Year Plan.

The most enthusiastic support came from an unusual source. Mirsky, a former lecturer in London at the School of Slavonic Studies, now resident in Russia[72] published a review of Fadeyev's *Last of the Udege* which stated bluntly that it was inferior to Fadeyev's earlier *The Rout* (1927). He argued that the new novel was written on too superficial a level for the second Five Year Plan and indicated, none too delicately, that the author was resting on his laurels: 'Soviet literature would not have reached its present level without Fadeyev's participation. In order to surpass this, Fadeyev has considerable work before him, in which he can scarcely avoid the prior admission that *Last of the Udege* is artistically mistaken'.[73] Yudin attempted a reply in *Pravda*: 'the article by a certain D. Mirsky in *Literaturnaya gazeta* is an irresponsible outburst by an opponent of Soviet literature',[74] but writers were unwilling to defend Fadeyev. On the contrary, Gladkov, Shaginyan and Jasienski publically criticised Yudin.[75] Moreover, Gorky remained loyal to Mirsky. In his handwritten preparations for the Congress,[76] Mirsky appears twice, down to give a speech on the works of Bagritsky and as rapporteur on English literature. The sequel to his article on literary manners, referred to 'D. Mirsky, an exceptionally well-educated man, knowledgeable critic, member of the English (*sic*) Communist Party, was absolutely right to state in print that the *Last of the Udege* does not enhance Soviet literature'.[77] Gorky suggested that the author himself realised it was a very poor work.

On the eve of the Congress, Gorky called for an improvement of literary manners. He complained that existing relations between writers were 'to put it mildly poor'. The collective spirit had atrophied while egotistical individualism ran wild. The 'anti-social and anti-Party' habit of seeing enemies everywhere persisted, notably in the behaviour of some former RAPPists. A little inconsistently, Gorky proposed that Averbakh, as Secretary of the *History of Factories* series, should address the Congress. Subsequently, he withdrew this proposal lest the suspicion arise of 'a return of the *RAPPovtsi* and RAPPist methods to the leadership of literature'.[78] He did, however, assail 'contemporary hooligans' including one

unfortunate young poet, P. Vasil'yev.[79] Without reconciliation between writers, he predicted, there would inevitably develop a
struggle between competing groups for the role of leader (*vozhd'*).
His stark warning '*vozhdism* is an illness'[80] seemed to point beyond
the literary sphere.

Stalin's attitude to the approaching Writers' Congress may be
reflected in his telephone call to Pasternak at the end of July. Their
conversation initially concerned the fate of Mandelstam, who had
been arrested on 13 May.[81] Since he had previously written and
recited a poem denouncing Stalin as 'the Kremlin mountaineer, the
murderer and peasant-slayer', his detention was hardly unexpected.[82]
Moreover, Mandelstam admitted authorship and was charged under
Article 58 of the criminal code with creating a 'counter-revolutionary
document without precedent'. None of his acquaintances doubted
that the penalty for such audacity would be death. Nevertheless,
attempts at rescue had been made. Akhmatova contrived to see
Yenukidze in the Kremlin, though he was non-committal.[83]
Nadezhda Mandelstam and Pasternak both approached Bukharin,
who was perturbed by the news and agreed to intercede with Stalin.
His letter doing so contained a postscript, mentioning that he had
been visited by Pasternak, who was upset by Mandelstam's arrest.
This was intended to indicate the concern of public opinion.[84] But the
literary intelligentsia was far from unanimous on this subject. Mandelstam had recently had a stand-up row with Alexei Tolstoy, who
responded with an attack on Acmeism and Mandelstam by name at
the Congress.

Stalin began the call to Pasternak by stating that Mandelstam's
sentence to forced labour on the White Sea Canal had been com-
muted to three years' internal exile. He then asked why Pasternak
had not taken up the case with writers' organisations or with Stalin
himself. Pasternak replied: 'The writers' organisations haven't
bothered with cases like this since 1927, and if I hadn't tried to do
something you would probably never have heard of it'. The poet then
requested a longer personal interview with the Party leader to discuss
'life and death'.[85] Stalin hung up at this point and Pasternak made
unavailing efforts to reconnect the line through the Kremlin switch-
board. Besides demonstrating that 'miracles' could occur, if only
Pasternak had appealed to him directly rather than through third
parties, Stalin's intervention had a further purpose. Pasternak was
told by Stalin's Secretary Poskrebyshev that the call could be made

public. Knowledge of this 'liberal' gesture spread through literary Moscow within a matter of hours. In Ehrenburg's opinion, Stalin's intervention 'transformed the programme of the Congress'.[86]

The First Congress of Soviet Writers opened in a carnival atmosphere hardly conducive to serious debate. Ehrenburg recalled a 'great and marvellous festival' at which writers accustomed to long hours at their desks found themselves in a public forum 'garlanded with all the flowers of an early Moscow autumn'.[87] Yashvili noted public enthusiasm 'which ran out onto the streets, the trams, factories and cafes' where writers formed the only topic of conversation on every side.[88] Delegates met in the Hall of Columns, formerly the Assembly Hall of the Moscow nobility, and notorious later as the venue for the 'show trials'. Its walls were hung with portraits of 'predecessors': Shakespeare, Cervantes, Pushkin, Gogol and Tolstoy. Ehrenburg sat opposite Heine 'youthful, dreamy and naturally mocking'.[89]

The proceedings were begun by an orchestra and were constantly interrupted by delegations of workers and peasants parading through, often in working clothes carrying the tools of their trade.[90] Such manifestations were meant to impress upon writers their social responsibilities. Their political allegiances were made explicit on the opening morning. Headlines in the press stated: 'Soviet writers have every right to call the great Stalin their best friend and leader'.[91] The Congress itself began with a message of greetings from the entire assembly:

Dear Iosif Vissarionovich!

We, representatives of Soviet literature, have gathered today for our first All-Union Congress. Our weapon is the word. Include this weapon in the arsenal of working class struggle . . . we will struggle to make our art a trusty and well-aimed weapon in the hands of the working class both at home and abroad and we will stand on guard over revolutionary literature of the entire world. We begin this historic day by greeting you, dear Iosif Vissarionovich, our teacher and friend. You, the foremost pupil of Lenin, truly and steadfastly continue his work . . . your name stands as the symbol of greatness, simplicity, strength and constancy, unites in itself everything that characterises the type and character of a Bolshevik.[92]

More nuanced greetings were sent to the Central Committee, Council of Ministers, Voroshilov and the workers of a paper factory.

Zhdanov's opening address declared they had convened at a time when 'The mighty banner of Marx, Engels, Lenin and Stalin has triumphed. It is to the victory of this banner that we owe the fact that the First Congress of Soviet Writers has assembled here. Were it not for this victory your Congress would not be taking place.' Soviet literature had now to emulate the success of socialist construction. Although 'the youngest of all literatures of all peoples and countries', it was already 'the richest in ideas, the most advanced and most revolutionary literature'. This could be seen in its unique subject-matter, the struggles of the working class and peasantry for socialism. 'There is not and cannot be in bourgeois countries a literature which consistently smashes every kind of obscurantism, every kind of mysticism, priesthood and superstition, as our literature is doing'. A Soviet writer took his 'images, artistic language and speech from the life and experience of the men and women of Dnieprostroi and Magnitostroi, from the heroic epic of the Chelyuskin expedition, from the experience of our collective farms, from the creative activity that is seething in all corners of our country'. His heroes were the active builders of the new life. Soviet literature was optimistic, not from 'inward animal instinct', but because it was the literature of the rising class of the proletariat, 'the only progressive and advanced class'.[93] 'Comrade Stalin has called our writers "engineers of human souls". What does this mean? What duties does this title confer upon you?' His answer provided the first authoritative statement of the new doctrine:

> In the first place it means knowing life, so as to be able to depict it truthfully in works of art, not to depict it in a dead, scholastic way, not simply as 'objective reality', but to depict reality in its revolutionary development. In addition, the truthfulness and historical concreteness of the artistic portrayal should be combined with the ideological remoulding and education of the toiling people in the spirit of socialism. This method in *belles-lettres* and literary criticism is what we call the method of socialist realism.[94]

To the objection that the portrayal of reality in its revolutionary development would oblige writers to subscribe to an ideological commitment, Zhdanov replied frankly 'Yes, Soviet literature is tendentious, for in an epoch of class struggle there is not and cannot be a literature which is not class literature, not tendentious, allegedly non-political'.[95] Taking up the issue raised by Lunacharsky at the Second Plenum, Zhdanov argued that socialist realism did contain an element of romanticism, not of the escape into fantasy or an unreal world, but romanticism of a new type: 'Revolutionary romanticism'. Soviet literature should be able 'to glimpse our tomorrow. This will be no utopian dream, for our tomorrow is already being prepared for today by dint of conscious planned work'.

Finally, turning to literary method, he came down cautiously on the side of diversity. 'One cannot be an engineer of human souls without knowing the technique of literary work and it must be noted that the technique of the writer's work possesses a large number of specific peculiarities.' Writers had 'many different types of weapon. Soviet literature has every opportunity of employing these types of weapon (genres, style, forms and methods of literary creation) in their diversity and fullness'. They were free to select from amongst the best created by the past, in order to assimilate it critically and advance it further. Considerable variety thus seemed to be permitted under the overall rubric of socialist realism. Indeed, Zhdanov endorsed the campaign for 'the culture of language, for quality of production. In this connection it is impossible to overrate the help that Maxim Gorky is rendering the Party and the proletariat in the struggle for quality in literature, for the culture of language'.[96]

Gorky himself entered a professional note. Rather than recite achievements, he dwelt on shortcomings. In contrast to Zhdanov and many later speakers, he offered no adulation of political leaders – Stalin was mentioned only twice in a long speech, both times in company with Marx and Lenin. His chosen mode was historical: the first half of his lecture was devoted to a resumé of world civilisation from neolithic times. He saw this as the sketch for a Marxian history of culture that had yet to be written. His outline dwelt on some politically 'difficult' subjects: on Dostoyevsky, portrayed as a genius but in judgement of character closer to 'the role of a medieval inquisitor'; Petr Struve and his contribution to *Vekhi*[97] and the role of both in the 'shameless decade' that followed in *belles-lettres*.[98] He then came to the contrast between the Russian literature of the nineteenth century based upon individuals and the central subject of Soviet literature, labour, 'i.e., a person organised by the processes of labour'. This rapidly advancing process was bringing out 'more powerfully the latent abilities and talents that are concealed in this mass of 170 million people'. Yet this 'raw material' of rapidly changing reality was as yet little appreciated. 'All of us – writers, factory workers, collective farmers – still work badly and cannot even fully master everything that has been made by us and for us.' Soviet writers were still poor observers. They neglected the changing external landscape and the psychological development through which 'human beings became aware of a sense of their own dignity and began to understand themselves as an active force actually changing the world'.[99] Such were Gorky's common injunctions on literary education, and their reiteration at the Congress was not surprising.

Much more novel was his abrupt shift of focus to literary critics. Their important functions were not being performed satisfactorily. In the 'discovery of new talent' they were 'simply negligent'. In promoting the literatures of the republics of the USSR they had a 'demoralising influence'. Such critics had forgotten Engels' most valuable idea: 'our teaching is not a dogma; it is a guide to action'. 'A critic cannot teach an author to write simply, clearly and economically if he himself is long-winded, obscure and perfunctory.' Further problems arose when a critic held close personal sympathies for an author or clique. He then became afflicted with leaderism (*vozhdism*), 'a contagious philistine disease'. In the inevitable conflict between the capitalist and the proletarian, the philistine sides with the former. He espouses an impoverished individualism, resulting in such festering sores as 'Ebert, Noske, Hitler and similar heroes of the capitalist world'. The philistine tries to climb above his colleagues, which, Gorky noted, was quite easily done given 'a certain mechanical cunning, an empty head and an empty heart'. Nor was this solely a western phenomenon. Such philistinism still existed in the Soviet Union and even in 'Lenin's party', despite numerous purges, it remained infectious and contagious. The disease had entered literary organisations: 'The Party leadership of literature must be thoroughly cleansed of all philistine influences'. Only then would it obtain moral authority in this sphere.[100] Philistinism would be replaced by collective responsibility for all that happened in their midst. Thereby cleansed, writers could be organised as a collective whole, as a mighty instrument of socialist culture. Although malign influences were not specifically located, it seems reasonable to assume in the light of his earlier statements that Gorky had in mind such party workers in literary criticism as Usievich and Yudin.

Finally, he discussed the reasons why the Writers' Congress had been organised and the purposes that would lie before the future Union. It would 'not have been worth so much effort' simply for the physical unification of writers. As a professional association, how-ever, the Writers' Union could 'pool its collective strength, give the clearest possible definition of various creative tendencies', and har-moniously merge into the unity which was 'now aiding all creative working energies of the country'. 'The idea of the Union is not to restrict individual creativity but to give it every possibility for future powerful development.'[101] Here Gorky was touching upon the cen-tral question of the reorganisation of literature: how could a single Union dedicated to the creation of a literature of socialist construc-tion be established without stifling individual initiative? He did not articulate this fully, but rather assumed that the general and the individual purposes were ultimately compatible. Where they still diverged the remedy was pedagogic: education was a primary task of the Writers' Union. He concluded his speech on a similar theme: 'our Congress should not only be a report to readers, not only a parade of our achievement. It should undertake the organisation of literature, the education of young writers on work of national significance, giving them a many-sided knowledge of our country's past and present'.[102]

Gorky's historical account 'which had stopped just at the point when bourgeois literature began to collapse' was brought up to date by Karl Radek. Once a Trotskyite, Radek had long since recanted. Even so, he addressed a problem which Stalin's leadership had been slow to recognise: the rise of Fascism. He situated Soviet literature in relation to this 'formative event' of the present day. 'On 10 May 1933, on the public squares of Berlin, the German Fascists burned not only works of Gorky, Stalin and German revolutionary writers such as Ludwig Renn and others, but also those of all humanitarian writers'. On that day 'all the world's writers were told there is no such thing as neutrality in the struggle now taking place in the arena of history'. Radek recognised that this had been appreciated by a 'number of revolutionary writers', forty of whom, including ten from Germany, attended the Congress.

Many others, while rejecting the cultural heritage of the bour-geoisie, still hesitated to align themselves with the communist parties of western countries. Radek depicted their dilemmas quite frankly. Some 'shied away from struggle in general', some 'underestimated the revolutionary forces in their own country' and others were held back by 'the idea of individualism' which led writers to think them-selves incapable of submitting to 'the discipline of the party'. Radek expressed their thoughts as follows: 'Being a writer, a worker of the mind, I cannot submit to any discipline. All parties mean blinkers. All parties tie down the artist. I want to be a freelance fighting for the revolution. I cannot be a soldier in the army of revolution'. There were also 'certain right-wing authors', who have adapted themselves to the revolution but 'in reality do not understand its greatness. They want to get away from Magnitogorsk, from 'Kuznetskstroi, from the great deeds of our country, to '"great art" which depicts the small deeds of small people. They want to escape from the stormy sea of revolution and take refuge in the stagnant waters of small ponds, in bogs where frogs croak'.[103] Admitting '*belles-lettres* is not my special province of work', Radek felt emboldened to advance a literary comparison. Writers could choose between socialist realism, the method of revolutionary art, in celebration of Soviet achievement, or retreat into the peculiar mode of Ulysses: 'a heap of dung, crawling with worms, photographed by a cinema apparatus through a microscope'. The choice was simple: 'James Joyce or Socialist Realism?'[104]

Several of the foreign guests protested at this formulation.[105] But Radek was unrepentant. Socialist realism was distinguished from all western literary experiments by its procedure:

Select all phenomena which show how the system of capitalism is being smashed, how socialism is growing, not embellishing it but showing that it is growing in battle, in hard toil, in sweat. Show how it is growing in deeds, in human beings. Do not represent each and every capitalist as he has been represented by *Agit-prop* brigades. No, show the typical in the individual. Do this, basing yourself on the criteria of the laws of historical development. That is what socialist realism means.[106]

But towards the visitors' defence of 'individualism', Radek was flexible. For Jean-Richard Bloch, aspects of the individual personality were positive and to be cherished. 'Individualism' was not synonymous with anti-social behaviour or unclubbability.[107] Radek accepted this correction and endorsed the principle of 'respect for the personality'. In conclusion, he reiterated his contention that artists in the west were 'coming over to the proletariat'.[108] Even so, the Writers' Congress did not achieve a 'united front' with western writers. No common platform emerged until the summer of 1935, when it was largely dictated by the Soviet representatives.[109]

Slowly, the Congress was coming to life. Now that the Party

preliminaries were out of the way, attention could turn – as Gorky had always intended – to writers themselves. Bukharin's speech was perfectly attuned to this transition. His address 'Poetry, Poetics and Problems of Poetry in the USSR' brought about the first major debate. Unlike previous spokesmen, he courted controversy. His account of the poetic past referred positively to Gumilev (who was quoted), Bal'mont (who had emigrated after the Revolution) and Bely. Sharp, sometimes hostile, characterisations were given of Blok, Esenin and Bryusov. The Formalist school of literary criticism was defended against 'Marxist literary critics [who] have regarded them with complete disdain'.[110] These opinions were received quite calmly. Passions arose, rather, from his assessment of contemporaries.

His opening remarks had given the campaign for quality a new impetus. He now warmed to the theme:

> It is not in the least accidental that in our time taken in the narrow sense of the word – I am talking about the period through which we are passing at present – that the problem of quality should be decisive on all fronts. The problem of quality is the problem of diversity, of the multiplicity of differing approaches to a question, of individualisation, of attaining greater depth, and so on. It is the fundamental problem in science, in economics, in the sphere of leadership, and in the sphere of ideas.

This led directly to literature.

> If we consider – and we all undoubtedly do so – that poetic work is one aspect of ideological creativity, that poetic work is also a special form of production, and that poetry, irrespective of whether it actually manages to be so or not, is one of the most potent factors in social development . . . If, as I say, we bear in mind this problem of quality, then the problem arises in our poetic work today: the problem of quality, the problem of mastering technique, of poetic creation, the problem of craftsmanship, the problem of assimilating the heritage of past literature and culture is now being put at the top of the agenda.

It was not the poet's business to paraphrase a newspaper or to show a 'standard knowledge of political science'. Soviet society had entered a new and more complex stage. Cultural requirements had grown immeasurably: 'there is a tremendous thirst to know everything, a tremendous desire to generalise, to rise on a new basis to an understanding of the process as a whole'.[111] Synthetic poetry was needed to summarise the epoch as a whole, not in a fragmentary manner but in all its complexity and diversity. For this purpose, the works of Demyan Bedny, immensely important and popular though they had been, were now inadequate. They did not take into account 'all the tremendous changes, the incredible growth of culture, its growing complexity, its richer content, its heightened tone, the changed dimensions of all our social life. Bedny takes new subjects but everything else remains almost as of old. For this reason he is becoming out of date, and here lies a manifest danger for him'.[112] Likewise, the whole galaxy of Komsomol poets, most notable amongst them Bezymensky, was in danger of becoming an anachronism:

> He was undoubtedly the poetic mouthpiece of the new generation of Komsomol and gave expression to the still unsifted elemental forces of communist youth of that time, with their militant fervour. He is primarily the poet of the 'light cavalry' in struggle and labour. He began to give place, however, when the heavy artillery of the literary front had to be called on, when life grew more intricate, when a more intensive survey, greater depth, greater variety, complexity and mastery of poetic expression were needed. Something similar to what happened to Demyan Bedny also happened to him: unable to divert his attention to more complex problems, he became elementary, began to get 'antiquated' and he was directly faced with the danger of simply repeating the slogan of the day in rhyme.[113]

Bukharin recognised that the influence of Mayakovsky on such poets had been enormous – 'Mayakovsky gave Soviet poetry so much that he has become a Soviet classic' – yet this inheritance was no longer sufficient. Even the most orthodox of Mayakovsky's followers, Aseyev, came in for criticism. 'He does not see that the "agitational pieces" of Mayakovsky can no longer satisfy, that they have become too elementary. What is required now is more diversity, more generalisation, the need is arising for monumental poetic painting, all the sources of lyric verse have been opened and the very conception of "actuality" is becoming a different one.' Lyricism was by no means precluded.

The new man that is being born and the whole world of his emotions, including even new erotics, if one may so express it, are therefore the province of socialist art. Lyric verse does not conflict with socialist realism because we are not here speaking of an anti-realistic form of lyric, seeking for a correct world beyond, but of a lyric which gives poetic shape to the spiritual experiences of the socialist man who is now coming into being. Socialist realism is not anti-lyrical.[114]

Bukharin's conclusion seemed designed to put the campaign for quality on a permanent footing. His remarkable statement of socialist pluralism praised the excellence of diversity:

The entire variety of life can and should serve as the material for poetic creation. Unity does not mean that we must all sing the same song at the same time – now about sugar beets, now about 'the living man',[115] now about the class struggle in the countryside, now about the Party card. Unity does not mean the presentation of the same ideal types and the same 'villains', nor the abolition – on paper – of all contradictions and evils. Unity consists in a single *aspect* – that of building socialism. All the richness of life, all tragedies and conflicts, vacillations and defeat, the conflict of tendencies – all this must become the material for poetic creation.[116]

There could be no forced unanimity on artistic issues. Socialist construction was a theme on which all writers should concentrate, but the variety of possible approaches to it was almost infinite. Differing perspectives were welcome until 'sufficiently broad generalisations are found'. 'Prohibitive measures are therefore absurd.' Although the RAPPist slogan of the 'living man' was 'one-sided', it did not follow that 'in connection with the change of leadership on the critical front this sort of portrayal should be relegated to the scrap-heap and in effect prohibited (*applause*)'. One dogma should not be super-ceded by another. Finally, he warned against the introduction of monopolistic institutions:

The danger of poetic work becoming departmentally alienated from life and bureaucratised, orders being issued by *Narkompros*, by the Commissariat of Means of Communication, by the Transport Workers' Trade Union, by the woodworking industries' trade union and so on. This, of course, is not art at all. In any case there is a very grave danger of this kind of art ceasing to be art. The way forward does not lie along these lines.[117]

Bukharin's speech was greeted with enormous enthusiasm. It ended with thunderous applause 'of the whole hall' rising to an ovation, 'cries of Hurrah with the assembly on its feet'.[118] This demonstration of approval could not have passed unnoticed. Bukharin himself foresaw the danger. At one point in his speech, he broke off to remark that he understood the applause coming from the audience was 'addressed to the Party as a whole, of which I am a member and which directed me to this meeting'.[119] An uncorroborated account describes Bukharin resuming his seat ashenfaced and commenting that the audience's reaction had signed 'his death warrant'.[120] This is surely apocryphal, for we do know that his speech had been vetted beforehand. Stetsky's secret report to the Central Committee 'on Bukharin's conduct at the Congress' (31 August 1934), states that Bukharin had shown a draft to the *Kul't-prop* Secretariat, in the knowledge that 'his remarks might be taken in the name of the Party'. Furthermore, these notes or 'theses' had been checked by Zhdanov for the Central Committee Secretariat.[121] It does seem that in some places Bukharin departed from the agreed text[122] and his reply to the debate was of course extemporary.

There was much to answer. Despite the ovation, many of those criticised spoke in the debate. Unable to address his main thesis on equal terms, a number of speakers resorted to abuse. Surkov purported to be scandalised that 'Comrade Bukharin forgot that the speech he was giving was on behalf of the Party' and deplored the fact that Bukharin had allowed his personal taste to influence the account of poetry.[123] More importantly he counterposed Bukharin's dismissal of Mayakovsky as *passé*, with his approval of Pasternak. Here were the makings of a myth. For many years, Bukharin's alleged denigration of Mayakovsky at the Congress was taken as the grounds on which to condemn his entire speech. Kirsanov defended Mayakovsky against Bukharin's attempt 'to withdraw poetry from its battle station in reality, to positions where it cannot influence contemporary life, cannot take part in class struggle, evacuating it to the rear'.[124] Several other followers, while denying that they were part of any 'cult of Mayakovsky', nonetheless came to his defence.[125] Still more enraged were those whom Bukharin had criticised by name. Demyan Bedny declared 'Bukharin brought here Esenin's corpse, stuck it on top of me and spread the ashes of Mayakovsky everywhere, rest in peace . . . I have come to the podium expressly to show you that I am not dead yet'.[126] Bezymensky was most fundamental in his complaint: Bukharin's report had omitted to identify those poets who were 'mouthpieces of the class enemy' of whom he named Gumilev, the peasant poets Klyuev and Klychkov, Gorky's recent antagonist Pavel Vasil'yev and Zabolotsky.[127]

Bukharin replied robustly:

> As I expected, the Congress has heard a number of bitter attacks on my speech. I must apologise in advance to those comrades with whom I in turn shall take issue in my concluding words. For I shall defend myself according to all the rules of art. As a further preliminary, however, I must say that unfortunately the value of the arguments directed against me – both cultural and specific – does not seem to me very great. (*applause*)[128]

Whereas he had attempted a general definition of poetry and socialist realism, his 'opponents' had almost invariably omitted to discuss substantive issues. They had 'united' in a single, unprincipled block: 'the fraction of the offended'. Their 'sharpshooter' Surkov alleged he had forgotten the speech was given on behalf of the Party but 'I myself have other information'. His main 'theses' had been scrutinised and confirmed by the appropriate Party authorities for 'this is one of the functions of Party leadership'. Surkov's other claim, that the speeches were delivered only on the authority of the *Orgkomitet*, was dispatched with style:

> Comrade Surkov seems to me to have adopted a harmful political conception. He says 'the Party doesn't come into it, it is a matter for the *Orgkomitet*'. But is not the *Orgkomitet* led by the Party? The consequence of this concept is to cut off writers' organisations from Party leadership. But I declare that Comrade Surkov will never achieve such a separation of our writers from the Party leadership. (*prolonged applause*)[129]

He rejected Surkov's claim that 'Bukharin is liquidating proletarian poetry'. Was he a 'liquidator' simply because he was unwilling to say "Bezymensky is a Shakespeare, Zharov a Goethe, and Svetlov a

Heine". Indeed, I did not want to say this!' (*applause*). He did not seek to 'liquidate' proletarian poetry, but simply 'to liquidate Communist conceit in poetry'.[130] He wanted to eliminate the exaggerated pretensions of proletarian writers towards what they had actually achieved. These were terms identical to the 1925 Party resolution on literature of which Bukharin was co-author.

The remainder of his reply poured scorn on the 'offended'. Kirsanov had been 'a mine of information in the negative, logically, morally and culturally'. Bezymensky had accused him of underestimating Mayakovsky. Pointing out that he had rated Mayakovsky very highly and even called him a 'classic of Soviet poetry', Bukharin reiterated his argument that even so great a man need not be idolised. Those who did so forgot that 'life keeps moving forward'. As for Demyan Bedny, at the slightest hint of criticism, he had turned into 'a corpse'. He summed up his main argument as follows:

> My opponents, striving to present me as a liquidator of proletarian poetry, rest on their laurels, are at a standstill and, since they consider themselves near-geniuses, are not exactly carried away with enthusiasm by the problem of severe and intense work. Nowhere else on the cultural front could one find such individualism, such lingering *oblomovism*, not infrequently developing into communist conceit.[131]

Bukharin's crushing retort did leave some questions about the authority for his speech unanswered. Faced with the choice between giving official endorsement to Bukharin, thus further offending the 'offended', or giving a rebuff, which in view of the ovation Bukharin had received would have been a hard task to undertake, Stetsky compromised. Proclaiming the Congress a success, he praised its lively discussion and predicted that after it 'literature will somehow become different, that it will rise to a new level. A future historian of literature will certainly divide the history of literature into periods before and after the first Congress of Writers'. (*applause*).[132] Only recently, RAPP had had its 'general line', 'General-Secretary' and 'general platform which it attempted to impose on all writers'. He recalled the 'bitter arguments which raged around every comma, every punctuation mark of this platform'. The Party had put a stop to this and paved the way for a Writers' Union. Their inaugural Congress, 'marked by freedom of creative discussion', was not 'passing any resolutions on creative questions which would be binding on all writers'. He admitted the 'open secret' that the *Orgkomitet* had consulted the Party over the appointment of the three main speakers. This did not mean, however, that every speech was intended as an 'official programme of which every comma and every word was immutable and binding'.[133] Nor was he aware of any party or government decision to hand out official evaluations of individual writers, nor 'to give prose writers or poets some kind of "decoration", of distinction, approval of blame'. Thus, turning to Bukharin, he stated:

> I know of no decision of our Party or government to 'canonise' Mayakovsky. Mayakovsky is a mighty poet, a poet of the revolution, but we have not made any decision that Soviet poetry must take Mayakovsky as its sole model. And if Comrade Bukharin in his report did give accounts of individual poets and poetic work, then this once again was for the purpose of raising literary questions for discussion. This does not mean at all that every poet at the Congress has received from the Party or the Government a mark of distinction which he may take with him on leaving this Congress. Such a thing would denote the worst kind of bureaucracy, and you know that there is no more irreconcilable opponent of bureaucracy than our Party.[134]

Not many months would pass before just such a 'canonisation' took place.

Stetsky's appraisal of Bukharin's speech was conciliatory but 'opponents' continued to protest behind the scenes. Bukharin succumbed to these pressures and unwisely offered his apologies[135] in the form of a 'Letter to the Congress Praesidium' which Fadeyev read out at the final session. It said:

> In view of the fact that the sharpness of my 'Concluding Word' has given rise to a number of misunderstandings and further questions, I consider it necessary to declare that I was indeed over-harsh in my comments and attacks addressed to some of our poet comrades, attacks which were intended to ward off various incorrect accusations addressed to me. I can, of course, in no way insist upon the correctness of these sharp polemical remarks.

If anyone had taken them to be some form of obligatory directive concerning those he criticised, they were mistaken. Literary assessments could not be put on a par with political assessments for 'in the

sphere of poetry there must be a wide-ranging, free competition'
Obligatory directives would lead to 'bureaucratisation'. Finally, Buk
harin stated 'I have in no way attempted, nor do I now attempt to
undermine the standing or discredit my opponents as poets and I in
no way wish to put this Congress under that kind of pressure'.[13]
Though carefully worded and following the Stetsky line, this was
clearly a climb-down and depressed his supporters at the Congress. I
was treated as a 'triumph' by the Surkov camp.

The other business of the Congress was to hear speeches from the
former fellow-travellers. Several abandoned their earlier indepen
dence. Vsevolod Ivanov described the path of non-party writer
towards *partiinost'* in literature. Since the early twenties, his col
leagues in the Serapions had shrugged off the influence of 'Russian
bourgeois literature' and started to learn from contemporary Soviet
life. They eventually rejected the old slogan 'against all tendentious
ness in literature'. He declared that they would now accept the
Zhdanov formula 'for a Bolshevik tendentiousness in literature'.[13]
The speech by Leonid Leonov also showed how far language had
changed since the early 1920s. He addressed the Congress in contem
porary cliché: 'we are happy to live in such a heroic period of world
history, this age may be the most capacious historical period of
all roads in human history, our age is the morrow of a new era'. He
declared that literature was to become 'one of the most mighty
instruments in the moulding of the new man'.[138] Tikhonov also
reminded writers of their social responsibilities. The Congress
showed 'how many we are, what an army' before which stands a 'big
social task'.[139] Some responded by calling their speeches 'reports to
readers'. Others more modestly apologised for their incurable indi
vidualism. Their highly personal utterances are eloquent testimony to
the inner accommodation of talented writers to Soviet conditions of
the 1930s.

Olesha noted that six years had passed since his short novel *Envy*
had portrayed the author's vision of the world.[140] He had undergone
a crisis of self-confidence when critics condemned his autobiographi
cal portrait. 'I wished to believe that the comrades who had criticised
me (they were communist critics) were right. And I did believe them
I began to think that what I had taken for treasure was in fact a sign
of poverty.' In the years that followed he attempted a five-year plan
novel but failed. Making 'a last attempt at a new subject',[141] Olesha
told the Congress 'I have given myself the task of writing about young
people'. The book will have 'a moral character writ somewhere

within me like the conviction that communism is not solely an economic but also a moral system and that our young men and women will be the first embodiment this side of communism'.[142] In this undertaking, though, he would also fail.

Babel's witty contribution was in a class of its own: rich in ambiguity, laconic even by the author's own standards, mostly made up of aphorisms. Thus he exclaimed (with Gorky) 'Philistinism is counter-revolution' and offered his famous dictum: 'if we speak of silence then it must be said that I am the great master of this genre'. He observed that the Party and government had deprived Soviet literature of only one right, 'that of writing badly' which was 'a very important right and their taking it away from us in no small matter' (*laughter*).[143] With this, he ended, as unexpectedly as he had begun.

Pasternak evidently observed the proceedings with disappointment. He had hoped for a 'gathering of Russian thinkers' making speeches of 'great philosophical importance'.[144] Only Gorky's had seemed to him in this class. Other matters he regarded as vital for the future of Russian literature had been left undiscussed. Towards the end of the Congress he came, reluctantly, to the microphone, explaining that he did so only lest it were taken amiss if he did not speak. A portion of his address was given to explaining a comic incident that had occurred earlier in the proceedings: 'When I was unaccountably moved to try and take that excavating tool, the name of which I do not even know, from the shoulder of the girl from the metro construction' who had marched through the Hall. A tussle had ensued when she refused to give it up. He tried to explain that 'comrades here on the platform who laughed at me for being an oversensitive intellectual could not have been aware that in some immediate sense I felt she was my sister and I wanted to help her, as though she were someone close to me whom I had known for a long time'.[145] His own contribution was extremely abbreviated: 'Poetry is prose . . . the voice of prose – prose in action, not at second hand. Poetry is the language of organic fact, that is, fact in all its living consequences . . .' He concluded with a curious admonition: 'the Party tells us to remain close to the masses. I myself have never earned the right to use that expression. Do not sacrifice your personality for the sake of a position . . . With all the enormous affection lavished on us by the people and the state, there is all too great a danger of one's turning into a literary office-holder'.[146] Perhaps Pasternak felt this could happen to him. Although a member of its Praesidium, he left before the meeting ended.

It is impossible to read the Congress's stenogram without experiencing a strong sense of the irony of history. As Ehrenburg recalled: '1934 was in general a good period, and we all thought that in 1937, when according to the statutes, the Second Congress of Writers was due to meet, we would be living in paradise'.[147] Precisely the opposite was to befall them. Yet simply because this was to be the final forum before their systematic exclusion and repression, the broader ideas and values expressed to the First Writers' Congress have a historical significance which transcends the particular event. Needless to say, the participants themselves were unaware of this.[148]

After the Congress, attempts were made to place the campaign for quality on a permanent footing. Gorky outlined an ambitious programme for educating writers through newly-established literary journals.[149] Bukharin turned to the *History of Factories* project, of which he was a board member. In a major speech to its editorial collective he called for the preparation of 'high quality books, which will stand the test of time'. Pointing out that the working-class had proved its ability in many other spheres, he now urged it to gain mastery over literature.[150] Under the inspiration of Gorky and Bukharin, the feeling became quite widespread that the Writers' Congress had brought about a fundamental change in cultural policy, ushering in a more liberal phase. The differentiation from the west, which both had sought since the beginning of the year, seemed to be about to be realised. Similar expectations were expressed by participants in a debate on socialist aesthetics promoted by M. I. Lifshits. Several argued that, with the defeat of 'class enemies' in literature, the question 'who whom?' had been resolved, making a policy of relaxation appropriate. The critic Zelinsky suggested it was possible to abolish limits on democracy and to discuss all problems openly and freely. Aseyev and Pil'nyak were reported to have spoken in the same vein.[151]

Kirov's murder, which Khrushchev rightly described as 'mysterious',[152] interrupted these expectations. According to Conquest, 'It is the keystone of the entire edifice of terror and suffering by which Stalin secured his grip on the Soviet people'.[153] Although his role in the assassination has yet to be clarified,[154] there is other evidence for this thesis. On 1 December 1934, he initiated the decree which made the death penalty automatic for 'terrorist' offences. This hurriedly-imposed resolution, made known as a result of Khrushchev's 'secret' speech, stated:

1. Investigative agencies are directed to speed up the cases of those accused of the preparation or execution of acts of terror.
2. Judicial organs are directed not to hold up the execution of death sentences, pending appeals for clemency by criminals of this category, since the President of the Central Executive Committee of the USSR does not consider it possible to countenance such appeals.
3. The organs of the Commissariat of Internal Affairs (NKVD) are directed to carry out the death sentences against criminals of the above-mentioned category immediately after such sentences have been issued.[155]

Further instructions ordered that such defendants were to be unrepresented at their trials, and that the whole process of investigation and sentencing had to be completed within a maximum of ten days. With hindsight, one can see that this is the moment at which the policy of relaxation associated with Kirov, Gorky and Bukharin was ended, though this was not immediately apparent.

At the outset, the Kirov murder was treated as a shocking but isolated occurrence without wider implications for Soviet policy as a whole. The tone of public statements was relatively mild. 'Grief and anger' were the emotions expressed in a statement by Leonov, Boris Lidin, Novikov-Priboi, Pasternak and Ehrenburg. A further group of 26 Moscow writers announced their condolences shortly afterwards. A rather different tone was adopted in Leningrad, where forty-seven writers including Zoshchenko, Kaverin, Zabolotsky, Shvarts, Eikhenbaum and Tynyanov wrote 'We loved Kirov, we were proud of him, we learned from him'.[157] Gorky's tribute referred to Kirov as 'a master of culture' and stated that his killing showed the need for greater 'vigilance'.[158] This was a developing theme. Arrests and executions of 'White Guards' took place at once, as apparently random reprisals. Victims came from Leningrad, Moscow and Kiev where a number of Ukrainian writers and intellectuals were summarily shot.[159] On 17 December *Pravda* for the first time attributed Kirov's assassination to an 'anti-Party group'. Its alleged leaders, Zinoviev and Kamenev, were sentenced to eight and five years' imprisonment respectively. The new explanation was put to Soviet writers by Radek in a speech on 21 December.[160] Bukharin was apparently convinced and referred in *Izvestiya* to the 'furtive rebirth of such people as Trotsky and Zinoviev and their supporters who refused to lay down their arms'.[161]

The murder's repercussions for writers were potentially serious. Kamenev, who had been reconciled to Stalin in 1933 reportedly through Gorky's good offices, had held several literary positions including a directorship of the "Akademiya" publishing house.[162] He had been attached to the board of the Writers' Union, attending some of its inaugural meetings. Several writers and critics were arrested in the last days of 1934, including the former RAPPists Lelevich, Gorbachov and I. Vardin.[163] Further arrests were put in hand by a top secret Party circular to all lower organisations demanding that 'enemies' be rooted out of the Party and from the population at large.[164] Direct connection between the Kirov assassination and the responsibility of writers was made in *Pravda* on 20 January 1935. An article by the notorious provocateur D. Zaslavsky[165] accused Gorky of connivance in the formation of 'counter-revolutionary intelligentsia'. It made a direct comparison between the 'liberal position' of Gorky and ideological 'class enemies' such as Zinoviev and Kamenev who adopted a 'Trotskyite position'. Although Gorky was able to reply, Zaslavsky returned to the attack, to which Gorky's second answer was not published.[166] If Gorky was no longer able to rebut his own critic, then his ability to defend other writers was clearly limited.

During February 1935, the Writers' Union began to adopt overtly political guidelines. They took the form of a document drawn up by the former *Litfrontist* Bespalov. His 'theses' pointed out that while critics might consider themselves part of the vanguard of literature, the actual leadership lay with the Party. Literary criticism was a political instrument. Enhanced vigilance was necessary: although the class enemy in the literary sphere was beaten and dispersed he 'still tries to offer his resistance to the victory of socialism and still sallies forth not infrequently in hidden form'.[167] Elaboration of Bespalov's 'theses' formed the central focus of a Second Plenum of the Writers' Union.[168]

According to this meeting, the intellectual level of Soviet criticism already stood 'immeasurably higher' than that of the capitalist and tsarist eras. Its greatest development had taken place in struggles against anti-Marxist theories and anti-proletarian influences in artistic production.[169] It had revealed:

The bankruptcy of the historico-cultural schools in literary theory (Sakulin, Piksanov and others), and their opposite, the formal method (Zhirmunsky, Shklovsky and others).[170] Defeated, are:

the anti-Marxist conceptions of Pereverzev, the Menshevik counter-revolutionary Trotskyite theory of culture and art and its various manifestations (Voronsky, Lelevich and others). Beaten are: the right-opportunist theory of culture of Bukharin. Overcome are the schematic and vulgarised platforms of *Litfront*, and the anti-Leninist contradistinction of proletarian with socialist cultures, as expressed in the opinions of Averbakh.[171]

The approved definition was explicitly political: 'The criteria for giving an account of literary facts or processes of Soviet art are given in the formula of Comrade STALIN with a definition of genius'.[172] It now demanded 'correct depiction of Soviet reality'. Soviet literature must include complete understanding of party-mindedness (*partiinost'*). 'The historically-concrete depiction of reality' must contribute to 'the task of the ideological re-moulding and education of workers in the spirit of socialism'.[173] The dogma now being propounded encountered only one dissentient voice.

In a bold and idiosyncratic speech, Shaginyan discussed 'What writers expect from critics'. In her experience, critics used book reviews as vehicles for preconceived notions. She traced the 'literary fate' of Ehrenburg's *Second Day*.[174] Commentary had begun as a duel between *Izvestiya* (Radek) and *Literaturnaya gazeta* (Goffenshefer). Neither of them gave any attention to the substance of the book but used it as a peg for their own opinions.[175] Another commentary was written in accordance with a 'typically RAPPist schematism' and tried to situate this work within Ehrenburg's overall political development. This was 'the height of formal analysis without concrete examples'. *Literaturnyi kritik* had taken a further view that the book was worthless, being written 'without *partiinost''*.[176] Shaginyan described this as an inadequate criterion with which to consign a book to oblivion. Her lone protest, which also extended to the 'literary fates' of works by Zoshchenko and Jasienski,[177] caused some embarrassment to the organisers of the Plenum. Summing up, they called for unanimity amongst critics so that 'particularist' platforms would disappear. Divergences from Party literary policies would then become rare and if any should occur, they would be dealt with by 'a responsible body of critics as a whole'.[178]

Control of literature was further enhanced by a series of bans and injunctions. A clutch of orders was sent to provincial libraries to withdraw books already in circulation. In the spring of 1935 libraries were instructed to remove the works of Trotsky, Zinoviev and

Kamenev.[179] Soon the blacklist was extended to include works by the economist Preobrazhensky and the critic Gorbachov. A further circular of 21 June ordered a 'general purge and removal of books' to be carried out forthwith.[180] Soviet librarians must have realised that question-marks now hung over works by Rykov, Bukharin and many others and that their interdiction was only a matter of time.

Central direction of cultural policy was increased further by a major overhaul of the Central Committee apparatus.[181] The *Kul't-prop* Secretariat was reconstituted in a series of departments, including a new one for 'Cultural-Enlightening Work'. Under its auspices were placed libraries and trade union clubs, cultural enlightenment in the countryside, workers in the cinema, radio and theatre, and the incipient or already established cultural unions. This department was led by Shcherbakov, who also headed the Writers' Union.[182]

A trend towards repressive policies was clearly evident. State legislation pointed the way. From 7 April, the death penalty could be imposed on twelve-year olds. It was accompanied by changes of leading personnel. Yezhov was made head of the Party Control Commission and Vyshinsky became Prosecutor-General. Stalin's personal Secretariat headed by Poskrebyshev and Shkiryatov was already in operation. Thus, by midsummer a nucleus of officials had been elevated to the posts from which they would later launch and administer the terror.[183]

Quite unexpectedly, there came a pause. For a few months, the slide into terror was delayed and a high-level commission appointed to prepare a new constitution for the USSR. Its centrepiece, the section concerning Soviet citizens' rights and obligations, was to be drafted by Bukharin.[184] By a terrible irony, the Soviet government was publically concerning itself with the need for legality on the eve of its greatest lawlessness. One impulse for the new policy was international. A period of *rapprochement* with western governments had been signalled by entry into the League of Nations.[185] Comintern policy had turned towards the 'Popular Fronts' and was to be sanctified by the Seventh Congress of Comintern in Moscow.[186] Many sections of Soviet society, including leading writers, were expected to foster this new image in international relations. The role given to writers was their participation in the International Congress of 'Writers for the Defence of Culture', to be held in Paris in June 1935. Gorky himself received a passport to travel – the last time he was to do so[187] – but did not use it. This meant that the Soviet delegation would be headed by officials of the Writers' Union. So Congress organisers approached the Kremlin, through diplomatic channels, to add some internationally-known writers to the delegation.[188] Though being in the lowest psychological condition, Pasternak dared not refuse the order given to him by Stalin's Secretary, Poskrebyshev, to attend.[189]

As Ehrenburg remarks 'it would have been absurd to do nothing but denounce Fascism for five days on end'.[190] So Soviet writers entertained their Paris audience with optimistic accounts of Soviet life. Kol'tsov spoke of the importance of satirical writing: 'our readers are fed up with the type of administrator who, distorting socialist principles, forces everyone into the same mould, making them eat, wear, speak and think the same things'. Babel expatiated upon the ordinary Russian's love of literature. Tikhonov gave an animated account of post-revolutionary poetry: 'Take Mayakovsky. There you have a master of the Soviet ode, of satire, of farce and comedy in verse'.[191] But Pasternak was in no mood for jollification. His reluctant statement on poetic craft was utterly at odds with the rest of the proceedings:

> Poetry will always remain that celebrated peak, higher than all the Alps, which lies in the grass at our feet, so that one has only to bend down and see it and pick it up from the ground; it will always be too simple to be discussed at meetings; it will always remain an organic function of the happiness of men endowed with the blessed gift of rational speech – thus, the more happiness on earth, the easier to be an artist.[192]

Marina Tsvetayeva recited to him in the corridors.[193] Others spent 'half a night in a small café arguing about Socialist Realism'. It ended when the head of the Soviet delegation 'trying not to fall asleep, abruptly asked: "Why bother to argue? It's all in the statutes"'.[194]

False optimism was now obligatory in the Soviet Union. Stalin had issued his famous dictum 'Comrades, life is better, life is happier', and so it had to be. A permanent holiday atmosphere pervaded public life.[195] Promethean achievements were recorded in communism's conquest of nature.[196] Even manual labour began to be glorified in surprising new ways. On 30 August 1935 Alexei Stakhanov mined a record 102 tons of coal in a single shift. Such astronomical output, made possible only through special equipment and supporting workers provided for him by the management, was now taken to be the benchmark for ordinary workers. Reports of Stakhanov's achievement in *Pravda* on 6 and 11 September were followed by the launching of the first Stakhanovite campaign.[197] *Literaturnaya gazeta* published an editorial on 'Literature and the Stakhanovite movement'. It explained that writers now had 'amazing new material' in the persons of Stakhanovites to bring before the public,[198] and demanded that they celebrate these new heroes of socialist labour, such as Busygin, the Stakhanov of the motor industry.[199] A Congress of Stakhanovites was addressed by Stalin on 17 November. He presented Stakhanovism as a 'profoundly revolutionary movement' from below, a spontaneous reaction against the conservatism and traditional attitudes of middle management.[200] There followed spectacular receptions in the Kremlin. As their autobiographies indicate, Stakhanovites typically approached the *vozhd'* with trepidation. On first seeing Stalin from afar they are dazzled by a 'blinding light'. But he soon reassures them, putting them at ease with his masterly simplicity.[201] None of them fails to mention that meeting Stalin was the turning-point of their lives. Further intimate connections between Stalin and these 'heroes of the Stalinist epoch' were claimed by innumerable editorials.[202]

In the latter part of 1935, the propagation of Stalin's personality reached unprecedented proportions. Gross falsification of history ensued, particularly after articles by Beria in *Pravda* had claimed that Stalin was foremost amongst the Russian revolutionaries.[203] As L. M. Zak has shown, Stalin arranged his presentation in art and cinema as the closest friend and adviser of Lenin.[204] In science, the label *coryphaeus* was gaining currency as the only description of Stalin's contribution. Stalin's views on *belles-lettres* were raised to the status of infallibility. Having previously restricted himself to negative appraisal of 'class hostile elements' in Soviet literature, Stalin now began to institute a positive canon. An editorial in *Pravda* on 5 December quoted Stalin's judgement: 'Mayakovsky was and remains the best and most talented poet of our era. Indifference to his memory and to his works is a crime'. The provenance of this statement was not explained and remained a mystery for many years. *Prima facie*, it seemed hard to relate the innovative works of Mayakovsky to any notion of socialist realism. However, the origin of the statement was later shown by Moscow *samizdat* to lie in a letter from Lili Brik to Stalin dated 24 November 1935.[205]

She began by explaining that she had received Mayakovsky's archive after his death and had prepared much of his material for publication. Public interest in Mayakovsky was growing year by year which showed 'his poetry is not only not out of date, but absolutely contemporary' and yet his works were virtually unobtainable. She complained that 'our institutions do not understand Mayakovsky's enormous significance – his agitational role, his contemporary revolutionary significance. They underestimate the exceptional interest he has for Komsomol and Soviet youth'. She appealed for Stalin's assistance in overcoming 'bureaucratic indifference and opposition' to realisation of 'the colossal revolutionary heritage of Mayakovsky'.[206] Stalin's response was brief and to the point:

> Com. Yezhov. Request you draw attention to Brik's letter. Mayakovsky was and remains the best, most talented poet of our Soviet epoch. Indifference to his memory is a crime. Unfortunately, I think Brik is right.[207]

Stalin ordered this to be mentioned to the editor of *Pravda* and declared himself ready to offer any personal assistance necessary to remedy the 'omission' over Mayakovsky's memory. The oversight was soon made good. Besides printing his *dictum*, instantly elevating Mayakovsky to the status of an obligatory and unquestioned classic of Soviet literature, *Pravda* published the section of 'At the Top of My Voice' which mentions Stalin.[208] Thereafter, Mayakovsky began to be introduced compulsorily 'like potatoes under Catherine the Great'.[209]

A side-effect of Mayakovsky's sudden canonisation was a further step in the humiliation of Bukharin. In the course of the poetry debate at the Congress, Bukharin had stated that he rated Mayakovsky 'very highly', but added the suggestion that even he could be, and perhaps was being, overtaken by the ever higher demands of the modern readership.[210] It will be recalled that Stetsky disclaimed all knowledge of any 'decision of party or government to canonise Mayakovsky' or to 'take our poetry *po-Mayakovskomu.*' He had denied that the Party awarded prizes to writers, any special class of 'decoration', 'orders' or other marks of distinction. Readers could judge for themselves, he said, without such indications of merit.[211] Those poets whom Bukharin had offended at the Congress quickly seized upon Stalin's statement. In several articles at the end of 1935, Surkov contrasted the Bukharin and the Stalin 'accounts' of Mayakovsky.[212] Selivanovsky joined the chorus of contrived indignation.[213] In reply, Bukharin wrote to Stalin, protesting his innocence and calling for a cessation of the campaign. He pointed out he had called Mayakovsky a 'Soviet classic' at the Congress and indeed had done so against the advice of the Central Committee Secretariat which wanted to excise this phrase from his speech 'so that it should not be thought that the Party wanted to compare poetry only with Mayakovsky'.[214] Bukharin's protest was to no avail. Until the 1960s, Soviet journals reiterated Surkov's line.[215]

A logical inference from Stalin's praise of Mayakovsky would have been that the Party wished to promote innovation and experiment in the arts. But critics burst into praise of the poet for quite different qualities, such as his 'simplicity and popular appeal'. As Ehrenburg comments, 'in one of his early Futurist poems Mayakovsky urged the hairdresser: "Please, trim my ears". He naturally did not know one could have more than one's ears trimmed'.[216] Rather than stimulate discussion of artistic issues, the consequence of Stalin's statement was to narrow literary debate. Instead of Futurist priorities, there began to be imposed a narrowly-defined, dogmatic and often backward-looking orthodoxy of socialist realism.

The signal was given on 17 January 1936. The respective chairmen of the Central Executive Committee (Kalinin) and the Council of Ministers (Molotov), declared that *Narkompros*, the governmental body which had administered theatres and the arts since the Revolution, could no longer provide the 'leadership of the arts' which the population 'demanded'. They added that in a period when 'technical means of communication' such as cinema and radio had greatly increased, more 'concrete and specialised' leadership was necessary.[217] Despite these alibis, the consequence of the decision was clearly to sever one of the remaining cultural linkages with the NEP period.[218] The same decree created a single Committee for Artistic Affairs, to administer theatres, cinemas, concert halls, exhibition centres, and other places of cultural activity. Its head was P. M. Kerzhentsev, the former *Proletkul'tist* and RAPP opponent, who had since presided over the State Committee for Radio.[219] It rapidly developed into the real instrument of Party political control over all the arts.

On the day the new Committee was announced, top Party leaders attended the Bolshoi Theatre for a performance of I. Dzierzynski's opera *The Quiet Don*. During the interval, Stalin and Molotov met the composer, librettist and musical director. According to a contemporary journal, Stalin and Molotov 'gave a positive account of the theatre's work in the sphere of creating Soviet opera and commended the significant ideological-political effect of staging *The Quiet Don*'. At the same time as noting such achievements, they revealed 'shortcomings' in the presentation of the spectacle which would have to be overcome before 'further positive successes' could be attained by Soviet opera.[220] An unpublished source adds that Stalin 'defined the "general line" for the development of Soviet music' and established the task of creating 'Soviet musical classics'.[221] Meetings of composers and of the Union of Art Workers (RABIS) were told that Comrade Stalin 'is personally interested' in questions of art.[222] From these hints behind the scenes, there emerged a public campaign of unprecedented ferocity.

The first target was Shostakovich's opera *Lady Macbeth of Mtsenk*. An unsigned editorial in *Pravda* on 28 January described it as 'Muddle instead of music'. The author – whom Shostakovich considered to have been Stalin himself[223] – claimed that the Soviet public 'demands better music' from its composers. Shostakovich's work was taken as an example of 'left art in general' whose 'deformation' was deplored, though not defined. Stalin attended the Bolshoi a few days later, for a ballet, *Bright Stream*, with music by Shostakovich. A second editorial, 'False Ballet', repeated and added to the earlier accusations.[224] After two attacks in ten days, it was widely assumed that Shostakovich would be arrested.[225] This did not happen, but the campaign was extended.

Unlike the 'anti-right' campaign of 1929, which singled out Pil'nyak and Zamyatin, that of 1936 went beyond individuals. Rather, new forms of pressure were mounted against entire categories of enemy. Numerous representatives of the 'social community' demanded the destruction of 'inimical' tendencies. An orchestrated campaign began to be directed against 'formalism' in the arts. Architecture was assailed on 20 February. Hurriedly assembled meetings denounced not only constructivists and utopian architects such as Mel'nikov, but also 'Sympathisers with Formalism'.[226] Painters were called to account after a *Pravda* editorial of 1 March. A general meeting of the Moscow Union of Artists accused various members of 'German formalist aesthetics'. In a courageous and dignified defence, D. P. Shterenberg demanded a more healthy atmosphere in the Union, and an end to 'surprise attacks' and the dragging up of alleged 'sins' from the distant past.[227]

Much of the cultural community took part in the campaign with great reluctance. A month after it began, Kerzhentsev castigated workers in cinema, architecture, radio, music, theatre and arts for their efforts thus far. He told them that Moscow meetings had been 'feeble'; in Leningrad merely the musicians had been called to account; there had been no meetings of any kind in the Ukraine, or other Republics. They had not realised that the *Pravda* articles referred to 'all the arts without exception'.[228]

The literary intelligentsia had been particularly recalcitrant. Even at this late stage, a few were fighting a rearguard action against the institution of Stalinism in literature. Their acts of resistance or non-cooperation were necessarily restricted: institutional channels for expression of dissent hardly existed. Even so, several poets made individual protests at the Third Plenum of the Writers' Union, held in Minsk during February 1936. Brave attempts were made by the former 'LEFists', Aseyev, Kirsanov, Shklovsky and Brik, to stem the tide.[229] An official of the Union reported that these writers 'attempted to interpret Stalin's account of Mayakovsky in their own way', as an 'absolution of the many previous formalist and political bias of their group'.[230] He admitted there were considerable difficulties in the way of 'consolidating poets' on the basis of self-criticism. Confirmation came from Moscow writers addressed by Stavsky. He called for a concerted effort to root out formalist 'deformations and contortions' in poetry and prose, citing works of Kirsanov and Pil'nyak as urgently in need of investigation. But self-criticism was not forthcoming. Instead, the speech was met by a 'bombastic and confused' statement from Kirsanov himself, and other writers responded with disdain.[231]

Pasternak's response was in a class of its own. He recalled:

Last winter there was a discussion in the papers about formalism. I don't know whether word about it reached you or not. It began with the article about Shostakovich and was extended to include the theatre and literature (with the same sort of insolent, sickeningly unoriginal, echolike, arbitrary attacks, on Meyerhold, Marietta Shaginyan, Bulgakov and others). It spread to the artists, and to the best of them, such as Vladimir Lebedev.

When the Writers' Union held open discussions of these articles, I was foolish enough to attend one of them. On hearing what utter nonentities said about the Pil'nyaks, the Fedins, the Leonovs (referring to them almost exclusively in the plural), I could not restrain myself and made an attempt to attack precisely this aspect of our press, calling everything by its real name. I was met first of all by sincere astonishment on the part of bigwigs and officials, who could not understand why I should come to the defence of my colleagues when no one had harmed me or even thought of doing

so. I was given such a rebuff that, later (again on official instigation), friends from the union – good friends, some even close
ones – were sent to inquire after my health. No one could believe
that I was feeling well and was able not only to sleep but even to
work. That, too, they took for rebelliousness.[232]

He wrote to Georgian friends, on 8 April 1936, of the 'worthless
critical semolina porridge which people have been gulping down so
touchingly over the past month'. In the recent campaign, he noted,
'truth was ladled out in a dismally weak solution'.[233]

In March, *Pravda* complained it had taken Soviet writers six weeks
to arrange a meeting 'to discuss formalist distortions in the sphere of
art'. Their response to a problem 'of wide social importance' had
been paltry and inadequate.[234] But Meyerhold made an impassioned
speech, against the 'central organ of the Party'. Travelling to Leningrad, he told his audience that it would be a terrible mistake to cut
off a promising artist, such as Shostakovich, 'in the spring of his
career'. He could not believe that was the intention of the editorials.
A more attentive reading, 'not on the lines, but between them',
would show their purpose was to raise art to a higher level, putting
greater demands on it, through serious criticism. The anti-formalists
had been 'too much concerned with generalities'. Precise reference
was needed to whichever artistic works contained 'formalist' and
other tendencies. He also complained that 'imitators' were 'really
destroying' him. He had chosen to speak in Leningrad, the home of
the majority of his pupils, rather than in Moscow where he had 'fewer
pupils but more imitators'. He referred to the Muscovites Radlov (a
pupil of his prior to 1917), and an actor under him, Okhlopkov, who
had become director of the Realistic Theatre, both of whom had
taken to incorporating 'meyerholdisms' into their productions. They
were doing him great damage. A campaign against 'imitators' rather
than 'formalists' was needed.[235]

While Meyerhold remained unrepentant, a Moscow meeting
heard Radlov make self-criticism. The Director of the Maly Theatre,
Amaglobely, similarly complied.[236] A third director, Tairov, admitted to serious 'errors' such as an 'idealistic tendency' in his choice of
plays with the result that only a handful of Soviet plays had been put
on at his theatre.[237] *Pravda* held Tairov's account to be a model of
self-examination which others were encouraged to adopt. But it
found Meyerhold's second speech, this time in Moscow, a great
'disappointment'.[238] Indeed, Meyerhold had considered the 'self-

criticism' of other directors insincere and implausible. Tairov, for instance, had admitted to producing only nine Soviet plays in the seven seasons since 1929 and promised to restore a balance in favour of Soviet material. But he failed to mention that the imbalance was brought about by the numerous interventions of the censorship.

Turning to his own work, Meyerhold offered a radically enlarged definition of self-criticism:

> Theatrical society expects me to move on in this speech from criticism of other theatres, to unsparing criticism of myself. My whole life in art, all my productions, have been nothing if not a permanent effort at self-criticism. I have never approached a new production without shaking myself free of the one before. The biography of every true artist is of a man tormented, ceaselessly, by dissatisfaction with himself.[239]

Meyerhold went on:

> Only a dilettante is entirely self-satisfied and has no inner doubts. A great master is always ruthless with himself and is devoid of complacency or conceit. There will be moments when an artist may seem complacent, self-assured and even arrogant. Vladimir Mayakovsky seemed to be so at times. But his self-assurance was only a means of defence against conservatives and their attacks.
>
> Should a master engage in unsparing criticism of himself at the earliest possible moment? No! Then he may see his mistakes dimly or indistinctly. For some, this happens rapidly; others take a long time to see their mistakes . . . Clearly it is the same with critics. It is difficult for them to take the measure of many artists.[240]

The defence Meyerhold used was ingenious. He supported the general purpose of the campaign but changed its direction. He referred to the tendency, on the appearance of *Pravda*'s articles, to exclaim: the 'golden mean!' Some considered the articles simply to exclude 'leftist experimental' and 'rightist, formalist' elements from repertoire. The reality, he argued, was much more complex. The Committee on Artistic Affairs should consider the problems of experimental art. While it should 'join with us in eliminating formalism, nihilism and harmful leftism', it should take care not to 'throw out the baby with the bath water'. The art of theatre was becoming more complex, and depended on the 'cross-fertilisation of diverse elements'.[241]

Although *Pravda* affected surprise that Meyerhold had chosen to defend the right to experiment and to innovate 'on which no-one has ever encroached', it is evident that the anti-formalist campaign was designed to eliminate both. In early April, *Pravda* hinted at further restrictions to come. Formalism, it stated, was 'not the only sickness of our art'. It was necessary to work out 'fresh directives' which would 'put in concrete terms' the task of 'constructing a socialist style'.[242] Uniformity was descending upon Soviet literature, despite the efforts of a few writers to prevent it. This inevitably led to the deterioration of artistic standards, to a loss of vitality and unwillingness to take risks. The outcome was bound to be conformism and imitation of 'safe' models: Gorky was an obvious example.

Gorky's response to the 'anti-formalist' campaign was silence. Nothing in his record suggested he would approve such an operation. Indeed, during the 'anti-right' campaign of 1929, he had been strongly critical of inquisitorial methods.

Between January 1936 when Stalin initiated the onslaught, and the end of March when officials summed up its 'results' for literature. Gorky remained aloof. His article 'On Formalism' appeared on 9 April. In contrast to the editorial line of *Pravda*, he argued that such bouts of public criticism were valuable only in so far as they contributed to raising the 'general level' of literary discussion. But 'reading the stenograms of the March discussions in Moscow' showed how little the leadership of literature was informed about the 'history of Soviet literary "currents" and modes'. Gorky noted a 'historical-cultural illiteracy' on the part of the new officialdom.[243] This was clearly less approving than the party leadership expected.

Was Gorky still a potential champion of the cultural intelligentsia? As the 'founder of Soviet literature' and first President of the Writers' Union, he was its standard-bearer at home and abroad. But these were honorific functions, quite distinct from day-to-day administration. Gorky's administrative energies were expended on the numerous pedagogic journals that he edited, rather than on running the Writers' Union. The political conclusion seems clear: after the Congress Gorky was necessary to the Party principally as a name. It is difficult entirely to accept the general proposition that 'on much Gorky was ill-informed'.[244]

During 1935, Gorky had still been consulted by the Writers' Union and tried on occasion to redirect or restrain its Secretariat. The correspondence opened in a courteous spirit, which seemed to promise future cooperation. The First Secretary played on Gorky's vanity and on his susceptibility to 'pragmatic measures', and he was complimented, in return, for his 'solid and business-like letters'.[245] In the autumn of 1934, Gorky declared his confidence in Shcherbakov as an 'energetic shepherd and organiser for literature' and praised his 'attentive leadership'. Following this, Shcherbakov wrote to assure him that the Praesidium was conducting literary affairs 'according to the principles we discussed', at an earlier meeting in the Crimea. But when it came to influencing the Secretariat's decisions, Gorky's letters seem to have done little to establish or alter policy.

His central objection to the Secretariat, its bureaucratic tendency, was never made effectively. An angry retort from Gorky after an announcement of the Secretariat could not change that policy. Despite the cautious diplomacy which Shcherbakov used, the note of exasperation in Gorky's letters grows. One has only to contrast the opening exchange of compliments with the final correspondence of early 1936 to see the change of tone. Nevertheless, Gorky manages to be ambivalent. For in the same letter that expressed criticism of 'bureaucratic tendencies', Gorky supported the suggestion that 'it is absolutely necessary to review the list of members in the Union of Writers and to free the Union of unnecessary and harmful ballast'.[246] Such formulae were an open invitation to high-handed 'administrative' methods in the Union.

His death on 20 June 1936 was not unexpected to those who knew his poor health. Wild rumours circulated that he had been thwarted in earlier attempts to protest against Stalin's regime and intended to do so when meeting a western writer – André Gide – on 17 June. Hearing this from Yagoda, so the story ran, Stalin ordered him to be killed. It is hard to know how claims of this nature could be disproven. Certainly the chances of Gorky speaking out against the purges seem remote. There was the practical point that Gorky, for all the mass circulation of his books and his access to *Pravda* and *Izvestiya*, could not automatically expect publication. His articles were closely scrutinised beforehand. There was no chance of any protest coming through the normal channels. As to unpublished protest, there were the police to cope with that. It seems rather that, with the inspiration of Stalin, Gorky's death was officially attributed to a 'poisoner'. Stalin used his death to stir up social antagonisms and to justify the launching of a new round of violence against imaginary enemies. As he did so, the debate on doctrine came, finally, to an end.

7 The Terror

Fear and the Muse
Stand watch by turns

Akhmatova, 1936[1]

Stalin's personal responsibility for the Terror (1936–9) was very great. According to one source: 'Yezhov came to Stalin almost daily with a thick file of papers. Stalin would give orders about arrests and tortures, and when an investigation was finished he would sanction the punishment recommended by the NKVD *before the trial*. Thus the court needed only a few minutes to rubber-stamp the sentence approved by Stalin.'[2] Documentary evidence presented to the 22nd Party Congress indicates that Stalin himself signed some 400 of Yezhov's lists for shootings which contained the names of approximately 44,000 persons, mostly Party or government officials, military men and cultural leaders.[3] There is every justification for the present Soviet leader's statement: 'the guilt of Stalin and his immediate entourage before the Party and the people for the mass repressions and lawlessness they committed is enormous and unforgivable. This is a lesson for all generations'.[4]

However, terror on such a scale could not have been the work of one small group alone. After all, the 44,000 names (many more than Stalin could have known in person) amount to an insignificant fraction of those deported or shot. At work was a huge mechanism of destruction, described in Bukharin's last letter as 'a hellish machine which, probably by the use of medieval methods, has acquired gigantic power, fabricates organised slander, acts boldly and confidently'.[5] Medvedev similarly refers to 'a real factory of lies'[6] and rightly distinguishes between preconditions and triggers which set a process in motion – the personality of Stalin seems essential here – and the implementation and inner dynamics of a process once it has begun. Indeed, it seems clear that the Terror rapidly developed dynamics of its own. Arrests and denunciations started to flood in to the 'investigative organs'. Some of those arrested apparently tried to turn this flood to advantage by denouncing everyone they knew, on the assumption that the authorities could not cope. This was sometimes a tragic miscalculation. More usual, though, was the operation of a centrally-directed mechanism of repression, well-described by Beck and Godin:

> NKVD files covered practically the whole population and everyone was classified in categories. Thus statistics were available in every town showing how many former Whites, members of opposition parties, people with foreign connections etc. were living there . . . As the statistics were regularly reported to higher authority, it was possible to arrange a purge at any moment, with full knowledge of the exact numbers of persons in each category.[7]

The Terror was madness but there was method in it. For while it was possible to prepare the Terror in secret, it was hardly possible so to conduct it. As Nadezhda Mandelstam suggests 'There are millions of witnesses and millions of them are still alive'.[8] Thus far only a handful have come forward: where are the confessions of torturers, the apologia of functionaries, the diaries of little people – cogs in the great machine?

Underlying this question is a third level of analysis: responses of the population as a whole. Scholarship on this vital question has hardly begun. According to Roy Medvedev the basis of Stalin's power was the deceived masses.[9] This is a difficult concept, not least for Marxism which maintains that the masses are the ultimate deciding-force in history. Certainly, though, the inclination to trust Stalin and disinclination to accept the evidence of one's own eyes seems to have been very strong. A professor of history in Kiev recalled of his own arrest 'the idea of establishing my innocence or disputing my guilt never entered my head . . . The NKVD knows what it is doing. If anyone is arrested, there must be important political grounds which no one may question'.[10] Stalin himself was widely regarded as a great protector. His projected personality exerted a hypnotic compulsion upon the public at large which – as if the Tsar had returned – dispatched millions of letters to him seeking the redress of wrongs. Usually these petitions to the Kremlin were burned unopened by the sack-load.[11] Members of the literary intelligentsia were not immune to such imaginings. Ehrenburg recalls, perhaps disingenuously, 'When I returned [to Moscow] from Spain at the end of 1937 and saw what was going on in people's homes and minds, I tried to reassure myself: there must be many things that Stalin does not know. If he had read the lists of all his victims, he would have had time for nothing else'.[12] The truth that Stalin did know what was happening and was behind it, was too hard to contemplate. There were powerful psychological reasons for clinging to this last illusion.

One purpose of the recent *glasnost'* in historiography is to strip away the layers of self-delusion, still tenaciously maintained amongst some Soviet citizens. The major impulse of *perestroika* is to find alternatives for the present and future. This cannot be done without declassifying the past, stripping away the layers of obfuscation that replaced thought, and putting an end to the age of myths. To face such terrible events requires an extraordinary courage when, for so many, they are within living memory. The Terror was insidious in requiring that the population at large take part by demanding death sentences, by giving false witness or engaging in other forms of moral complicity. There is a shared sense of shame amongst the older generation and, coming with it, a strong psychological urge to suppress the past. Yet as Nadezhda Mandelstam points out, collective amnesia is a serious disease whose sole remedy is the recovery of memory through 'the ability once more to think in the first person'. When this happens, a person has returned to health. A final cure is reached through a 'retroactive restoration of all the omitted elements in their organic interdependence'.[13] These, though, are hardly matters on which an outsider can apportion blame. The purpose of this chapter will be simply to outline the course of the Terror and indicate some of its impact upon members of the literary intelligentsia. To attempt more would be presumptuous: 'Only those who have lived through history, have experienced it at first-hand, can make judgements about it'.[14]

August 1936 was not the date from which the Party began to use Terror as an instrument of policy. The employment of systematic violence had been necessary to ensure victory in the Civil War, and that memory remained fresh although its force was diminished during the Twenties. A reversion to terror, against the old technical intelligentsia and then the peasantry, marked the first Five-Year Plan. Famine followed through much of the countryside. When, therefore, Khrushchev declared that 'after the criminal murder of S. M. Kirov, mass repression and brutal acts of violation of socialist legality began', [15] he was really referring to the extension of terror to the one stratum on which it had not been turned before: Party members themselves. With characteristic cynicism, Stalinism blamed this extension on its victims.

According to the indictment of the major 'show trial' held in Moscow in August 1936, Zinoviev and Kamenev had formed a 'united terrorist centre' with Trotskyites in 1932 whose purpose was 'to seize power at all costs'. Their chosen and only method was to be political assassination. The prosecution alleged that Trotsky had suggested Stalin be assassinated first, at some major public occasion, such as the Congress of Comintern. An assassin with a Browning pistol had entered the hall 'but could not carry out his criminal intention because he sat too far away from the Praesidium'.[16] The murder of other Politburo members was to follow. However, not a single shot was fired. To say the least, the 'conspirators' were bungling incompetents. This was demonstrated in the 'evidence' of one Pikel', a playwright at the Kamerny Theatre and member of the Writers' Union, who had also headed Zinoviev's Secretariat for many years. Pikel' admitted in court to taking part in preparations for an attempt on Stalin's life in autumn 1933 and again in 1934. Although abroad in Spitzbergen during the 'conspiracy', he explained that this journey was a cover funded by the Writers' Union. On his return, he had resumed terrorist works, attempting to kill 'Kaganovich, Voroshilov and other leaders of the Party and government'.[17] His final 'plea' admitted: 'we represent a most brutal gang of criminals who are nothing more nor less than a detachment of international fascism. The last years of my life have been years of baseness, years of terrible, nightmarish deeds, (*sic*). I must bear my deserved punishment'.[18]

Two features of the trial deserve further attention. The first, and most notorious, concerns the nature of 'evidence' accepted by the court. With the exception of 'acts' carried out abroad – all of which were rapidly disproven – the indictment rested solely upon the confessions of the accused. In the aftermath of the Moscow Trials, there was much speculation concerning the motivations of men who so incriminated themselves and indeed confessed to crimes they could not possibly have committed. Koestler advanced the romantic notion of 'last service to the Party' to explain their conduct. The truth, though, was more simple. As *Pravda* recently put it 'inadmissable methods of investigation' (i.e. torture) were extensively employed.[19] A number of intended defendants died at this stage. In addition came straightforward blackmail: only the cooperation of the accused in court would provide their closest relatives with a chance of survival. It is in this context that the Soviet Supreme Court has now stated that guilt cannot be established by the confession of an accused person unless this is supported by other evidence.[20] Accordingly, after an interval of fifty years, the Moscow Trials have been officially declared null and void.

A second feature of the trials has also been re-examined and found wanting. This concerns the use of language by the Chief Prosecutor. Under Andrei Vyshinsky, abuse replaced analysis. He referred to Zinoviev and Kamenev as 'liars and clowns, insignificant pigmies, puppies snarling at an elephant – that is what this gang represents'.[22] Besides reiterating Stalin's notorious thesis that 'class struggle intensifies' as socialism approaches, he added his own infamous demand: 'Shoot the mad dogs, every one of them'.[23] His recent biographer, Arkady Vaksberg, is deeply concerned to expunge Vyshinsky's legacy from Soviet jurisprudence. But he notes that for many years 'he was very popular in the country. His name inspired a reverential fear. He was able to inspire terror through his self-esteem, his air of importance, his erudition'. As Vaksberg explains: 'This mass psychosis, mass delusion, submission to the fascination of accusatory abuse, is a very important lesson to us not to fall again under the spell of fine-sounding and frightening words'.[24]

The execution of Lenin's close comrades broke a taboo, as other potential victims were not slow to realise. Vyshinsky had stated at the trial that leaders of the former 'right' were now under investigation. After an exchange with Stalin, Tomsky committed suicide on the spot. Rykov tried to do the same but was restrained by relatives, a fact they much regretted later on. Bukharin, who had been on holiday, returned in haste to plead his innocence. But Stalin had gone to Sochi 'for a rest' and ignored his many protestations.[25] Pikel''s involvement made the prospects for writers almost as ominous.

Predicting the guilty verdict, the Writers' Union sent numerous collective letters supporting the prosecution.[26] Their views were also expressed in doggerel by Demyan Bedny. His plea to the judge 'No Mercy!' declared:

Here are the ones who murdered Kirov! . . .
They were going for Stalin!
But they failed to get their bandit mugs into him!
    WE HAVE GUARDED STALIN
    WE CANNOT BUT GUARD HIM!
    WE GUARD HIM AS OUR HEAD,
        WE GUARD HIM AS OUR OWN HEART! . .
Where is Trotsky? Without him your poisoned, filthy,
Your foredoomed group

Is lacking, empty –
But Proletarian justice will pursue
The hated Judas everywhere.[27]

Immediately after the trial, the Writers' Union held an emergency meeting at which they tried to establish collective innocence. As a first step, greetings and congratulations were sent to Yagoda of the NKVD and Voroshilov. The question of a communiqué to Stalin was raised. Voices from the hall demanded an immediate telegram.[28] Under the banner headline 'The Decision of the Proletarian Court is our Decision' the press reported their resolution:

> The Praesidium of the Union of Soviet Writers warmly greets the decision of the proletarian court to execute the Trotskyite-Zinovievite agents of fascism, terrorists and diversionists, who killed Kirov and were preparing to kill the leaders of our party and our great Stalin.
>
> The court fulfilled the will of millions of Soviet citizens and millions of friends of the USSR abroad. Greetings to the revolutionary vigilance of the NKVD and the steadfastness of the proletarian court.
>
> Greetings to Stalin! In Stalin is expressed the genius, the strength, the monolithic *ideinost'* of our Party, the will of the whole country, the Socialist programme. Death to all those who threaten his life.[29]

This was signed by Leonov, Pogodin, G. Lakhuti and Stavsky.

Stavsky's 'political conclusions' were presented to a series of writers' meetings. His constant theme was the need for renewed vigilance in the face of threats from Trotskyite 'terrorist centres'. The treachery of 'Gestapo-agent Pikel'' showed the urgency of rooting-out double-dealers from writers' organisations. His first candidates for exclusion were Galina Serebryakova, author of a biographical novel, *Marx's Youth*, and the playwright Tarasov-Rodionov, author of an uncompleted trilogy on 1917. Stavsky asked rhetorically: 'who can guarantee that there are no more sworn enemies of the working-class in our midst'[30] As Roy Medvedev observes, no-one could guarantee it.[31] The net was widened by M. M. Rozental' in a speech 'For Militant Party Organisation' of the Writers' Union. He warned that it was naive to imagine that class enemies would not try to infiltrate the Writers' Union. Soviet literature had a long history of struggle with 'alien groups', Trotskyite and other anti-communist tendencies. He named as potential enemies the former RAPP critics: Selivanovsky, Lelevich, Semyon Rodov, Vardin and Gorbachov, and the former *Pereval'tsy* Ivan Katayev, Boris Guber and N. Zarudin. Extending the investigation, he pointed out that the traitor Pikel' had been published in *Teatri dramaturgiya* (by Afinogenov) and *Novyi mir* (by Gronsky).[32]

The point was elaborated by *Oktyabr'*, where an editorial 'The Vermin Squashed!', declared that 'enemies of the Party and people infiltrated editorial boards of journals, publishing houses, the Writers' Union, wherever they could, carrying out their infamous, vile, base deeds'. The recent court decision 'taught us to be vigilant every day, every hour, of our Party, of our leader of genius – Stalin'. It rejoiced that 'By joining their voices in the national chorus of wrath against the Trotskyite-Zinovievite gang, Soviet writers have unanimously condemned Trotskyite agents on the literary front and expelled them from their ranks'.[33]

However, hysterical demands for revolutionary vigilance subsided in the early autumn. Intermittent assaults were still mounted upon easy targets. For instance, Pil'nyak was arraigned by a familiar panel of accusers: Stavsky, Usievich and the playwright Vishnevsky.[34] But no connection was suggested between his current work and the Party 'right'. Indeed, judicial investigation of the 'right' was dropped on 10 September 'for lack of evidence'. This was probably in deference to the next act of Stalinist duplicity: the new Constitution. Introducing this innovation to the world's press, Stalin foresaw 'very lively election campaigns' with keenly-fought contests between multiple candidates.[35] Bukharin, too, a major author of the document, appeared to believe its introduction would bring legality to the Soviet system.[36] The text gave the intelligentsia more formal status and security than at any time since the Revolution. In an inaugurating speech, Stalin referred to a great transformation of the 'old hidebound intelligentsia, which tried to place itself above classes but which actually, for the most part, served landlords and capitalists'. It had become 'Our Soviet intelligentsia, an entirely new intelligentsia, which by its very roots is bound up with the working class and peasantry'. He added that the intelligentsia 'was never a class and never can be a class – it was and remains a stratum', recruiting members from all sections of society. But whereas 'formerly it had to serve the wealthy classes, for it had no alternative, today it must serve the people'. To facilitate that 'we need an atmosphere of certainty, we need stability'.[37] His statement seemed to secure the role of the intelligentsia by conferring upon it the duty of serving socialism, the country and the nation, but also granting it rights and social respectability.

The 'Stalin Constitution' was greeted with great hyperbole by writers' representatives. Stavsky led the way by calling it 'a codification of the conquests of our great motherland, its joy, its happiness, the basis for all future struggle'.[38] Frenzied enthusiasm concluded the speech by the Ukrainian writer Mikitenko to the Congress of Soviets at which the document was formally adopted:

> Long live the Stalin Constitution! Long live our leader the great Stalin! Glory to Stalin! (*All delegates stand, thunderous applause, cried of 'Hurrah', 'Hurrah for Comrade Stalin!' 'Hurrah for our Leader the great Stalin'! 'Greetings to the Great Comrade Stalin!'*)[39]

Much was made of contrasts with the west, still in deep recession, and between Nazi tyranny and the liberty of life under the new Stalin Constitution. But how many Soviet citizens can have believed on the basis of personal experience that domestic arbitrariness would be tamed?

An eye-witness to the opposite is Ol'ga Freidenberg, best known as a cousin and correspondent of Pasternak, who had spent ten years preparing a study of *Poetics of Plot and Genre*. Under scurrilous attacks designed to terminate her career, she boldly appealed to Stalin. She recalls that:

> Like hundreds of thousands of others, I still sincerely believed in acts of sabotage, the tricks of local scoundrels, and the deliberate distortion of Party instructions. It was said that Stalin wished to do right and that he read all letters addressed to him. I resolved to act in my usual way, by personally appealing to the highest authority, without intermediaries, half measures, and compromises. Disarmed as I was, one weapon was left to me: my pen, my honesty, and my passionate conviction.
>
> The letter was my secret. It was a political secret, which I had no right to divulge.
>
> I wrote it at the beginning of October. Immediately I felt more calm. The time of waiting set in. But the days dragged on, no reply was forthcoming, and the consequences of the defamation I had

been subjected to made themselves felt. People avoided me so as not to have to speak to me. My friends ceased calling me on the phone.

No one who has not lived in the Stalin era can appreciate the horror of our uncertain position. A person's life was poisoned secretly, invisibly, as witches and sorcerers were hounded in the Dark Ages. Something mysterious was accumulating under the earth and coming to the boil. A person felt at the mercy of an inescapable force aimed at him and certain to crush him.

I went on giving lectures and attending meetings at which students despised me and colleagues isolated me in a ring of empty chairs. No chairman would give me the floor, always finding an excuse. In those days I learned to know what cowardice is, what the complexion of baseness is, what mediocrity, servility, and dishonour look like.[40]

The atmosphere of uncertainty continued with the arrests of further leading public figures, including Pyatakov and Radek. This strongly suggested that a new 'show trial' was under preparation. Stalin and Zhdanov sent a top-secret telegram to Kaganovich, Molotov and 'other members of the Political Bureau'. It insisted on the immediate appointment of Yezhov, hitherto almost unknown, to head the NKVD. The telegram maintained that 'Yagoda has proved himself to be incapable of unmasking the Trotskyite-Zinovievite bloc. The OGPU is four years behind in this matter. This is noted by all Party workers and by the majority of the representatives of the NKVD'.[41] Although the reference to 'four years' is obscure, it may refer to the autumn 1932 meeting of the Politburo which discussed the 'Ryutin platform'. Stalin proposed the death penalty for authors of this extensive *ad hominem* critique of his leadership, but was defeated on a majority vote. Alternatively, it may simply refer to the trial's indictment of 'Trotskyite' conspiracy from 1932. In any case, Yagoda's removal for 'incapability' was sure to have severe repercussions for both politics and literature. He had close personal relations with leading writers and critics. With the loss of his protection their future looked uncertain. His successor moved swiftly to install a new team of interrogators and torturers. Prisoners soon started confessing, including Radek, who may even have assisted his captors in devising the next trial 'scenario'.[42]

According to the new indictment, unveiled on 23 January 1937, the 'Trotskyite-Zinovievite bloc' exposed the previous August had 'a so-called reserve, parallel centre, formed on the direct instructions of L. D. Trotsky'. It consisted of well-known *ex*-Trotskyites, Pyatakov, Radek, Sokol'nikov and Serebryansky. Beside routine charges of terrorism and wrecking, the prosecution alleged an attempt to kill Molotov (making up for his omission from the last trial) and a scheme to grant territorial concessions to the Axis powers. Pyatakov admitted an offer to hand over the Ukraine to Germany and the Amur region to Japan, thus beginning the dismemberment of the USSR. He attributed this plan to Trotsky, whom he claimed to have met in Oslo – this was later proved impossible – but defended it on these grounds: 'If we missed the opportunity', the danger would arise of stabilisation of the Stalinist state for decades 'supported by certain economic achievements and particularly by the new young cadres who had grown up and been brought up to take this state for granted, to regard it as a socialist, Soviet state – they did not think of any other states and could not conceive of any other'.[43] Apart from this quite sensible analysis, called in court 'Trotsky's philosophy', the indictment was rather thin. Indeed, the rambling 'evidence' of a certain 'Arnold', a master of alibis and holder of numerous passports who claimed to believe he was being tried for Freemasonry,[44] reduced proceedings to a farcical level.

Although the Writers' Union was not directly implicated this time, six leading writers – Fadeyev, A. Tolstoy, Pavlenko, Tikhonov, Jasienski and Nikulin – attended the opening session. They publicly demanded death penalties while the court was in session.[45] Reviewing the trial on its third day, the Writers' Union accepted the prosecution's case in full. Amongst those names appended to the Resolution 'If the Enemy does not surrender – he must be annihilated' were Afinogenov, V. Ivanov, Gladkov and Pil'nyak.[46] A series of denunciations appeared in *Literaturnaya gazeta*,[47] including Fedin's 'Agents of International Counter-Revolution'; Olesha's 'Fascists before the National Court'; Leonov's 'Case of Reptiles'; and Babel's 'Lies, Treachery, *Smerdyakovshchina*'.[48] Immediately after the trial, all the major defendants, except one, were shot. Perhaps as a reward for cooperation, Radek was sentenced to ten years in a labour camp, where he was murdered by a fellow prisoner.[49] A different fate befell the writer Galina Serebryakova, formerly married to two leading defendants.[50] After twenty years in Siberia, she was rehabilitated and returned to Moscow, where she continued to uphold Stalinist policies in opposition to the Khrushchevian 'thaw'.[51]

Political 'conclusions' from this trial were drawn by a meeting of

Moscow writers on the day the death sentences were announced. Bezymensky referred to the 'decontamination of Trotskyist ideology'. Fedin spoke of a successful struggle with 'the masked enemy'. Others followed Stavsky's call for 'closing writers' ranks' against the threat of fascism and its Soviet agents. Fadeyev insisted that battle was still raging: many more enemies had still to be uncovered.[52] The hunt continued with attacks on *Novyi mir*.[53] Its former editor Gronsky was said to have harboured and protected the 'enemy' Pavel Vasil'yev, who was immediately arrested. According to one account, this young poet had bravely refused to join the ritual denunciation of those accused in the January trial and to have called such statements 'pornographic scribblings on the margins of Russian literature'.[54] He was shot on 16 July, aged 26. Further identified as Trotskyites were Makarov (a board member of *Novyi mir*), and Zarudin (formerly of *Pereval*).[55]

At the same time, the net closed on the former 'Right'. Top of the agenda for the February 1937 Central Committee Plenum was simply 'N. Bukharin and A. Rykov'.[56] Realising that he could do nothing to influence its discussion, Bukharin declared a hunger strike.[57] On the eve of this meeting, the Commissar of Heavy Industry, 'Sergo' Ordzhonikidze, died suddenly. Although this was officially ascribed to a heart attack, he may have been murdered, or, since Ordzhonikidze could no longer work normally, in order to avoid clashing with Stalin and sharing the responsibility for his abuse of power, he decided to take his own life.[58]

After a week's postponement for the funeral, the Plenum began. Proceedings were almost entirely *in camera*. A fragment of Yezhov's report, 'Lessons Flowing from the Activity, Diversion and Espionage of the Japanese-German Trotskyite Agents', became known in 1956. Khrushchev's 'secret' speech contained a short extract concerning the laggardliness of the NKVD in rooting out these 'most inexorable enemies of the people'.[59] Similar reticence surrounds Stalin's speech 'On Deficiencies in Party Work and Measurers for Liquidating Trotskyites and other Double-Dealers'. After a delay of six weeks a cut version appeared in *Pravda* on 29 March (front page) and 1 April (page two). Khrushchev speaks of menacing passages omitted from the published text.[60] This was probably the occasion on which Stalin demanded of Postyshev 'What are you actually?'. Postyshev replied 'A Bolshevik, comrade Stalin, a Bolshevik'.[61] But boldness did not save him. Postyshev and some other leading politicians perhaps intended to use the Plenum to halt the purge, thereby effecting an eleventh-hour rescue for themselves and the most vulnerable members of the government apparatus. But while reading a statement which rejected suggestions that loyal Party members could have been recruited as Trotskyites in 1934, he lost confidence – perhaps after interruptions by Stalin – and gave way.[62] Stalin then attacked the 'theories' advanced by opponents of a further purge. He assailed the 'rotten' notions that 'an individual who is not always engaged in wrecking cannot be a wrecker', that 'since we Bolsheviks are many, while the wreckers are few – then we can afford to disregard the handful of wreckers'. To the claim that 'with each advance we make, class struggle diminishes', he counterposed his familiar 'class struggle intensifies' argument.[63] The published version indicates only two interruptions for applause and at the end an unprecedented omission: no ovation.

The Plenum considered the fates of Bukharin and Rykov, both present as Central Committee members. Bukharin spoke in his defence, denying all charges and declaring 'I am no Zinoviev or Kamenev. I'm not going to tell lies against myself'. To this, Molotov shouted from his seat, 'No confession! That proves you're a Fascist hireling'.[64] Bukharin replied that the real conspirators were Yezhov and the NKVD fabricating evidence in the Lubyanka. He proposed they should be examined by a special commission. Stalin remarked 'We'll send you down there to see for yourself'.[65] Instead, a special commission was set up for an immediate review of the Bukharin-Rykov case.[66] When the Plenum reconvened after a forty-eight hour recess both men were arrested in the antechamber and driven directly to the Lubyanka.[67]

Bukharin's views on poetry were condemned while the Party Plenum was still in session. A plenary meeting of the Writers' Union was then still in progress, ostensibly to commemorate the centenary of Pushkin's death. But Party speakers had rather more contemporary concerns. Bezymensky attacked Bukharin's attempt to belittle 'revolutionary poetry'.[68] Others attacked Pasternak. Alexander Gladkov explains:

> this was the price he had to pay for the praise lavished on him by Bukharin in his speech on poetry at the First Congress of Soviet Writers. Particularly harsh words were spoken by A. and X.[69] At first sight it seems strange that X. should have made such a speech – how could X., a genuine poet of great subtlety, associate himself with this crude and demogogic assault on Pasternak? It can only be understood against the background of the psychology of those

times, when fear seeped into every pore and abject cravenness
became the normal standard of behaviour. Look at any newspaper
from those days and you will see how tomorrow's victims, trying to
save their own skins, heaped abuse on today's.[70]

Pravda strongly endorsed this line in an article serenading the 'revolutionary poets' Bezymensky and Surkov (another of Bukharin's
adversaries at the Writers' Congress). It also heaped praise upon the
critic Usievich for her recent article condemning the cultural views of
Bukharin.[71]

Pasternak did not respond directly to this attack, but used the few
means at his disposal to distance himself from the new campaign.
Privately, he assured Bukharin's wife, in a handwritten note, that he
had no doubt of her husband's innocence.[72] In a more public gesture,
he refused to sign a collective protest against Gide's book *Retour de
L'URSS* (1936) in which the author repented of his earlier enthusiasm for the Russian Revolution.[73] Gladkov recalls that Pasternak's
excuse that he had not read the book

> struck others as affected and provocative, though nothing could
> have been further from what he intended. I remember a writer
> called V. who had signed and was quite genuinely indignant with
> Pasternak: 'Well, he didn't read it, but so what? Neither did I.
> Does he think any of the others did? Why does he want to be
> different? The book was denounced as lies in *Pravda*, wasn't it?'[74]

After the Plenum, denunciations were redoubled. Gronsky was
guilty of 'very serious political mistakes' by giving space in *Novyi mir*
to 'Enemies of the People'.[75] *Krasnaya nov'* had published 'vile
scoundrels'.[76] Further arrests were signalled by Postyshev's demotion
and the next day by a purge of the purgers themselves. Yezhov
denounced his predecessor Yagoda and his entire team, some 3,000
of whom were soon executed.[77]

Fresh charges reached literature in early April. The cue was given
by Stavsky to an all-Moscow writers' meeting. Taking as his text the
'speech of genius of Comrade Stalin', part of which had appeared in
print the previous day, he identified enemies on all sides, above all
his former colleagues of RAPP.[78] The first casualty was Averbakh, a
relation by marriage of Yagoda, who had been arrested on 3 April.
His own arrest followed in mid-April.[79] The press revealed his
double-dealing between Trotskyist slogans ('Ally or Enemy?') and

Bukharinite conceptions ('For Plekhanovite orthodoxy').[80] Yudin
used the fifth anniversary of RAPP's abolition to invent new charges.
He alleged Averbakh had set up a 'parallel centre' in literature, on
the lines of those exposed in the previous 'show trial' and had also
recruited an 'inner circle' of accomplices: Kirshon, Makar'yev,
Korabel'nikov, Maznin and Bruno Jasienski.[81] All of them were first
identified as 'enemies of the people' and then investigated in writers'
meetings of May and June 1937.

Their fates varied. Jasienski was attacked at a Party session by
Yudin, Stavsky, Panfyorov and others. He denied all charges, particularly the existence of a RAPPist 'wrecking' clique.[82] He was
arrested on 31 July 1937 and died in a transit prison. Some of his last
thoughts are expressed in a prison poem:

A harbinger of Communism's immortal ideas,
One celebration, the magnificence of our times,
I lie behind bars, like an enemy and criminal,
What could be more absurd?
But I do not reproach you, Nativeland – mother,
I know that only by losing faith in your own son,
Could you have faith in such a heresy
And break my song like a sword.[83]

Kirshon was assailed by his old antagonist Vishnevsky, who asked
why he had associated with an 'enemy of the people' (Averbakh) for
fourteen years, why he had opposed the 1932 Resolution and why he
had proposed Averbakh as a delegate to the Congress.[84] His self-
defence was unavailing: he was expelled from the Party and put
under investigation. Fadeyev revealed the next step: 'I was called in
by the NKVD and asked what I thought of Kirshon, after his arrest. I
said that Yagoda, Averbakh and Kirshon were all of a kind. I was
used to thinking like that. But my reply could have been fateful'.[85]
Averbakh was shot immediately, and Kirshon's execution followed a
year later.[86] The RAPPist Makar'yev was sentenced to a labour camp,
apparently after the same testimonial. Extraordinarily, he survived and
came back to Moscow after fifteen years to confront his accuser.[87]
Fadeyev committed suicide shortly after, in 1956. A handful
of RAPPists were more fortunate. Afinogenov escaped lightly with
expulsion from the Party, and his membership was restored a year
later. In a debate over his expulsion from the Writers' Union, he was
defended by Seyfullina.[88] He died in an air raid at the beginning of

the war. Libedinsky's home was searched: Fadeyev, evidently ap-
praised of this, had removed his correspondence with Libedinsky the
previous day. His expulsion from the Party was debated but he was
not arrested.[89] He lived on until 1959. The longest life was enjoyed by
Sutyrin, the only leading RAPPist to survive into the 1970s.

Writers' investigations were interrupted on 12 June by the abrupt
announcement that most of the military High Command had been
shot.[90] The list of victims was headed by Marshal Tukhachevsky,
leader of the campaigns against Poland in 1920 and Kronstadt the
following year, and General Yakir, who had written a protestation of
innocence from the Lubyanka. Stalin amused himself by covering it
with obscenities.[91] As in the 'show trials', great pressure was put
upon public figures to approved the executions. At very short notice,
Bezymensky managed some blank verse welcoming the liquidation of
the 'fascist spies' and Demyan Bedny produced a fifty-four-line
'poem' incorporating the names of the condemned within the
rhyme-scheme.[92] A collective letter of congratulation to Yezhov and
the Supreme Court was drawn up by the Writers' Union and circulated for signature. Pasternak caused consternation by his refusal to
sign. He recalled that:

The Secretary of the Writers' Union at that time was a certain
Stavsky, a great scoundrel. He was scared stiff he would be accused
of not watching things more closely, the Union of Writers would be
called a hotbed of opportunism, and he would have to pay the
price. They tried to put pressure on me, but I wouldn't give in.
Then the whole leadership of the Union of Writers came out to
Peredelkino – not to my *dacha*, but to another one, where they
summoned me. Stavsky began to shout at me and started using
threats. I said that if he couldn't talk to me calmly, I wasn't obliged
to listen to him, and I went home.

We expected I would be arrested that night. But, just imagine, I
went to bed and at once fell into a blissful sleep. Not for a long time
had I slept so well and peacefully. This always happens after I have
taken some irrevocable step. My close friends urged me to write to
Stalin – as though we were regular correspondents and exchanged
cards at holiday seasons? But I actually did send him a letter. I
wrote that I had grown up in a family with very strong Tolstoian
convictions, which I had imbibed with my mother's milk, and that
my life was at his disposal, but that I could not consider I had a
right to be a judge in matters of life and death where others were

concerned. To this very day I cannot understand why I was not arrested there and then.[93]

Stalin made no direct response to this appeal. However, the Writers' Union took no chances: Pasternak's signature was added to the rest.[94]

The military massacre caused further perplexity to the intelligentsia. Ehrenburg recalls a 'terrible day' at Meyerhold's apartment where a number of writers were discussing art history. A middle-ranking officer, Belov, who served on the Military Collegium of the Supreme Court, arrived unannounced. 'Ignoring us completely, he began to describe the trial of Tukhachevsky and other top officers'. He noted that the judges were observing the Collegium in an unambiguous manner: 'Uborevich[95] looked me straight in the eyes'. Belov confidently predicted, and was soon proved accurate, 'tomorrow I'll be in the dock too'. Ehrenburg glanced at their host: 'Meyerhold sat with his eyes shut like a wounded bird'.[96]

Those present wondered about the meaning of the trial and tried to fathom its significance. The charges seemed so fantastic. Most of them considered that 'Stalin knew nothing of the senseless violence committed against communists and the Soviet intelligentsia'. Meyerhold stated 'They conceal it from Stalin', and Ehrenburg quoted Pasternak's wish 'If only someone would tell Stalin about it'.[97] Pasternak's real thoughts were perhaps more accurately related by Alexander Gladkov, who met him in the street at the height of the terror. 'He stopped to talk to me with quite extraordinary outspokenness'. All that Gladkov felt able to record in his diary was 'Gogol's Boulevard, Pasternak' – his brother had just been arrested. But in his memoir Gladkov adds: 'This was in the autumn of 1937, at the height of arrests and executions. He talked while I listened embarrassed by the unexpected vehemence of his diatribe, until he suddenly checked himself almost in mid-sentence'.[98] Pasternak had been 'very worked up and kept referring to Dostoyevsky – I remember a phrase about Shigalyov'. This was a reference to the nihilist in *The Possessed* who envisaged a utopia based upon mutual denunciation and surveillance. In his *Essay in Autobiography* Pasternak employs the notion of *shigalyovshchina* to describe 1937.[99]

The year is more commonly known as the *Yezhovshchina* (Yezhovism) and rests in popular memory as the apex of mass executions. The macabre data of this slaughter have never been published. Solzhenitsyn asked:

What legal expert, what historian of crime will provide us with verified statistics for those 1937–1938 executions? Where is that *Special Archive* we might be able to penetrate in order to read the figures? There is none. There is none and there never will be any. Therefore we dare report only those figures mentioned in rumours that were quite fresh in 1939–1940, when they were drifting around under the Butyrki arches, having emanated from the high- and middle-ranking Yezhov men of the NKVD who had been arrested and had passed through those cells not long before. (And they really knew!) The Yezhov men said during those two years of 1937 and 1938 a *half-million* 'political prisoners' had been shot throughout the Soviet Union, and 480,000 *blatnye* – habitual thieves – in addition. (The thieves were all shot under Article 59–3 because they constituted 'a basis of Yagoda's power'; and thereby the 'ancient and noble companionship of thieves' was pruned back.)

How improbable are these figures? Taking into consideration that the mass executions went on not for two full years but only for a year and a half, we would have to assume (under Article 58 – in other words, the politicals alone) an average of 28,000 executions per month in that period. For the whole Soviet Union. But at how many different locations were executions being carried out? A figure of 150 would be very modest. (There were more, of course. In Pskov alone, the NKVD set up torture and execution chambers in the basements of many churches, in former hermits' cells. And even in 1953 tourists were still not allowed into these churches, on the grounds that 'archives' were kept there. The cobwebs hadn't been swept out for ten years at a stretch: those were the 'archives' they kept there. And before beginning restoration work on these churches, they had to haul away the bones in them by the truck-load.) On the basis of this calculation, an average of six people were shot in the course of one day at each execution site. What's so fantastic about that? It is even an understatement! (According to other sources, 1,700,000 had been shot by January 1, 1939.).[100]

Roy Medvedev is in broad agreement with this analysis. His original estimate that 700,000–800,000 persons were shot soon after their arrest during 1937 or 1938 has been revised upwards. Now recognising that many were shot on secret orders in the 'corrective labour' camps, he puts the number of death sentences at one million.[101]

The Terror struck deeply into every section of the intelligentsia. Amongst the professions, it was revealed that in history the so-called school of Pokrovsky became a base for wrecking, as the NKVD has discovered; a base for enemies of the people, for Trotskyite-Bukharinite hirelings of fascism, for wreckers, spies, and terrorists, who cleverly disguised themselves with the harmful anti-Leninist concepts of M. N. Pokrovsky. Only unforgivable, idiotic carelessness and loss of vigilance by people on the historical front can explain the fact that this shameless gang of enemies of Leninism long and safely carried on their wrecking work in the field of history.[102]

Many Old Bolsheviks active in historical research perished while several of those formerly termed bourgeois historians found new status and property. Thereafter, the Russian past became a major area of research, especially the lives of Ivan the Terrible and Peter the Great, while study of revolutionary history and socialism dwindled.[103] Soviet philosophy was devastated under the slanderous accusations of Mitin, Yudin and Konstantinov. Dozens of philosophers were arrested. They included Jan Sten, Stalin's reluctant tutor in Hegelianism, seized on the direct instructions of Stalin, who declared him a 'Menshevik idealist'. He was shot in prison on 19 June 1937. His last article, 'Dialectical Materialism', was nonetheless published in the *Large Soviet Encyclopaedia*, attributed to 'M. B. Mitin'.[104] Similar campaigns assailed the social sciences, where such disciplines as law, economics and pedagogy were ravaged by denunciations and disappearances.[105] The campaigns within natural science have been particularly well-documented, notably in biology and agronomy where numerous specialists were executed. In the words of one researcher 'most of the repressed people were genuine scientists and technicians, professionals with a strong commitment to their disciplines'.[106] Indeed, D. N. Prashnikov, chairman of a meeting in 1937 that was supposed to condemn soil scientists recently arrested, ruled such condemnation out of order. He silenced those speakers who wished to echo articles in the press entitled 'Prisoners of pseudoscientific theories' or 'Root out Alien Theories in Agronomy' by confining them to scientific issues: 'You are not the Procurator nor the NKVD'.[107] Before long, *Pravda* denounced him as a protector of 'enemies.[108] There were widespread losses in such apolitical areas as medical science and mathematics.

The literary losses were certainly amongst the highest. The quarrels of the two previous decades here reach a bloody climax in which adherents of previous schools and tendencies are decimated, often almost totally. Among the hardest hit were former members of *Pereval*. First to be arrested was Ivan Katayev in the spring of 1937. He was soon joined in prison by Boris Guber, Zarudin and A. Lezhnev. Unlike the other two, Lezhnev still harboured some illusions of a fair trial. None received one and all were dead within the next two years.[109] The fate of Esenin's friends was no less terrible. As a Soviet author concedes: 'From 1934 until the War, Esenin was not published for his fellow-countrymen. RAPP theorists and critics from the early 1930s on began more and more frequently to call him, and his elder brother Klyuev, a *"kulak"* poet. People began to utter the name Esenin more rarely and quietly in official circles, with a shade of hostility'.[110] Klyuev, who had been exiled to Tomsk in 1934, and was rearrested in 1937, died in prison.[111] His 'kulak' counterpart, Klychkov, was arrested outside Moscow on 31 July 1937. He is reported to have faced his ordeal in the Lubyanka with great fortitude. Then, in the absence of any evidence of guilt, he was shot by one of the interrogators.[112] None of his confiscated verses were returned. A similar fate befell other poets. Amongst those arrested in 1937 were Pavel Vasil'yev[113] and Boris Kornilov, husband of Ol'ga Berqqol'ts. The purges destroyed literary critics in large numbers, such as Gorbachov, Lelevich and I. Bespalov (all adherents of *Litfront*), Benedikt Liushits, the historian of Futurism[114] and Mirsky.

The death toll amongst prose writers was also great. Victims of repression in these years included Panteleimon Romanov, Artyom Vesyoly and Tarasov-Rodionov. The fate of Boris Pil'nyak is particularly poignant. During the summer of 1937, he continued to write, though no longer with any prospect of publication. An epic novel, *The Salt Barn*, set between the revolutions of 1905 and 1917, was thereby completed. He buried the manuscript by instalments in his garden at Peredelkino. Only his wife and an old nanny knew this secret.[115] Anticipating arrest, he destroyed all other documents including correspondence that could be used in 'evidence' against him. Since he had no income, his family supported itself by the sale of possessions. The NKVD arrived on 2 October, during his three-year-old's birthday party. They took him away 'for a chat with Nikolai Ivanovich (Yezhov)', saying he would be back within an hour or two.[116] Pil'nyak had in fact known Yezhov since the late 1920s and used to supply Victor Serge with gory details of prison executions.[117] He was also on good terms with the sinister Pavlenko, who sometimes boasted of witnessing NKVD interrogations.[118] However, such connections did not help save him. Pil'nyak never returned to his

family. The only 'evidence' to substantiate the charge of terrorism fo
which he was executed appears to have been a toy pistol found whe
he was arrested.

The Terror was not confined to Moscow and Leningrad. It cu
sharply into the upper echelons of every Union Republic. A cam
paign of political extermination was orchestrated 'from above'. In th
late summer and autumn of 1937 'Stalin sent special authorise
representatives of the Central Committee to the Republics, terr
tories and regions. He wanted to organise and ensure in the localitie
the fulfillment of his personal instructions on stepping up repressiv
measures'.[119] Many Politburo members led these murderous ex
peditions. Kaganovich, for example, arrived to supervise the mass
acre of the Yaroslavl' and Ivanovo Regions in August 1937. 'Durin
his stay . . . he phoned Stalin several times a day to report th
number of those arrested and the course of their investigation'. Afte
such conversations, he ordered the local NKVD Chief to speed up th
number of arrests and the extraction of confessions. As he put it t
Stalin: 'I'll press the NKVD Department heads not to be too liber:
and to maximally increase identification of "enemies of th
people"'.[120] Special 'troikas' were established to pass death sentenc
without trial – the procuracy had no access to such bodies – accordin
to centrally-defined quotas. An initial target of 1,500 shootings w:
given to the Ivanovo troika. This sufficed to wipe out most of th
Party and state functionaries, together with all Communists co:
nected, however indirectly, with Trotskyism, Anarchism or Menshe
ism.[121] The use of troikas, which was adopted across the who
country, was supplemented by a nationwide wave of 'open' trials i
the second half of 1937. These arraigned 'little people' at *oblast'*, an
raion level, whether in the local Party organisations or in *kolkhe*
administration. Medvedev notes that 'usually the same rank of of
cials were put on trial everywhere, indicating a uniform schem
worked out at the centre'.[122] Not all of those accused were execute
Instead, the state hastily built dozens of new prisons, convert
former monasteries, childrens' homes or stables, and established
vast new *GULag* empire of concentration camps in the Far Eas
Urals, Siberia and Kazakhstan.[123]

Mass repression of leading writers took place in every Unic
Republic. In Georgia, this was led by Beria, whose intentions
purge literature and art were made plain in a speech on literature a:
art published in June.[124] Following this, the outstanding poet Tabid
was arrested. His colleague, the poet Yashvili, received sever

summonses to the NKVD headquarters. Instead he went to the Union of Georgian Writers, of which he was Secretary, and committed suicide with a shotgun. The execution of Tabidze was announced on 16 December. Moving tributes to their widows appear in Pasternak's *Letters to Georgian Friends*.[125] In Armenia, the revolutionary poet E. Charents perished, together with many others.[126] One who survived, the poet G. Maari, spent two years in confinement prior to a three-minute trial at which he confessed to 'terrorist acts, the wish to separate Armenia from the Soviet Union and to unite her to the imperialist camp and the intention to kill Beria'.[127] Miraculously, he returned to Erevan in 1954. The pattern of arrests and executions was repeated in Azerbaijan and Kazakhstan.

Still more severe was the repression in the Ukraine. Already subjected to earlier ravages,[128] the Ukrainian purges of the latter half of 1937 were exceptionally destructive. One account states 'It is no exaggeration to state that during these terrible years an entire Ukrainian intelligentsia perished in labour camps and the execution chambers of the NKVD'.[129] The terror struck hard at the literary intelligentsia. The former President of the Ukrainian Writers' Union Senchenko, and its Secretary, Epin, both perished. So too did the nationally famous writer and literary official Mikitenko[130] and many lesser-known figures. Tremendous devastation took place amongst Belorussian writers. As one historian notes 'In addition to the usual charges of anti-proletarianism, decadence and formalism, Belorussian writers were also liable to be accused of the even more heinous crime of bourgeois nationalism . . . few literary figures of any consequence survived Stalin's reign and the price paid by survivors was high indeed'.[131] Recently, the author Vasil' Bykov applied in his capacity of Deputy to the Republic's Supreme Soviet for information concerning the several dozen Belorussian writers who simply vanished during Stalin's purges. It turned out that a good number had been posthumously rehabilitated. There was, however, 'no information' concerning the fate of eighteen of the writers who had disappeared.[132]

Such silence illustrates the difficulty in reaching overall figures for the numbers of writers who died during Stalin's terror. Some calculations have put the number arrested above 600, that is almost one-third of the membership of the Writers' Union,[133] but this is certainly too low. Ehrenburg compared the names of delegates to the 1934 and 1954 Writers' Congresses. He found that all but fifty of some 700 original delegates failed to reappear.[134] Given that their average age was under forty, this could not be explained by natural causes and the war. Indeed, the turnover amongst Praesidium members was even faster. Jack Matlock estimates that of the original 37 in 1934, only five were still members in 1939.[135] This suggests an even more rapid rate of replacement than in the Party hierarchy. We know that 70 per cent of 1934 Congress delegates perished over the same five years. A much higher figure for literature was recently provided in the Soviet press. A correspondent announced that he had been listing Soviet writers who died or were executed in Stalinist camps or prisons. The list had 1,300 names. He added that the list was unfortunately far from complete. The example of Bykov in Belorussia had shown how hard this research was to complete. However, he considered it could be accomplished one day:

> All talk about NKVD archives being lost or destroyed is naive: hundreds of people who recently turned to the Military Judicial Board to find out when their repressed relatives really died were given those dates. Incidentally, admirers of Boris Pil'nyak and Artyom Vesyoly can cross out their false dates of death from every book mentioning them . . . both were shot in April 1938. This means that such a list of names – the absence of which was once lamented by Anna Akhmatova – does actually exist.[136]

This astonishing illustration of *glasnost'* concluded with the hope that it would 'not take decades' to obtain such a complete list.

Other independent research into Stalin's victims is also in hand. A young researcher at the Moscow Archival-Historical Institute, D. G. Yurasov, has compiled a personal card index of people who had been repressed. His index contains 80,000 names. He reported that all those condemned for anti-Soviet crimes from 1929 onwards were recorded in a filing system of the Special Department of the Ministry of Internal Affairs. Such evidence, to which he had not had access, did, however, exist. He warned, though, that this source was disappearing fast. Materials from the later 1930s 'have already been partly destroyed, because the period for preservation has expired'. It had also been decided to transfer subsequent material to the KGB 'because there was nowhere to store it'.[137] Such admonitions give added urgency to the recent appeal from the Archival-Historical Institute:

> We must establish a public commission including scientists and representives from newly-established public organisations or those

being established, such as Memorial, the Soviet Cultural Fund, the Moscow Tribune etc. The commission should have at its disposal the archival *fonds* of the CPSU (b) Central Committee, the OGPU-NKVD (joint Chief Political Administration of the Commissariat of Internal Affairs), the NKGB (Commissariat of State Security), the procurator's office and court, and the personal *fonds* of unlawfully repressed Party leaders, government officials, economic executives, scientists, cultural workers and artists.[138]

The Commission should prepare a White Book on 'Stalin and his Regime', using 'scientific methodology and authentic documentary material'. Without access to the latter, they concluded, 'any serious scientific approach to the problem is impossible'.[139]

As the 1930s proceeded, scientific criteria were increasingly rejected and cultural policy became steadily more dependent on the utterances of one man. It would be naive to regard Stalin as solely responsible for this outcome. He warned repeatedly against a 'cult of personality'. When the Central Archival Administration requested materials for an exhibition of the 'revolutionary activity of I. V. Stalin', to be mounted at the Society of Old Bolsheviks in 1933, he pronounced against it. 'Such small beginnings', he prophesied, 'would lead to a strengthening of a "cult of personality", harmful to and incompatible with the spirit of our Party'.[140] The exhibition was prevented and the Society of Old Bolsheviks was afterwards abolished. When *Detgiz* proposed a volume of stories about 'Stalin's childhood' in 1937, he also opposed the idea. He found the proposed collection to be full of 'factual distortions, untruths, exaggeration and unwarranted encomia', supplied by 'lovers of fairy tales, liars (perhaps "honest liars") and timeservers'. Furthermore the book 'tends to inculcate in the Soviet people (and people in general) the cult of personality of the leader (*vozhd'*) and of infallible heroes', which was 'dangerous and harmful'.[141] He recommended that the book be burnt. But these admonitions did not prevent Stalin from arranging, and even writing, lavish tributes to himself.

A hagiographer, however, had yet to be found. Stalin's biographer Boris Souvarine begun work in 1930. His critical study, the first in any language, appeared in 1935 to a mixed reception. André Malraux, who had refused to recommend the typescript to Gallimard, explained 'I think you and your friends are right, Souvarine, but I will come over to you only when might is on your side'.[142] Stalin read the book in a specially prepared translation of one copy. He replied in a subsequent speech which named a non-existent 'Souvarine group' as a reserve force of Trotskyite wreckers.[143] Clearly, though, Stalin sought other answers. Two literary visitors, L. Feuchtwanger and André Gide, were approached to write a biography but declined. Under great pressure, Gorky reluctantly took on the task. Vast piles of documents were supplied by Central Committee couriers. He pored over them in his study day after day. Then suddenly he emerged to announce cheerfully to his own biographer and friend, V. Desnitsky, that the results were too saccharine. He called a halt and never touched the material again.[144] Eventually the French communist writer Barbusse was prevailed upon to perform, or lend his name, to this duty. To convey the flavour of his sickeningly uncritical account, we need look no further than the preface: 'if the cobbles in the street could talk, they would say: Stalin'.[145]

Soviet writers, practically without exception, made their obeisance to the burgeoning 'cult'. Unlike Barbusse, however, they did so involuntarily. Beginning in the Five Year Plan and reaching a climax during the purge years, they praised Stalin's childhood and youthful political activities. An established 'safe' theme was Stalin's birthplace, Gori, and the modest circumstances of his origins. Nikolai Tikhonov described this at length[146] and was rewarded with the Stalin Prize (three times). The subject was treated in numerous variations by Ukrainians, Armenians and Georgians themselves. Typical was Georgy Leonidze's 'Stalin' poem of 1939 which stressed Stalin's love of nature and of peasants, his boyish playfulness and scholarly achievements.[147] Treatment of his revolutionary debut, in particular his stormy relationship with the Tbilisi Party which expelled him on more than one occasion, was necessarily more tentative. Most writers left well alone. Bulgakov took up the subject in *Batum* but the play was banned.[148] The Georgian playwright Dadyan did manage to stage *From the Spark*, showing Stalin at the head of a street demonstration, fearless under fire from Tsarist forces. There was little historical basis for such an episode, nor to justify the statement in the *Short Biography* that in his Batum period (aged twenty-two) Stalin was 'already known' as a teacher of the workers.[149] His period in exile and imprisonment are mostly passed over in silence, perhaps as too similar to those of other Old Bolsheviks.

'Stalin in the Civil War' became a major theme. The genre had begun with Voroshilov's articles about the southern front,[150] and was extended by him throughout the 1930s. Amongst literary works, two were most notable for their inaccuracy and sycophancy. A. Tolstoy, at other times a talented writer, produced his *Bread* in 1937. Its glorification and distortion of Stalin's role reduced all other participants to insignificance. In the same year, Pogodin's play *Man with a Gun* provided not only the first stage portrayal of Lenin (played by B. V. Shchukin) but also, in Act Two, of Stalin. The 'tension' is gradually built up. First Lenin consults him on the 'phone, then asks 'Where is Stalin?'. At last, he actually appears and delivers a stirring address to revolutionary soldiers.[151] Although both works exaggerated Stalin's contribution during the Revolution and Civil War beyond all proportion, accounts of his subsequent career do not pale by comparison. On the contrary, the qualities noted earlier of historical vision and decisive leadership appear on even grander scales. During the Five Year Plan, Gorky repeatedly referred to the indomitable will, indefatigable efforts, organisational abilities and colossal energies of the Party leader. A number of statements at the height of Gorky's influence in 1934 seem to place Stalin on a par with Lenin, not just as an activist but as a theorist too: 'The Soviet working class is proud and happy to have such a leader (*vozhd'*) as Stalin'.[152] As we have seen, his inner doubts were expressed privately.

Public adulation of Stalin reached its climax during the 'election' campaign of June–December 1937. Stalin was adopted as a candidate by all 3,346 electoral districts.[153] Writers reached new heights of enthusiasm. Verses appeared entitled 'On Stalin, My Greatest Song'. The journalist Mikhail Kol'tsov entitled a column 'The Great Author Iosif Stalin'.[154] According to others, Stalin was the 'highest mountain', the 'genius of the World'. He sometimes surpassed these attributes by possessing sublime or immortal qualities. The literary journals held an unspoken contest in hyperbole, prefacing literary portraits with his photographs and speeches.[155]

How sincere was all this adulation? In the absence of contrary testimony written at the time, we must refer to memoirs. Those of Il'ya Ehrenburg tell us: 'It would be an overstatement to say that I liked Stalin, but for a long time I believed in him and feared him. Like everybody else, I referred to him in conversation as the "Boss"'.[156] He likens this to the Jewish attitude towards their God: 'They could not really have loved Jehovah; he was not only omnipotent but pitiless and unjust. He heaped every calamity on the head of the virtuous'. Yet Ehrenburg himself seems dissatisfied with the 'book of Job' theory. He notes in the passage which follows:

Although I had been brought up on nineteenth-century free-thinking and had written *Julio Jurenito*,[157] I proved not to be immune to the epidemic of the Stalin cult . . . Faith, like fear and some other emotions, is infectious . . . The faith of others weighed on me, preventing me from looking clearly at what was happening[158] . . . Poets whose integrity is above question such as Eluard, Jean-Richard Bloch,[158] Hernandez, Nerval – extolled Stalin. He became a banner, an immaculate godhead.[159]

Perhaps not surprisingly, Ehrenburg carries less conviction when he attempts to find more rational reasons for belief. He pleads ignorance of the scale of the terror, claiming 'In 1937, I knew only of isolated crimes, even today I am not fully informed'. He stresses Stalin's cunning, shown by his critique of collectivisation, 'Dizzy from success', and later denunciation of 'excessive' arrests under the *Yezhovshchina*. The international context is also used, if not to argue that Stalinism was a 'lesser evil', at least to suggest that crusading western business interests and militarists 'helped to consolidate the Stalin cult'.[160] In the end, however, he reverts to a form of pragmatism: 'Yes, I knew about many crimes, but it was not in my power to stop them'. After all 'far more influential and better informed people'[161] could do nothing. Perhaps recognising the incompleteness of this analysis, he concludes on an apologetic note:

> In a previous volume of these memoirs, I promised to return to the subject of Stalin and to try to discover and sum up the reasons for our errors . . . I have started writing this Chapter several times, crossing out and tearing up as I went along. In the end I have to acknowledge that I could not keep my word.[162]

It is worth noting that almost a generation has passed by since Ehrenburg wrote this apology and that the analysis he was attempting in his memoirs remains far from complete.

As he had noted, and Medvedev has echoed in his curious point that the basis of Stalin's power was the deceived masses, Stalinism involved a complex relationship between the leader and popular feeling. Other literary memoirs provide important evidence of the ways in which this was brought about. A number were witnesses to Stalin's rare, stage-managed and increasingly theatrical appearances in the Thirties. Paustovsky recalls the last day of a Komsomol Congress in the Kremlin:

Stalin had not yet made an appearance. All delegates hoped he would, if only at the final session . . . They cried out – individually or in unison – 'We want comrade Stalin, Stalin, Stalin'. Occasionally this would give place to 'Glory to Stalin, the genius and father of us all'. This would be drowned by thunderous applause and stamping of feet.

It was getting late. The whole Praesidium was on its feet, waiting for Stalin's entry. And then it happened! Stalin emerged suddenly and silently out of the wall behind the Praesidium table, right out of one of the walnut panels. Everyone jumped up. There was frenzied applause. At any moment, one felt, the ceiling would come crashing down. Stalin raised a hand. Instantly, there was a deathly hush. In that hush, Stalin shouted abruptly and in a rather hoarse voice, with a strong Georgian accent: 'Long live Soviet youth!'. Then he vanished into the wall as suddenly and mysteriously as he had appeared.[163]

To use the Weberian notion of charisma seems not entirely appropriate, but the relationship between the ruler and the ruled certainly contained elements of magic. Followers would not have been able to give a rational account of their willingness to be led.

Stalin and the writers exerted a mutual fascination. According to Paustovsky, Bulgakov 'sent' enigmatic letters to Stalin almost daily, signing them 'Tarzan'. In this gentle fantasy, Stalin is presented as surprised, even frightened, each time a letter arrives. He orders the author to be brought before him. Eventually Bulgakov is caught and taken to the Kremlin:

Stalin gives him a searching, not unfriendly look, and puffing on his pipe, begins an amiable conversation;
'So it's you: Bulgakov?'
'It is, Iosif Vissarionovich.'
'Why those patched trousers, those worn-out shoes. A shame, such a shame.'
'Oh, it's just that my earnings are a bit on the low side, Iosif Vissarionovich.'
Stalin turns to the Commissar for Supplies:
'Why are you sitting here doing nothing. Can't you clothe a man? Your people can steal all right, but when it comes to clothing a writer, it's beyond them. Why have you gone so pale? You're not frightened? Clothe him at once. Just look at your boots! Take them off this instant and give them to this man.'[164]

Thus clothed and shod, Bulgakov takes to visiting Stalin. He strikes up an unexpected friendship with the recluse in the Kremlin. Sometimes Stalin is depressed and complains to Bulgakov: 'You see, they all bawl "Genius, genius". And yet there's no-one to share a glass of brandy'.[165] This dialogue has the mark of authenticity. One may well consider that the more courtiers extolled Stalin's genius, the more he doubted their sincerity.

Some of Bulgakov's conversations with Stalin were not imaginary. In the early 1930s, Stalin spoke to him on the telephone, concerning the writer's despair at unemployment. Stalin promised to 'put in a word' for Bulgakov with the Moscow Arts Theatre (MKhAT). Though an actual event, Bulgakov could not resist a fictionalised account of Stalin's intervention: 'Is that MKhAT? Stalin here. Don't ring off. Where's the Director? What? Died? Just this instant? Well really, people are so nervous nowadays!'[166] In February 1938 at the height of the terror, during which he suffered much anguish,[167] Bulgakov appealed to Stalin on behalf of a close colleague:

Permit me to turn to you with a request concerning the playwright Nikolay Robertovich Erdman, who has fully completed his three-year sentence of exile in the towns of Yeniseisk and Tomsk, and who is currently living in the town of Kalinin.

Confident in the fact that literary gifts are extremely highly prized in our fatherland, and knowing at the same time that the writer Nikolay Erdman is currently deprived of the opportunity to practise his skills as the result of the negative attitude which has developed towards him, and which has been sharply voiced in the press, I take the liberty of asking you to turn your attention to his fate.

In the hope that the lot of the writer N. Erdman might be relieved if you were to think it worthwhile considering this request, I ask wholeheartedly for N. Erdman to be given the possibility of returning to Moscow and of working in literature without hindrance, so that he might escape from his solitary state and his spiritual depression.[168]

Perhaps as the result of this letter, Erdman was rehabilitated. He returned to Moscow and obtained employment, which later included sketch-writing for an NKVD ensemble.[169]

The problem of the 'cult of personality' is not a simple one, and deserves more extended treatment than can be given here. We may conclude this section by noting that public attitudes towards Stalin remain deeply controversial to this day. *Komsomol'skaya pravda* states in a recent editorial:

> When we began to print material concerning revision of the attitude to Stalin as the 'dear father' 'faithful Leninist' and 'inspirer of all our victories' (definitions which he coined for himself and skillfully instilled in the masses), not all our readers understood us.
>
> A telephone call: 'What are you doing? After your article, my mother and I and my two sisters spent the whole night in the kitchen, talking, crying and reminiscing. We cannot accept this! Has our whole life been for nothing? Do you realise what you've done to us?'.
>
> We did realise. We understood that for people who have spent a quarter of their lives, half their lives, or even their whole life with the personality cult in their hearts, the operation to extract it cannot be painless.[170]

His recent Soviet biographer D. A. Volkogonov has argued: 'Stalin was alongside. He was part of the fabric of our life and thus became as if an organic element of it. People believed in this very strongly'.[171] Precisely because so much of their own experience was bound up with the Stalin era, it is a period that many citizens are reluctant to revise.

There are, however, the beginnings of a revision even for the most difficult period. The trial of Bukharin (2–13 March 1938) has been exposed as fraudulent and the guilty verdict quashed for all defendants except one. The Supreme Court has declared that there was no anti-Soviet 'Bloc of Rights and Trotskyites' engaged in espionage or treason, nor were there acts of wrecking. The charge of assassination is annulled, thus refuting the prosecution's claim that: 'The murder of Soviet public figures completed the circle of heinous state crimes by which this band of contemptible apostates of our country, provocateurs of the Tsarist secret police and hirelings of foreign intelligence services, who were selling our land and liberty to foreign capitalists, strove to carry out a fascist plan for the overthrow of the Soviet system and the restoration of capitalism.'[172] Amongst their victims had, supposedly, been Gorky. According to one defendant, this had been at the instigation of Trotsky: 'he referred to Gorky's extremely close friendship with Stalin and said that Maxim Gorky's utterances were definitely driving away from Trotsky many of his followers amongst the European intelligentsia and bringing them closer to the position of the Party leadership'.[173]

Gorky's death was attributed at the trial to a medical murder. Dr Levin, thought to have been a forced collaborator with the Cheka since 1918,[174] provided the 'medical evidence', claiming that Gorky had been given 'heart stimulants in large quantities', including camphor, caffeine and cardiosial with the intention of killing him. This had been done on the instructions of Yagoda (who has not been rehabilitated). The administration of wrong treatment was confirmed by Gorky's secretary, Kryuchkov, who had been arrested and denounced in *Pravda*. Yagoda, however, flatly denied this submission: 'It is all lies'.[175] The charges were indeed absurd. Ehrenburg was in Moscow as they came out: 'When it was announced on the radio that Gorky's murderers were being put on trial, and that doctors had been involved, Babel, who knew Gorky well, came rushing in, sat on the bed and tapped his forehead: they were insane'.[176]

Bukharin, similarly, denied involvement. Instead, he told the court that Dr Levin had been a Menshevik immediately after the Revolution.[177] As several western scholars have shown, he did the same with every specific charge, most vehemently denying that of an attempt on Lenin's life. While accepting overall responsibility for 'the sum total of crimes committed by the counter-revolutionary organisation, irrespective of whether or not I knew of, or whether or not I took a direct part in any particular act',[178] he attempted to indicate subtly that the proceedings were fraudulent. But the vast majority of his contemporaries did not take the point: Bukharin's individual denials were so overwhelmed by the fact of confession to general crimes, that few looked further for corroboration. Stalin's instinct that the world would believe the lie was well-founded. Only after fifty years have we been told officially that the trial was false.

In his last 'testament', Bukharin had predicted that his death would lead inevitably to many thousands of others. In addition to the eradication of his former 'school', there took place further decimation of the cultural intelligentsia. The poet Zabolotsky was arrested a week after Bukharin's execution. He was exiled to camps in the Far East and Kazakhstan and released only in 1948, returning to Moscow in broken health.[179] During his imprisonment, he is thought to have written to Tikhonov, a fellow Leningrad writer, asking for an intercession on behalf of himself and other prisoners. It is not known whether Tikhonov responded.[180] Mandelstam's destruction soon followed. Through the good offices of Bukharin in 1934, he had had three years' respite in Voronezh. Even there, he had to endure denunciation. His rehabilitation commission has recently uncovered a collection put out by the local Writers' Union in November 1937. Entitled *Literary Voronezh*, it included the statement: 'Supported by enemies of the people, the Trotskyites Stefan, Aich, Mandelstam and Kaletsky, who arrived in Voronezh in 1934, tried to cordon off the writers' collective by introducing a debilitating spirit and political apathy. Their attempt was foiled. The groups was exposed and cut off, despite a clearly liberal attitude towards them on the part of the former regional Party committee (Genkin and others) who proposed "reforming" this band'.[181] Then, after some months of release in Moscow, Mandel'stam was abruptly dispatched to the countryside. He was arrested on 2 May 1938. His widow has no doubt that Stavsky had deliberately set the trap:

> Evidently the police had to wait for a decision from Stalin or someone close to him – without such authorization it was impossible to arrest M. on account of Stalin's personal order in 1934 to 'isolate but preserve' him. Stavsky must have been told to arrange for M. to stay for the time being in some definite place so they wouldn't have to look for him when the moment came. In other words, to save the 'organs' any tiresome detective work, Stavsky had obligingly sent us to a rest home. The 'organs' were desperately overworked and a good Communist like Stavsky was always glad to help them. He had even been careful in his choice of a rest home: it was not a place you could easily get out of in a hurry – twenty-five kilometers to the nearest station was no joke for a man with a weak heart.
>
> Before sending us to Samatika, Stavsky had received M. for the first time. This also we had taken as a good sign. But in fact Stavsky probably wanted to see M. only to make it easier for him to write his report – the sort of report always written on a man about to be arrested.[182]

On 2 August 1938, he was sentenced to a labour camp. On 9 September, the convoy of prisoners left Butyrki prison. He reached Vladivostok on 12 October. A last letter to his brother and wife was sent from there:

> My health is very bad, I'm extremely exhausted and thin, almost unrecognizable, but I don't know whether there's any sense in

sending clothes, food and money. You can try, all the same. I'm very cold without proper clothes.

My darling Nadia – are you alive, my dear? Shura, write to me at once about Nadia. This is a transit point. I've not been picked for Kolyma and may have to spend the winter here.[183]

He did not survive. The official date of death, 27 December 1938, has never been verified.

Political terror had continued throughout 1938. Postyshev was arrested in March or April, Eikhe on 29 April and Kossior soon followed. At the end of July, many senior Stalinists were shot.[184] Cultural repression was turned on the theatre. Already, stringent censorship had emptied the repertoire. Now particular producers came under direct attack.[185] Meyerhold's theatre was shut and he was arrested, and shot after extraordinary tortures, details of which have recently been revealed.[186] No trial was held.[187] Towards the end of 1938, Stalin called a halt. A number of other trials thought to be in preparation, including those of former diplomats, failed to be held, or were held *in camera*. On 8 December 1938, Yezhov was replaced by Beria as head of the NKVD.[188] There remained only Stalin's hypocritical denial of the whole procedure.

He solemnly assured the 18th Party Congress 'We shall have no further need to resort to the method of mass purges. Even so, the purge of 1933–36 (*sic*) was unavoidable and its results, in general, beneficial'. He condemned both anarchistic criticism of intellectuals (*makhaevshchina*) and specialist-baiting (*spetseydstvo*) and instead introduced his notion of the 'new Soviet intelligentsia'.[189] Amongst the writers, Sholokhov was prominent as a Congress speaker.[190] Indeed, the joyful new relationship between politics and literature had already been consummated.

An order of the Supreme Soviet on 31 January 1939 conferred state awards on favoured writers. Twenty-four Soviet writers were given the Order of Lenin (including Gladkov, V. Katayev, Pavlenko, Pogodin, Tikhonov, Fadeyev and Sholokhov). Forty-nine writers were given the Order of the Red Banner of Labour (recipients included Zoshchenko, Vsevolod Ivanov, Leonov, Panfyorov, Seyfullina, Tynyanov, Fedin, Shaginyan and Shklovsky). A lesser degree of distinction was conferred on 102 other writers.[191] By a cruel irony, the awards were announced on the day Mrs Mandelstam received the news of her husband's death.[192]

Mandelstam once divided literature into the parts written with and without permission. Even for the Stalin period described above, this seems too simple. All writers compromised, more or less: even he made an (unsuccessful) attempt to write an 'Ode to Stalin'. The categories need refinement into a series of sub-questions: the question was not of overt resistance, which could only be suicidal, but of the extent to which writers managed to preserve something of their personal integrity. Were individual writers able to retain sufficient distance for the horrors around them to think private thoughts, and thereby to incorporate the recognition of great evils into their own thinking? Was it possible for an element of moral autonomy to survive?

Some survival strategies were precluded. The emigration of Zamyatin in 1931 was a rarity, not a precedent, as Bulgakov discovered when he attempted to follow suit.[193] The protection of writers by politicians or policemen (even Yezhov, as Pil'nyak found on his arrest) was unstable and fleeting. Rather more promising were strategies which involved a change of genre. Here a range of possibilities were open. Some writers (such as Shklovsky) turned to the cinema, or (in the case of Bulgakov) to adapting novels for the stage. Forms of scholarship were also explored: editing or lexicography, or researching into 'safe' subjects, such as Gorky or Mayakovsky. There was always translation, with which Pasternak was heavily involved.[194] Other writers turned to children's literature, or from contemporary concerns to Aesopian or non-Aesopian historical novels. From this has arisen considerable discussion amongst commentators about the role of ambiguity in Bulgakov's *Molière*, Akhmatova's Pushkin studies, and even of Shklovsky's alleged strategy of 'mock surrender.[195] It is also noteworthy that a number of Soviet writers took Babel's advice at the Writers' Congress and added to the 'genre of silence'. It must be recognised that a far more common response, fully understandable in the desparate circumstances of the time, was conformity. Amongst numerous, terrible examples of the costs this imposed upon the writers concerned, perhaps one simple illustration will suffice. It comes from a letter addressed to Alexei Tolstoy, some months after his election to the Supreme Soviet in December 1937. An architect wrote about the arrest of his brother, sentenced to eight years' hard labour, leaving behind three children under ten:

> I know you can't do anything to help me. You receive hundreds of letters like mine. I'm not asking you about my brother, I have

something else in mind. You are writing a biography of the great man, mention the name of the person who didn't tell him about the horrors of 100 per cent collectivization. Such a man must have existed. Isn't there any protection from careerists, bootlickers and cowards who cash in on every slogan – yesterday on collectivization, today on vigilance – who lump honest people together with Trotskyites, mercenary plenipotentiaries, poisoners and murderers. Are you deputies only meant to shout hurray to Stalin and applaud Yezhov?

It's not for nothing that Feuchtwanger so bitterly ridiculed you with the Rembrandt exhibition, and Stalin himself on that occasion described you very aptly. Give this letter to Stalin. Don't be afraid. I'm not crazy. I am a living person with family and a job that I like. I am neither a careerist nor a lickspittle . . . A coward? Maybe, but not more than others. But for me now the feeling of truth is stronger than the fear of 10 years in a camp.[196]

There was not total conformity, however, even in this terrible period. A handful of writers were still able to consider posterity, either writing for the drawer, or retaining an undercurrent of nonconformity akin to the counter-culture in the concentration camps.[197] The recent publication of three women writers may serve to establish this point. In her Preface to *Rekviem* (1935–40), Akhmatova consciously evokes the role of witness to the *Yezhovshchina*:

In the terrible years of the Yezhov terror I spent seventeen months waiting in line outside the prison in Leningrad. One day somebody in the crowd identified me. Standing behind me was a woman, with lips blue from the cold, who had, of course, never heard me called by name before. Now she started out of the torpor common to us all and asked me in a whisper (everyone whispered there):
'Can you describe this?'
And I said: 'I can.'
Then something like a smile passed fleetingly over what had once been her face.[198]

This was published in the Soviet Union for the first time by *Oktyabr'* in March 1987.[199] Likewise, her friend and biographer, Lydiya Chukovskaya, wrote a novella, *Sof'ya Petrovna*, in 1939–40. During the Khrushchev thaw, when submitting the manuscript for publication, she explained 'In content it was a protest against the mass repression of Soviet citizens that occurred in 1937–8'.[200] Finally, Ol'ga Berq-qol'ts, whose first husband Boris Kornilov had been arrested in 1936 and shot as an 'enemy of the people', was herself arrested in December 1938. Although soon released, she remained faithful to those who suffered the ordeal in full. In 1955, as survivors of the *GULag* were being released after 'seventeen years – always seventeen years', she wrote of those returning 'from the bottom of the sea, from the canals':

Should you, then, suddenly, somehow
Stumble over these lines
Written in contorted pain, as if
A dead circle left around the fire,

Should our scorching legend
Reach you now if only as cold smoke,
Well, then, honour us with silence
As we keep silent in front of you.[201]

The purpose of this study was not to make moral judgements about the conduct of individuals. It is hardly the place of outsiders to presume to do so. Rather, we should simply conclude with Max Hayward: 'The majority of writers have acquitted themselves with honour in a situation which required more courage, patience, intelligence and fortitude than could ever be imagined by people who live in more fortunate circumstances. One day it will perhaps be shown that not only Russia, but the whole world, is indebted to Soviet literature for keeping alive, in unimaginable conditions, that indefinable sense of freedom which is common to all men'.[202]

8 Stalinism in Literature

> Unanimity did not fall from the skies. It was eagerly created by
> thousands of supporters.
>
> Nadezhda Mandelstam[1]

'Stalinism in literature' has been described in three stages. The first
and most dynamic lasted from 1929 to 1932 while the country was
transformed by revolution from above. In this short space, proletarian writers managed by skilful manoeuvring to establish an institutional hegemony. Their harassment and persecution of the literary
intelligentsia brought fellow-travelling to an end. That done, they
found themselves rejected as anachronistic by an ungrateful Party
leadership. Thereafter, the technique of class warfare was abandoned, coercion was much reduced and former fellow-travellers were
rehabilitated, but on new terms. At the second stage, inaugurated in
1932, fresh principles were laid down for treatment of the literary
intelligentsia. It was recognised that their special skills and abilities
could only be secured for the state by granting them special status
and rewards as in early NEP. Now, though, such expertise could only
be contained within a rigid framework. They were obliged to become
'Soviet writers', organised in a single Union and equipped with a
compulsory orthodoxy: socialist realism. Its introduction was prefaced by a wide-ranging debate on theoretical issues promoted by
Gorky and Bukharin. Under their non-exclusive auspices a wide
variety of opinion was tolerated within a broadly-defined notion of
socialist realism. The climax of their campaign for quality was the
First Writers' Congress. Afterwards, diversity was rapidly eliminated.

In a third stage, from the winter of 1935, Stalin assumed a major
role as cultural leader. His *ex cathedra* statements severely restricted
the limits of permissible debate. The anti-formalist campaign served
notice that writers and artists must conform to state-sponsored for
mulae and institutions. Gorky was pushed aside. Following his death
the literary intelligentsia felt the full force of terror and destruction
Subsequent stages of Stalinism lie beyond the scope of this book.[2]
However, it is possible to identify continuities during the pre-war
period sufficient to warrant the 'Stalinist' appellation. This conclud
ing chapter offers an account of Stalinism in literature which sum

marises and extends the evidence presented above in a more analytical form.

INSTITUTIONS

The first authoritative prospectus of Bolshevik policies, the *ABC of Communism* (1919), devoted much space to education which was given precedence over sections on agriculture and industry, but made no mention of literature beyond a passing reference to the need to reassemble private libraries in public collections.[3] Although written in haste and in crisis – at the height of the Civil War – this omission might seem surprising. The author of the cultural sections was Bukharin, later a prominent advocate of pluralism in literature and the arts. Yet the absence of a firm statement on this subject was not an oversight. It reflected the fact that, like so much in the new state, Soviet policy towards literature would have to be improvised.

In the early years after the Revolution, institutional supervision of the arts was left to the government through *Narkompros*. The distinction between Party and government was a real one. As Commissar, Lunacharsky always insisted that while the Party reserved the right to intervene on one side or another in high cultural debates, the state must stay neutral between competing views.[4] The state's cultural functions were conducted by 'chief administrative organs' overseeing higher education, political education and science; an 'academic centre' with powers to direct 'theoretical, scientific and aesthetic work' in an overall policy-making sense but without executive authority, and finally an 'organisational centre' in charge of finance, supply and inter-departmental matters.[5] Those initially employed in government administration of the arts included the Symbolist V. Bryusov, the proletarian writer A. Serafimovich and very briefly Mayakovsky. But the Arts Sector of *Narkompros* did not survive the reorganisation of the whole Commissariat at the end of the Civil War. Lenin had proposed it be retained. He told Lunacharsky that *Narkompros* should 'leave the Arts Sector as a single section, appointing "politicians" from amongst Communist Party members . . . in all leading aspects of this sector'. However, when this idea was put to a Party meeting, only members of the pre-existing sector supported the proposal. They called for a separate Department, or at least a Chief Directorate of the Arts (*Glaviskusstvo*), but no-one else agreed. The meeting merely accepted the need for a *Glavkom* within the 'academic' centre, whose functions were left undefined.[6] This body led a shadowy existence until 1928, when a *Glaviskusstvo* was belatedly created.[7] By this time, 'governmental passivity' towards arts policy was under fatal attack from Party members.

The Party's role in literary policy developed slowly. At first it followed Trotsky's line that the sphere of literature was not one in which the Party was called upon to command. The rubric of Party institutions was narrowly defined. Supervision of journals and publishing lay with the Press Department of the Central Committee, initially headed by the proletarian writer I. Vardin, and Vareikis who chaired the 1924 debate on literature. The Old Bolshevik S. I. Gusev took over in 1926, and was subsequently described by Trotsky as Molotov's right-hand man in cultural repression.[8] A second Central Committee Department, *Agit-prop*, was principally concerned with the Party schools and enrollment of Party members in tertiary education.[9] Its heads were Knorin and Krinitsky, with Kerzhentzev as Deputy. From mid-1930 it was headed by Postyshev. In the same year, however, the Central Committee set up a *Kul't-prop* Department,[10] under which the Party's control over literary groups rapidly increased. At once, the officials of RAPP, while jealously determined to assert their own political independence, were required to send in regular and detailed reports of its activities.[11] *Kul't-prop* exercised wide powers over literary appointments. For instance, the RAPP activist Sutyrin was transferred to the editorship of *Na kino postu* and the critic Makar'yev posted to party work in Rostov-on-Don in the spring of 1930.[12] These measures, accompanied by the banishment of Averbakh to Smolensk 'for political mistakes', considerably depleted RAPP's leadership. At first, appeals were of no avail. Sutyrin's posting was confirmed by the Central Committee's *Orgburo*. The Party Secretariat remained deaf to RAPP's protestations. Eventually they relented: an instruction reassigned Averbakh for 'leading work' in the 'party fraction' of RAPP from August 1930.[13]

The functions of *Kul't-prop* were further elaborated in a statute of January 1932. This set up twelve sections:

1. The Party textbooks and political education
2. The teaching of Leninism in higher and secondary schools
3. Mass propaganda of Leninism and Party policy
4. National education and overseeing *Narkompros*
5. Scientific research institutions
6. Production-technical propaganda

7. Cultural provisions for factories and *kolkhozes*
8. Newspapers
9. Journals
10. Scientific literature
11. Creative literature (*belles-lettres*)
12. Art (theatres, cinemas etc.)[14]

The increased rubric indicated the enlarged scope of its activities including the new section for literature under Sergei Dinamov and a diminution of those of *Narkompros*, which was now explicitly subordinated. A further rationalisation of its structure took place in 1935 when *Kul't-prop* was then rearranged into five departments:

1. Party Propaganda and Agitation
   - inner Party work (higher schools)
   - mass agitation
2. Press and Publishing
3. Schools
4. Cultural-Enlightening work
   - libraries and clubs
   - cultural work in the countryside
   - cinema, radio and drama
   - the organisations of writers, artists, architects etc.
5. Science and Technology.[15]

Here was the real locus of institutional control over literature through Department 4 under Shcherbakov, whose duties included supervision of the Writers' Union.

While *Kul't-prop* was an extension of Party institutions previously in existence, the Writers' Union was an institution of an entirely new type. It arose from the most fundamental cultural edict from the Stalin period: the Central Committee Resolution of April 1932. This abolished all existing literary and artistic organisations and ordered the establishment of new, monopolistic associations.[16] The pace of enactment varied. Thus the Union of Composers and the Union of Architects were both set up in 1932. The formation of the Writers' Union was achieved by mid-1934 after surmounting the many difficulties we have documented in this book. The Union of Cinematographers and the Union of Artists were not formed until 1957.

Membership was not confined to Party writers. Although the inaugural Congress had claimed an absolute majority of Party delegates, by including those who had candidate status in the Party or membership of Komsomol,[17] Party members numbered only one-third of the new Union. The limitation may be accounted for in two main ways. First, there was an emphasis on professional qualifications: whereas RAPP had claimed 4,000 members in its heyday,[18] the Writers' Union was restricted to 2,000. 1,500 of the original applicants were refused as 'not coming up to the requirements demanded in the Statutes'. It was explained that rejection did not arise 'from malice on the part of the interviewing commission': refusal meant simply that an applicant should work hard to raise his or her qualifications.[19] To this end, the adoption of members with 'candidate status' was agreed in an amendment to the Statutes.[20]

A second and more substantial reason was that the Party simply lacked sufficient cadres to obtain an overall majority. The bulk of established writers were not Party members. Two-thirds of the Moscow members had been professionally engaged in literature at least since the Civil War,[21] and had had experience of earlier literary associations. Most had to be brought into the Union, if Soviet literature was to be worthy of the name. When the Writers' Union was given a governing board (*pravlenye*), those elected at the first Plenum – by acclamation – had wide appeal. Gorky's name, which headed the list, was greeted with an ovation. Thereafter came 100 other writers, including many prominent figures: Ehrenburg, Pasternak and Pil'nyak were included. The presence of Pogodin and Vishnevsky, Afinogenov and Kirshon, allowed a wide spectrum of opinion on dramaturgy.[22] Babel, Olesha and V. Katayev were added to the review commission of the Union. These appointments appeared to further the spirit of reconciliation between Party and non-Party writers. Indeed, this pattern was reflected in intellectual and cultural life as a whole. The Party did not attempt political 'saturation' overnight by appointing an overwhelming number of its own ranks. Even social science graduates included only 35 per cent of Party members by the end of the 1930s. All other subjects had a lower proportion of Party members, and in the lowest – art and medicine – Communist graduates numbered only about one in ten.[23]

While Union membership and the governing board were widely inclusive, the real locus of authority was narrowly defined. From the outset the Party pursued the policy of maintaining formally broad institutions while controlling them from within. We must distinguish between the 'dignified' bodies, such as the *pravlenye* and the 'efficient' bodies through which the Party ensured its leadership of literature.

These included its Secretariat, for day-to-day administration, consisting of four Party members, Shcherbakov, Stavsky, the Ukranian writer Kulik, and G. Lakhuti, and a single non-Communist, Vsevolod Ivanov,[24] and its Praesidium, to which general issues were normally referred. The Praesidium also supervised plenary sessions, preceding them by intensive rehearsals, even surpassing those before the Writers' Congress. For instance, the Praesidium told Gorky in a letter of 19 November 1934 of its outline for a Second Plenum, adding that 'the Central Committee of the Party has approved this agenda'.[25] The main subject to be discussed was literary criticism. The Praesidium considered it 'imperative' that Gorky deliver a major speech. He declined but did suggest changes in some of those that were to be given.[26] The Praesidium itself reviewed the main speeches prior to delivery, thus ensuring they would present an approved position. Many corrections were called for to sharpen 'cowardly' or 'diplomatic' critics who were thought too mild in their reviews. When Pasternak tried to defend the principle of moderation, he was upbraided for an 'abstract notion' of honesty in criticism.[27] This degree of supervision did not encourage non-Party participation. Many rank-and-file writers recognised this tacitly: public meetings called to discuss the Plenum were sparsely attended. At one, many promptings from the chair were unavailing. Those present preserved an 'obstinate silence'.[28] The meeting adjourned after a fruitless two hours.

Plenary sessions were equally vacuous. Reports delivered by Union officials had a purely formal character and the subjects under discussion had little to do with contemporary literary administration.[29] The latter was done by fiat. Thus at the conclusion of his speech to the Second Plenum, Shcherbakov commented:

'Now about the Plan. The Plan was distributed. There was time to read it through. I propose that if there are no objections in principle that the Plan be confirmed. Any corrections, additions or improvements may be given to the Praesidium for its consideration in editing the final version' (*applause*) *President*: 'Are there any objections to Comrade Shcherbakov's proposal on the Plan?'(*no objections*) (Interval announced).[30]

The real locus of authority was the Party group of writers within the Union. Its inner workings were rarely published but there are scanty references in the literary press and journals to Party group meetings, though without details of who took part.[31]

To regard the Writers' Union as a political institution and hence susceptible to analysis along lines that would be used in the study of the Party may appear misleading. The Union was a corporate entity separate from the Party (although overseen by the Central Committee's *Kul't-prop*) and a majority of its rank-and-file were not party members, yet the analogy is compelling. As with the Party, the Union contained only a single channel of communication, from the top downwards; there was no provision for a two-way flow of information, initiative or ideas. Popular involvement in the Union's activities, as shown in early 1936, was restricted to obligatory participation in mass campaigns. Their main purpose was to express unanimous approval for policy statements emanating from above. In their political style, the leadership of the Union also emulated the Party. As Fadeyev conceded after the Second Writers' Congress (in 1954), 'over the past twenty years, the collective principle has not always been observed'. 'Too much power' had been concentrated in the hands of 'individual leaders' whereas most writers would have preferred 'a relatively broad Praesidium, with full authority to settle Union matters between plenary sessions of the governing body'.[32] No such admission was made in Stalin's lifetime.

Alongside these formal institutions, Stalinism offered substantial rewards for the production of the required literature of socialist construction. Other, negative, instruments came to constitute an increasingly formalised system of sanctions for nonconformity. While recognising that in their practical workings these methods served a single end, it may be useful to consider each in turn.

Positive inducements and rewards were channeled through *Litfond* (the literary fund) of the Writers' Union. This provided grants, travelling scholarships, study, recreational and holiday facilities. Although first announced in July 1934,[33] no members were admitted for twelve months. One cause of delay was the difficulty of finding writers to head its 'governing body'. In November 1934, Vsevolod Ivanov was adopted as first president, with Slonimsky as President of the Leningrad branch, thus placing non-Party figures at the head of this 'material-welfare' administration. V. Ivanov appears to have accepted the appointment with misgivings. He tendered his resignation in early 1936, with the approval of Gorky, but agreed to stay on pending the appointment of a new president. One wonders whether the reason he gave, of not wishing to be burdened by administrative duties, was the full story.[34] At the end of 1935, a plenum of *Litfond* criticised the 'inadequate control' of the central organ over its subordinate bodies. It suggested that funds were being misused, called for an independent auditing and for bringing the responsible officials to account.[35] Such charges were extended in August 1936 when it was suggested that funds of the Novosibirsk branch had been misappropriated to finance a 'terrorist centre'. The Praesidium of the Writers' Union then noted that the conduct of *Litfond* raised important issues of 'writers' ethics'. Some writers were boasting about the size of their stipendia: even more shocking was the fact that some members managed to make five trips annually to the Crimea, all at the expense of *Litfond*.[36] The system of financial and other privileges that developed under the Writers' Union was described in detail by a non-beneficiary: Bulgakov's account of MASSOLIT hardly appears to be a caricature.[37]

A state system of awards, honours, distinctions and prizes was elaborated for writers and artists who enjoyed the special favour of the political authorities. In 1936 the title 'National Artist' was created and first awarded to figures from the theatrical community: Stanislavsky, Nemirovich-Danchenko and the actor Shchukin.[38] The Stalin Prize for literature was instituted later. Prominent writers combined literary and state offices. Some were deputies to the Supreme Soviet. Sholokhov even joined the Central Committee.[39] Such a system of positive rewards made explicit the connection between service to literature and to the Stalinist state.

Negative instruments for the control of literature were greatly extended during the 1930s, above all the censorship. The apparatus of censorship had ancient rank, dating at least from Catherine the Great's time. Much nineteenth-century literature was written in defiance of the Tsarist censors, several of whom left illuminating memoirs.[40] Indeed, one team of censors decided to pass *Das Kapital* for publication in Russia on the not implausible grounds that 'few will read it, fewer still will understand it'. It did not take long before the Revolution restored this instrument of the *ancien régime*. Literary censorship, *Glavlit*, was codified in 1922, and that of the performing arts, *Glavrepertkom*, received its statute the following year. These charters were elaborated in the early 1930s. Both documents officially proclaimed the purpose of censorship to prohibit:

1. Agitation and Propaganda against Soviet power and the dictatorship of the proletariat

2. Revelation of State Secrets
3. Fomenting of national and religious fanaticism
4. Pornography.[41]

The statute of *Glavrepertkom* added further prohibitions, of mysticism and various 'anti-artistic' tendencies. It covered spectacles of 'all types: theatre, music, screen, cinema, gramophone recordings, art, radio and others'.[42] Yet another, by *Narkompros*, the Commissariat of Justice and the OGPU of February 1934, confirmed the previous documents.[43]

In practise, censorship took several forms. The formal institutions set out above were supplemented in three main ways. First *Litkontrol* OGPU/NKVD provided secret police surveillance and supervision both of writers and of officials employed in *Glavlit* and *Kul't-prop*.[44] This top-secret mode of double-checking shows the intricacy of Stalinist institutions. A second source of censorship, by Stalin personally, is somewhat better documented. We have the testimony of Leonov, who possessed the manuscript of his *Russian Forest* with Stalin's corrections in red pencil.[45] There is also the extraordinary case of a work by Afinogenov which came to Stalin's attention.

In the spring of 1933, Afinogenov finished the first 'variant' of his play *Lozh'* (*The Lie*) and sent it to Gorky. A covering letter explained the play was written 'in response to many, many questions in my life as a writer' and to the many thoughts, doubts and 'undecided issues' that were then being turned over in his mind. The central doubt, as the title of the play made clear was the 'collision of truth and lies' in the contemporary reality.[46] The main charater, Nina, is struck by the 'contradiction between word and deed' in the conduct of the other characters in the play: all of whom with one exception, were party members. This theme was hardly designed to endear the author to Stalin, who is supposed to have written many exclamations in the margin of the manuscript, and to have dismissed the play as 'Dismal and tedious. Gibberish'. Gorky's reply suggested that *The Lie's* fault lay in its content. In his view, such a theme could be presented only to 'a few thousand literate socialists', and could never be shown to an audience in which there were 'not socialists but the bitches' children of the past, in exile from the shambles of their bourgeois life'.[47] Whether Gorky was correct in this opinion need not be considered here: having accepted some of his recommendations including the excision of the monologue by Nina, in which she spoke about her doubts, Afinogenov sent the manuscript to Stalin. Meantime, the play went into rehearsal at no less than 300 Soviet theatres, in Moscow and across the Union Republics.

It would seem that Afinogenov's request for Stalin's opinion was not only in recognition of the obvious fact that the play raised sensitive issues of party life and the desirability of communicating them to wider audiences. There may also have been the thought that, in his reply, Stalin would assist the playwright to overcome certain of his own 'doubts and indecisions'. But Stalin subjected the play to annihilating criticism which can only have confirmed Afinogenov's forebodings. To analyze the first and second variants of this play – as Karaganov has done – is to see

> the hundreds of changes that Stalin recommended ignored the central issue raised by Afinogenov's play. Subjecting the play itself to extensive criticism and blame, Stalin introduced new cues, proposed the introduction of 'unmasking' episodes, changed one character with another, and even proposed to alter the language of the heroine.[48]

The meaning of all these corrections and substitutions is not in doubt: any attempt by writers to treat the genuine doubts of a character such as Nina was inadmissible. Any attempt at serious psychological portrayal would be met by administrative reaction. In so doing, he pronounced his verdict not on one play alone but on the permissible course for the whole of Soviet literature. For, by 1933, the personal opinions of Stalin were already beginning to take a determining influence on the course of literary life and criticism: laying down directives, making aesthetic judgements, pontificating on theoretical aspects, and using the party cultural apparatus at his disposal for making indisputable assessments as to the value of this or that work. As Karaganov comments: 'in this period when the position of capitalist elements in town and countryside was destroyed, once and for all, Stalin put forward his lying (*lozhnii*) and ominous thesis about the strengthening and aggravation of class struggle as socialism approaches'. 'Stalin's approach to the play *Lozh*' was closely connected with this thesis'.[49]

On reading the second variant which was duly supplied, Stalin gave an entirely negative evaluation – without further explanation. As Afinogenov noted, 'the play was dead, nothing can be begun again'.[50] It was taken out of rehearsal in every Soviet theatre except one. The Theatre of Russian Drama in Kharkov staged the premiere of

Afinogenov's play, with a programme note supplied by the author.

The final category is self-censorship.[51] Both the formal institutions, and intermittent intervention by Stalin, helped to produce an atmosphere of conformity which was bound to influence a writer even before he began to put pen to paper. Lest he forget, there were those on hand to remind him. While the editorial staff in publishing houses and journals, for instance, had only low Party rank, they were nonetheless of great importance in 'translating' the instructions and directives from above. As one contemporary has noted, though an editor was 'only the humble channel by which instructions were handed down, he [served] as mentor, judge and final authority'. In the first place orders to be fulfilled by writers were 'passed down from unimaginable heights in the form of suggestions and recommendations of the most general nature, eventually reaching those for whom they were intended via an army of editors'.[52] Such supervision took place while writers were still casting around for a legitimate subject. Once they had produced their draft, a second stage began: the 'editorial processing of the completed order, the organisation of a low-level debate about the published work, followed by new recommendations this time more specific and taking account of "errors" and "achievements".'[53] Both writer and editor were also highly dependent upon any change of instruction or personnel above. In such a situation they could only err on the side of caution and avoid all controversial material.

From this brief survey of the Central Committee's *Kul't-prop*, the censorship and the Writers' Union, it can be seen that the Party developed a plenitude of instruments for the imposition of 'Stalinism in literature'. Institutional regulation of Soviet *belles-lettres* was well in hand before the terror was turned on writers themselves.

IDEAS

The precise relationship between Soviet writers and their rulers was never a simple one, and cannot be reduced even for the Stalin years to the desire of the latter to exercise 'political control'. Political control was exercised but we need to know how and to what extent, and we also need to know for what purpose. This leads us into a wider set of questions concerning the Party's intentions for society and the means by which they intended the writers to influence the public.

At its broadest, the general purpose of Stalinist literary policy was to create a new literature serving the Soviet state. In this it broke radically with the expectations of the 1920s. Then, significant cultural and social pluralism existed within the Party's political monopoly. Accordingly, the intelligentsia enjoyed sufficient space in which to explore ideas that had not been previously approved 'from above'. A forward-looking and critical element within their ranks provided many ideas, and sometimes whole disciplines, whose implications are still far from exhausted in our day. They could, moreover, have contributed greatly to the Soviet Union's industrialisation drive. Economists, for instance, had advanced many valuable insights into planning and provided a rich debate between 'genetic' and 'teleological' development.[54] Social theorists were in a position to analyse the impact of industrial and urban development, and calculate the consequences of rapid social mobility.[55] Not the least useful could have been a political sociology of Stalinism, first sketched out by Bukharin, which could have helped to explain the rapid growth of bureaucracy and reduce the bewilderment of many Old Bolsheviks who found that they were constructing nothing less than a 'new Leviathan'.[56] Instead, independent centres of thought were rapidly eliminated and it was left to a handful of historians to hint, in Aesopian language, that this was happening.[57]

Natural science was subordinated to practical activity. From 1929, the statutes of the Academy of Sciences made statements about the need to redirect research towards the policies of socialist construction. Industrial goals began to loom large on its agendas, symbolised by its transference to the jurisdiction of the Council of the National Economy. New Institutes were founded for Chemistry and Biology (1934), Physics (1935) and Geophysics (1937). The number of scientific researchers trebled and new scientific centres were opened across the whole country. Looking back in a report of March 1936, Krzhizhanovsky stated that work had been undertaken on such national priorities as electrification, prospecting for minerals and natural gas, motor fuels and automisation.[58] Indeed, scientific activity was given full coverage in the press and journals of the mid-1930s. Heroic accounts of Promethean assaults upon the forces (and sometimes laws) of nature made daily headlines. Soviet expeditions traversed the Arctic, intrepid minerologists explored the frozen north or west, fearless aviators crossed the pole or Siberia. Two pilots even took on the stratosphere in a spectacular ascent timed to coincide with the Seventeenth Party Congress. When the news came that they had

perished, at record heights, the proceedings were halted while delegates trooped out for a memorial meeting in Red Square.[59] Naive
though some of these brave pioneers may seem, they caught the
mood of early Stalinist Russia: that there was nothing that will-power
could not achieve. In such an atmosphere, any obstacle to scientific
or applied research was liable to be rejected as 'subjectivism' and
those who pointed to objective difficulties were accused of defeatism,
Menshevism or even wrecking.

At the outset of the industrialisation drive, many writers took on
new tasks with genuine enthusiasm. The social realism of the nineteenth century, concerned with underprivileged classes in society,
took on a new complexion of socialist realism, dedicated to the
purposes of the state. An open political commitment was now required, but was legitimised by the claim that this would simultaneously help writers overcome their previously incurable
individualism and drew closer to 'the people'. Literature must now be
tendentious, Zhdanov declared, and carry out social functions. In
order to do so, writers had to become partners with the state,
performing tasks which the Party itself, a vanguard leadership, pre-
scribed for society as a whole. A classic response was that of Il'in, whose
Great Conveyor (1934) described the younger generation of Stalinist
workers devoting themselves to the 'mastering of technique', a major
goal of the second Five Year Plan. The text included Stalin's speech of
February 1931[60] on the mastering of technology almost verbatim.
Indeed, Il'in presents Stalin's audience as captivated by the logic of
his arguments, which offered them brilliant answers to hitherto
unresolved questions. The speech is taken by every participant in the
hall as a personal instruction. According to the author this proved the
profound and unshakeable connection between the Party leadership
and the rank-and-file.

Parallel ideas upon upbringing and the importance of discipline
were advanced by another curious character of the mid-thirties,
Nikolai Ostrovsky. He, too, put his pedagogical precepts into semi-
fictionalised form; entitled *How the Steel was Tempered*, serialised
from 1932 to 1934.[61] Its leading character, Pavel Korchagin, is perhaps the first personality in Soviet literature to be portrayed in
complete conformity with society. He displays unshakeable confidence in the Soviet system with the Party as an organised embodiment of society's ideals. The story shows several stages of his life: as a
peasant making his career in the Civil War, as a Komsomol organiser, and amongst the incurably ill. At each stage, his behaviour is

exemplary: disciplined, moral, absolutely disinterested, courageous, hardworking. He is principled in making his decisions and steadfast once they are taken. Encouraged by the success of his 'novel' – which appeared in sixty-two reprintings in his lifetime – Ostrovsky began a sequel. Its portrayal of revolutionary struggle and Ukrainian revolt against the Polish gentry and PPS nationalists, provides an equally oversimplified account of total virtue overcoming utter darkness. It remained mercifully unfinished.

Ostrovsky himself had been seriously wounded in the Russo-Polish war of 1920 at the age of sixteen, and became completely paralysed in 1926. Blindness followed, yet he overcame all his physical handicaps to become an author.[62] The last months of his life were truly heroic. On 1 October 1935 he was awarded the Order of Lenin. His note of thanks addressed Stalin as 'Leader and teacher, dearest to me of all men'.[63] In December he arrived in Moscow and was carried from the train via a special ambulance to 40 Gorky Street, from which he made contact with the Writers' Union. *Izvestiya* carried his piece, 'My Happiest Years' on New Year's Day 1936.[64] During the tenth Komsomol conference (April 1936) his hospital room was connected by direct lines to the conference hall in the Kremlin. He joined in the singing and planned a speech, which was not delivered, on the duty of writers to portray 'new feelings'. This contained his political testament: 'the training of courage and valour, a selfless devotion to the Revolution and hatred for the enemy: such are our laws'. He also offered literary advice reminiscent of Stalin's:

> Let there be fewer books if need be, but the books must be good. There is no room on our bookshelves for the mediocre. No-one has the right to steal time, to steal honest workers' hours of leisure. Our reader has become a severe and merciless critic. Let none dare to try to feed him chaff.[65]

His funeral, which followed shortly afterwards, was a national event.

The Soviet authorities had hoped that Ostrovsky's example would inspire a literature of socialist realism. Its failure to materialise caused some embarrassment. Reporting to the 1935 Plenum of the Writers' Union, V. Ivanov complained that many writers had reneged on their commitment to prepare literary works in celebration of socialist construction. In particular, their willingness to write collectively had flagged: 'despite numerous declarations and undertakings' their response had been 'completely inadequate'.[66] Later in the year, Shcherbakov raised the same question at a widened session of the Presidium. He contrasted the impetus given by the 1932 Resolution, which was followed by important new works from Gorky, Sholokhov and Panfyorov, and the lack of major writing since the First Congress. He bravely referred to the period as 'a pause for growth'.[67] It transpired, however, that literature was fundamentally unsuited as a vehicle for such purposes as economic exhortation, the propagation of technical knowledge, pedagogic or didactic principles. Such tracts lacked the elements of suspense or tension, conflict, and development of plot which are essential to retaining the reader's interest. The theory of socialist realism, with its tendentiousness and positive heroes, proved in practice unworkable. Instead, as political demands became more strident, and the onset of the purges made any attempt at experiment or deviation foolhardy, Soviet writers sought refuge in 'safe' models. Gorky was an obvious example.

Even though written before the Revolution by a non-Party member, Gorky's *Mother* (1906) came to be regarded as an exemplar of socialist realism. It shows the evolution of a god-fearing, illiterate peasant into an intrepid revolutionary. Yet even this first model contained strong 'Menshevik' understones, such as the admonition that social backwardness could endanger the success of a political revolution and an awareness – later made explicit by Trotsky in *The Culture of Everyday Life* – that the new socialist state needed to provide secular rituals if it was to substitute for religion. Many re-writings were found necessary before the novel passed into the socialist realist genre. The critic Bespalov, writing for the *Literary Encyclopedia* in 1929 was still able to protest that the main character, Pavel, was presented 'schematically and somewhat bookishly'.[68] Gorky himself regarded the work as rather poor and ephemeral.[69] Nevertheless for all its shortcomings, Gorky's *Mother* was retrospectively adopted as the founding novel in the canon of socialist realism. It became a paradigm: the essentials of the plot were repeated innumerable times.[70]

The retrospective canon was soon enlarged to overcome the absence of new writings. Their common feature was an absolute conviction of the outcome of the historical process – the victory of socialism – though the manner of its presentation offered great variety. The chosen battleground could be local (in a farm or factory), national (the Civil War) or even cosmic, such as A. Tolstoy's *Aelita* (set on Mars), a rare example of socialist realist science fiction. Amongst the earliest works to be accepted as canonical was *Chapayev* by Dmitri

Furmanov, published in 1923 and later made into a successful film. Indeed, Stalin was devoted to the screen version and once called in Dovzhenko to tell him '*Chapayev*: that's how you should make films'.[71] The original story shows an archetypical positive hero, the Red Army commander in the Civil War, who learns his politics the hard way in conflict with the elemental forces of nature and Russian backwardness. Gorky was enamoured of the work, while warning the author tactfully that 'the historical and ideological merit of the work exceeds its artistic significance'.[72] Lunacharsky wrote a preface to the revised 1925 edition. There followed other stories on almost identical themes, such as Gladkov's *Cement* (1925), in which a Civil War veteran returns home to employ his military experience on the 'economic front' and Fadeyev's *The Rout* (1927), in which Red partisans fight the Whites and Japanese in the Far East. All three novels show the heroism of selflessly dedicated commanders fighting for socialism against long odds. In the case of *The Rout*, as of *Mother*, while the underlying message is one of optimism, the actual outcome is defeat.

To these founding novels of socialist realism, all written long before the doctrine itself was formulated, were added the works of selected fellow-travellers. None of them was adopted in their entirety. Leonov's *Sot'* and *Skutarevsky* were accepted but his *Thief* was excluded; Ehrenburg's *Second Day* entered the canon, while his earlier work did not. Fadeyev's *Young Guard* was re-written at intervals to accord with current demands. Much of Sholokhov's work was included, as was Valentin Katayev's *Time, Forward!* As this list[73] shows, social origin was not in itself grounds for inclusion, though the preponderance of writers from the intelligentsia, and indeed of non-Party members, made itself felt. We should also note, with Rufus Mathewson, the important role of the radical democrats in the founding canon of socialist realism. He notes that ' it was not until after 1932 that the pre-revolutionary critics rose to a position of influence on a level with Marx and Engels. By 1946, they seemed to have gained absolute ascendancy'.[74] Then, Zhdanov asserted that 'the finest aspect of Soviet literature is its continuation in the best traditions of nineteenth-century Russian literature, traditions established by our great revolutionary democrats; Belinsky, Dobrolyubov, Chernyshevsky and Saltykov-Shchedrin'. All these had been 'spokesmen of art for the people, demanding that art should have a worthy educational and social significance'. Zhdanov named these radical democrats nineteen times; Lenin and Stalin received seven and six references respectively. His report did not mention Marx or Engels at all.[75]

The failure of socialist realism to inspire a lively literature of socialism was not admitted in Stalin's lifetime. Rather, publishers relied upon reprints of established classics, or their current variants and a vast output of feeble imitations. Some of the middle-brow literature that reached the reading public in the post-war Stalin period has been analysed by Vera Dunham. She shows how the unadventurous and hackneyed quality of this writing found wide resonance amongst the new elite.[76] At the same time, the public appetite for western and escapist literature continued unabated. Perhaps in recognition of the failure of doctrine, its revision was debated at the Second Writers' Congress (1954). The statute of 1934 had stated:

> Socialist realism, the basic method of Soviet literature and literary criticism, demands of the artist truthful, historically concrete representation of reality in its revolutionary development. At the same time, truthfulness and historical concreteness of artistic representation of reality must be combined with the task of ideologically remoulding and training working people in the spirit of socialism.[77]

After discussion, the second sentence was deleted as redundant. Harold Swayze regards this as evidence of 'the trend toward a less dogmatic application of Zhdanovist doctrines'.[78] However, it was a generation later before the doctrine itself was abandoned.

INDIVIDUALS

Both the totalitarian thesis and the notion of the 'cult of the individual' imply that cultural policy came from Stalin and the upper echelons of the party leadership; it was passed down through a network of subordinate political and cultural institutions, in the form of both general and specific directives, and finally reached those for whom it was intended: the writers and artists themselves. The major corollary is that lower individuals, whether of the party or of the cultural unions, did not participate in policy formation.

The degree of correspondence of this model with many of the known cases of Stalin's activity in culture is striking. The abolition of

RAPP, for instance, took not only the proletarians themselves but the whole literary intelligentsia by surprise, and seemed to typify the mode of sudden, unexpected interventionism. It is the hallmark of the 'cult of the individual', and of 'totalitarian' leadership to act apparently without consultation, regard for precedent or any pre-existing platform or ideas. There are other cases in which arbitrariness is combined with ambiguity, calculated to bewilder or atomize the intelligentsia. The 'Letter to the Editors of *Proletarskaya revolyutsiya*' was clearly such a case. On this occasion, Stalin's intervention over a minor matter of historical interpretation was likely to cause confusion and argument over the 'party line', as ' conclusions' were extrapolated from Stalin's letter and applied to historiography, the social sciences and other areas of the ideological 'front'.

A major feature of Stalin's literary interventions is this suddeness, a failure to consult. Such interventions often came over the heads of existing 'authorities' and outside the 'normal channels' of policy transmission. Their style is unpredictable and sinister, characteristic of autocratic leadership. They are also, throughout the Stalin period, hasty, slipshod and careless in their formulation. It is only necessary to compare the months of drafting and re-formulation that preceded the Resolution of 1925 with the abrupt and cryptic decree of 1932, to see the decline in the quality of party leadership after Stalin's ascendancy. But the signalling of political intentions in a highly-simplified form, almost as a cypher or code to be translated by others, meant necessarily that great onus was left with the 'interpreter'. To a limited extent this had been the case in the 1920s, when proletarian writers tried – and eventually managed – to reinterpret the Central Committee's declaration of 1925 as a decision in their favour. A much clearer example of the need for 'interpretation' followed the Resolution on literature of 1932, which failed to provide any detailed measures or instructions for giving effect to its announced provisions. As we have seen, this led to the call for further high-level intervention to clarify and enforce the original Resolution. When such statements could not be effected through existing channels because they circumvented or even abolished those that did previously exist, interpretation and implementation was necessarily done by others. Procedures through which implementors were selected, instructed and in the course of their activities themselves scrutinized, still lay within Stalin's sphere of influence. But the intractable nature of many cultural questions – such as the formulation of socialist realism –

seems also to have required the delegation of authority to subordinates, who exercised a limited autonomy within their designated fields.

Major changes of policy in the literary sphere proceeded from initiatives by Stalin and were issued at the level of the Politburo. At the same time, other individuals contributed to policy formation on a lower level. The remainder of this section will define more closely the type and form of high-level interventionism, and then suggest a more precise relationship between these and other levels of policy formation.

High-level interventions in literature performed the primary function of establishing the major political priorities of the moment. Thus the unpublished letter to the 'Writer-Communists from RAPP', of February 1929,[79] first indicated a 'right danger' and designated Pil'nyak as the leader of the political deviation. In this case Stalin's intention was evidently to use cultural policy, through the spokesmanship of RAPP, as part of a wider campaign against the 'Right' in politics. But the relatively fleeting nature of this re-direction is also obvious in the light of the sudden disavowal of the communist militants of the cultural revolution in October 1931. Then, Stalin's 'Letter to the Editors of *Proletarskaya revolyutsiya*,' which made a devastating attack on a minor historical deviation in describing the Second International, was subsequently broadened into an ideological offensive against the left, including special brigades, which were organised to seek out 'Trotskyist contraband' in historiography and social sciences. Thereafter, the designation of cultural and intellectual deviations as 'left' and 'right' diminished. But the establishment of political guidelines continued. In 1936, it was the turn of the *avant-garde* in music, opera, and other arts to be derided as a 'formalist' deviation and to be the victim of a public campaign initiated by Stalin and Zhdanov. At this time too, the Formalist school in Soviet criticism, which had actually ended some years earlier, was retrospectively condemned as a phase of 'vulgar sociology'. Though it does not appear to have had the support of any published statement by Stalin, this attack fully reflected his earlier strictures on *dia-mat* and the proletarian 'hegemony'.

Having first established a political framework for the literary policy, the second function of high-level interventionism was to lay down a practical ideological perspective within which the literary intelligentsia was supposed to operate. The *locus classicus* of this category was Stalin's meeting with writers of October 1932. Stalin not only criticised *dia-mat* on that occasion, but also laid out the general theoretical direction which Soviet writers were expected to follow. They were to 'know the theory of Marx and Lenin'; but they should also 'know life' and express it truthfully in their writings. That, Stalin said, 'will be socialist art; that will be socialist realism'.[80] But it is obvious that such injunctions towards writing the truth and its assumed concomitant of doing so from the socialist perspective were very general. Stalin left the task of formulating the method of socialist realism in which they were to be expressed more fully to others. The effect of his intervention was rather to draw attention to certain favoured areas such as tendentiousness, and to exclude others such as *dia-mat* and any exclusive reliance on the Marxian 'classics'.

Towards writing for the theatre, however, Stalin's ideological interventions do seem to have been given more precise articulation. That plays, rather than *belles-lettres*, should have been the object of greater and more specific attention may have been simply a result of Stalin's personal patronage of theatres, which was accompanied later, and perhaps replaced, by his penchant for the cinema. Equally, Stalin's attention may have been drawn to theatre as the most immediately political of the literary genres. In his treatment of Afinogenov's *The Lie*, Stalin showed the political potential of dramatic conflict, in the rapid unfolding of plot, and in the denouement which was compounded by his awareness of the 'educational' potential of the stage.[81] The great importance which Stalin attached to the *impact* of a drama on audiences is seen best, perhaps, in his treatment of two works by Bulgakov.

The Days of the Turbins, Stalin wrote in 1929, could be tolerated for just as long as it took proletarian dramatists to write something better. It was still permissible 'because we have not enough of our *own* plays that are suitable for staging'. Proletarian drama could not be introduced by fiat: it would have to compete with the best of non-proletarian writing and earn its place. *The Days of the Turbins*, though obviously written 'from sympathy with the Turbins' plight', would do 'less harm than good' to the Bolshevik cause. The audience, in Stalin's view, would take it as 'a demonstration' of the all-conquering power of the Bolsheviks – despite the author's intentions.[82] There was, however, a curious afterthought to this judgement. Just the opposite effect would come from staging *Flight* (1922), in which Stalin considered that Bulgakov had tried to evoke pity, or at least sympathy, for 'certain sections of the anti-Soviet emigration'. *Flight* was an effort to justify 'white-guardism', while *The Days of the*

Turbins, apparently, was not. Only after the addition of further scenes would an audience grasp the fact that the *Flight* took place, not by a 'caprice of the Bolsheviks', but by the party's rightful execution of 'the workers' and peasants' will' that such 'supporters of exploitation and parasites' be driven into emigration.[83] *Flight* was thus prohibited and *The Days of the Turbins* came off a few weeks afterwards. But Bulgakov made a personal appeal to Stalin to have the ban removed. Stalin asked to see the play again. After a few days of hectic preparation, the Moscow Arts Theatre put on a special performance for Stalin alone. After making amendments, he permitted it to return to the repertoire, and it ran continuously until 1941.[84] This ambivalent attitude (which the playwright reciprocated) may serve to indicate the perspective with which Stalin approached works of art. His approval of *The Days of the Turbins* appeared to show that the positive ideological impact of a play on the audience could, on occasion, be more important, from the vantage point of censorship, than the intentions of an author.

A further criterion for interventionism, particularly prominent in the second half of the thirties, was the notion of what was 'popular' in literature and art. 'Popularity' was not defined by any testing of public opinion: in book sales, for instance, or in box office takings at theatres, opera or cinema. It was designated 'from above'. Rather than providing the productions which the population wanted, therefore, the party leadership intended to supply the art or literature which they thought that it should have. The point was made by reference to a production of *Bogatyr'*, a comic opera, which opened at the Kamerny in the 1936–7 season. Bedny's libretto made a mockery of the boyars, in contrast to the more dignified and exalted portrayal of Kievan brigand bands. This drew down several charges on the playwright's head, as well as the injunction that the producer, Tairov, should himself be investigated.[85] His treatment of history was condemned as 'false'; tarred apparently with Pokrovsky's brush. But beyond the 'falsification' of national history (in which it was the boyars who were held to have played the positive role, and the brigands, to have behaved as brigands do), Bedny was held guilty of the further crime of disrespect for national traditions. His script was an 'insult' to the Russian, and even, it was said, to the Slavonic peoples. It was surprising to find the poet Bedny taking such liberties with Russian history, however far into its past. He had previously been warned, in a letter from Stalin, against discrediting (on that occasion in verse) the great 'revolutionary processes of the Russian working class'. This was a clear injunction against any future liberties.[86] But the attack on *Bogatyr'* had wider relevance. At a time when Soviet patriotism was coming back into vogue, it served a warning to dramatists and writers generally of the need to bow to nationalist sentiments.

Other theatres were less fortunate than the Kamerny in their encounters with the national principle or *narodnost'* in art. A Resolution signed by Stalin and Molotov, on 27 February 1936, stated that the Moscow Arts Theatre II had done 'too little to justify' its continued existence. There was 'no need for the preservation of such a theatre in Moscow'.[87] This view was made even more explicit on the closure of Meyerhold's theatre at the end of 1937. According to an official declaration, Soviet audiences had 'no need' of such a theatre. Its spectacles were 'alien' to them, and therefore they had ' failed to attend'.[88] But the reality of these closures is rather different. Such populist arguments were a disguise and rationalisation for a political decision. Nevertheless, in proscribing what it did not consider to be 'popular' in Soviet literature and the arts, the party leadership was reflecting accurately its own tastes, and it cannot be said with certainty that the distinction between its own notion of what was popular, and the art that the consumers of mass culture wanted, was always very great.

These three categories of high-level interventionism are too general to permit the thesis that Stalin formulated literary policy in detail. The notions of *partiinost'*, *ideinost'* and *narodnost'* established an overall theoretical framework for literary controls.[89] Moreover, the principles overlap, and are to a considerable extent contained within each other. In particular, the principle of party-mindedness seems to be assumed by the other two. Similarly, the establishment of ideological perspective could hardly operate without designation of the political context beforehand and the idea of 'popularity' in culture was imposed by the political authorities. Thus, in book production, literary criticism or censorship, the three principles establish general guidelines. They provide broad standards for the evaluation of a particular work: its truthfulness or party-mindedness; its pedagogic potential for mass enlightenment; and the degree to which the ideological content would be intelligible to the masses. They become a context within which those working in culture, as artists or as officials, could operate, without offering detailed instructions for implementation. However, in practice, numerous questions of application and interpretation arise. Such a division of labour is not surprising: it helps to resolve the otherwise puzzling question of how a single leader or party leadership could control literature without consultation or delegation of day-to-day responsibility.

To turn from high-level policy statements on literature by Stalin or by the Politburo to lower levels of the party apparatus, is to see a more complicated and differentiated picture. The policy process cannot be reduced to a single channel of commands issued 'from above', and carried out below. If we include pressures emanating from outside the party apparatus, a considerably fuller account of 'Stalinism in literature' starts to emerge.

In the late 1920s and early 1930s narrow cliques of communist intellectuals (RAPP, the Communist Academy) actively competed for Stalin's ear. They also sought to seize control of cultural facilities – journals and publishing-houses – and authoritative status as the 'party's leadership' in literature. Such activities undoubtedly absorbed much time and energy amongst both the contestants themselves, and the higher party echelons (be they partisans or mediators), particularly in the years between the dismissal of Voronsky from *Krasnaya nov'* (1927) to the abolition of *Na literaturnom postu* (in 1932). Averbakh and others continued this after RAPP's abolition. It seems unlikely that the RAPP leadership could have acted so boldly, or held together for so long as a distinct 'creative' grouping (both before and after its formal abolition), without a significant measure of high-level protection. In the case of Averbakh and his clique, protection probably came from his brother-in-law Yagoda. If to the influence of these individuals is added the activity in culture of many graduates of the Institute of Red Professors – including Dinamov, Surkov, Nusinov and Gronsky – it then seems reasonable to assume a measure of competition, even of conflict, at lower levels of policy formation. However, these cantankerous rivals, whose 'furious jealousies' are so well-chronicled by S. Sheshukov,[90] were steadily replaced as the Stalinist period developed. They were replaced by officialdom of new kinds. Four main categories have been identified in this book.

Cultural bureaucrats

Cultural policy does appear to have been one field in which communist officials of a lower rank did actually try to initiate policy changes, as a conscious act of insubordination to their immediate

superiors or even, in the case of RAPP, to the Central Committee.
The 'Letter' to *Proletarskaya revolyutsiya* may be a case in point.
According to Avtorkhanov, then a junior official of the Press Department at the Central Committee, the basic 'theses' of this letter – such
as the idea of 'Trotskyist contraband' in history, and the notion of
'anti-Leninist distortions' in literature – were proposed to Stalin by a
middle-ranking official of the department (Ingulov), over the heads
of his immediate superiors (Stetsky and Kerzhentzev). He states that
this was 'the Stalinist idea, not yet formulated by Stalin himself' of a
sharp reversal of policy on the intellectual front, subsequently accepted by the Organisational Bureau of the Central Committee,
whih, in turn, agreed that Stalin should publish articles both on
historiography and literature.[91] Confirmation of this account comes
not only in the fact that the article on history appeared in the autumn
of 1931, and the one on literature (actually by Yudin) in the spring of
1932,[92] but that Ingulov himself replaced Kerzhentsev as Stetsky's
deputy, and later took charge of *Glavlit* – a further promotion.[93]

While it may perhaps be objected that a monolithic political party,
in which directives were transmitted only from above, did not have
the channels for communication of alternative ideas or proposals on
culture, such an objection seems circular. It presupposes that cultural
policy was dictated from above. In view of the frequent changes in
the institutional structure of cultural administration in the 1930s –
Kul't-prop, for instance, was reorganised three times between 1930
and 1935 – the failure of such channels to establish themselves should
be less surprising.

Party delegates

The second category of officialdom consists of those posted by the
Party to literature in order to resolve problems of which they had no
previous experience. The appointment of the ideologist Yudin to the
Orgkomitet and to chair the Commission on Socialist Realism is the
best illustration. As we have seen, Gorky appears to have opposed
Yudin's growing authority, and to have reacted with extreme irritation when preparations for the Congress made it necessary for them
to meet. Romanovsky, who reports this in his unpublished dissertation, is inclined to blame Averbakh and the continuing intrigues with
what remained of his clique for poisoning the relations between
them.[94] So too was Stetsky, when in a report to Stalin, he blamed
Averbakh for surrounding Gorky with a 'web of conspirators and

squabblers', and using all means to 'isolate Gorky from the *Orgkomitet*'.[95] No doubt, Averbakh still believed that, with Gorky's help, he could displace Yudin as Secretary of the future Union.[96] But this should not disguise the substance of Gorky's complaint, the conduct of Yudin himself. According to an unpublished letter in the Central Party Archive, Gorky's criticism culminated in a bitter outburst in the spring of 1934 in which he called Yudin 'a poor communist' and a 'dishonest one'. His conduct of literature had 'disorganised the communist fraction' and 'driven off non-party writers', and generally done 'great damage' to literary affairs.[97] Gorky was certainly concerned that non-party writers should willingly accede to the Writers' Union. Little writing of value would result if they joined grudgingly, through coercion, or from fear that professional literary activity could not be carried on outside the Union. Moreover, writers would need to adhere voluntarily if the newly-proclaimed solidarity of Soviet Writers was to find a convincing expression at the Writers' Congress. By contrast, Yudin represented the intimidatory element in party policy.

Subsequently, Yudin attempted to take over the Writers' Union. This led to an exchange in the contemporary press on the 'party leadership of literature' between *Literaturnyi kritik*, which Yudin edited, and spokesmen of the Union. The Writers' Union had established a Critics' Section in the autumn of 1934. Its early meetings revealed some differences of opinion between speakers who thought the section should restrict itself to the education of its members, while others proposed a more active policy. A furious altercation took place between the Critics' Section and *Literaturnyi kritik*. It heard a report from Rozental' who concluded that little progress had been made in the journal's task of establishing higher quality of publicism and criticism.[98] Yudin replied with a sharp defence of its activity. He distinguished two stages in the development of Soviet literature. The first, polemical and publicistic, had been concerned with rooting out the harmful tendency of *dia-mat* in literature and other 'remnants'. Now this was completed a second stage based on reconciliation could begin. *Literaturnyi kritik* was better equipped than the Critics' Section, to take over 'the leadership of Soviet literature'.[99] But the Writers' Union brushed Yudin's suggestion aside. The Critics' Section was to take the 'offensive' on the literary front. Accordingly an inner bureau of the section was established under Bespalov, who undertook to formulate a 'unified Programme'.[100] Thus rebuffed, Yudin returned to editorial duties with his journal, which continued to publish controversial pieces in the later 1930s. He had, though, outlived his usefulness to the Party in the sphere of literature. In the later Stalin period he was sent abroad as Soviet envoy to Tito and ended his career as a plenipotentiary to Mao-tse-Tung.[101]

'Diplomats'

An acute observer noted the changing manner of literary officialdom under Stalinism:

> Until the middle of the twenties we had been dealing with former members of the old revolutionary underground and their younger assistants of a similar type. They were brusque, utterly self-righteous, and often ill-mannered, but they loved to hold forth and argue. There was about them something of the seminarists and Pisarev. Gradually they were replaced by round-headed, fair-haired types in embroidered Ukrainian shirts who affected a cheerful familiarity, cracked jokes and liked to be taken for bluff, straightforward fellows. It was all completely put on. These were superseded in their turn by diplomats who weighed every word, never gave anything away or made any promises, but at the same time tried to create the impression that they were men of power and influence.[102]

One of the first such 'diplomats' in literature was Shcherbakov, a full-time Party official whose career was made entirely outside of literature. Following *Kul't-prop* work in Nizhnii Novgorod, where he had been introduced to Gorky on his 1928 visit, he was transferred to the Central Committee *Agit-prop* in Moscow. He graduated from the Institute of Red Professors in 1932. At the Writers' Congress he was abruptly proposed as the first Secretary of the Writers' Union. Of his relationship with Gorky, a masterpiece of tactful duplicity, we have already seen. His successor as Union Secretary was Stavsky, whose early career, as already noted, had been in RAPP. But he had made a timely defection to Stalin on the eve of the April Resolution, and alone of the RAPP secretariat argued in May 1932 that the Resolution meant an end of their organisation.[103] In the period of the *Orgkomitet*, Stavsky had specialised in work with younger writers and had reported on this topic to the Congress.[104] The uncontroversial nature of this work stood him in good stead for the later period of the Purges. He became First Secretary of the Writers' Union in 1937.

Non-Party authorities

A final influence on literary policy, which has been partly noted in western literature, is that of non-party authorities. Such figures did not arise in contradistinction to the power exercised by the party, nor did they simply fulfil its wishes: they rather reflected a decision of the Party leadership to delegate a limited responsibility to selected figures in the cultural sphere. There were perhaps two principal reasons for this delegation. One was the previous insubordination of competing communist groups such as RAPP towards the party leadership in the Five Year Plan. This may well have led the Party to prefer a division of function, in fact practised throughout the later 1930s between communist administrators, and non-party figures with status in their own field, but without administrative authority. A second reason was that a majority of writers and artists were non-communist. The fostering of non-party 'authorities' in literature, the theatre, and some academic disciplines, might therefore help to reassure that part of the intelligentsia. In literature, it would seem that authority was exercised in two distinct forms by different figures: the power of administrative decision was exercised by Shcherbakov (and later Stavsky), and the power of limited patronage and status was held by Gorky. Shcherbakov maintained regular contacts with the highest party echelons. His function was evidently that of literary consultant, to the Central Committee and to Stalin. He acted not as a representative of the interests and wishes of the literary profession, but rather as an informed source on writers' attitudes in general, and their likely reaction to measures – such as the 'anti-formalist' campaign of 1936 – to be launched from above. As Union Secretary, he executed high-level orders. As *Kul't-prop* Secretary, he simultaneously took general supervisory powers over all spheres of culture and the cultural Unions.[105]

The position of Gorky, as President of the Writers' Union, was quite different. He was a major writer and widely recognised as such by the literary community. His past association with Lenin could not be claimed by other literary administrators. He had an international reputation and thus represented Soviet literature to 'revolutionary' writers abroad. These sources of influence and authority were assiduously fostered by the political authorities, who used them to reconcile Soviet writers and dignify the Writers' Union, and also to foster a link between the leaderships of literature and the Party, as a propaganda instrument of great potential value to the latter. It may be that Gorky tried to resist this second usage, and that his warm relationship with Stalin did cool. There is an evident disjunction between Gorky's optimism on his first return at the end of the 1920s – reflected in the further celebrations of September 1932 – and the restrictions imposed on Gorky's influence and movements in his final years. Already in 1932 there were indications that Gorky attempted to withhold his full endorsement of the cult of Stalin. When the State Publishing House asked him for a biography of Stalin, and supplied the materials, he left the order unfulfilled. Nor did he add to the fulsome tributes that were made by many of Stalin's former political opponents as the price for their 'returns'. His personal connection with Stalin seems to have declined thereafter. By the summer of 1934 Gorky began to express doubts, amongst his innermost circle, about the nature of leadership and the 'legitimate aspirations of the people'.[106] These private misgivings did not greatly reduce his status as a cultural authority in his own lifetime but it is noticeable that the cult of Gorky was greatly extended after his death. This is partly attributable to the rapid decline of the political situation into show trials and arrests on a mass scale which made Gorky a comparatively safe topic for literary composition.[107] It was also the case that his status as an authority was as easy or easier for the party leadership to sustain when Gorky himself was dead.

A second 'non-Party authority' of importance in the literary sphere was A. S. Makarenko, who became, under Gorky's auspices, a major figure within the Writers' Union, and leading pedagogue. He had founded a labour colony for delinquents which Gorky had visited on his return to Russia in 1928. It was run on military lines: the colonists were awoken by a bugle at 6.00 a.m. and worked according to partisan detachments headed by commanders. Its basic principle was reformation through active work, requiring traditional discipline: 'until a community spirit is developed. So long as the children are without tradition and have not acquired elementary habits of life and labour, the teacher not only may but ought to use force if necessary . . . Children should be educated to be strong and hard as nails, fitted to carry out unpleasant and boring tasks, if the community interests require it'.[108] Only after principles of discipline and collective spirit had been instilled would it become possible, in Makarenko's view, to proceed with education. This consisted both of technical qualifications and instilling a strong sense of community. The ideal hero in his 'Pedagogical Poem: The Road to Life' (1933–5), was uncomplicated, dedicated to good work and optimistic of the future. Makarenko considered his contribution to be to show how much heroes of the time could have their personalities formed.

He wrote in the first person of his own experiences. For book learning he had utter contempt: 'you're all for reading and reading but if we give you a real human being to deal with he'll say he'll cut your throat! "Intelligentsia!"'[109] In an autobiography he notes that 'in the winter of 1920 the more I read, the more I realised I knew nothing whatever about education and that there were no ready-made theories for me to work upon and that I had to work out my own theory from everyday experiences. And I realised I needed not a formula but immediate action on the basis of my own analysis of the situation.'[110] This does not sit readily with the return to formal learning and educational textbooks of the 1930s. Nonetheless Makarenko had enjoyed a great vogue. He toured the country as a lecturer on such themes as parental authority, education by work and discipline. *Krasnaya nov'* began to publish *A Book for Parents* in 1937, planned in four volumes, of which only the first was written.

It has been suggested that Gorky was a 'prototype' of cultural authority, which was established in some other spheres of cultural and intellectual life during the thirties. The case of Stanislavsky has been put forward as a 'non-party authority' in theatre. The similarities are indeed considerable. In addition to sharing non-party status, Stanislavsky's professional reputation, like Gorky's, predated the revolution. He too, was adopted by the party leadership and received extensive public recognition of his services to theatre in a high government award (of 1933), and the title of National Artist (in 1936). Even though he was a retiring individual, and not a public figure, his acting system was 'canonised' increasingly after his death in 1938. To attempt to answer the question whether this pattern of non-party 'authorities' may be located elsewhere in intellectual life – with figures such as Pavlov in psychology, Marr in linguistics and the biologist Lysenko – would go beyond the limits of this book.

We have, however, established the existence of actors other than Stalin in literary policy. This section identified: cultural bureaucrats (Stetsky, Ingulov); party delegates (such as Yudin); 'diplomats' (Shcherbakov later Stavsky) and non-Party authorities (notably Gorky and Makarenko). The system could not have come into being without them. Stalinism in literature was also their creation.

Notes and References

'M.' means the place of publication was Moscow; 'L.' that it was Leningrad; 'M.-L.' that the work was published in both cities.

1 THE REVOLUTION

1. The origins of this notion are contested. R. Pipes, '*Intelligentsia* from the German *Intelligenz*'?: A Note' *Slavic Review*, 1971 (3) pp. 615–18, advances the claim for 'die Intelligenz', used in German from 1849. This had been noted by L. B. Namier, *1848: The Revolution of the Intellectuals* (London, 1944) p. 22. It had certainly been used in Poland at the beginning of the 1840s, see Andrzej Walicki, *A History of Russian Thought from the Enlightenment to Marxism* (Oxford, 1980) p. xv, note 3. However, another Polish scholar suggests the term entered Russian vocabulary, with Belinsky, in 1846: see: A. Gella, 'The Life and Death of the Old Polish Intelligentsia', *Slavic Review*, 1971 (3) p. 4. During the nineteenth century, of course, the term covered a great variety of political and social tendencies: populist, radical, liberal, anarchist and revolutionary. For a twentieth-century appraisal of the evolution of the concept see Karl Mannheim, *Ideology and Utopia* 'The Sociological Problem of the *Intelligentsia*' (n. date, first published 1936) pp. 153–63. In the post-war Russian context, L. G. Churchward, *The Soviet Intelligentsia* (London, 1973) pp. 1–6.
2. W. H. Chamberlain, *The Russian Revolution, 1917–1921*, vol. 1 (Cambridge, Mass., 1935) p. 109.
3. K. D. Muratova, *M. Gor'kii v bor'be za razvitiye sovetskoi literatury* (M.-L. 1958) pp. 27–8.
4. *Literaturnoye nasledstvo* vol. 65 (M.1958) p. 546. Gorky's speech appears in V. Pertsov, *Mayakovsky: Zhizn' i tvorchestvo* (M.1950) pp. 414–18.
5. Charles Rougle, 'The Intelligentsia Debate in Russia, 1917–1918', in N. A. Nilsson (ed.) *Art, Society, Revolution: Russia, 1917–1921* (Stockholm, 1979) p. 59.
6. Rougle, pp. 73–4.
7. G. Janecek (ed.) *Andrei Bely. A Critical Review* (Lexington, 1978) pp. 196–7.
8. Rougle, pp. 76–9.
9. The views of the Polish anarchist J. W. Machajski (A. Vol'skii, 1899–1926) are collected in his *Umstvennyi rabochii* (New York, 1968).
10. S. A. Fedyukin, *Velikii oktyabr' i intelligentsia* (M.1972), translated as *The Great October Revolution and the Intelligentsia* (M.1975) p. 25.
11. Sheila Fitzpatrick, *The Commisariat of Enlightenment: Soviet Organisation of Education and the Arts under Lunacharsky, October 1917–1921* (Cambridge, 1970). For the background see p. 113.

12. Vahan D. Barooshian, *Brik and Mayakovsky* (The Hague, 1978) pp. 17–18.
13. Rougle, pp. 81–2.
14. Two excellent studies of this process are Robert C. Williams, *Culture in Exile: Russian emigrés in Germany, 1881–1941* (Ithaca, 1972); and Simon Karlinsky and Alfred Appel, Jr (eds), *The Bitter Air of Exile: Russian Writers in the West, 1922–1972* (Berkeley, Calif., 1977).
15. See, for instance, the exchange between the proletarian writer Serafimovich and his detractors in Fedyukin, *Great October*, p. 28.
16. See Avril Pyman, *The Life of Aleksandr Blok*: vol. II, *The Release of Harmony: 1908–1921* (Oxford: 1980) p. 119.
17. Pyman, vol. II, p. 223.
18. See M. Bowra, *Poetry and Politics, 1900–1960* (Cambridge, 1965) pp. 49–50. According to Sergei Hackel, *The Poet and the Revolution* (Oxford, 1975) pp. 84–190, Blok intends a 'compilative Christ', in which theological and populist connotations are combined.
19. 'Intelligentsia and Revolution', first published in *Znamya truda* 19 January 1918, is translated in Marc Raeff, *Russian Intellectual History: An Anthology* (New Jersey, 1978) pp. 364–71.
20. Discussed by J. D. Elsworth, *Andrey Bely* (Letchworth, 1972) pp. 92–3.
21. Its meanings are considered by Pyman, vol. II, p. 292, n. v.
22. Analysed by Stefani Hoffman, 'Scythian Theory and Literature, 1917–1924', in Nilsson, (ed.) *Art, Society, Revolution*, pp. 138–64.
23. Leonard B. Schapiro, *The Origin of the Communist Autocracy* (London, 1955), Chapter 7.
24. *The Memoirs of Ivanov-Razumnik* (pen-name of Razumnik Vasilevich Ivanov, 1878–1946) (Oxford, 1965), pp. 15–56. His debate with Zamyatin, who had contested the notion of 'Scythian' and, more generally, of the intelligentsia offered in Ivanov-Razumnik's *History*, is described by A. M. Shane, *The Life and Works of Evgenii Zamyatin* (Berkeley, Calif., 1968) pp. 17–21.
25. The poem was printed in *Izvestiya VTsIK*, 22 August 1918.
26. Gordon McVay, *Esenin: A Life* (London, 1976) p. 107.
27. *Memoirs of Ivanov-Razumnik*, pp. 21–5.
28. Pyman, vol. II, p. 345.
29. Pyman, however, argues that the speech 'rose above the conflicts of the day to make broad statements about art', *ibid*. 367–70.
30. Eyewitness accounts are given in Nina Berberova, *The Italics are Mine* (London, 1969) pp. 125–8. Photograph: Pyman, vol. II opposite p. 377.
31. Reprinted in the collection by N. L. Brodski *et.al* (eds) *Literaturniye manifesty: ot Simvolizma k Oktyabryu* (M.1929).
32. Nadezhda Mandel'stam: *Hope Against Hope* (London, 1971) p. 264, and *Hope Abandoned* (London, 1974) pp. 45–6.
33. 'Pushkin and Scriabin: Fragments', in Jane Gary Harris (ed.) Mandelstam, *The Complete Critical Prose and Letters* (Ann Arbor, Michigan, 1979) pp. 90–5, and the important 'Notes' pp. 596–602.
34. 'Sumerki svobody' was published in *Znamya truda*, 24 May 1918. See the analysis by Steven Broyde, *Osip Mandel štam and His Age* (Cambridge, Mass., 1975) pp. 47–62.

35. Anna Akhmatova, *Stikhotvoreniya i poemi* (L.1976) p. 229. Trans. by Stanley Kunitz, *Poems of Akhmatova* (London, 1974) p. 69.
36. Her memoir of Mandelstam appears in *Russian Literature Triquarterly* vol. 9 (Ann Arbor, 1974) pp. 239–54.
37. Ibid., p. 244.
38. Akhmatova, *Stikhotvoreniya*, p. 152; Kunitz, *Poems of Akhmatova* p. 75.
39. See the introduction by Max Hayward to Alexander Gladkov, *Meetings with Pasternak: A Memoir* (London, 1977) pp. 7–30; and Andrei Sinyavskii 'Poeziya Pasternaka', preface to Boris Pasternak, *Stikhotvoreniya i poemi* (M.1965) pp. 9–62.
40. Olga Hughes, *The Poetic World of Boris Pasternak* (Princeton, 1974).
41. Boris Pasternak, *Safe Conduct: An Early Autobiography and Other Works* (London, 1959), p. 187.
42. See David Magarshack (trans.) Konstantin Stanislavsky, *Stanislavsky on the Art of the Stage* (London, 1961).
43. See Edward Braun, *The Theatre of Meyerhold* (London, 1979) pp. 102–13.
44. Vladimir Markov, *Russian Futurism: A History* (London, 1969) pp. 147–51.
45. This compendium (of January 1914) was confiscated by the censorship. See Wiktor Woroszylski, *The Life of Mayakovsky* (London, 1972) pp. 88–9.
46. Raymond Cooke, *Velimir Khlebnikov: A critical study* (Cambridge, 1983) pp. 82–9.
47. The challenge was signed 'amidst a sea of boos and indignation' by Burliuk, Kruchenykh and Mayakovsky. See Woroszylski, *Mayakovsky*, pp. 43–51.
48. V. V. Mayakovsky, *Sochineniya*, vol. I (M.1970) p. 41. Of some 120 members of the Petrograd intelligentsia summoned to a meeting at the Smolny Institut by the new authorities, only six (including Blok, Meyerhold and Mayakovsky) attended.
49. 'Open Letter to Workers' (15 March 1918) and 'Order No. 1. On the Democratisation of Art', Woroszylski, *Mayakovsky*, p. 194.
50. Published in *Iskusstvo kommuny*, 15 December 1918.
51. Set up in January 1918. See Fitzpatrick, *The Commissariat of Enlightenment*, chapter 6.
52. Quoted in ibid., pp. 125–6.
53. Woroszylski, *Mayakovsky*, pp. 212–13.
54. See Edward J. Brown, *Mayakovsky: A Poet in the Revolution* (New Jersey, 1973 pp. 204–6.
55. Barooshian, *Brik and Mayakovsky* pp. 39–40.
56. The theme of retribution is prominent in his post-revolutionary poetry. 'Night in the Trench' (brought out by the Imaginist publishing house in 1921) shows Civil War struggles through the implacable eyes of Scythian stone statues who interrupt the Red victory to prophecy a typhus epidemic. In 'Night Search', he shows a group of Red sailors looting and carousing, prior to being suffocated by the wife and mother of a soldier they had murdered. See further Vladimir Markov, *The Longer Poems of Velimir Khlebnikov* (Berkeley, 1962) chapters 7 and 8.

272 *Notes and References*

57. Ibid., pp. 146–53.
58. See Richard Stites, *Revolutionary Dreams: Utopian Visions and Experimental Life in the Russian Revolution* (Oxford, 1989).
59. Quoted by D. G. B. Piper, *V. A. Kaverin: A Soviet Writer's Response to the Problem of Commitment* (Pittsburgh, 1970) p. 33.
60. V. I. Lenin, 'On Party Organisation and Party Literature', 15 November 1905, *Polnoe sobraniye sochinenii* (M.1958–65) vol. 12, pp. 99–105.
61. For instance, N. I. Krutikova (ed.) *V. I. Lenin o literature i iskusstve* (M.1967); see also V. P. Shcherbina, *Problemy literaturovedeniya v svete naslediya V. I. Lenina* (M.1971); A. K. Dremov, *Partiinost' literatury i sovremennost' ucheniyi Lenina* (M.1980).
62. See Peter Reddaway, 'Literature, the Arts and the Personality of Lenin', in Leonard Schapiro and Peter Reddaway (eds), *Lenin: The Man, the Theorist, the Leader* (London, 1967) pp. 37–70.
63. Ya. M. Strochkov, 'O stat'e V. I. Lenina', *Voprosy istorii* 1956 (4) pp. 29–37.
64. *Kommunist*, 1957 (3) pp. 22–3. This is an editorial.
65. See the entries on 'Lenin' and 'Partiinost' v literature' in *Kratkaya literaturnaya entsiklopediya* vol. 4 (M.1967) and vol. 5 (M.1968).
66. Quoted by Robert V. Daniels, 'Intellectuals and the Russian Revolution', *Slavic Review*, April 1961, pp. 272–3.
67. V. I. Lenin, *Sochineniya*, vol. 51, pp. 47–9.
68. Fedyukin, *Great October*, p. 45.
69. N. I. Bukharin and E. Preobrazhensky, *The ABC of Communism* (London, 1922, reprinted 1969) p. 295.
70. A. V. Lunacharsky. 'Khudozhestvennaya politika sovetskogo gosudarstva', *Zhizn' iskusstva*, 1924 (10).
71. Fitzpatrick, *The Commissariat of Enlightenment*, p. 236 ff.
72. Sheila Fitzpatrick, 'The Emergence of *Glaviskusstvo*', *Soviet Studies*, October 1971.
73. Decree of 13 November 1917. See Ernest J. Simmons, 'The Origins of Literary Controls' in *Survey*, April 1961, pp. 78–84. The article is concluded in *Survey*, July 1961, pp. 60–7.
74. Decree on state publishing: *Gosizdat* 21 May 1919. See also the article on 'freedom of books' under the Revolution, by Luncharsky in *Pechat' i revolyutsiya*, 1921. (1).
75. A copy of the *Narkompros* circular, signed by Krupskaya in 1920 (renewed in 1923) entitled 'Guide to the removal of anti-artistic and counter-revolutionary literature from libraries serving the mass reader' is kept in the Boris Nicolaevsky Collection of the Hoover Institution, Stanford. See citations in Bertram D. Wolfe, *The Bridge and the Abyss: The Troubled Friendship of Maxim Gorky and V. I. Lenin* (London, 1967) pp. 143–5.
76. A. M. Gor'kii, *O russkom krest'yarstve* (Berlin, 1922).
77. Herman Ermolaev (ed.) Maxim Gorky, *Untimely Thoughts* (London, 1968) p. 47. Article of 12 June 1917.
78. Ibid., 18 April 1917 (Mayday, new style), p. 6.
79. Ibid., 7 November 1917, p. 85.

80. An article 'Maxim Gorky and *Narkompros*', *Izvestiya TsIK* 10 September 1918, confirmed his change of position.

81. A. M. Shane, *The Life and Works of Evgenij Zamyatin* (Berkeley, Ca., 1968) p. 27.

82. 'World Literature' was formally instituted, by agreement with *Narkompros*, on 4 September 1918. It is described in *Pamyat'*, V, pp. 287–91.

83. The House of Arts, on Nevsky Prospekt, opened officially in December 1919. It forms the backcloth to a novel by Ol'ga Forsh, *Sumasshedshii korabl'*, (L.1931). The Petrograd Union of Writers had been formed earlier, in March 1918, and lasted for about a year. See the article by P. P. Shirmakov in *Voprosy sovetskoi literatury* vol. 7 (M.1958). Memoirs of Gorky's involvement include K. I. Chukovsky, *Sovremenniki: Portrety i etiudy* (M.1962) pp. 328–30 and K. Zelinsky, *Na rubezhe dvukh epokh: Literaturnye vstrechi, 1917–1920 godov* (M.1959) p. 266. See also, N. Luker, *Alexander Grin* (Letchworth, 1973) pp. 70–1.

84. On the intercessions, see V. F. Khodasevich, 'Gor'kii' in *Nekropol: vospominaniya* (Brussells, 1939); Pyman, *Blok*, vol. 2, p. 375; and T. E. O'Connor, *The Politics of Soviet Culture: Anatolii Lunacharskii* (Ann Arbor, Mich., 1983) pp. 146–7.

85. G. Struve and B. Fillipov (eds), *Sobraniye sochinenii* (Washington, DC, 1962) vol. I, pp. xc–xci. However, it was recently confirmed that no documentary evidence had been found to warrant Gumilev's sentence: *Novyi mir* 1987, (12). An interview with a Gumilev appeared in *Soviet Weekly*, 14 May 1988.

2 NEP IN LITERATURE

1. Moshe Lewin, 'The Social Background of Stalinism', in Robert C. Tucker (ed.), *Stalinism: Essays in Historical Interpretation* (New York, 1977) pp. 111–13.

2. V. I. Lenin, *Sochineniya*, XXVII, pp. 392–4.

3. See Stephen F. Cohen, *Bukharin and the Bolshevik Revolution, 1888–1938: A Political Biography* (New York, 1973) pp. 134–55.

4. Lenin, *Sochineniya*, loc. cit.

5. See S. A. Fedyukin, *Sovetskaya vlast' i burzhuaznye spetsialisty* (M.1965).

6. Stanisław Ossowski, *Struktura klasowa w spotecznej świadomośći* (Łódz, 1957) pp. 26–38 for fuller definition of this term.

7. L. D. Trotsky, *Literature and Revolution* (New York, 1925) p. 57.

8. Ibid., p. 58.

9. For a fuller account see: Baruch Knei-Paz, *The Social and Political Thought of Leon Trotsky* (Oxford, 1978) pp. 289–301.

10. Their name was adopted from *The Stories of the Serapion Brothers* (1819–1821) by E. T. A. Hoffmann.

11. Lev Lunts, contribution to *Literaturnie zapiski* (Petrograd, 1922) in *Russian Literature Triquarterly* (*RLT*) vol. 2 (Ann Arbor, 1972) pp. 176–9.

12. Trotsky, *Literature and Revolution* p. 70.
13. Discussed by Gary Kern, 'The Serapion Brothers: a Dialectics of Fellow traveling' *RLT*, vol. 2, pp. 234–7.
14. Ibid., p. 226.
15. Robert A. Maguire, *Red Virgin Soil: Soviet Literature in the 1920's* (Princeton, NJ., 1978) ch. 1.
16. *Krasnaya nov'*, 1922 (6). Trans. in *RLT*, vol. 2, pp. 153–75.
17. *Krasnaya nov'*, 1921 (1).
18. V. P. Polonsky (pen-name of Vyacheslav Pavlovich Gusin, 1886–1932).
19. Stalin complained about this portrayal. See *The Foundations of Leninism* (M.1924).
20. See Leonard Schapiro, *Russian Studies* (London, 1986) pp. 84–7, notes 91–2.
21. See E. H. Carr, *The Bolshevik Revolution* vol. 1 (London, 1966) pp. 375–6.; *Socialism in One Country*, vol. 1 (London, 1970) pp. 69–71, 73–4. The major convert was the writer A. Tolstoy who returned to Russia.
22. See Alexander Solzhenitsyn, *The GULag Archipelago*, vols 1, 2 (London, 1974) p. 372.
23. Central Party Archives, cited by A. F. Ermakov in *Obogashchenie metoda sotsialisticheskogo realizma i problema mnogoobraziya sovetskogo iskusstva* (M.1967) p. 358.
24. Ibid., pp. 357–9.
25. For the famous 'ban on factions' of the Tenth Party Congress (March 1921), see Leonard B. Schapiro, *The Origin of the Communist Autocracy* (London, 1955) ch. XVII.
26. Trotsky, *Literature and Revolution*, p. 218.
27. See I. M. Gronskii, 'Predisloviye' to *Assosiatsiya khudozhnikov revolyutsionnoi Rossii: Sbornik vospominanii statei dokumentov* (M.1973).
28. S. Sheshukov, *Neistovye revniteli: Iz istorii literaturnoi bor'by 20-kh godov* (M.1970) pp. 18–25.
29. Averbakh (born 1903) was a rising star. He was related both to Sverdlov and Yaroslavsky; Trotsky contributed a preface to his first book: *Voprosy yunosheskogo dvizheniya i Lenin* (M.1923). See E. H. Carr, *Socialism in One Country* vol. 2 (London, 1970) p. 87.
30. *Na postu*, June 1923, (1). Manilov was the lazy landowner in *Dead Souls*.
31. A. V. Lunacharsky, 'Khudozhestvennaya politika sovetskovo gosudarstva', *Zhizn' iskusstva*, 1924 (10), p. 1.
32. 'O khudozhestvennoi politike Narkomprosa', in *Literaturnoe nasledstvo*, vol. 82 (M.1970) p. 408.
33. Ermakov, *Obogashchenie metoda* pp. 361–2; Sheshukov, *Neistovye revniteli* pp. 15–16.
34. Ermakov, ibid.
35. Ibid.
36. G. Lelevich, *Na literaturnom postu* (Tver, 1924) p. 166.
37. Politburo debate quoted by Nina Tumarkin, *Lenin Lives! The Lenin Cult in Soviet Russia* (Cambridge, Mass. 1983) p. 174.
38. L. D. Trotsky, *Sochineniya* vol. XXI (M.1927).
39. Tumarkin, *Lenin Lives!* chap. 7.

40. See *Zvezda*, 1924 (3) and I. Maiskii (ed.), *Proletariat i literatura: sbornik statei* (L.1925).
41. See John Biggart, 'Bukharin's Theory of Cultural Revolution' in A. Kemp-Welch (ed.) *The Ideas of Nikolai Bukharin* (Oxford, 1991).
42. 'V. I. Lenin i proletarskaya kul'tura', *Pechat' i revolyutsiya*, 1927 (7); and 'V. I. Lenin ob iskusstve i literature' *Novyi mir*, 1927 (11). Further thoughts were printed in V. Polonsky, *Ocherki literaturnogo dvizheniya revolyutsionnoi epokhi* (M.1928). His views were translated as a 'supplement' to Max Eastman, *Artists in Uniform: a Study of Literature and Bureaucratism* (New York, 1934) pp. 217–52.
43. See Zenovia Sochor, *Revolution and Culture: the Bogdanov-Lenin Controversy* (Ithaca, NY, 1988).
44. *Proletarskaya kul'tura*, August 1918, quoted by Herman Ermolaev, *Soviet Literary Theories, 1917–1934: The Genesis of Socialist Realism* (New York, 1977) p. 13.
45. V. I. Lenin, 'Zadachi soyuzov molodezhi', *Sochineniya*, vol. 30, pp. 403–17.
46. Central Committee, 'Letter to the Proletkul'ts', 1 December 1920.
47. Fitzpatrick, *The Commissariat of Enlightenment*, pp. 236–42.
48. Reasons for Trotsky's rejection of proletarian culture are given in Chapter 6 of *Literature and Revolution*.
49. A. V. Lunacharsky, in Ermakov, *Obogaschenie metoda*, p. 38 ff.
50. The full text appears in *Voprosy kul'tury pri diktature proletariata* (M.1925), pp. 56–139.
51. Voronsky, op. cit.
52. Vardin, op. cit.
53. Trotsky, op. cit.
54. Lunacharsky, op. cit.
55. Bukharin, op. cit.
56. Ibid, p. 139. The Party statement is in *Pravda*, 1 June 1924.
57. *Arkhiv A. M. Gor'kogo* vol. xii, *M. Gor'kii i sovetskaya pechat'*, p. 15 (29 January 1925).
58. Ibid, pp. 16–17 (12 February 1925).
59. Ibid, p. 16.
60. Ermakov, *Obogashchenie metoda*, pp. 37–78. On the role of Frunze, see Ermolaev, *Soviet Literary Theories*, pp. 46–8.
61. LEF was formed in 1922–3.
62. See Ermakov, *Obogashchenie metoda*, p. 371.
63. *Pravda*, 18 February 1925.
64. Ermakov, pp. 373–4.
65. 'Proletariat i voprosy khudozhestvennoi politiki', *Krasnaya nov'* 1925 (4).
66. Ermakov, *Obogashchenie metoda* pp. 376–7.
67. *Literaturnoye nasledstvo*, vol. 74 (M.1965) pp. 29–37.
68. Published in *Pravda*, 1 July 1925.
69. In English: E. Preobrazhensky, *The New Economics* (Oxford, 1965); *A. V. Chayanov on the Theory of the Peasant Economy* (Homewood, Ill., 1966); E. B. Pashukanis, *Law and Marxism: A General Theory* (London, 1978); L. G. Vygotsky, *Mind in Society* (Cambridge, Mass.,

1978); and A. R. Luria, *The Making of Mind: a personal account of Soviet psychology* (Cambridge, Mass., 1980).

70. The institutional story of this body and its dozen attendant specialist journals remains to be written. For an important hint by the keeper of its archives, see *Voprosy istorii*, 1988 (5) pp. 75–6.

71. L. B. Schapiro, *The Communist Party of the Soviet Union* (London, 1960) p. 343.

72. See, for instance, Camilla Gray, *The Russian Experiment in Art 1863–1922* (London, 1962); Christina Lodder, *Russian Constructivism* (New Haven, Conn., 1983); S. Frederick Starr; *Melnikov: Solo Architect in a Mass Society* (Princeton, N. J., 1978); W. G. Rosenberg (ed.), *Bolshevik Visions* (Ann Arbor, Mich., 1984).

73. English translation by Michael Scammell (New York, 1962).

74. Struve, *Russian Literature*, pp. 102–5.

75. See A. Rannit, 'Zabolotskii' in Nikolai Zabolotskii, *Stikhotvoreniya* (New York, 1965).

76. E. K. Beaujour, *The Invisible Land: A Study of the Artistic Imagination of Iurii Olesha* (New York, 1970) pp. 30–7 ff.

77. The reception of *The Rout* is described by Sheshukov, *Neistovye revniteli*, pp. 128–32.

78. Quoted from typed copy, State Literary Museum (Moscow) by Gordon McVay, *Esenin: A Life* (Ann Arbor, 1976) p. 251.

79. Ibid.

80. Cited in McVay, *Esenin*, pp. 220–21.

81. Leonov, 'Umer poet', *30 dnei*, 1926 (2), cited by McVay, p. 294.

82. Trotsky, 'Pamiati Sergeiya Esenina', in *Pamiati Esenina* (M.1926).

83. N. I. Bukharin, 'Zlye zametki', *Pravda*, 12 January 1927, reprinted in *Etiudy* (M.1932 and 1988). It is worth noting that unlike Mayakovsky (who was later canonised) Esenin never mentioned Stalin in a poem.

84. Nadezhda Mandelstam, *Hope Abandoned*, p. 202. Bukharin was editor of *Prozhektor*. The ban was confirmed by Narbut, head of the *Zemlya i fabrika* publishing house.

85. 'Burya i natisk', *Russkoye iskusstvo*, January 1923. Trans. in Mandelstam, *The Complete Critical Prose and Letters* (Ann Arbor, 1979) pp. 170–80.

86. Discussed by Amanda Haight, *Anna Akhmatova: A Poetic Pilgrimage* (Oxford, 1976) pp. 82–4.

87. Ivanov-Razumnik, *Pisatel'skiye sud'by* (New York, 1952) pp. 28–9. Not unnaturally, she referred to this as a 'pre-Gutenberg' era.

88. Nadezhda Mandelstam, *Hope against Hope*, p. 117.

89. 'Anna Akhmatova' in *Literaturnaya entsiklopediya*, vol. 1 (M.1929).

90. G. Lelevich, 'Anna Akhmatova' in *Na postu*, 1923 (2/3).

91. Speech of 1922, quoted by Haight, *Akhmatova*, p. 71.

92. Aleksei Kruchenykh, *Vechernyaya Moskva*, 9 October 1925. See Woroszylski, pp. 379 ff.

93. Cited from N. Punin's diaries at the University of Texas, Austin, by Lazar' Fleishman, *Boris Pasternak v tridtsatiye gody* (Jerusalem, 1984) p. 12. This is probably the episode attributed to an otherwise unrecorded 'meeting *with Stalin*' in Olga Ivinskaya, *A Captive of Time*

(London, 1979) p. 62. See Neil Cornwell in *Irish Slavonic Studies*, 1980 (1) p. 134.

94. *Izvestiya*, 25 and 27 February 1927.
95. *Literature and Revolution*, ch. 5 'The Formalist School of Poetry and Marxism'. Trotsky observes: 'The Formalists are followers of St. John. They believe that "in the beginning was the Word". But we believe that in the beginning was the deed.'
96. See A. V. Lunacharsky, in V. Erlich, *Russian Formalism: History-Doctrine* 3rd ed. (New Haven, Conn., 1981) pp. 105–7.
97. Bukharin, 'O formal nom metode v iskusstve', *Krasnaya nov'*, 1925 (3).
98. Erlich, pp. 107–9.
99. Erlich, ch. VII.
100. *Third Factory* (Ann Arbor, Mich., 1977) p. 49.
101. Shklovsky, *Gamburgskii schet* (L.1929; M.1989) p. 109 cited by Piper, *Kaverin*, p. 101.
102. V. Shklovskii, *Tret'ya fabrika* (M.1926).
103. R. Sheldon (trans. and ed.), *Zoo, or Letters not about love* (Ithaca, 1971) pp. 103–4. See the debate between V. Erlich and R. Sheldon in *Slavic Review*, 1976 (1), pp 111–21.
104. See Piper, *Kaverin*, p. 107–9.
105. Maguire, *Red Virgin Soil*, pp. 252–9.
106. Vera T. Reck, *Boris Pil'niak: A Soviet Writer in Conflict with the State* (Montreal, 1975) p. 28.
107. See the account by E. H. Carr, *Soviet Studies*, 1958 (2) pp. 162–4.
108. A. Voronskii, 'Pis'mo v redaktsiiu', *Novyi mir*, 1926 (6) p. 184.
109. *Literaturnoye nasledstvo*, vol. 70, p. 79.
110. *Arkhiv A. M. Gor'kogo*, xii (M.1965) p. 38.
111. Ibid., p. 39 (24 July 1926). Pil'nyak's own retraction was made much later. He addressed V. Polonsky (on *Izvestiya* notepaper) on 24 December 1926, TSGALI f. 1328, opis 1, ed.khr. 275. Attributing the delay to absence abroad, he now considered it 'greatly mistaken to have written and published such a *Tale*'. Polonsky approved this for publication in *Novyi mir*, 1927 (1) p. 256.
112. Voronsky's catholic approach is discussed in Maguire, *Red Virgin Soil*, esp. pp. 392–416.
113. *Krasnaya nov'*, 1927 (4).
114. Letter of 10 March 1927. *Literaturnoye nasledstvo*, vol. 70, p. 907. He also expected V. Polonsky to be dismissed.
115. The book was *Tvorcheskii teatr'. Puti sotsialisticheskogo teatra* (Petrograd, 1918).
116. *Arkhiv A. M. Gor'kogo*, xii, p. 50 (Letter of 23 March 1927).
117. Reference to H. G. Wells's novel, *Krasnaya nov'* 1927 (6) pp. 238–49.
118. *Pravda*, 30 April 1927.
119. See Leonard B. Schapiro, *The Communist Party of the Soviet Union* (London, 1960) pp. 278–9.
120. See above, n. 29.
121. TSGALI f.1698, opis 1, ed.khr. 916. Averbakh spoke on 'cultural revolution' and Fadeyev on the need for an artistic 'proletarian hegemony'.

122. His views were elaborated at the First All-Union Conference of Proletarian and Revolutionary Writers (15–16 November 1927). See also Lunacharsky's article of the same day in *Revolyutsiya i kul'tura*, 1927 (1). This was the first number of a new 'thick' journal, edited by Bukharin, Deborin, Pashukanis and others.
123. *Na literaturnom postu*, 1927 (22/23).
124. M. Lewin, *Russian Peasants and Soviet Power: A Study of Collectivisation* (London, 1968) ch. 10 'Stalin Changes Course'.
125. 'Pravii uklon'. Unlike the left, it was never called an 'opposition'.
126. The first two were regarded as either 1905 and 1917 or February and October 1917.
127. J. V. Stalin, *Sochineniya*, VI.
128. Interview with A. I. Ovcharenko (Moscow, October 1977).
129. J. V. Stalin, *Sochineniya*, VII, records that on 7 February 1925 he met 'a delegation of the *Proletkul't* concerning its future work'.
130. TSGALI, fond 457, opis 3, ed.tcbr. 101 (23 October 1926).
131. See above pp. 42–3.
132. S. M. Krylov (ed.) *Puti razvitiya teatra* (M.1927).
133. Luncharsky, ibid., pp. 15–41.
134. Knorin, introduction to op. cit., pp. 5–13, and speech, op.cit., pp. 245–60.
135. Averbakh, ibid., pp. 222–4.
136. B. S. Ol'khovy (ed.), *Puti kino* (M.1929). Krinitsky's career is described in *Voprosy istorii KPSS*, 1964 (12) pp. 96–9.
137. *Puti kino*, p. 439.
138. 'The Emergence of *Glaviskusstvo*: "Class War on the Cultural Front" (Moscow, 1928–29)', *Soviet Studies*, October 1971. Its first head, Svidersky, a former Minister of Agriculture, was clearly on his way down.
139. Ibid., pp. 238–41.
140. Libedinsky and Fadeyev's speeches appear in *Tvorcheskie puti proletarskoi literaturi* (M.1929). See also Sheshukov, *Neistovye revniteli*, pp. 160–73.
141. Krinitsky, *Pravda*, 5 May 1928.
142. *Na literaturnom postu*, 1928 (11/12); A. V. Lunacharsky, *Sobraniye sochinenii*, vol. 8, pp. 17–18.
143. See P. Desai (ed.) *Marxism, central planning, and the Soviet Economy: Economic essays in honor of A. Erlich* (Cambridge, Mass. 1983).
144. The shorthand name given to Stalin's grain-collecting campaign conducted at gun-point in early 1928. It may have been his last visit to the countryside.
145. Stalin, *Sochineniya*, XI (13 February 1928) p. 15.
146. Ibid., (18 April 1928) p. 46.
147. It lasted, with daily press coverage, for six weeks. See Kendall E. Bailes, *Technology and Society under Lenin and Stalin: Origins of the Soviet Technical Intelligentsia, 1917–1941* (New Jersey, 1978) ch. 3.
148. Stalin, *Sochineniya*, XI (April 1928) p. 53.
149. *Sochineniya*, X (5 August 1927) p. 61.

150. Speech to the Eighth Congress of Komsomol (16 May 1928) *Sochineniya*, XI, pp. 70–4.
151. Ibid., p. 77.
152. See Bailes, *Technology and Society*, pp. 81–5.
153. On Tomsky's role see Cohen, *Bukharin*, pp. 283–91.
154. Houghton Library, Harvard, Trotsky Exile Papers T. 1588.
155. Stalin, *Sochineniya*, XI, p. 216.
156. Bukharin, 'Proletariat i voprosy literatury', which stated 'our domestic policy does not follow the line of fanning class struggle but, on the contrary, goes some way towards dampening it down', *Krasnaya nov'*, 1925 (4).
157. Krinitsky, quoted in Fitzpatrick, *Soviet Studies*, October 1971, p. 243.
158. *Izvestiya TsK VKP (b)*, 1928 (16/17) p. 14. This was a *Sovnarkom* resolution of 13 April 1928: *Sobraniye uzakonenii RSFSR*, 1928 (41).
159. *Spravochnik partiinovo rabotnika: Vypusk VII (i)* (M.1930) pp. 410–16 and pp. 421–2.
160. Depletion of the original board, by death or disgrace, was rapid and soon almost total. Rarely can a great scholarly enterprise have begun at a less auspicious moment.
161. *Vestnik kommunisticheskoi akademii*, 1928 (2) p. 244.
162. *Kratkii otchet o rabote Kommakademii za 1928/1929 gg.* (M.1929) pp. 38–42.
163. *Partiinoye stroitel'stvo*, 1930 (2) p. 24.
164. See the study by Peter Ferdinand, 'The Bukharin group of political theoreticians. Their ideas and their importance to the Soviet Union in the 1920's'. Unpublished D.Phil. dissertation, University of Oxford, 1984.
165. Stalin, *Sochineniya*, XI pp. 81–97 (28 May 1928).
166. See A. Avtorkhanov, *Stalin and the Soviet Communist Party* (New York, 1959) pp. 43–47. 'Theoretical brigades' headed by Yudin and Shcherbakov were explicitly directed towards cultural policy.
167. F. M. Vaganov, 'Pravy uklon v VKP(b) i evo razgrom', unpublished doctoral dissertation (M.1970) pp. 500–02.
168. Ibid.
169. 'K teorii imperialisticheskogo gosudartsvta' (1916). Translated in Richard B. Day, *N. I. Bukharin: Selected Writings on the State and the Transition to Socialism* (Nottingham, 1982) p. 31; *Ekonomika perekhodnovo perioda* (M.1920). Partly trans. in Day, *Selected Writings*, p. 84.
170. Stalin, *Sochineniya*, XI, pp. 167–72.
171. Kamenev's report to Zinoviev is available at the Houghton Library, Harvard University, T.1897.
172. The balance of forces is discussed by Cohen, *Bukharin*, pp. 296–9.
173. Stalin, *Sochineniya*, XI, pp. 215–17.
174. Bailes, *Technology and Society*, pt. 3; Sheila Fitzpatrick, *Education and social mobility in the Soviet Union, 1921–1934* (Cambridge, 1979) pt. 2.
175. Fitzpatrick, 'The Emergence of *Glaviskusstvo*', p. 242.
176. See 'V Glavrepertkome', *Na literaturnom postu*, 1928 (20/21) p. 137.

177. Shane, *Zamyatin*, pp. 63–4. The play had been inspired by a proposal from Gorky in 1919.
178. Published in Evgenii Zamyatin, *Litsa* (New York, 1967) pp. 277–82 (dated 'June 1931'). Stalin acceded to the request to emigrate. Zamyatin died in Paris in 1937.
179. See A. Colin Wright, *Mikhail Bulgakov: Life and Interpretations* (Toronto, 1978) p. 126.
180. See E. Proffer, *Bulgakov: Life and Works* (Ann Arbor, 1984) pp. 614–15.
181. Wright, *Bulgakov*, p. 127.
182. *Komsomol'skaya pravda*, 23 October 1928.
183. Averbakh and Kirshon, 'Pochemu my protiv *Bega* M. Bulgakova', *Na literaturnom postu* 1928 (20/21) pp. 48–50.
184. Wright, *Bulgakov*, pp. 128–9.
185. Stalin, *Sochineniya*, XI, p. 327 (2 February 1929, first published 1949).
186. Ibid., pp. 328–9.
187. *Crimson Island* (1929) by M. Levidov (1891–1942).
188. See E. Braun, *The Theatre of Meyerhold* (London, 1979) ch. 9.
189. Quoted from *Komsomol'skaya pravda*, 31 August 1928, by Fitzpatrick, 'The Emergence of *Glaviskusstvo*', p. 249. Further critique appeared in *Zhizn' iskusstva*, 1928 (34) and the weekly *Novyi zritel'* began a major campaign on 9 September 1928, with an editorial 'Meyerhold's Crisis'.
190. Telegram of Meyerhold to Lunacharsky (19 September) in *Pravda*, 20 September 1928. Telegram to Rykov, *Vechernyaya Moskva*, 27 September 1928.
191. *Novy zritel'*, 1928 (39), 23 September 1928, p. 6. This was preceeded by an editorial, 'On Meyerhold's Theatre'.
192. IMLI f.40, opis 1, ed.khr. 71, p. 452.
193. Article by Kerzhentsev in *Pravda*, 21 September 1928.
194. Fitzpatrick, 'The Emergence of *Glaviskusstvo*', p. 249.
195. Editorial: *Na literaturnom postu*, 1928 (20/21).
196. IMLI f.40, opis 1. ed.khr. 1153 (28 February 1929).
197. Stalin's earlier remarks on Pil'nyak had appeared in *Foundations of Leninism* (1924).
198. Old Bolshevik and deputy-head of *Agit-prop* 1928–30.
199. Edited by Kerzhentsev.
200. The phrase is Voronsky's from the 1927 campaign.
201. See Cohen, *Bukharin*, pp. 296–9.
202. The full text was first published in A. Kemp-Welch (ed.) *The Ideas of Nikolai Bukharin* (Oxford, 1991).
203. Robert C. Tucker, *Stalin as Revolutionary 1879–1929* (London, 1973) p. 452.
204. See Moshe Lewin, *Russian Peasants*, p. 317. Also Robert V. Daniels, *The Conscience of the Revolution*, ch. 13.
205. Vaganov, 'Pravy uklon' p. 500–02.
206. Ibid.
207. 'Politicheskoye zaveshchaniye Lenina', *Pravda*, 24 January 1929.
208. Cited by Rudzutak, *XVI s"ezd VKP (b)* (M.1930) p. 200.
209. Stalin, *Sochineniya*, XII (M.1949) pp. 1–107.

210. XVI *konferentsiya VKP (b): aprel' 1929 goda* (M.1962).
211. See Peter Ferdinand's thesis (n. 164 above).
212. Lynne Viola, *The Best Sons of the Fatherland: Workers in the Vanguard of Soviet Collectivisation* (Oxford, 1987).
213. This point is elaborated in 'Introduction', to A. Kemp-Welch (ed.) *The Ideas of Nikolai Bukharin.*
214. Nadezhda Mandelstam, *Hope Against Hope*, p. 117.
215. *Annali, 1966* (Milan, 1966) pp. 648–9; *Isaac Babel: The Lonely Years*, (London, 1966) p. 134.
216. Letter to Gorky (2 April 1931). *Arkhiv A. M. Gor'kogo* xii, pp. 78–9.
217. One chapter appeared in *Novyi mir*, 1964 (8) pp. 228–39.
218. *Pechat' i revolyutsiya*, 1929 (2/3).
219. TSGALI f.1328, opis 2, ed.khr. 172. Letter of Friche to V. P. Polonsky (20 February 1929).
220. Fragments appeared in S. A. Fedyukin, *Sovetskaya vlast'*, p. 244, and M. P. Kim (ed.) *Kul'turnaya revolyutsiya v SSSR, 1917–1965 gg.* (M.1967) pp. 314–25. Lunacharsky's earlier attempts to reply included 'Class struggle in Art', *Iskusstvo* 1929 (1/2); 'Politics and Literature', *Vechernyaya Moskva*, 25 February 1929.
221. IMLI f.40, opis I. ed.khr. 3.
222. Ibid.
223. Ibid.
224. *Na literaturnom postu*, 1929 (9) pp. 2–3.
225. IMLI f.40, opis 1, ed.khr. 873.
226. David Iosipovich Zaslavsky (1880–1965) attacked Mandelstam in *Literaturnaya gazeta*, 7 May 1929, and again on 20 May 1929.
227. *Literaturnaya gazeta*, 10 May 1929.
228. *Literaturnaya gazeta*, 13 May 1929. Leningrad writers' organisations refused to intervene and an investigation by the Writers' Federation (FOSP) proved inconclusive.
229. *Pravda* and *Izvestiya*, 21 April 1928.
230. *Komsomol'skaya pravda*, 26 May 1928.
231. An article by Astrov, a member of Bukharin's 'school', 'Gor'kii i komchvanstvo' appeared in *Pravda*, 2/3 June 1928. Also *Na literaturnom postu* 1928 (11/12). See Sheshukov, *Neistovye revniteli*, p. 220.
232. IMLI f.40, opis I, ed.khr. 2 (29 August 1928).
233. A delegation, headed by Kirshon and Fadeyev, visited the Central Committee Secretariat, asking for the decision to be rescinded: IMLI f.40, opis 1, ed.khr. 2.
234. *Letopis' zhizni i tvorchestva A. M. Gor'kogo*, vol. 3 (M.1959) pp. 593–673.
235. It was also addressed by Yaroslavsky, Mayakovsky and Demyan Bedny: *Pravda*, 11 June 1929.
236. *Letopis'*, vol. 3, pp. 729–48. He also visited the 'Gigant' kolkhoz: see paper by R. W. Davies in Abramsky, C. (ed.), *Essays in Honour of E. H. Carr* (London, 1974) p. 261.
237. Feliks Kon was a 'veteran Polish Bolshevik'. See: E. H. Carr, *The Bolshevik Revolution*, vol. III (London, 1966) p. 215.
238. This unusual epithet became standard form for Stalin.

239. Stalin, *Sochineniya*, XII, p. 114.
240. Ibid.
241. Sheshukov, *Neistovye revniteli.*
242. Ibid, p. 225.
243. *Nastoyashchee*, quoted by Sheshukov, ibid. Gorky complained about this treatment to M. A. Savel'iev (Stalin's appointment to *Pravda*) on 13 September 1929.
244. This occured later. Central Committee Resolution: 'O vystuplenii chast i sibirskikh literatorov i literaturnikh organizatsii protiv M. Gor'kogo', 25 December 1929.
245. *Literaturnaya gazeta*, 26 August 1929.
246. IMLI f.40, opis 1, ed.khr. 3.
247. *Literaturnaya gazeta*, 2 September 1929. See also Reck, *Pil'niak* pp. 92–3; Gary Browning, *Boris Pilniak: Scythian at a Typewriter* (Ann Arbor, 1985) pp. 39–49.
248. IMLI f.40, opis 1, ed.khr. 3 (2 September 1929).
249. *Literaturnaya gazeta*, 9 September 1929.
250. *Literaturnaya gazeta*, 16 September 1929.
251. See the account by Shane, *Zamyatin*, pp. 72–6.
252. Gizetti, quoted in *Literaturnaya gazeta*, 30 September 1929.
253. Ibid.
254. Letter of 24 September 1929, translated in *A Soviet Heretic: Essays by Yevgeny Zamyatin* (Chicago, 1970) pp. 301–04.
255. *Literaturnaya gazeta* 9 and 16 September 1929.
256. 'O trate energii', *Izvestiya*, 15 September 1929. It also appears in N. F. Bel'chikov (ed.) *M. Gor'kii o literature: Stat'i i rechi, 1928–1936*, 3rd. ed. (M.1937) pp. 47–50, dated simply '1930'. Gorky's reply to criticism of the above article was not published.

3 PROLETARIAN HEGEMONY

1. This may be analogous to Gramsci's notion of 'hegemony' as a dual process of displacement. Communist intellectuals displace the hegemony of the bourgeoisie 'from above', while 'from below' the masses bring forth a new social order based on their labour. See A. Gramsci, *Selections from the Prison Notebooks* (London, 1971). According to Gramsci, this is achieved through combining all forces opposed to capitalism into a 'new, homogenous politico-economic historical bloc, without internal contradictions'. See John Cammett, *Antonio Gramsci and the Origins of Italian Communism* (Stanford, 1967) p. 204. The present chapter also describes the fragmentation and eventual failure of such a 'bloc'.
2. Described by Lynne Viola, *Best Sons*, pp. 90 ff.
3. S. Fitzpatrick, *Education and Social Mobility in the USSR, 1921–1934* (Cambridge, 1979) pp. 137–63.
4. For an elaboration of this concept see Kendall E. Bailes, *Technology and Society under Lenin and Stalin* (Princeton, 1978) ch. 7; and the discussion between Bailes and Fitzpatrick in *Slavic Review*, June 1980.

5. S. Frederick Starr, 'Visionary Town Planning during the Cultural Revolution', in S. Fitzpatrick (ed.) *Cultural Revolution in Russia, 1928–1931* (Indiana, 1978) pp. 207–40.
6. See below, Chapter Four.
7. The unpublished stenogram is IMLI f.40, opis 1, ed.khr. 72–80.
8. IMLI f.40, opis 1, ed.khr. 72.
9. Ibid.
10. IMLI f.40, opis 1, ed.khr. 72. Fadeyev's speech is further discussed by L. Kiseleva, 'Problema khudozhestvennogo metoda', in *Iz istorii sovetskoi esteticheskoi mysli: sbornik statei* (M.1967) pp. 426–45.
11. Libedinsky, quoted by Edward J. Brown, *The Proletarian Episode in Russian Literature* (New York 1953) pp. 67–8.
12. S. Sheshukov, *Neistovye revniteli: Iz istorii literaturnoi bor'by 20-kh godov* (M.1970) pp. 182–5.
13. IMLI f.40, opis 1, ed.khr. 73 pp. 151–2. Mayakovsky and Brik had left *Novyi LEF* in August 1928.
14. Discussed in Vahan D. Barooshian, *Brik and Mayakovsky* (The Hague, 1978) pp. 61 ff.
15. IMLI f.40, opis 1, ed.khr. 73, p. 257.
16. V. Mayakovsky, *Polnoye sobraniye sochinenii* (M.1955–1961) vol. 12, p. 381; IMLI f.40, opis 1, ed.khr. 73 pp. 195–201. Critical appraisals of the Plenum, both entitled 'Itogi', were published by B. Ol'khovy, *Pravda*, 20 October 1929 and *Pechat' i revolyutsiya*, 1929 (10).
17. IMLI f.41, opis 1, ed.khr. 873.
18. *Izvestiya TsK VKP (b)* 1929 (23), p. 23.
19. *Literaturnaya gazeta*, 4 November 1929 and *Vechernyaya Moskva*, 16 November 1929.
20. A. I. Stetsky was formerly head of the Leningrad *Agit-prop* and a Central Committee member since 1927. He, alone of Bukharin's major followers, defected to Stalin (in March 1929). See Stephen F. Cohen, *Bukharin and the Bolshevik Revolution* (New York, 1973) p. 308.
21. P. M. Kerzhentsev was an Old Bolshevik (Party member since 1904) who had held a number of government and diplomatic posts before becoming Deputy Head of *Agit-prop* in Moscow in 1928. He, too, played a part in the downfall of Bukharin and in the Stalinisation of the Communist Academy, whose Vice-President he became in 1930.
22. S. Ossowski, *Struktura klasowa*, pp. 26–38.
23. IMLI f.41, opis 1, ed.khr. 454 (14 March 1930).
24. IMLI f.40, opis 1, ed.khr. 873.
25. *Pechat' i revolyutsiya*, 1929 (10) accused *Na postu* of being 'right deviation in practice'.
26. See Sheshukov, *Neistovye revniteli*, p. 224.
27. The new editor, Lev Mekhlis, was Stalin's man. See Robert C. Tucker, *Stalin as Revolutionary*, pp. 294, 465.
28. By B. Ol'khovy, *Pravda*, 20 October 1929. Shatskin was held responsible for a 'Komsomol deviation' concerned with the entitlement of lower echelons to criticise their leaderships. It has yet to be documented.
29. It will be recalled that Bukharin made precisely the same criticism of proletarian writers in 1925, and wrote it into the Resolution.

30. *Pravda*, 4 December 1929.

31. J. V. Stalin, *Sochineniya*, XII, pp. 141–2.

32. *Pravda*, 10 February 1930.

33. B. T. Ermakov, 'Bor'ba K. P. za perestroiku raboty nauchnikh uchrezhdenii v godi pervoi pyatiletki', unpublished candidate's thesis (M., 1955) pp. 284–5. See also David Joravsky, *Soviet Marxism and Natural Science* (London, 1961), and David Bakhurst,' 'Deborinism versus Mechanism: A Clash of Two Logics in Early Soviet Philosophy', *Slavonic and East European Review*, July 1985, pp. 422–8.

34. *Pravda*, 7 June 1930.

35. 'On the Journal *Pod znamenem marksisma*', *Pravda*, 26 January 1931.

36. The best overview is John Barber, 'The Establishment of Intellectual Orthodoxy in the USSR, 1928–1934', *Past and Present*, May 1979 pp. 141–64.

37. Loren Graham, *The Soviet Academy of Sciences*, chs. IV and V.

38. Prospectus for 1930–1.

39. For Pereverzev's summaries of his views, see Preface to his *Tvorchestvo Dostoyevskogo* (3rd. ed. M.1928) or V. F. Pereverzev (ed.) *Literaturovedeniye.Sbornik statei* (M.1928) pp. 10–12.

40. See *Vestnik kommunisticheskoi akademii*, 1927 (24). Proletarian writers of RAPP, soon to be the severest critics of Pereverzev, concurred. Their attacks on Gorky were rejected by a Central Committee Resolution 'On the speeches of Siberian writers and literary organisations against M. Gorky', as 'profoundly mistaken and verging on hooliganism'. *Pravda*, 25 December 1929.

41. H. Ermolaev, *Soviet Literary Theories*, p. 95. For a fuller study see H. G. Scott, 'An Experiment in Sociology of Form: A Re-evaluation of the "crude sociologism" of V. F. Pereverzev', unpublished PhD dissertation, University of Chicago, 1981.

42. The stenographic account is *Protiv mekhanisticheskogo literaturovedeniya. Diskussiya o kontseptsii V. F. Pereverzeva* (Moscow Communist Academy, 1930).

43. Variously issued: *Pravda*, 18 December 1929; *Pod znamenem marksisma* 1930 (1); and even in a special booklet, *Dve kritik (Plekhanov-Pereverzev)* (M.1930).

44. Averbakh's earlier critique, given in the Communist Academy on 5 December 1929, was reissued twice: *Na literaturnom postu* 1930 (1/2); and *Oktyabr'*, 1930 (1/2).

45. *Protiv mekhan, lit.*, p. 110.

46. Sutyrin, p. 81.

47. Ibid.; Nusinov, p. 78; Gel'fand, pp. 84–5.

48. The article by Bespalov, Gel'fand and Zonin appeared in *Pravda*, 25 January 1930.

49. B. T. Ermakov, 'Bor'ba K. P.', unpublished dissertation, (M.1955). The Communist Academy Secretariat on 25 February: TSGALI f.1698, opis I ed.khr. 931, gave Averbakh and his followers muted approval.

50. V. Mayakovsky, *Polnoye sobraniye sochinenii*, XII, p. 387.

51. Barooshian, *Brik and Mayakovsky*, p. 102.

52. To Alexander Serebrov-Tikhonov, cited by Wiktor Woroszylski, *The Life of Mayakovsky* (London, 1971) pp. 500–1.

53. Yu. Libedinsky, *Sovremenniki* (M.1961) p. 180.
54. This is, of course, poetry not prose. See Wovoszylski, pp. 492–7.
55. *Vechernyaya Moskva*, 8 February 1930.
56. Libedinsky, *Sovremenniki*, pp. 180–2.
57. Viktor Shklovsky, *Mayakovsky and his Circle* (London, 1974) pp. 200–1.
58. TSGALI f.969.
59. IMLI f.54, opis I, ed.khr. 45.
60. IMLI f.54, opis 1, ed.khr. 19. (18 April 1930).
61. IMLI f.40, opis 1, ed.khr. 6.
62. Ibid.
63. *Pravda*, 9 March 1930.
64. *Vechernyaya Moskva*, 13 March 1930. Ermilov replied ibid, 17 March 1930.
65. For further criticisms see E. J. Brown, *Mayakovsky*, pp. 333–5.
66. Woroszylski, p. 510.
67. A. Dovzhenko, reminiscences, *Literaturnaya gazeta*, 16 November 1962.
68. 'Samoubiistvo V. Mayakovskogo', *Byulleten' oppozitsii*, no. 11 (1930) pp. 39–40.
69. E. J. Brown, *Mayakovsky* pp. 362–3.
70. *Literaturnoye nasledstvo* vol. 65 (M.1965) p. 199.
71. IMLI f.40, opis 1, ed.khr. 25 (17 April 1930).
72. *Komsomol'skaya pravda*, 20 April 1930.
73. *Pravda*, 10 May 1930. For a recent Soviet discussion of Mayakovsky's final years, including his relationship with RAPP, see *Oktyabr'*, 1987 (6).
74. On Pereval's history see G. Glinka, *Na Perevale* (New York, 1954). Other studies referring to the group include: René Śliwowski, *Dawni i nowi. Szkice o literaturze radzieckiej* (Warsaw, 1967) pp. 73–111; and M. Geller, *Andrei Platonov v poiskakh schast'ya*, (Paris, 1982).
75. *Na literaturnom postu*, 1930 (5/6) and *Komsomol'skaya pravda*, 8 March 1930.
76. *Kotlovan* was first published in *Novyi mir*, 1987 (6).
77. 'The Foundation Pit': Andrei Platonov, *Collected Works* (Ann Arbor, 1978).
78. *Novyi mir*, 1928 (6) Only one chapter was published.
79. *Literaturnoye nasledstvo*, vol. 70, p. 103; pp. 313–15.
80. *Chevengur* was published in *Druzhba narodov*, 1988 (3) and (4).
81. *Krasnaya nov'*, 1931 (3).
82. For RAPP's resolution, see IMLI f.40, opis 1, ed.khr. 25; also see L. Averbakh, *Iz rappovskovo dnevnika* (L.1931) pp. 59–73.
83. *Krasnaya nov'*, 1931 (5/6); *Izvestiya*, 3 July 1931.
84. N. M. Mitrakova, *A. P. Platonov (1899–1951) Materiali k bibliografii* (Voronezh, 1969) p. 20.
85. *Literaturnaya gazeta*, 10 March 1930.
86. *Protiv burzhuaznogo liberalizma v khudozhestvennoi literature: Sbornik statei* (Moscow, Communist Academy, 1931) p. 11.
87. A. Lezhnev, pp. 31–8.
88. *Rovesniki*, vol. 7 (Moscow, 1932).

89. See Chapter Five.
90. *Pechat' i revolyutsiya*, 1930 (5/6).
91. *Leningradskaya pravda*, 15 June 1930.
92. TSGALI f.1029, opis 2, ed.khr. 22 (dated 'April 1930').
93. *Tvorcheskaya diskussiya v RAPPe. Sbornik stenogram i materialov III oblastnoi konferentsii LAPPa (15–21 May 1930g.)* (M.1930). Gel'fand's speech appears on pp. 202–41. It was reprinted in pamphlet form, with his 'concluding word' in *O tvorcheskom metode proletarskoi literaturi i ob oshibkakh napostovtsev* (M.1930). At the conference, Fadeyev replied for RAPP. An excerpt appeared in *Pechat' i revolyutsiya*, 1930 (5/6) p. 113.
94. Kirshon's speech appeared in *Tvorcheskaya diskussiya*.
95. IMLI f.40, opis 1, ed.khr. 8 p. 63; pp. 75–6.
96. IMLI f.40, opis I, ed.khr. 25.
97. See also Sheshukov, *Neistovye revniteli* pp. 273–5.
98. *The Shot* (1930) caused a political sensation.
99. Stalin, *Sochinenii*, XII, pp. 200–1.
100. *Na literaturnom postu*, 1930 (2) (Sutyrin) and 1930 (4) (Ermilov) were particularly venomous.
101. *XVI s'ezd VKP(b): sten'otchet* (M.1931) p. 281.
102. Ibid, pp. 698–9.
103. IMLI f.40, opis 1, ed.khr. 25.
104. Ibid.
105. The most important appeared on 15 August 1930.
106. IMLI f.40, opis 1, ed.khr. 25.
107. IMLI f.40, opis 1, ed.khr. 865 (27 June 1930).
108. IMLI f.40, opis 1, ed.khr. 865 (22 July 1930).
109. *Pravda*, 3 September 1930.
110. IMLI f.40, opis 1, ed.khr. 25 (11 September 1930).
111. *Pravda*, 23 September 1930.
112. IMLI f.40, opis 1, ed.khr. 16.
113. IMLI f.40, opis 1, ed.khr. 873 (23 November 1930).
114. Sheshukov, *Neistovye revniteli* p. 290.
115. Roy Medvedev, *Let History Judge* pp. 110–33, rejected their legality. This is now confirmed by the Supreme Court.
116. IMLI f.40, opis 1, ed.khr. 25.
117. The evidence is evaluated by R. W. Davies, 'The Syrtsov-Lominadze Affair', *Soviet Studies*, 1981 (1) pp. 42–5.
118. IMLI f.40, opis 1, ed.khr. 25.
119. N. Mandelstam, *Hope Against Hope*, p. 165.
120. IMLI f.54, opis 1, ed.khr. 45; f.40, opis 1, ed. khr. 18 and 25.
121. *XVI s"ezd VKP(b): sten'otchet* (M.1931) pp. 500–3.
122. Ibid.
123. See, for instance, the appeal 'To all Workers in Literature and Art': 'We writers, poets, composers, artists and actors, consider it our vital duty at the present stage of development of Soviet art, to reflect in our works the gigantic task of construction now taking place, particularly that in the Urals'. The Urals brigade included the writers Leonov, V. Ivanov, Bezymensky, Pavlenko, Shaginyan and Vishnevsky, as well as Meyer-

hold, Tairov and Shostakovich. *Soviet Cultural Review*, 1932 (5).

124. V. Polonsky, *Magnitostroi* (M.1930) p. 12.

125. Valentin Katayev, *Time, Forward!* (M.1933), trans. reprinted Bloomington, Indiana, 1976, p. 193.

126. L. Leonov, *Sot'* (M.1931). Introduction.

127. On *izgoi*, see: *Den' vtoroi* (M.1933) pp. 41–3. On the writing of the novel: Ilya Ehrenburg, *Men, Years, Life*, vol. III, pp. 230–5. A valuable study is Robert Louis Jackson, *Dostoyevsky's Underground Man in Russian Literature* (The Hague, 1958).

128. Victor Serge, *Memoirs of a Revolutionary, 1901–1941* (Oxford, 1967) pp. 269–70.

129. For this, see Max Eastman, *Artists in Uniform*, ch. 11.

130. The 'Industrial Party' Trial (25 November–7 December 1930) was presided over by Vyshinsky. See Roy Medvedev, *Let History Judge*, pp. 114–21; Loren Graham, *The Soviet Academy*, pp. 174–5 and A. Solzhenitsyn, *The GULag Archipelago* (London, 1974) vols 1/2 pp. 376–99.

131. See 'OGPU-Orden Lenina', *Pravda*, 13 November 1930. Meeting of VOAPP, 17 November 1930. See *VOKS*, 1931 (1) p. 68.

132. *Izvestiya*, 14 December 1930. It has been suggested that the article was prompted by gratitude to Stalin, who had sent him a personal letter granting him permission to visit the USA. See Browning, *Pilniak*, pp. 53–4 and p. 203 (n. 13).

133. 'Neobkhodimost' perestroiki mne iasna', *30 dnei*, 1932 (5) pp. 67–8.

134. Arkady Belinkov: *Sdacha i gibel' sovetskogo intelligenta: Yury Olesha* (Madrid, 1976).

135. *Pervyi vsesoyuzny s"ezd sovetskikh pisatelei* (M.1934) pp. 234–6.

136. See Beaujour, *Invisible Land*, pp. 115–30.

137. See the autobiographical essay 'Ocherk raboty' (1964) in 'Introduction' to H. Oulanoff, *The Prose Fiction of Veniamin A. Kervin* (Cambridge, Mass., 1976) pp. 6–7. On *'Skandalist'* see Piper, *Kaverin* pp. 125–65.

138. V. Kaverin, 'An Undelivered speech to the Serapion Brothers', *Russian Literature Triquarterly* (Ann Arbor) vol. 2. (Winter, 1972) pp. 470–4.

139. V. Katayev, *The Holy Well* (London, 1967).

140. Nadezhda Mandelstam, *Hope Abandoned* pp. 526–35.

141. Mandelstam, *The Complete Critical Prose and Letters* (Ann Arbor, 1979) pp. 312–25.

142. He had long acted as 'protector'. See Nadezhda Mandelstam, *Hope Against Hope*, pp. 112–18. The subsequent trip to Armenia, arranged through him, is mentioned on pp. 250–1.

143. *The Complete Critical Prose*, pp. 344–78.

144. Published first in *Zvezda*, 1933 (5). The sacked editor was Tsezar' Volpe. Further details of the scandal appear in Nadezhda Mandelstam, *Hope Abandoned*, p. 410.

145. Nadezhda Mandelstam, *Hope Against Hope*, pp. 150–1.

146. *Hope Against Hope*, p. 149.

147. See Max Hayward, 'Introduction' to Olga Ivinskaya, *A Captive of Time: My Years with Pasternak* (London, 1978) p. xxvii.

148. *Stikhotvoreniya i poemi* (1965) pp. 350–1.

149. A Selivanovsky, 'Poeziya opasna?' *Literaturnaya gazeta*, 15 August 1931.
150. See Roy Medvedev, *On Stalin and Stalinism* (Oxford, 1979) p. 78. This also appears in Robert C. Tucker, (ed) *Stalinism: Essays in Historical Interpretation* (New York, 1977) p. 212.
151. See Smolensk Archive, WKP 260 (23–8 February 1930) pp. 34–42.
152. Smolensk Archive, WKP 162, Central Directives on Collectivisation.
153. *Literaturnaya gazeta*, 14 May 1986.
154. Teodor Shanin, *The Awkward Class* (Oxford, 1972).
155. L. M. Zak, 'Stroitel'stvo sotsialisticheskoi kul'tury v SSSR, 1933–1937', unpublished doctoral dissertation, (M.1966).
156. See the data from Central Party Archives in F. M. Vaganov, 'Pravyi uklon' (unpublished doctoral dissertation).
157. I. Babel, 'Kolyvushka', trans. Max Hayward in *Isaac Babel: The Lonely Years, 1925–1939* (New York, 1964) p. 5.
158. I. Babel, 'Gapa Guzhva', *Novyi mir*, 1931 (10). Translated in ibid., p. 34.
159. Public Record Office (London), Russian Correspondence, 1929–39.
160. Cited by H. Ermolaev, *Mikhail Sholokhov and His Art* (Princeton, 1982) p. 29. Stalin's own attitude was ambiguous. In the letter to Feliks Kon, 3 July 1929, *Sochineniya*, XII, p. 112, he referred to Sholokhov as 'a prominent writer of our time who has made in his *Quiet Don* a number of blunders and outright erroneous assertions'. When this was published, in 1949, Sholokhov immediately wrote for chapter-and verse. Stalin did not reply.
161. Ermolaev, *Sholokhov*, pp. 29–30 and p. 308 (n. 82).
162. Written at the Politburo's behest, *Pravda*, 3 March 1930.
163. See Lynne Viola, *Best Sons*, ch. 2.
164. Moshe Lewin, 'Who was the Soviet kulak?' in M. Lewin, *The Making of the Soviet Union* (London, 1985).
165. For instance, A. F. Britikov, *Masterstvo Mikhaila Sholokhova* (M.1964).
166. Ermolaev, *Sholokhov*, p. 32.
167. See Britikov, *Masterstvo Mikhaila Sholokhova*, pp. 47–8, cited from archives.
168. 'Razgovor s Sholokhovym', *Izvestiya*, 10 March 1935.
169. F. Panfyorov, *Bruski: A Story of Peasant Life* (London, 1930) p. 201.
170. M. Kantor, *Bol'shevik*, 1933 (23); Vasil'kovsky, *Oktyabr'*, 1933 (10).
171. See chapter Six below.
172. See the entry on VOKP in *Literaturnaya entsiklopediya* (M.1929) in vol. I.
173. Ibid.
174. Ibid.
175. O. Beskin, 'Kulatskaya literatura', *Literaturnaya entsiklopediya* (M.1931) vol. V. Also the same author's *Kulatskaya khudozhestven-naya literatura i opportuniistcheskaya kritika* (Moscow, Communist Academy, 1930).
176. N. A. Klyuev (1887–1937).
177. S. A. Klychkov (1889–1940). See Gordon McVay, 'Nikolay Klyuev and

Sergei Klychkov: Unpublished Texts', *Oxford Slavonic Papers*, vol. 17 (Oxford, 1984) pp. 90–108.

178. In meetings on 26 April, 14 May and 1 November 1932. By 1936, he could only publish translations and adaptions of folklore. Arrested 31 July 1937.

179. This is gradually being admitted in Soviet publications.

180. Stalin, *Sochineniya*, XIII (M.1952) pp. 69–73.

181. Ibid., pp. 72–3.

182. See Sheila Fitzpatrick, 'Culture and Politics under Stalin', *Slavic Review*, 1976 (2) p. 231.

183. As pointed out by Jerry Hough, 'Preface', to V. Dunham, *In Stalin's Time: Middle-class Values in Soviet Fiction* (Cambridge, 1976).

184. The present author's 'Stalinism and Intellectual Order' in T. H. Rigby et. al. (eds) *Authority, Power and Policy in the USSR: Essays dedicated to Leonard Schapiro* (London, 1980).

185. IMLI f.40, opis 1, ed.khr. 2 (29 August 1928) and ed.khr. 3 (2 October 1929) threatening resignation.

186. IMLI f.40, opis 1, ed.khr. 25 (11 March 1930) referring to his departure.

187. IMLI f.40, opis I, ed.khr. 873 (11 July 1930) appeal for return. This was agreed from 1 August. He was back on 13 August 1930.

188. IMLI f.40, opis 1, ed.khr. 873.

189. Edward J. Brown, *Proletarian Episode*, p. 95.

190. Ibid., p. 96.

191. *Na literaturnom postu*, 1931.

192. IMLI f.96, opis 1, ed.khr. 15 (no date).

193. Ibid.

194. IMLI f.96, opis 1, ed.khr. 16 (23 September 1931).

195. Excerpts from this letter (to A. Serafimovich) were first published in A. Plotkin, *Partiya i literatura* (L.1960) pp. 170–1.

196. IMLI f.40, opis 1, ed.khr. 730 (8 September 1931).

197. RAPP extended the technique of literary 'brigades' begun in 1929. Now they accepted the value of fact-finding exercises, earlier derided as 'empiricism' when practised by the Panfyorov group, and issued a call 'Face to Production'.

198. E. J. Brown, *Proletarian Episode* pp. 162–7. The membership figures appear in *Vsya Moskva*, 1931.

199. IMLI f.40, opis 1, ed.khr. 730 (8 September 1931) also Il'yenkov, 'Gruppa t.Panferova', *Na literaturnom postu* 1931 (23).

200. IMLI f.40, opis 1, ed.khr. 730.

201. A. Isbakh, *Na literaturnikh barrikadakh* (M.1964) pp. 203–6.

202. Ibid., p. 204.

203. IMLI f.40, opis 1, ed.khr. 49 (8 December 1931). See also Panfyorov, Il'yenkov, Isbakh and others in *Pravda* 1 September 1931.

204. A. Kosarev, *Bol'shevistskomu pokoleniyu–leninskoye rukovodstvo* (M.1931) pp. 22–3.

205. The campaign was launched at a Komsomol Plenum in early October 1931.

206. *Literaturnaya gazeta* (now edited by the RAPPist Selivanovsky) 22 October 1931.

207. IMLI f.40, opis 1, ed.khr. 877 (21 October 1931).
208. IMLI f.40, opis 1, ed.khr. 45.
209. *Pravda*, 10 November 1931.
210. IMLI f.40, opis 1, ed.khr. 46 (11 November 1931).
211. *Pravda*, 19 November 1931; see also the editorial of 24 November 1931.
212. Stalin, *Sochineniya*, XIII, pp. 86–104.
213. John Barber, *Soviet Historians*, pp. 134–35.
214. See John Barber, 'Stalin's "Letter to the Editors of *Proletarskaya Revolyutsiya*"' *Soviet Studies*, 1976 (1) pp. 21–41.
215. S. Dinamov delivered a speech on 'Militant tasks of Marxist criticism' to the Institute on 28 December 1931, rehearsing these earlier discussions. A reworked version appeared in *Marksistko-leninskoye iskusstvoznaniye*, 1932 (1) p. 3–34.
216. Ibid.
217. *Pravda*, 23 December 1931. See also the tortuous attempt to explicate 'Comrade Stalin's *Letter* and Party Tasks on the Literary Front', by Sergei Malakhov, *Protiv trotskizma i men'shevisma v literaturovedenii* (M.1932) esp. the first half on 'Trotskyist contraband', pp. 3–51.
218. Speech of 11 January 1932 quoted in Barber, *Soviet Historians*, pp. 135–6.
219. TSGALI f.457, opis 4, ed.khr. 27 (6 June 1930).
220. IMLI f.40, opis 1, ed.khr. 46 (11 November 1931).
221. A. K. Romanovsky, 'Iz istorii podgotovki pervovo s"ezda sovetskikh pisatele', unpublished candidate's thesis (M.1958).
222. Romanovsky, pp. 139–43.
223. Ibid.
224. Isbakh, *Na literaturnikh barrikadakh* (M.1964). Also, the same author's memoir of Serafimovich in *Voprosy literatury*, 1958 (11) p. 175.
225. *Pravda*, 23 April 1932.
226. Isbakh., *op. cit.*
227. Nadezhda Mandelstam, *Hope Against Hope*, p. 233.

4 THE NEW ORDER

1. Quoted by Max Eastman, *Artists in Uniform*, p. 161 and note 159 (p. 257).
2. Gleb Struve, *Russian Literature under Lenin and Stalin, 1917–1953* (London, 1972) p. 253.
3. Max Hayward 'Introduction' to Hayward and L. Labedz (eds) *Literature and Revolution in Soviet Russia, 1917–62* (Oxford, 1963) p. xiii.
4. B. Suvarin, 'Poslednie razgovori s Babelem', *Kontinent*, 1980 (23) p. 348.
5. *XVII s'ezd VKP(b): sten'otchot* (M.1934) p. 565. See also p. 564, where the school reform of 1931 is also attributed to Stalin. It is worth noting that other speakers were less effusive.
6. Ibid.

7. *Pravda*, 24 April 1932.
8. RAPM: The Russian Association of Proletarian Musicians.
9. Other cultural Unions were formed at intervals, the latest in 1957.
10. Discussed in A. Kemp-Welch (ed.) *The Ideas of Nikolai Bukharin*.
11. See the report, by B. Rest, in *Literaturnaya gazeta*, 5 May 1932.
12. IMLI f.40, opis 1, ed.khr. 70. Thirty-one fellow-travellers signed the letter.
13. Romanovsky, unpublished thesis, pp. 110–11 (27 April 1932).
14. Romanovsky, p. 145.
15. IMLI f.40, opis I, ed.khr. 70.
16. Ibid.
17. Ibid. This was later confirmed: P. Pavlenko, *Golos v puti* (M.1952) p. 125; M. Slonimkii, 'Pervyi s"ezd sovetskikh pisatele' in *Leningradskii al'manakh*, 1954, Book 9 p. 274.
18. IMLI f.40, opis I, ed.khr. 70.
19. 'Na uroven' novykh zadach', *Pravda*, 9 May 1932. It was widely reprinted. See special supplement to *Marksistko-leninskoye iskusstvoznaniye*, 1932 (4).
20. *Na literaturnom postu*, 1932 (12). 15 May 1932.
21. Romanovsky thesis, p. 149.
22. A. Afinogenov, *Tvorcheskii metod teatra. Dialektika tvorcheskogo protsessa* (M.-L., 1931) and his entry 'Sovetskaya dramaturgiya', in *Bol'shaya sovetskaya entsiklopediya*, XXIII (M.1931).
23. Interview with I. M. Gronsky (Moscow, November 1974). But note the discrepancies between this interview and that with S. Sheshukov, in his *Neistovye revniteli*, pp. 337–8.
24. Romanovsky thesis, p. 149.
25. Ibid.
26. 'Sovetskaya literatura na novom pod"eme', *Komsomol'skaya pravda*, 15 May 1932.
27. Editor of *Izvestiya* until early 1934, when replaced by Bukharin.
28. A literary critic and specialist on Dostoyevsky, working in the Leningrad branch of the Communist Academy. See *Ves' Leningrad*, 1931, p. 43. He also headed the Central Committee's literary section from 1932 until 1936.
29. IMLI f.41, opis 1, ed.khr. 438.
30. Ibid.
31. *Pravda*, 14 May 1932. The apology came (Resolution of 15 May) in *Literaturnaya gazeta*, 17 May 1932.
32. IMLI f.41, opis 1, ed.khr. 438 (28 June 1932).
33. Comment by Illyés: *Sovetskaya literatura na novom etape: sten. otchot. 1-ogo plenuma orgkomiteta* (M.1933) pp. 215–16.
34. IMLI f.41, opis 1, ed.khr. 438.
35. *Na literaturnom postu*, 11 June 1932.
36. Those shut included: *Proletarskaya literatura, Proletarskii avangard* (the journal of *Kuznitsa*) and *Marksistsko-leninskoe iskusstvoznaniye*.
37. IMLI f.41, opis 1, ed.khr. 438 (26 May 1932).
38. IMLI f.41, opis 1, ed.khr. 438 (7 June 1932).

39. Ibid (28 June 1932).
40. Yu. Libedinsky, *Sovremenniki*, p. 237.
41. *Literaturnaya gazeta*, 15 August 1932.
42. A. Fadeyev, *Pis'ma, 1916–1956* (M.1967) pp. 83–5.
43. *Literaturnaya gazeta*, 23 and 29 June 1932.
44. Ye. Usievich, *Za chistotu leninizma v literaturnoi teorii* (M.1932), preface by Yudin. Makar'yev replied, on behalf of RAPP, in the journal *Rost* (edited by Kirshon) 1932 (20) pp. 26–32.
45. *Literaturnaya gazeta*, 23 July 1932. See also the Communist Academy's earlier denunciation of these views, *Za povorot na filosofskom fronte* (M.1931). Discussed by David Joravsky, *Soviet Marxism and Natural Science* (N Y 1961) ch. 15. It will be recalled that Averbakh's opinion of the fellow-travellers was, in fact, the opposite of that held by Trotsky as outlined in Chapter Two.
46. Fadeyev, *Pis'ma*, p. 85.
47. It was later shown that Kuibyshev's statement had been made in January 1930, while RAPP had not adopted this slogan until its Fourth Plenum (September 1931). See Subotsky, *Pervii plenum*, p. 44.
48. The series appeared thus: (1) 'Ally or Enemy?' and where the chief danger lies (11 and 17 October); (2) *Belles-lettres* and questions of cultural revolution (23 October); (3) Tasks of Marxist-Leninist criticism (23 October); (4) Questions of artistic creation (29 October and 11 November).
49. *Literaturnaya gazeta*, 11, 17, 23 August; 11, 17 September 1932.
50. IMLI f.41, opis 1, ed.khr. 668.
51. V. F. Pim, *Vospominaniya o Litinstitute, 1933–1983* (M.1983) p. 6.
52. *Pravda o Gor'kom: sbornik* (M.1932) pp. 41–9.
53. Ibid., pp. 55–62.
54. Ibid., pp. 65–6.
55. Yet to be published. See quotations in: A. I. Ovcharenko, 'Sovetskaya deistvitel'nost' v publitsistike Gor'kogo (1928–1936)' in *Nauchnye doklady wysshei shkoly*; *Filologicheskie nauki* (M.1959) no. 2 pp. 3 ff.
56. Stalin *Sochineniya*, vol. XIII.
57. This took place in July 1931. See Ermolaev, *Sholokhov*, p. 31.
58. See the brief reference in *Sochineniya*, XIII, which mentions that Gorky read out 'Death and the Maiden'.
59. *Pravda*, 10 October 1931.
60. Ibid.
61. See L. M. Zak, (ed.) *A. M. Gor'kii i sozdaniye istorii fabrik i zavodov* (M.1959) p. 44.
62. Letter to Gruzdev of 18 February 1932: see *Arkhiv A. M. Gor'kovo*, xi, p. 287. Also his comments on Averbakh in *Literaturnoye nasledstvo*, vol. 70, p. 542.
63. Consultation with Professor A. I. Ovcharenko (Moscow, October 1977).
64. 'Vstrecha pisatelei s I. V. Stalinym u A. M. Gor'kogo (26 October 1932)' unpublished manuscript, Arkhiv A. M. Gor'kogo.
65. Ibid.
66. The Emil Ludwig interview appears in *Sochineniya*, vol. XIII. Bernard

Shaw went to Russia in July 1931. He met various Soviet writers and also held a long conversation with Stalin.
67. 'Vstrecha pisatelei s I. V. Stalinym'. Arkhiv A. M. Gor'kogo (26 October 1932).
68. Ibid.
69. Consultation with Professor Ovcharenko (Moscow, October 1977).
70. 'Vstrecha pisatelei s I. V. Stalinym', Arkhiv A. M. Gor'kogo.
71. *Voprosy literatury*, 1967 (5) pp. 25–33.
72. *Neistovye revniteli*, pp. 337–8.
73. Interview with I. M. Gronsky (Moscow, November 1974). Gronsky's article appeared in *Literaturnaya gazeta*, 23 May 1932. See also Ermolaev, *Soviet Literary Theories*, pp. 144–7.
74. Roy Medvedev, *On Stalin and Stalinism*, p. 32.
75. *Pervyi plenum*, pp. 2–5.
76. Ibid., pp. 37–58.
77. Ibid., pp. 159–60. For the fuller version of his speech, see Gordon McVay, 'Klyuev and Klychkov: Unpublished Texts', *Oxford Slavonic Papers* (1984) pp. 104–6.
78. *Pervyi plenum*, pp. 37–58.
79. Ibid., pp. 95–101.
80. Ibid., p. 166.
81. Ibid., p. 190.
82. They spoke on 1 November 1932 (the fourth day).
83. *Pervyi plenum*, p. 66 (Prishvin was 59).
84. Ibid., p. 69 (Bely was 52).
85. V. Kirpotin, *Voprosy literatury*, 1967 (5) p. 30. The enforcing document was 'Postanovlenie Ts.K KP(b) B', 27 May 1932. See *Sovetskaya literatura na novom etape: sbornik* (M.1932) pp. 44–5. Later enforcement included a further statement of the Belo russian Central Committee in October 1932, criticising the slow tempo of reconstructing literary groups and of reeducating writers. See I. V. Ermakova, 'Deyatel'nost'' K. P. po podgotovke I-ogo s'e'zda sovetskikh pisatele', in *Nekotorye voprosy istorii KPSS* (M.1973) p. 263.
86. The overall background is found in James E. Mace, *Communism and Dilemmas of National Liberation* (Cambridge, Mass., 1983). The standard work on writers is George S. N. Luckyj, *Literary Politics in the Soviet Ukraine, 1917–1934* (New York, 1956). The official version of events appears in *Literatura Ukraini* (M.1934). This reports on Ukrainian Party resolutions on culture, notably those of 14 December 1932 and of the January 1933 plenum. The 'colossal assistance' of Party Secretary P. P. Postyshev is acknowledged in extirpating 'nationalist deviations'.
87. Set up on 26 May 1932, its activities are reported in Ermakova (1973).
88. A decision of 9 May 1932, to liquidate KazAPP and set up a 'Union of Soviet Writers organised in sections: music, art, theatre cinema etc' – clearly misunderstanding the cryptic Moscow Resolution – appears in *Sovetskaya literatura na novom etape*, pp. 46–7. Further developments are reported in *Materialy plenuma Orgkomiteta C SSPK* (Alma-Ata/ Moscow, 1933). Moscow's emissary to this meeting referred solely to

Moscow developments. Absolutely no local initiatives, other than fulfilling central directives, were countenanced. Speech by Berezovsky in ibid., p. 8–15.

89. The delegation included Uzbeks. See M. Sh. Shukurov, *Bor'ba K. P. Uzbekistana za razvitiye sovetskoi literatury, 1917–1936* (Tashkent, 1971) on further enforcing action by the local Central Committee on 3 and 23 May 1932, following which UzAPP was liquidated.
90. *Pervyi plenum*, p. 90.
91. Ibid., pp. 165–8.
92. Ibid., pp. 194–200.
93. Ibid., pp. 160–5.
94. Ibid., pp. 116–23 (Gronsky's interruptions are on p. 120).
95. Ibid., pp. 247–56.
96. Ibid., pp. 200–1.
97. Ibid., pp. 247–56.
98. Accounts of her mother are found in Svetlana Alliluyeva, *Letters to a Friend* (London, 1967).
99. *Literaturnaya gazeta*, 17 November 1932. The signatories included Leonov, Shklovsky, Olesha, V. Ivanov, Il'f and Petrov, Pil'nyak and five former RAPPists.
100. See Max Hayward, 'Introduction', to Alexander Gladkov, *Meetings with Pasternak* (London, 1977) pp. 15–16.
101. Olga Ivinskaya, *A Captive of Time*, p. 154.
102. On Beria's role see Alliluyeva, *Letters to a Friend, passim*.
103. First announced in *Pravda*, 2 December 1930.
104. The first Soviet author to confirm this case is Arkady Vaksberg, 'Kak zhivoi s zhivymi', *Literaturnaya gazeta*, 26 June 1988. On other oppositional activities see Roy Medvedev, *Nikolai Bukharin: The Last Years* (New York, 1980) pp. 64–5.
105. Vaksberg, *op. cit.*
106. Stalin, *Sochineniya*, XI, pp. 179–80.
107. Central Committee Resolution 'On Overcoming the Personality Cult and its Consequences' (30 June 1956). See *The Anti-Stalin Campaign and International Communism* (New York, 1956) p. 290.
108. Sources quoted in Robert Conquest, *Harvest of Sorrow* (London, 1986) p. 324. Khrushchev's own accounts vary between *Khrushchev Remembers* (London, 1971) pp. 57–61, which broadly denies knowledge and *The Last Testament* (New York, 1976) p. 109, from which the quotation comes.
109. *Pravda*, 16 May 1964.
110. M. Alekseev, *Drachuny* (M.1982).
111. Steven Rosefielde, 'Excess Collectivization Deaths, 1929–33: New Demographic Evidence', *Slavic Review*, April 1984, pp. 83–8, partly based on Lorimer, *Population of the Soviet Union* (Geneva, 1946). See also forthcoming article by Stephen Wheatcroft, based on archives in *Voprosy istorii*.
112. See R. W. Davies, *Détente* (9/10) pp. 44–5.
113. *Pravda*, 10 March 1963.

114. H. Ermolaev, *Sholokhov*, p. 35. Also see Sholokhov's article 'The Results of Unconsidered Concern', *Pravda*, 23 March 1933.
115. Reply cited in *Pravda*, 10 March 1963.
116. H. Ermolaev, *Sholokhov*, p. 36. See also Sholokhov's memoir, *Sovetskaya Rossiya*, 19 May 1985; and his letter on the devastating effects of grain procurements on the peasantry of the Lower Volga region (written on 18 June 1929) *Moskovskiye novosti*, 12 July 1987. The article states that this was forwarded to Stalin and notes that it preceded by a matter of days his reference to Sholokhov in the letter (of 3 July 1929) to Feliks Kon.
117. Lev Kopelev, *The Education of a True Believer* (New York, 1980) pp. 11–12.
118. Ye. F. Usievich, *Literaturnyi kritik*, 1934 (1). Gorky also used this euphemism: *Sobraniye sochinenii*, vol. 30, p. 283.
119. An account of the criticism appears in G. Struve and B. Fillipov (eds), *Nikolai Zabolotsky, Stikhotvoreniya* (Washington, 1965) LXIII–LXIV.
120. N. Zabolotsky, 'Autobiografiya', ibid., p. 3.
121. Beskin, *Literaturnaya gazeta*, 11 July 1933; Ermilov, *Pravda*, 21 July 1933. Usievich, *Literaturnyi kritik*, 1933 (4). Other reactions, both public and private, were more positive: *Krasnaya nov'*, 1933 (9) pp. 177–81; Ehrenburg was 'astonished and captivated', *Men, Years-Life*, vol. 4, p. 53;
122. Yu. Afanas'yev, *Sovetskaya kul'tura*, 21 March 1987.
123. Elizar Mal'tsev, *Literaturnaya gazeta*, 18 February 1987.

5 SOCIALIST REALISM

1. This part of Stalin's speech, documented above from archives, became commonly known. See for instance, the comments of Libedinsky, *Sovetskii teatr*, 1933 (2/3) and Panfyorov, *Rezets*, 1933 (17/18) p. 3. A somewhat garbled account is offered in *Aleksandr Fadeyev: Materialy i issledovaniya, Vypusk II* (M.1984) p. 41.
2. Stephen F. Cohen, *Bukharin* pp. 332–3. Also A. Avtorkhanov, *Stalin and the Communist Party* (London, 1959).
3. David Joravsky, *Soviet Marxism and Natural Science 1917–1932* (New York, 1961) pp. 170 ff.
4. David Joravsky, *The Lysenko Affair* (Cambridge, Mass. 1970); Zhores A. Medvedev, *The Rise and Fall of T.D. Lysenko* (New York, 1971).
5. Discussed by Sheila Fitzpatrick, *Slavic Review*, 1976 (2) pp. 224–30.
6. J. V. Stalin, *Marxism and Linguistics* (M.1951).
7. Argued, for instance, by N. K. Piksanov, *Sotsialisticheskii realizm: bibliograficheskii ukazatel'* (M.1934).
8. No stenogram of the proceedings was ever published. We have, therefore, relied upon archives and journal articles.
9. A. V. Lunacharsky, *Sovetskii teatr*, 1933 (1) pp. 16–19. The full text is published in his *Sobraniye sochinenii*, vol. 8 (M.1967) pp. 491–515 and pp. 613–17.

10. Ibid.
11. A. Afinogenov, *Tvorcheskii metod teatra: Dialektika tvorcheskogo prot-sessa* (M.-L.1931). See also *O zadachakh RAPPa na teatral'nom fronte* (M.1932) and the editorial in *Sovetskii teatr*, 1931 (10/11).
12. *Literaturnaya gazeta*, 23 March 1933.
13. A 'corrected version' appeared in *Teatr i dramaturgiya*, 1933 (1) and a full text was published posthumously: V. Kirshon, *Stat'i i rechi o dramaturgii, teatre i kino* (M.1962).
14. Vishnevsky's article, under this title, was printed in *Sovetskii teatr*, 1933 (2/3), pp. 65–70.
15. Kirshon, V. M., *O literature i iskusstve: stat'i i vystupleniya* (M.1967).
16. A point argued by S. I. Andreyeva, 'Iz polemiki v sovetskoi dramaturgia 1930-kh godov', *Vestnik Leningradskogo universiteta* 1957 (20) p. 184.
17. Lunacharsky, 'concluding word', *Literaturnyi kritik*, 1933 (1) pp. 11–35.
18. IMLI f.41, opis 1, ed.khr. 45.
19. Ibid.
20. IMLI f.41, opis 1, ed.khr. 440.
21. A. Fadeyev, *Pis'ma* pp. 90–1.
22. IMLI f.41, opis 1, ed.khr. 671 (29 March 1933).
23. IMLI f.41, opis 1, ed.khr. 671 (3 April 1933).
24. *Literaturnaya gazeta*, 28 April 1933. Socialist realism was here described as the 'chief theoretical question in the period of preparation for the Congress'.
25. Ibid.
26. *Literaturnaya gazeta*, 17 May 1933.
27. V. D. Pel't, *Gor' kii-zhurnalist, 1918–1936* (M.1968) p. 371. Kirpotin's contributions to the establishment of socialist realism were widely published during this period: *Pravda*, 7 May 1933; *Literaturnaya gazeta*, 5 June 1933; *Kniga i proletarskaya revolyutsiya*, 1933 (8); and *Literaturnyi kritik*, 1933 (3) (August).
28. Arkhiv A. M. Gor'kogo (15 July 1933).
29. *Literaturnaya gazeta*, 17 May 1933.
30. IMLI f.41, opis 1, ed.khr. 440 (I June 1933).
31. Ibid.
32. Ibid.
33. Arkhiv A. M. Gor'kogo (11 July 1933).
34. *Aleksandr Fadeyev. Materialy*, p. 511.
35. Following this approach, Radek was appointed to deliver a speech.
36. Held from 16–17 July 1933.
37. The new agenda was published in *Literaturnaya gazeta*, 15 August 1933.
38. Seven brigades were established to prepare speeches for the Congress: *Literaturnaya gazeta*, 7 September 1933.
39. Arkhiv A. M. Gor'kogo (15 July 1933).
40. Preface to Ya. Il'in, (ed.) *Lyudi Stalingradskogo traktornogo* (M.1933). His further thoughts on socialist realism were expressed in *Pravda*, 10 July and 27 August 1933.
41. *Literaturnaya gazeta*, 17 August 1933.
42. Avtorkhanov, *Stalin*, ch. 6. Nor did Yudin's assaults upon the 'right' end here. Although defeated in politics, Bukharinite ideas still carried

weight in cultural debates and would return to prominence during 1934. Meantime, Yudin kept up constant vigilance. In October 1933, he published a sharp attack upon Bukharin's views as 'mechanism not Marxism' and for allegedly 'dissociating cultural questions from political revolution, economic revolution, technical revolution and culture in general'. P. F. Yudin, *Marxsism-leninism o kul'ture i kul'turnoi revolyutsii* (M.1933) pp. 27–8. The edition was 50,000.

43. Arkhiv A. M. Gor'kogo. Gorky-Yudin Correspondence (1933–4). This first item is dated 'mid-August 1933: no earlier than 15 August'.
44. *Literaturnoye nasled stvo*, vol. 70 (M.1963), p. 278.
45. Romanovsky thesis, p. 158.
46. Ibid.
47. IMLI f.41, opis 1, ed.khr. 445.
48. T. H. Rigby, *Communist Party Membership in the USSR, 1917–1967* (Princeton, 1968) pp. 202–05. In the Ukraine, however, the cultural purge under Postyshev was far more severe. A reign of unparalled terror was unleashed on the region. Postyshev decimated the cultural 'front' for alleged 'bourgeois nationalist deviation': P. P. Postyshev, *Ot XVI do XVII s"ezda: Stat'i i rechi* (M.1934) p. 59. Institutions purged included these of linguistics, philosophy, the Shevchenko Institute of Literary Scholarship and the Ukrainian Publishing House. *Narkompros*, whose local head, Skrypnik, committed suicide in June 1933, was also decimated. Smaller-scale purges were also conducted at cultural institutions in other Republics.
49. *Literaturnaya gazeta*, 5 September 1933.
50. *Literaturnaya gazeta*, 29 August 1933. For a note on Parfyonov in prison see *Shipwreck of a Generation: The Memoirs of Joseph Berger* (London, 1971) pp. 39–43.
51. *Literaturnaya gazeta*, 5 September 1933.
52. *Literaturnaya gazeta*, 17 September 1933.
53. IMLI f.52, opis 1, ed.khr. 85 (19 September 1933).
54. Ibid.
55. *Dramaturgiya: Sbornik* (M.1933).
56. IMLI f.41, opis 1, ed.khr. 445.
57. Brilliantly analysed by S. S. Prawer, *Karl Marx and World Literature* (Oxford, 1976).
58. Ibid., p. 94.
59. Ibid.
60. See, for instance, Leszek Kolakowski, *Main Currents of Marxism* vol. 1 (Oxford, 1978) pp. 172–3.
61. Partial text in David McLellan (ed.), *Karl Marx: Selected Writings* (Oxford, 1977) pp. 189–90.
62. M. Lifshits, *Marks i Engel's ob iskusstve* (M.1933).
63. On this, see also Prawer, op. cit.
64. Mikhail Lifshits, *The Philosophy of Art of Karl Marx* (London, 1973) pp. 55–9. Background is provided by Kolakowski, vol. 1, pp. 120–2; and David McLellan, *Marx before Marxism* (London, 1980) pp. 82–97.
65. F. Shiller, *Engel's kak literaturnyi kritik* (M.1933).
66. Lee Baxandall and Stefan Morawski (eds), *Marx and Engels on Litera-*

ture and Art: A selection of writings (St Louis and Milwaukee, 1973) p. 109.

67. Ibid. Also: Peter Demetz, *Marx, Engels, and the Poets* (Chicago, 1967) pp. 107–15.
68. In Baxandall and Morawski (eds), p. 113. Also discussion in Demetz, pp. 127–33.
69. Letter to Margaret Harkness (1888) in Baxandall, p. 116.
70. P. I. Lebedev-Polyansky (1882–1948).
71. See Hebert E. Bowman, *Vissarion Belinski 1811–1848* (Cambridge, Mass., 1954) and Victor Terras, *Belinskij and Russian Literary Criticism* (Madison, Wisconsin, 1974).
72. Isaiah Berlin, *Russian Thinkers* (London, 1978) p. 181.
73. Cited in the standard work by Rufus W. Mathewson, Jr., *The Positive Hero in Russian Literature*, 2nd. ed. (Stanford, Ca., 1975) p. 40.
74. L. D. Trotsky, *Literature and Revolution* (New York, 1925) pp. 209–10.
75. See *Preface* to the withdrawn edition (M.1933).
76. V. I. Lenin, *Collected Works*, vol. 35, p. 31.
77. V. Kirpotin, *M. E. Saltikov-Shchedrin* (M.1939).
78. *Sobraniye sochinenii*, 20 vols (M.1933–41).
79. I. Berlin, *Russian Thinkers*, pp. 150–85.
80. See *Sobraniye sochinenii*, ed. P. I. Lebedev-Polyansky, 6 vols (M.1934–41); Lebedev-Polyansky, *N. A. Dobrolyubov: Mirovozzreniye i literaturno-kriticheskaya deyatel'nost*, 2nd. ed. (M.1935).
81. See especially Dobrolyubov, 'What is Oblomovism?'. See Mathewson, pp. 50–51.
82. See especially his *Aesthetic Relations of Art to Reality* (1855).
83. V. Kirpotin, 'Chernyshevsky' in *Publitsistiki i kritiki* (M-L.1932) and *Sobraniye sochinenii* 16 vols (M.1939–53). See also the important study by William F. Woehrhin, *Chernyshevskii* (Cambridge, Mass., 1971).
84. N. Valentinov 'Chernyshevsky i Lenin', *Novyi zhurnal* 1951 (27), cited by Mathewson, p. 82.
85. Quoted by Mathewson, p. 81.
86. Nadezhda Krupskaya, *Memoires of Lenin* (London, 1970)
87. Ibid. See also the contribution 'V. I. Lenin i russkiy revolyutsionniye demokraty' in *Naslediye Lenina i nauka o literature* (L.1969) pp. 63–92.
88. *Literaturnyi kritik*, 1933 (3) pp. 3–11; the board consisted of: Yudin (ed.), *Rozental'* (ed. sec.) and members: Gronsky, Dinamov, *K. Zelinskii*, Illyés, Kirpotin, Kirshon, Lebedev, Serafimovich, Sutyrin and *Ye. F. Usievich*. Those in italics were Commission members. Their original editorial 'Marxism–Leninism and Belles-Lettres' appeared in *Literaturnii kritik*, 1933 (3) pp. 3–11.
89. M. M. Rozental', 'Mirovozzreniye i metod', *Literaturnyi kritik*, 1933 (6).
90. P. F. Yudin, (ed.) *Lenin i literatura* (M.1933).
91. Ibid.
92. Lenin, 'On Party Organisation and Party Literature' (1905). For a valuable collection of related documents see C. Vaughan James, *Soviet Socialist Realism Origins and Theory* (London, 1973).

93. A. V. Lunacharsky, 'Lenin i literaturovedeniye', *Literaturnaya entsiklopediya* (M.1932).
94. *Literaturnaya entsiklopediya* (M.1967) also: *Kratkaya literaturnaya entsiklopediya* vol. 4 (M.1967).
95. P. F. Yudin (ed.) *Pisateli k XVII parts"ezdu* (M.1934) p. 6.
96. IMLI f.41, opis 1, ed.khr. 434.
97. *Literaturnyi Leningrad*, 3 February 1934.
98. IMLI f.41, opis 1, ed.khr. 434.
99. The outcome was *Belomorsko-Baltiiskii kanal imeni Stalina: Istoriya stroitel'stva* (M.1934).
100. Ibid, pp. 113–15.
101. See L. M. Zak (ed.), *A. M. Gor'kii i sozdaniye istorii fabrik i zavodov: sbornik dokumentov* (M.1959) p. 232.
102. *Belomor*, Preface.

6 DEBATE ON DOCTRINE

1. Kirov's Leningrad speech (*Pravda*) 24 January 1934, quotes substantially from that of Gorky to a Moscow Party conference in *Pravda* and *Literaturnaya gazeta*, 20 January 1934. There is some evidence of Kirov's role as a 'protector' of writers: L. Bykovtseva, *Gor'kii v Moskve, 1931–1936* (M.1968) p. 121.
2. 'Krizis kapitalisticheskoi kul'tury', *Izvestiya*, 18 and 30 March 1934. He also appointed Radek, who wrote in the same vein.
3. Boris Nicolaevsky, *Power and the Soviet Elite* pp. 45–6.
4. F. Benvenuti, 'Kirov in Soviet Politics', Birmingham Discussion Paper (Birmingham, CREES, 1974).
5. Ibid.
6. The vote was reported in Roy Medvedev, *Let History Judge*, p. 156; also Anton Antonov-Ovseyenko, *The Time of Stalin* (New York, 1983) pp. 80–3.
7. See the testimony of L. S. Shaumyan, *Pravda*, 1 December 1964.
8. Discussed above, Chapter Three.
9. Vasil'kovsky, *Oktyabr'*, 1933 (10).
10. M. Kantor, *Bol'shevik*, 1933 (23).
11. Gorky, *Pravda*, 28 January 1934.
12. *XVII s'ezd VKP (b): stenotchot* (M.1934) pp. 623–6.
13. As we have seen above, formulation of this was taking place *in camera*.
14. *XVII s'ezd VKP (b): stenotchot* p. 646.
15. His 'Open Letter to A. S. Serafimovich' appeared in *Literaturnaya gazeta*, 14 February 1934.
16. 'O boikosti', *Pravda* and *Izvestiya*, 28 February 1934.
17. *Literaturnaya gazeta*, 8 March 1934.
18. Ibid.
19. Ibid.
20. Cohen, *Bukharin*, p. 308.
21. *Literaturnaya gazeta*, 10 March 1934.
22. Aseyev, *Literaturnaya gazeta*, 10 March 1934.

23. Kirsanov, ibid. Collected essays of A. Selivanovsky from this period appear as *Ocherki po istorii russkoi sovetskoi poezii* (M.1936).
24. Utkin, *Literaturnaya gazeta*, 10 March 1934.
25. Surkov, ibid.
26. Fadeyev, *Literaturnaya gazeta* 14 March 1934. Also article in *Literaturnyi kritik*, 1934 (4), reprinted in A. A. Fadeyev, *Sobraniye sochinenii*, vol. 5.
27. Kirpotin, *Literaturnaya gazeta*, 14 March 1934.
28. Kirshon, *Literaturnaya gazeta*, 4 April 1934.
29. Like all eclipses, it was temporary. Fadeyev succeeded Stavsky as First Secretary of the Writers' Union in 1939.
30. *Literaturnaya gazeta*, 12 March 1934. Plenary resolutions were published in *Literaturnaya gazeta*, 10 March 1934, and discussed in an editorial of 16 March 1934.
31. See below pp. 181–8.
32. 'O yazyke', *Pravda*, 18 March 1934. An editorial note added that the campaign for quality was paramount 'in industry and agriculture, in the spheres of culture and government'.
33. *Literaturnaya gazeta*, 4 April 1934 (V. Ivanov and Slonimsky) and 16 April 1934 (Leonov).
34. *Literaturnaya gazeta*, 18 April 1934.
35. *Literaturnaya gazeta*, 6 March 1934.
36. IMLI f.41, opis 1, ed.khr. 440.
37. IMLI f.41, opis I, ed.khr. 433.
38. IMLI f.41, opis I, ed.khr. 492.
39. In particular, the legal advice, dated 26 May 1933, noted the failure to distinguish clearly between the powers of the 'Pravleniye' (or ruling body) and plenary session of the incipient Union. These were paragraphs 25 and 27 of the draft document.
40. *Literaturnaya gazeta*, 6 May 1934.
41. The latter phrase was rescinded when the statutes were revised in 1954. See H. Swayze, *The Political Control of Literature in the USSR, 1946–1959* (Cambridge, Mass., 1962) pp. 112–13.
42. This was admirably pointed out by his *nom-de-plume*: Abram Tertz, *On Socialist Realism* (New York, 1960) pp. 24–9.
43. Fitzpatrick, *Education and Social Mobility*, ch. 8.
44. *Pravda*, 8 May 1934.
45. Ibid.
46. Ibid.
47. *Literaturnaya gazeta*, 20 May 1934.
48. These were left unspecified.
49. Debate of 1894. Quoted by Ermolaev, *Soviet Literary Theories* pp. 171–72 and p. 233 (note 48).
50. *Leninskii sbornik*, vol. 26 (M.1934); *Sochineniya*, vol. 34, pp. 379–82.
51. *Literaturnaya gazeta*, 20 May 1934.
52. IMLI f.41, opis 1, ed.khr. 448.
53. IMLI f.41, opis 1, ed.khr. 448.
54. *Literaturnaya gazeta*, 27 May 1934.

55. 'Proletarskii gumanizm', *Pravda*, 22 May 1934; 'Literaturnye zabavy', *Pravda*, 14 June 1934.
56. M. Peshkov died on 11 May 1934.
57. From V. Ivanov, A. Tolstoy, Babel, Leonov and others: *Literaturnaya gazeta*, 12 May 1934.
58. A full analysis of the makers of cultural policy appears in Chapter Eight.
59. This was openly recognised when the Secretariat was reorganised in mid-1935.
60. Despite his declared intentions (see Ch. Five, n. 21 above).
61. His contact with Gorky had begun in 1929.
62. See Swayze, *Political Control*, ch. 2: 'The Heyday of Zhdanovism, 1948–1953'.
63. Arkhiv Gor'kogo, 'Komissiya po podgotovke s''ezda' (17 March 1934). Its decisions were confirmed by the Orgkomitet, IMLI f.41, opis I, ed.khr. 448 (15 June 1934).
64. See the mémoire of N. Tikhonov, *Voprosy literatury*, 1967 (4), p. 29, and letter to him on 3 July 1934 by P. A. Pavlenko, *Znamya*, 1968 (4) p. 133.
65. Arkhiv A. M. Gor'kogo, 'Preparations for the First Congress' (March-August 1934).
66. See the annotation to the letter of Kirshon to Gorky (27 May 1934) in *Literaturnoye nasledstvo* vol. 70 (M.1963) pp. 192–3.
67. The editorial boards of such ventures were normally honorific, but Bukharin turned up at the House of Soviet Writers on 9 July 1934 to deliver a substantial address. A summary account appeared in *Literaturnaya gazeta*, 12 July 1934.
68. There is a fuller discussion of this notion in Edward J. Brown, *Proletarian Episode* pp. 64–6.
69. Further discussion of his views on culture appears in John Biggart, 'Bukharin's Theory of Cultural Revolution' in A. Kemp-Welch (ed.) *The Ideas of Nikolai Bukharin*.
70. *Literaturnaya gazeta*, 12 July 1934.
71. A. Tolstoy's reflections on 'The People of the Five-year Plan' appeared in *Literaturnaya gazeta*, 22 July 1934.
72. Prince Dmitry Petrovich Svyatopolk Mirsky. See Gleb Struve, *Russian Literature under Lenin and Stalin*, pp. 270–1.
73. *Literaturnaya gazeta*, 24 June 1934.
74. *Pravda*, 23 July 1934.
75. See Lazar' Fleishman, *Boris Pasternak v tridtsatye gody* (Jerusalem, 1984), p. 194, n. 162.
76. Arkhiv A. M. Gor'kovo, 'Preparations for the First Congress' (March-August 1934).
77. The latter part of 'Literaturnye zabavy' was published in *Pravda*, 24 January 1935.
78. Arkhiv A. M. Gor'kogo, 'Preparations for the First Congress' (March-August 1934).
79. *Pravda*, 14 June 1934.

80. I. Shkapa, *Sem' let s Gor'kim* (M.1964) p. 249.
81. Nadezhda Mandelstam, *Hope Against Hope*, pp. 4–25.
82. These lines are from the original version, which came to the notice of the authorities. The text, which was never written down, is offered in the English translation of *Hope Against Hope*, p. 13. No-one doubted that despite this precaution the penalty for the poem would be death. Mandelstam himself foretold his arrest 'Ya k smertiu gotov' (February 1934). See Akhmatova, *Sochineniya* (M.1968) vol. 2, p. 179.
83. *A Captive of Time: My Years with Pasternak: The Memoirs of Olga Ivinskaya* (London, 1979) p. 67.
84. Mandelstam had recited the poem to Pasternak in the street, who sensibly replied 'I didn't hear this and you didn't recite it to me'. Ivinskaya, *Captive of Time*, pp. 64–5.
85. There exist several versions of this phone call. The most reliable are: Nadezhda Mandelstam, *Hope Against Hope*, pp. 145–9 and Ivinskaya, *Captive of Time*, pp. 66–8. Further accounts include: *Pamyat': Istoricheskii sbornik* vol. 2, pp. 438–41 and vol. 4, pp. 316–17.
86. Cited by Lazar' Fleishman, *Boris Pasternak*, p. 187. One further effect was the embarrassment of Bukharin. He did not hear about the poem until afterwards, when Yagoda recited it to him from memory. Bukharin refused to receive Nadezhda Mandelstam afterwards. Even so, her white lie helped gain Mandelstam three years' grace.
87. Ehrenburg, *Men, Years-Life* vol. IV p. 40.
88. *Pervyi vsesoyuznyni s"ezd sovetskikh pisatelei* (M.1935), hereafter *Pervyi s"ezd*, p. 281.
89. Ehrenburg, *Men, Years-Life*, vol. IV *op. cit.*
90. This gave rise to a comic incident involving Boris Pasternak, described below.
91. *Literaturnaya gazeta*, 21 August 1934.
92. *Pervyi s"ezd*, p. 19.
93. Ibid., pp. 2–4.
94. Ibid., p. 4.
95. Ibid.
96. Ibid., p. 5.
97. See Leonard Schapiro 'The *Vekhi* Group', *Russian Studies* (London 1986) pp. 68–92.
98. *Pervyi s"ezd*, pp. 12–13.
99. Ibid., p. 13.
100. Ibid., p. 17.
101. Ibid., p. 18.
102. Ibid.
103. Ibid., pp. 308–15.
104. Ibid., p. 315.
105. Forty foreign guests attended the Congress. Their names are listed in *Pervyi s"ezd*, Appendix IV, p. 699.
106. Ibid., p. 317.
107. Ibid., pp. 351–2. His speech was translated by Il'ya Ehrenburg.
108. *Soviet Writers' Congress*, p. 182.
109. The international congress in defence of culture (Paris, May 1935) is

described by Ehrenburg, one of the organisers, in vol. 4, pp. 72–80. See also V. Serge, *Memoirs of a Revolutionary*, pp. 317–19.

110. *Soviet Writers' Congress*, pp. 189–207.
111. Ibid., pp. 185–6, p. 245.
112. Ibid., p. 220.
113. Ibid., p. 225.
114. Ibid., pp. 222–3, 240–55.
115. RAPP slogan, see Sheshukov, *Neistovye revniteli*, pp. 173–5.
116. *Soviet Writers' Congress*, pp. 246–7.
117. Ibid., pp. 247–9.
118. *Pervyi s"ezd*, p. 504.
119. *Pervyi s"ezd*, p. 493.
120. John Berger, *Shipwreck of a Generation* (London, 1971) pp. 106–7.
121. L. M. Zak, dissertation, p. 768.
122. Indeed he said so: 'I wish to make one further deviation from my printed report. I have omitted to mention such an outstanding poet – this is my personal opinion, but I feel obliged to express it . . .' *Soviet Writers' Congress*, p. 241.
123. *Pervyi s"ezd*, p. 512. Surkov added that 'at our Congress, all the speeches are delivered on the authority of the Orgkomitet', p. 513.
124. Ibid., p. 524.
125. Notably the former Futurist Aseyev, *Pervyi s"ezd*, pp. 567–9.
126. Ibid., p. 557.
127. Ibid., p. 550.
128. Ibid., p. 573.
129. Ibid., pp. 573–4.
130. Ibid., p. 574. He had used the same word (*komchvanstvo*) in 1925.
131. Ibid., pp. 574–7. Again, he received 'thunderous applause'.
132. *Soviet Writers' Congress*, p. 261.
133. Ibid., p. 263.
134. Ibid., p. 264.
135. *Pervyi s"ezd*, p. 671.
136. Ibid., See also Roy Medvedev, *Bukharin*, p. 91, and Lazar' Fleishman, *Pasternak*, p. 213.
137. *Pervyi s"ezd*, pp. 229–30.
138. Ibid., p. 151.
139. Ibid., pp. 504–12. He also contributed a memoire of the Congress to *Voprosy literatury*, 1967 (4) p. 31.
140. Discussed in Chapter Two above.
141. See Beaujaer, *Invisible Land*, ch. 6, 'The Last Attempt' and R. Mathewson, 'The First Congress: A Second Look' in M. Hayward and L. Labedz, *Literature and Revolution*.
142. *Pervyi s"ezd*, pp. 235–6.
143. Ibid., pp. 278–80.
144. Ivinskaya, *Captive of Time*, p. 74. See the interpretations in Fleishman, *Pasternak*, pp. 146–7.
145. *Pervyi s"ezd*, p. 549.
146. Ibid.
147. Ehrenburg, *Men, Years-Life*, p. 48.

148. It may well have been clearer to non-participants. Akhmatova had received an application form, but declined to reply. Mandelstam was in exile. Bulgakov was also absent.
149. Prominent amongst these was *Literaturnaya uchoba*, see Gorky, *Sobraniye sochinenii*, vol. 25, p. 102. A new journal appeared in September 1934, *Kolkhoznik*, edited by Gorky. See V. A. Maksimova, *Gor'kii-redaktor, 1918–1936* (M.1965).
150. Some thirty writers were present (but not Gorky). See *Literaturnaya gazeta*, 10 October 1934. The speech was attacked by Usievich in *Literaturnyi kritik*, 1934 (10) pp. 92–112.
151. *Literaturnyi kritik*, 1935 (2) pp. 219–50; thesis, p. 898.
152. On its unpublished investigation, see Roy Medvedev, *Khrushchev* (Oxford, 1982) ch. 9.
153. The argument from Robert Conquest, *The Great Terror* (London, 1968), was recently restated in the same author's *Stalin and the Kirov Murder* (Oxford, 1989).
154. In addition to Khrushchev's hints, there is the statement of Academician A. Samsonov, *Knizhnoye obozreniye*, 1988 (8) that Stalin was implicated.
155. *The Anti-Stalin Campaign and International Communism* (New York, 1956) p. 25.
156. *Literaturnaya gazeta*, 2 and 4 December 1934.
157. *Literaturnaya gazeta*, 4 December 1934.
158. Ibid.
159. Medvedev, *Let History Judge*, pp. 164–5; Hryhory Kostiuk, *Stalinist Rule in the Ukraine* (London, 1960) pp. 98–100.
160. Speech at the House of Soviet Writers, *Literaturnaya gazeta*, 24 December 1934.
161. *Izvestiya*, 22 December 1934. See Medvedev, *Bukharin*, pp. 96–8, who states that they were on good terms. Also Nadezhda Mandelstam, *Hope Against Hope*, p. 118.
162. Kamenev was also Director of the Pushkinskii Dom (IRLi) and attached to the Board of the Writers' Union, attending several of its earliest meetings.
163. Serge, *Memoirs*, pp. 121–2.
164. Smolensk Archive WKP 499. Medvedev, *K sudu istorii* (2nd ed.) (New York, 1974) pp. 325–32. Serge, *Memoirs* pp. 313–14. For some counter-arguments, see J. Arch Getty, *Origins of the Great Purges* (London, 1985) ch. 3.
165. Zaslavsky's attack was launched in *Pravda*, 20 January 1935. According to the 'Old Bolshevik' Nicolaevsky, *Power and the Soviet Elite*, he wrote 'on instructions from Yezhov and Stetsky'. His further tirade appeared in *Pravda*, 25 January 1935.
166. Gorky replied in *Pravda*, 24 January 1935. See also Panfyorov (settling an old score with Gorky) in *Pravda*, 28 January 1935. Gorky's reply was not published.
167. *Materialy ko vtoromu plenumu soyuza sovetskikh pisatelei* (M.1935).
168. *Vtoroi plenum pravleniya soyuza sovetskikh pisateli: stenotchot*

(M.1935) (hereafter *Vtoroi plenum*) pp. 5–41. The meeting was held from 2–7 March 1935.

169. *Materialy*, p. 1.
170. See V. Erlich, *Russian Formalism* (The Hague, 1955).
171. *Materialy*, ibid.
172. Ibid.
173. Ibid.
174. Discussed above in Chapter Three. The reviewers included Radek, *Izvestiya*, 24 May 1934 and Goffenshefer, *Literaturnii kritik*, 1934 (7/8).
175. *Vtoroi plenum*, pp. 41–61; *Krasnaya nov'*, 1935 (54) p. 212.
176. *Krasnaya nov'*, p. 212.
177. *Krasnaya nov'*, pp. 223–4.
178. See Bespalov, *Vtoroi plenum*, pp. 369–75.
179. Merle Fainsod, *Smolensk under Soviet Rule* (Cambridge, Mass., 1958) pp. 374–77. Such instructions remained in force until 1988.
180. See M. Fainsod, 'Censorship in the USSR – A Documented Record', *Problems of Communism*, 1956 (March/April).
181. *Pravda*, 14 May 1935.
182. The role of Shcherbakov is considered more fully in Chapter Eight.
183. See Robert Conquest, *The Great Terror*, pp. 123–7.
184. Medvedev, *Bukharin*, p. 102.
185. E. H. Carr, *The Twilight of the Comintern 1930–1935* (London, 1982).
186. Ibid.
187. Interview with A. I. Ovcharenko (M. October 1977).
188. Ivinskaya, *Captive of Time*, p. 75; also Serge, *Memoirs*, pp. 317–19.
189. Ivinskaya, p. 75.
190. Ehrenburg, *Men, Years-Life*, vol. 4, p. 74.
191. Ibid., p. 75.
192. Ivinskaya, p. 76.
193. *Letters to A. Tesková* (Prague, 1969).
194. The head of delegation was Shcherbakov, whose words are reported by Ehrenburg, vol. 4, p. 76. Official accounts of the proceedings appeared in *Zvezda*, 1935 (9); *Pravda*, 21–25 June 1935 and *Literaturnyi kritik*, 1935 (8).
195. Well described by Roy Medvedev, *Bukharin*, pp. 100–07.
196. Discussed by L. M. Zak, unpublished dissertation, Chapter 5.
197. See, for instance, Lewis H. Siegelbaum, *Stakhanovism and the Politics of Productivity in the USSR, 1935–1941* (Cambridge, 1988).
198. *Literaturnaya gazeta*, 29 October 1935.
199. *Literaturnaya gazeta*, 5 November 1935.
200. *Literaturnaya gazeta*, 24 November 1935.
201. K. Clark, *The Soviet Novel: history as ritual* (Chicago, 1981).
202. Editorials appeared, for instance, in *Literaturnaya gazeta* on 5 August and 15 September 1936. See also I. Gudov, *Put' stakhanovtsa: Rasskaz o moyei zhizni* (M.1938) and A. Stakhanov, *Rasskaz o moyei zhizni* (M.1937).
203. Discussed by Amy Knight 'Beria and the Cult of Stalin', in *Soviet Studies* (forthcoming).

204. Zak thesis, pp. 859 ff.
205. *Pamyat'. Istoricheskii sbornik*, no. I (M.1976; New York, 1979) pp. 308–10.
206. Ibid.
207. Ibid.
208. *Pravda* (editorial), 5 December 1935.
209. The phrase is Pasternak's in *An Essay in Autobiography* (London, 1959) p. 103. He added: 'This was his second death. He had no hand in it'.
210. *Soviet Writers' Congress*, p. 257.
211. *Soviet Writers' Congress*, p. 264.
212. In 'theses' for the Third Plenum of the Writers' Union (Minsk, February 1936), some of which appeared in *Literaturnaya gazeta*, 15 January 1936, *Pravda* 31 January 1936 and also *Literaturnaya gazeta*, 13 February 1936, the Surkov-Pasternak enmity was in its infancy. The state of their relations in 1948 is described by an eye-witness, Max Hayward, 'Introduction' to Alexander Gladkov, *Meetings with Pasternak*.
213. A. Selivanovsky, *Ocherki po istorii russkoi sovetskoi poezii*, pp. 4, 296–7.
214. Zak thesis, p. 760.
215. E.g. A. Demen'tyev in *Novyi mir*, 1966 (10) p. 258.
216. Ehrenburg, vol. 4, p. 96.
217. *Sovetskoye iskusstvo*, 1936 (4) (22 January 1936).
218. See Chapters One and Two above.
219. He had held that post since 1933.
220. *Rabochii i teatr*, 1936 (2) p. 4.
221. Zak thesis, p. 899.
222. Ibid., p. 900.
223. 'Muddle in place of Music', *Pravda*, 28 January 1936. See *Testimony: The Memoirs of Dmitri Shostakovich* related to S. Volkov (London, 1981) pp. 85–6.
224. *Pravda*, 6 February 1936.
225. Shostakovich, *Testimony*, p. 86.
226. This followed a *Pravda* attack of 20 February 1936. See also Ehrenburg, vol. 4, p. 96. Mel'nikov designed the Soviet pavilion for the 1924 Paris exhibition.
227. Zak thesis, pp. 904–5.
228. *Pravda*, 20 February 1936.
229. *Arkhiv A. M. Gor'kogo*, vol. X (i) pp. 383–5.
230. Shcherbakov in ibid.
231. *Literaturnaya gazeta*, 13 March 1936.
232. *The Correspondence of Boris Pasternak and Olga Freidenberg, 1910–1954* (London, 1982) pp. 158–9.
233. 'Letters to the Tabidzes', *Voprosy literatury*, 1966 (1) pp. 178–9. Trans. as *Letters to Georgian Friends* (London, 1971) pp. 58–9.
234. *Pravda*, 11 March 1936.
235. A. Fevral'sky (ed.) *V. E. Meyerhold: Stat'i, pis'ma, rechi, besedy* (M.1968) vol. 2, p. 331. See also his letter to Shostakovich, ibid. p. 372.
236. *Pravda*, 4 April 1936.

237. Ibid.
238. Ibid.
239. *Teatr i dramaturgiya*, 1936 (4) pp. 207–10. Fevral'sky, *Meyerhold*, p. 348.
240. Fevral'sky, pp. 348–9.
241. Ibid., pp. 355–6.
242. *Pravda*, 4 April 1936.
243. *Pravda*, 9 April 1936.
244. Zak thesis, p. 889.
245. *Istoricheskii arkhiv*, 1960 (5).
246. Gorky, *Sobraniye sochinenii*, vol. 30 (M.1955) pp. 370–1.

7 THE TERROR

1. 'Voronezh. To O.M.' (Osip Mandelstam), 1936.
2. Testimony of Stalin's bodyguard between 1937–8, in Medvedev, *Let History Judge*, p. 296.
3. Khrushchev in *The Anti-Stalin Campaign and International Communism*, p. 38, and documents read to the Twenty-Second. (1961) Party Congress. See *Let History Judge*, pp. 293–4.
4. For the background see R. W. Davies, *Soviet History in the Gorbachov Revolution* (London, 1989).
5. First published in the Soviet Union in *Moskovskiye novosti*, 6 December 1987, p. 12.
6. *Let History Judge*, p. 301.
7. F. Beck and W. Godin, *Russian Purge and the Extraction of Confession* (London, 1951) pp. 201–2.
8. Nadezhda Mandelstam, *Hope Against Hope*, p. viii.
9. *Let History Judge*, pp. 350–4.
10. Beck and Godin, *Russian Purge*, p. 158.
11. Grigory Svirsky, *Na lobnom meste* (London, 1979) p. 47.
12. Ehrenburg, *Men, Years-Life*, vol. 6: *Post-War Years* (London, 1966) p. 306.
13. Nadezhda Mandelstam, *Hope Abandoned*, ch. 18.
14. Goethe, quoted by M. Heller in *Survey*, 1982 (2) p. 189.
15. *The Anti-Stalin Campaign*, p. 24.
16. *Report of Court Proceedings: The Case of the Trotskyite-Zinovievite Terrorist Centre* (Moscow, 1936). (Hereafter: *Zinoviev Trial*) pp. 26–7.
17. According to a defector source, Pikel' was a personal friend of some NKVD officer who promised him his life in return for giving evidence against Zinoviev. Both were executed. See: A. Orlov, *The Secret History of Stalin's Crimes* (London, 1954) p. 53.
18. *Zinoviev Trial*, p. 168.
19. *Pravda*, 6 February 1988.
20. *Izvestiya*, 7 February 1988, contains an important interview with Judge Marov, explaining 'How the 4 February 1988 USSR Supreme Court Plenum was prepared and held'.
21. Judicial annulment was confirmed by a special Politburo Commission

on the 'supplementary study of materials connected with the repressions of the 1930's, 1940's and early 1950's'. See *Pravda*, 6 February 1988.
22. *Zinoviev Trial*, p. 122.
23. *Zinoviev Trial*, p. 164.
24. *Literaturnaya gazeta*, 27 January 1988, p. 13.
25. Roy Medvedev, *Bukharin*, pp. 121–7.
26. Sixteen Moscow writers in *Pravda*, 21 August 1936; others in *Literaturnyi Leningrad*, 23 August 1936.
27. Demyan Bedny in *Literaturnaya gazeta*, 27 August 1936.
28. Session of 25 August 1936. *Literaturnaya gazeta*, 27 August 1936.
29. Ibid.
30. *Literaturnaya gazeta*, 27 August 1936.
31. *Let History Judge*, p. 231.
32. *Literaturnaya gazeta*, 27 August 1936. See the same author's series of articles in ibid., from 10 September 1936, re-published as M. Rozental', *Protiv vul'garnoi sotsiologii v literaturnoi teorii* (M.1936).
33. *Oktyabr'* 1936 (9), editorial.
34. His accusers included *Literaturnaya gazeta*, 28 October 1936.
35. Stalin to Roy Howard (I March 1936): *Pravda*, 5 March 1936.
36. Nicolaevsky, *Power and the Soviet Elite*, p. 22. A draft constitution was published on 12 June 1936. See comments on it by *Izvestiya*, 14/15 June 1936. These may have been Bukharin's last published articles.
37. Stalin's speech of 27 November appears in *Sochineniya* (Stanford, 1967) vol. XIV.
38. His speech to the Eighth Congress of Soviets (5 December 1936) appeared in *Literaturnaya gazeta*, 6 December 1936.
39. *Literaturnaya gazeta*, 1 December 1936.
40. *The Correspondence of Boris Pasternak and Olga Freidenberg*, pp. 163–4.
41. Cited by Khrushchev, see *The Anti-Stalin Campaign*, p. 26. Further commentary appears in J. Arch Getty, *Origins of the Great Purges* (Cambridge, 1985); and on Yezhov personally (by I. Sats) in Medvedev, *On Stalin*, p. 100.
42. Medvedev, *Bukharin*, p. 129.
43. *Report of the Court Proceedings in the Case of the Anti-Soviet Trotskyite Centre* (M.1937) pp. 61–2.
44. Ibid., pp. 302–25.
45. *Pravda*, 24 January 1937.
46. *Literaturnaya gazeta*, 26 January 1937.
47. Ibid.
48. This campaign is also discussed in Fleishman, *Pasternak*, pp. 385–93.
49. Conquest, *The Great Terror*, pp. 254–55. See also: Jim Tuck, *Engine of Mischief: An Analytical Biography of Karl Radek* (London, 1988).
50. G. Serebryakova had been the wife of both Serebryakov and Sokol'nikov.
51. Conquest, *Great Terror*, p. 183.
52. *Literaturnaya gazeta*, 26 January 1937.

53. *Izvestiya*, 12 February 1937.
54. See Conquest, *The Great Terror*, p. 442; Cohen, *Bukharin and the Bolshevik Revolution*, p. 475 (note 3) and Vasily Grossman, *Forever Flowing*, p. 33.
55. *Izvestiya*, 12 February 1937.
56. Medvedev, *Bukharin*, p. 134.
57. Ibid.
58. *The Anti-Stalin Campaign*, p. 89.
59. *The Anti-Stalin Campaign*, p. 27.
60. Ibid., p. 29. Also, Robert H. McNeal, *Stalin: Man and Ruler* (London, 1988) p. 196.
61. Quoted from Khrushchev, by Conquest, *Great Terror*, pp. 268–9. See fragment from Postyshev in *The Anti-Stalin Campaign*, p. 29.
62. Conquest, *Great Terror*, p. 269.
63. *The Anti-Stalin Campaign*, p. 30.
64. Medvedev, *Bukharin*, p. 135.
65. Ibid., p. 136.
66. It had thirty members, ibid.
67. Medvedev, *Bukharin*, p. 138.
68. 'Speech to Moscow Writers on 30 January 1937': *Literaturnaya gazeta*, 1 February 1937.
69. Lazar' Fleishman states that 'A' was D. M. Altauzen, *Pasternak*, p. 397, n. 13. 'X' is not identified.
70. *Meetings with Pasternak*, p. 34.
71. *Pravda*, 28 February 1937 (unsigned editorial, p. 4).
72. Medvedev, *Bukharin*, p. 138.
73. See Gladkov, *Meetings with Pasternak*, pp. 34–5. Guy de Mallac, *Boris Pasternak: his life and art* (London, 1983), p. 158.
74. Gladkov, *Meetings with Pasternak*, pp. 34–5. Pasternak earlier replied to accusations from Stavsky in *Literaturnaya gazeta*, 5 January 1937. See Fleishman, *Pasternak*, pp. 385–6.
75. *Pravda*, 27 February 1937. The 'enemies' included P. Vasil'yev (already under arrest).
76. Ibid. This was blamed on the editor, Ermilov.
77. Conquest, *Great Terror*, p. 275.
78. *Literaturnaya gazeta*, 6 April 1937. Stalin had in fact spoken on 5 March – one month before it was reported.
79. He was accused of driving Mayakovsky to suicide: *Pravda*, 27, 29 April 1937.
80. This was a RAPP slogan. See the editorial in *Literaturnaya gazeta*, 20 April 1937. Further attacks were mounted in *Pravda*, 17 May 1937 (Kirpotin) and *Pravda*, 26 May 1937 (which also accused Jasienski). Yudin's contribution appeared in *Oktyabr'*, 1937 (6) (not without a hint of anti-Semitism).
81. *Pravda*, 23 April 1937. The further issue of 26 April 1937 included an editorial attacking RAPP and an article on 'Averbakhovshchina'.
82. *Pravda*, 27 April 1937.
83. Cited by Medvedev, *Let History Judge*, p. 232.
84. *Pravda*, 29 April 1937.

85. Svirsky, *Na lobnom meste*, p. 54.
86. Kirshon was accused of Trotskyism; *Literaturnaya gazeta*, 30 May 1937; *Pravda*, 15 June 1937. He was expelled from the Party: *Literaturnaya gazeta*, 10 August 1937.
87. Svirsky, *Na lobnom meste*, p. 49.
88. *Pravda*, 29 April and 26 May 1937.
89. Svirsky, *Na lobnom meste*, p. 54. For the investigation of Libedinsky see *Literaturnaya gazeta*, 20 May 1937.
90. Conquest, *The Great Terror*, ch. 7.
91. Ibid., p. 305.
92. Both appeared in *Pravda*, 12 June 1937.
93. Ivinskaya, *A Captive of Time*, pp. 141–2.
94. Ibid.
95. Army Commander of the Belorussian military district. Candidate Member of the Central Committee, prior to arrest.
96. *Men, Years-Life*, vol. 4, p. 197.
97. Ibid., pp. 196–7.
98. Gladkov, *Meetings with Pasternak*, p. 34.
99. Shigalyov is a conspirator in Dostoyevsky's *The Devils* who 'set out from boundless freedom and arrives at total despotism' in which all become 'slaves and equal in their slavery'.
100. Solzhenitsyn, *The GULag Archipelago*, bk. 1, pp. 438–9.
101. *Moscow News*: Special Supplement 'Memorial', 27 November 1988.
102. Official directive quoted by Medvedev in *Let History Judge*, p. 223.
103. John Barber, *Soviet Historians*, pp. 140–1.
104. Medvedev, *Let History Judge*, pp. 224–5.
105. Zak dissertation, pp. 667–98.
106. David Joravsky, *The Lysenko Affair* (Cambridge, Mass., 1970) p. 123.
107. Cited by Zhores A. Medvedev, *The Rise and Fall of T. D. Lysenko* (New York, 1969) p. 98. The meeting is described in Joravsky, *Lysenko*, p. 124.
108. *Pravda*, 16 November 1937. However, he was not arrested.
109. The campaign began with an editorial on 'Voronshchina': *Literaturnaya gazeta*, 5 June 1937. It continued in the issue of 26 June 1937. See also Gleb Glinka, *Na Perevale*, pp. 407–9.
110. A. E. Reshetov, quoted by Gordon McVay, 'Yesenin's posthumous fate', *Modern Language Review*, 1972 (3) p. 596.
111. Sergei Subbotin, 'Nikolai Kluyev (1887–1937)', *Soviet Literature* 1988 (6) pp. 143–4.
112. On 31 July 1937, Klychkov was arrested at his dacha. See Nadezhda Mandelstam, *Hope Against Hope*, pp. 259–60. His date of death was given as 1937 in *Arkhiv A. M. Gor'kogo*, xii, p. 24.
113. See above, p. 215; p. 309, n. 54.
114. B. K. Livshits, *Polutoraglazyi strelets* (Leningrad 1933, reprinted 1989).
115. Vera Reck, *Pil'niak*, p. 6. It was published in 1964.
116. See Gary Browning, *Boris Pilnyak*, pp. 132–87.
117. Serge, *Memoirs of a Revolutionary*, pp. 269–70.
118. Reck, p. 8.
119. See Mikhail Shreider, 'Ivanovo, 1937: From the notes of a Chekist-

Operative', *Moskowskiye novosti*, 'Memorial', 27 November 1988.
120. Ibid.
121. Ibid.
122. Medvedev, *Let History Judge*, Ch. 9, is still the fullest ana. sis.
123. Solzhenitsyn, *The GULag Archipelago*, Bk. 2.
124. *Literaturnaya gazeta*, 5 June 1937.
125. Yashvili's suicide was on 22 July 1937. See Boris Pasternak, *Letters to Georgian Friends* (London, 1968).
126. See K. S. Khudaverdyan, *Kul'turnaya revolyutsiya v Sovetskoi Armenii* (Yerevan, 1966) p. 244.
127. Conquest, *The Great Terror*, pp. 443–4.
128. Noteworthy is the fate of Mykola Khvylovy, a proletarian writer, who committed suicide during the famine, on 13 May 1933. He left a letter to the Ukrainian Central Committee accusing the Party of betraying the Revolution. He called the terror in the Ukraine the start of a new Thermidor. His funeral in Kharkov became a national demonstration. Stalin had already protested against 'Khvylovy's demand that the proletariat in the Ukraine be immediately de-Russified, his belief that Ukrainian poetry should keep as far away as possible from Russian literature and style'. Stalin also condemned the writer's 'ridiculous and non-Marxist attempt to divorce culture from politics'. Letter to Kaganovich, of 26 April 1926: *Sochineniya*, VIII.
129. See the commentary in *Mykola Khvylovy, The Cultural Renaissance in the Ukraine: Polemical Pamphlets, 1925–26* (Edmonton, 1986) p. 25: 'In the latter half of 1937 almost the entire Central Committee of the Ukrainian Communist Party and government was executed. It is no exaggeration to state that during those terrible years, an entire Ukranian intelligentsia perished in labour camps and the execution chambers of the NKVD'.
130. *Literaturnaya gazeta*, 5 October 1937. See also James Mace, *Communism and Dilemmas of National Liberation*. The intended trial of 'bourgeois nationalist' Ukrainian officials – including Postyshev and Kossior as well as many scholars and scientists – did not take place: see Beck and Godin, *Russian Purge*, p. 181.
131. Amongst those arrested were the poets Astapenko and Taubin, and the writer Platon Golovach, who had attended the Writers' Congress. Writers who perished in camps or prisons included Ciška Hartny, Michas Carot, Symon Baranavych, Platon Halavac and Uladzimir Chadyka. All were posthumously rehabilitated. See A. McMillin, *Die Literatur der Weibrussen*, [a history of Byelorussian literature] (Giessen, 1977); A. Adamovich, *Opposition to Sovietization in BeloRussian Literature* (New York, 1958).
132. E. Bel'tov in *Moskovskoye novosti*, 27 November 1988.
133. Medvedev, *Let History Judge*, p. 321.
134. *Men, Years-Life*, vol. 4, p. 41.
135. J. J. Matlock, 'The "governing organs" of the Union of Soviet Writers', *American Slavonic and East European Review*, 1956 (October) pp. 382–99.
136. E. Bel'tov, *Moskovskiye novosti*, 27 November 1988.

137. Quoted by R. W. Davies, *Soviet History*, pp. 169–70, 138.
138. *Moskovskiye novosti*, 27 November 1988.
139. Ibid.
140. Zak dissertation, p. 889.
141. Letter dated 16 February 1938: *Voprosy literatury*, 1953 (11) p. 21.
142. Michel Heller, 'Boris Souvarine, 1895–1984', translated by Teresa Cherfas, in *Survey*, Winter 1984, p. 201.
143. Stalin, *Sochineniya*, (Stanford) vol. XIV, p. 218.
144. Interview with A. I. Ovcharenko (Moscow, October 1977).
145. H. Barbusse, *Stalin: A new world seen through one man* (London, 1935) p. vi.
146. See Zak, unpublished dissertation, p. 802.
147. Ibid.
148. E. Proffer, *Bulgakov*, ch. XXVIII.
149. *Joseph Stalin: A Short Biography* (M.1949) pp. 15–16.
150. The theme was developed in K. E. Voroshilov, *Stalin i Krasnaya Armiya* (M.1937), where, on p. 7 for instance, we read of Stalin's activity on the Southern front. It was followed by the same author's *Stalin i stroitel'stvo Krasnoi Armii* (M.1941).
151. See also Pogodin's 'Tovarishch Stalin' in *Literaturnaya gazeta*, 12 September 1937.
152. Such as Gorky's 'Pravda sotsialisma', Preface to *Belomor* (M.1934), reprinted in *Sobraniye sochinenii*, vol. 27 (M.1953) p. 126.
153. Getty, *Origins of the Great Purges*, pp. 180–1.
154. *Literaturnaya gazeta*, 26 November and 5 December 1937.
155. See the 'poetical' selection in *Oktyabr'*, 1937 (12) such as p. 16, 'Stalin'.
156. *Men, Years-Life*, vol. 6, p. 302.
157. *The Extraordinary Adventures of Julio Jurenito and his Disciples* (1922) was under a ban in Stalin's lifetime.
158. See above, pp. 206–7.
159. *Men, Years-Life*, vol. 6, pp. 302–7.
160. Ibid.
161. Ibid.
162. Ibid., p. 302.
163. K. Paustovsky, *The Restless Years: Memoirs* vol. 6 (London, 1979) pp. 133–4.
164. Reported by Paustovsky, op. cit., pp. 63–5.
165. Ibid.
166. Ibid.
167. J. Curtis, *Bulgakov's last decade: the writer as hero* (Cambridge, 1987) p. 204.
168. Ibid., pp. 205–6.
169. Ibid., p. 206.
170. *Komsomol'skaya pravda*.
171. D. A. Volkogonov, 'Triunfi tragediya. Politicheskii portret I. V. Stalina', *Oktyabr'*, 1988, 10–12.
172. *Report of the Court Proceedings in the case of the anti-Soviet 'Bloc of Rightists and Trotskyites'* (hereafter *Bukharin Trial*) (M.1938) pp. 28–9.
173. *Bukharin Trial*, p. 64.

174. See also: *Stalin's Doctor, Stalin's Nurse: A Memoir* by N. Romano-Petrova (Princeton, N.J., 1984).
175. *Bukharin Trial*, pp. 529–30.
176. *Men, Years-Life*, vol. 4, p. 197.
177. *Bukharin Trial*, p. 548. The same, of course, was true of Vyshinsky.
178. Ibid., p. 370.
179. Ivanov-Razumnik, *Pisatel'skiye sud'by*, p. 44.
180. Struve, *Russian Literature*, p. 193.
181. *Moskovskiye novosti*, 9 April 1989. Part of the information given here was provided by V. M. Markelov, Senior Research Assistant, Central KGB Archives.
182. Nadezhda Mandelstam, *Hope against Hope*, p. 367.
183. Ibid., p. 373.
184. Conquest, *The Great Terror*, p. 606.
185. *Literaturnaya gazeta*, 20 December 1937.
186. See the account by Stephen Wheatcroft, *Australian Slavonic Papers*, vol. I, no. 1.
187. Several had been mooted, such as the trial of Meyerhold, Pil'nyak and Babel as a 'diversionary organisation of literary people'. Medvedev, *Let History Judge*, p. 309. The arrest of Babel is discussed by Nathalie Babel, 'Preface' to Isaac Babel, *You Must Know Everything* (London, 1970) pp. vii–viii. Also *Ogonyok*, 1989 (39) pp. 6–7; 22–3.
188. Medvedev, *On Stalin*, pp. 108–111 describes Yezhov's last months, as Commissar for Water Transport.
189. Stalin, *Sochineniya*, vol. I(XIV) pp. 364–66. His speech was also carried by *Literaturnaya gazeta*, 11 March 1939, pp. 1–5.
190. *Literaturnaya gazeta*, 11 March 1939. The extraordinary details of a NKVD action against him in late 1938 are described by Ermolaev, *Sholokhov*, pp. 41–2.
191. *Literaturnaya gazeta*, 5 February 1939. The awards were presented in the Kremlin: *Literaturnaya gazeta*, 10 February 1939.
192. Nadezhda Mandelstam, *Hope against Hope*, p. 3.
193. See Wright, *Bulgakov*, pp. 143–7; M. Chudakova, *Zhizneopisaniye Mikhaila Bulgakova* (M.1989), ch. 4.
194. See A. K. France, *Boris Pasternak's translations of Shakespeare* (Berkeley, 1978).
195. See the debates in *Slavic Review*, 1976(1) pp. 111–21.
196. Letter to A. Tolstoy of 'August 4–October 5 1938', in *Moskovskiye novosti*. Its references are to Tolstoy's *Bread* (1937) or a new book glorifying Stalinism and to L. Feuchtwanger, *Moscow, 1937. My visit described for my friends* (London, 1937).
197. Counter-culture in the camps is described by Solzhenitsyn, *GULag*, bk. 2, pp. 471–4. Inevitably, it is mostly lost.
198. For the background, see Amanda Haight, *Akhmatova*, pp. 97–9;. *Zvezda* special issue 1989 (6).
199. On its publication in the USSR, see *Literaturnaya gazeta*, 22 April 1987.
200. See Stephen F. Cohen, (ed.) *An End to Silence* (New York, 1982) pp. 162–7.
201. Ibid., pp. 91–2.

202. M. Hayward, 'Introduction', *Dissonant Voices in Soviet Literature* (London, 1964) p. xlii.

8 STALINISM IN LITERATURE

1. Nadezhda Mandelstam, *Hope Abandoned*, p. 411.
2. The best account of post-war Stalinism in literature is Harold Swayze, *Political Control of Literature in the USSR, 1946–1959* (Cambridge, Mass., 1962).
3. N. I. Bukharin and E. Preobrazhensky, *The ABC of Communism* (London, 1922, 1969) p. 295.
4. *Zhizn' iskusstva*, 1924 (10) p. 1.
5. Sheila Fitzpatrick, *The Commissariat of Enlightenment*, ch. 6.
6. Sheila Fitzpatrick, 'The Emergence of *Glaviskusstvo*', *Soviet Studies*, October 1971.
7. Ibid.
8. His role in the debate with Voronsky is described by Maguire, *Red Virgin Soil*, pp. 180–3.
9. Set up in 1920, it was merged with the Central Committee's Press Department in 1928: *Izvestiya TsK VKP(b)* (16/17) 25 May 1928.
10. *Partiinoye stroitel'stvo*, 1930 (2). The decision was explained by Kaganovich in *ibid.*, pp. 9–13.
11. IMLI f. 40, opis I, ed. khr. 876.
12. Ibid.
13. Ibid.
14. *Partiinoye stroitel'stvo*, 1932 (6). This was a Central Committee Resolution of 17 January 1932.
15. *Pravda*, 14 May 1935.
16. *Pravda*, 24 April 1932.
17. *Pervyi vsesoyuznyi s"ezd sovetskikh pisatelei: stenotchot* (M.1935) pp. 669–70.
18. *Vsya Moskva, 1929*, p. 130.
19. *Literaturnaya gazeta*, 14 May 1934.
20. *Pravda*, 2 September 1934.
21. *Pervyi s"ezd*, Appendix V, p. 710.
22. Ibid., Appendix VI.
23. T. H. Rigby, *Communist Party Membership in the USSR, 1917–1967* (Princeton, 1968) p. 444.
24. *Pervyi s"ezd*, Appendix VII.
25. *Arkhiv A. M. Gor'kovo*, vol. X (i) (M.1964) p. 362.
26. *Istoricheskii arkhiv*, 1960 (5) p. 17.
27. *Literaturnaya gazeta*, 20 February 1935.
28. Ibid., 26 February 1935.
29. The pattern of later plenary sessions, held at lengthier intervals until the war, confirm this picture of vacuity. A useful account of this process is J. J. Matlock, 'The "governing organs" of the Union of Soviet Writers', *Slavic Review*, October 1956, pp. 382–99.
30. *Vtoroi plenum pravleniya soyuza sovetskikh pisatelei: stenotchot* (M.1935) p. 495.

31. Matlock, op. cit., provides the available evidence.
32. *Literaturnaya gazeta*, 27 December 1954.
33. Ibid., 30 July 1934.
34. *Arkhiv A. M. Gor'kogo*, vol. X (i) pp. 282–3.
35. *Literaturnaya gazeta*, 24 December 1935.
36. Ibid., 26 August 1936. Further details are set out in *Literaturnyi fond SSSR: ustav* (M.1934); and V. V. Ivanov, *The Position of the Author in the USSR* (M.1934).
37. M. Bulgakov, *The Master and Margarita* in *Romani* (M.1973) pp. 469 ff.
38. *Pravda*, 7 September 1936.
39. See H. Ermolaev, *Sholokhov*, p. 45 on his earlier honours. His Central Committee election took place at the Twenty-Second Party Congress.
40. See for instance, Aleksandr Nikitenko, *The Diary of a Russian Censor* ed. H. Jacobson (Massachusetts, 1975). For the pre-revolutionary background: Charles A. Ruud, *Fighting Words: Imperial Censorship and the Russian Press, 1804–1906* (Toronto, 1982).
41. *Sobraniye uzakonenii RSFSR* 1931 (31) article 273 (6 June 1931).
42. Ibid., 26 February 1934 (confirming statutes of *Glavrepertkom* for 9 February 1923) in ibid., 1923 (14) para 177 and 1927 (19) para 134.
43. L. G. Fogelevich (compiler), *Osnovnye direktivy i zakonodatel'stvo o pechati*, 5th ed. (M.1935) pp. 122–3.
44. See R. Gul', 'Tsenzura i pisatel' v SSSR', *Sovremennye zapiski* (Paris, 1938) no. 66 pp. 438–449.
45. Max Hayward, in M. Dewhirst and R. Farrell (eds), *The Soviet Censorship* (New Jersey, 1973) p. 17.
46. *Literaturnoye nasledstvo*, vol. 70 (M.1963) p. 30.
47. Ibid., p. 31.
48. A. Karaganov in *Znamya*, 1963 (1) pp. 202–16 and *Zhizn' dramaturga: tvorcheskii put'* A. *Afinogenova* (M.1964) pp. 279 ff.
49. Ibid.
50. A. Afinogenov, *Stat'i, dnevniki, pis'ma. Vospominaniya* (M.1957) p. 105.
51. A recent exploration of this neglected area is Miklos Haraszti, *The Velvet Prison: Artists under State Socialism* (London, 1988).
52. Nadezhda Mandelstam, *Hope Abandoned*, p. 410.
53. Ibid., p. 409.
54. An overview is provided by Moshe Lewin, *Political Undercurrents in Soviet Economic Debates* (London, 1975), ch. 6.
55. See for instance Anatole Kopp, *Town and Revolution: Soviet Architecture and City Planning, 1917–1935* (New York, 1970) and S. Frederick Starr, 'Visionary Town Planning during the Cultural Revolution' in Sheila Fitzpatrick (ed.) *Cultural Revolution in Russia, 1928–1931* (London, 1978) pp. 207–40.
56. See Richard Day, *N. I. Bukharin: Selected Writings*, pp. 31, 42 and note, p. 84.
57. For instance Ia. V. Starosel'sky, *Problema yakobinskoi diktatury* (M.1930).
58. See *Ustav Akademii nauk SSSR* (M.1936).
59. Zak dissertation, pp. 568 ff.
60. Stalin's speech is discussed by Bailes, *Technology and Society*, Ch. 6.

61. *Molodaya gvardiya* April-September 1932. The remainder came out in 1934.
62. S. Tregub, *The Heroic Life of Nikolai Ostrovsky* (M., n.d.)
63. Ibid.
64. He mentioned: 'There can be no measure to a fighter's happiness, if his will, his perseverance, have gained his country's praise, if on his breast, where the heart beats, he wears the Order of Lenin'.
65. Ibid.
66. *Vtoroi plenum pravleniya*, pp. 513–14.
67. *Literaturnaya gazeta*, 16 October 1935.
68. *Literaturnaya entsiklopediya*, vol. 2 (M.1929) p. 652.
69. Letter to Gladkov (1927).
70. R. Mathewson, *The Positive Hero in Russian Literature* 2nd ed. (Stanford, 1975) pp. 174–5.
71. Recounted to Ehrenburg, see vol. 4 of his autobiography, p. 98.
72. *Letopis'*, 3 (M.1959) pp. 421–2; Letters of 27 August and September 1925.
73. See Max Hayward, 'The Decline of Socialist Realism', reprinted in *Writers in Russia, 1917–1978* (London, 1983) pp. 153–63.
74. Mathewson, *The Positive Hero*, ch. 2.
75. Zhdanov, 'Doklad o zhurnalakh *Zvezda* i *Leningrad*', *Pravda* 21 September 1946.
76. Vera Dunham, *In Stalin's Time: middle class values in Soviet fiction* (Cambridge, 1976).
77. *Pervyi s"ezd*, p. 716.
78. Swayze, *Political Control of Literature*, p. 114.
79. See above, Chapter Two.
80. Arkhiv Gor'kovo (26 October 1932).
81. Ibid.
82. Stalin, *Sochineniya*, XI pp. 326–9.
83. Ibid., p. 328.
84. According to records in the Moscow Art Theatre Museum, Stalin saw the play fifteen times. V. Petelin, 'M. A. Bulgakov i *Dni Turbinykh*' *Ogonyok* 1969 (11) pp. 25–7. I owe this reference to Dr L. Milne.
85. *Pravda*, 29 October 1936; P. M. Kerzhentsev, *Protiv fal'sifikatsii narodnogo proshlogo* (M.1937).
86. Stalin, *Sochineniya*, vol. XII pp. 23–7.
87. Zak dissertation, p. 917.
88. Ibid.
89. These notions are analysed more fully in Swayze, *Political Control of Literature*, pp. 11–16.
90. S. Sheshukov, *Neistovye revniteli* (M.1970).
91. A. Avtorkhanov, *Stalin and the Soviet Communist Party* (London, 1959) p. 186.
92. *Literaturnaya gazeta*, 23 April 1932.
93. L. G. Fogelevich, *Osnovnye direktivy* (M.1935).
94. See p. 149, above.
95. Ibid.
96. He paced the corridors of the Writers' Congress with the *White Sea Canal* which he had co-edited.

97. See p. 149, above.
98. *Literaturnaya gazeta*, 28 November 1934.
99. *Literaturnyi kritik*, 1934 (12) pp. 8–10 and 1935 (2) pp. 165–84.
100. *Materialy ko vtoromu plenum soyuza sovetskikh pisatelei* (M.1935) p. 1.
101. E. J. Brown, *The Proletarian Episode*, p. 277, n. 54.
102. Nadezhda Mandelstam, *Hope against Hope*, pp. 140–1.
103. IMLI f. 40, opis 1, ed. khr. 70.
104. *Pervyi s"ezd*, pp. 578–97.
105. *Pravda*, 14 May 1935.
106. I. Shkapa, *Sem' let s Gor'kim* (M.1964) pp. 241–57. Reissued 1989.
107. A vast army of Gor'koved assembled between mid-1937 and end 1938, when 333 articles were devoted to him: Sheila Fitzpatrick 'Culture and Politics under Stalin', *Slavic Review* 1976 (2) note 30, pp. 223–4.
108. A. S. Matkarenko, *The Road to Life* (London, 1936) p. 161.
109. Ibid., p. 9.
110. Ibid., p. 19.

Bibliography

ARCHIVES

Institut mirovoi literatury pri AN SSSR (IMLI)

Fond 40: Rossiskaya assosiatsiya proletarskikh pisatelei (RAPP) 1928–1932

Protocols and stenograms of the Secretariat and Party 'fraction'
1 Secretariat (May-December 1928)
3 Secretariat (January-December 1929)
6 Constructivists (4 April 1930)
8 'Litfront' (19 June 1930)
16 'Litfront' (29 September 1930)
18 *Kuznitsa* (24 October 1930)
25 Secretariat (January-December 1930)
45 'MORP' (5 November 1931)
46 '*Pravda*' (11 November 1931)
49 Secretariat (January-December 1931)
66 Secretariat (1931-May 1932)
70 'CC Resolution' (3 May 1932)

Stenograms, resolutions and protocols of plenary sessions
71 I Plenum (1–4 October 1928)
72–80 II Plenum (20–29 September) 1929
83–86 III Plenum (18–20 February 1931)
87–90 IV Plenum (31 August-4 September 1931)
92–100 V Plenum (2–6 December 1931)

'Litfront' and 'Pereverzev'
650–657 'Litfront'
712 'Pereverzev' (11 May 1930)
713 Institute of Red Professors (24 November 1930)
714 Resolution of above meeting (19 December 1930)

Correspondence with the Central Committee (1930–31)
728 Letter to Stalin (November 1930)
729 Letter to *Kul't-prop* (8 August 1931)
730 Letter to Central Committee Secretariat (8 September 1931)

General Correspondence
736 On literary Constructivism
742 To 'Novaya Kuznitsa'
855 To *Glaviskusstvo* NKP (1928–32)
861 With Communist Academy (1930–1)
865 With Institute LiYa (Communist Academy)

872 With Central Committee (1928–9)
873 With Komsomol (1929–31)
874 To Stetsky (1930)

Correspondence with Stalin
875 To Stalin (December 1931)
876 To Central Committee Secretariat (1931)
900 To Stalin, draft (15 November 1929)
1153 'Answer to Writer-Communists of RAPP'

Fond 41: Soyuz sovetskikh pisatelei, 1932–6

33–45 Second Plenum of the *Orgkomitet* (12–19 February 1933)
52 Discussion on socialist realism (April-May 1933)
73 *Orgkomitet*, All-Union meeting (15 August 1933)
76 Praesidium of the *Orgkomitet* (7 September 1933)
429 Party Cell (1933)
432 *Litfond* (7 September 1934)
433 Secretariat of the *Orgkomitet* (1933)
434 'Party fraction' (1933–4)
438 Praesidium of the *Orgkomitet* (1932)
440 Praesidium of the *Orgkomitet* (1933)
445 'Buro' of the Praesidium (1933)
448 'Buro' of the Praesidium (1934)
454 Draft Central Committee resolution (March 1930)
484 Membership rules (undated: spring 1934)
492 Statutes (1934)
494–7 'Plans of Work' (1932–34)
526 Preparations for Congress (1933)
527 Instructions on Congress (May-July 1933)
533 'Bulletin' of All-Union *Orgkomitet* (January 1934)
668 Commission on Gorky's Jubilee (1932)
671 Commission on Socialist Realism (1933)
691 Commission on Dramaturgy (1933)
890–93 Leningrad *Orgkomitet*
968 Correspondence with *VseRossKomDram*
982 Correspondence with Communist Academy

Fond 52: VseRossKomDram

69 Plenary sessions (February-July 1933)
75 Praesidium (April-December 1933)
85 Purge Commission (19 September 1933)
98 'Creative sections' (January 1934)
114 Speech of Shklovsky (27 May 1933)
175 Secretariat (1931–3)
206 Reorganisation Commission (1933)
230 Autonomous Section for Dramaturgy (1934)

Fond 54: Kuznitsa

19 Letter from RAPP (18 April 1930)
22 Agreement with RAPP (17 January 1931)
27 Membership of *Kuznitsa*
45 Correspondence with RAPP (1930–1)

Fond 96: F. V. Gladkov (1883–1958)

15 Letter to Averbakh (1931)
16 Averbakh's reply (23 September 1931)

Fond 147: P. F. Yudin (1898–1968)

10 Letter from Zarudin (14 May 1934)
15 Letter from Makar'yev (7 June 1934)
28 Letter from Serafimovich (27 May 1934)
31 Letter from Tikhonov (20 June 1934)

Arkhiv A. M. Gor'kovo (pri IMLI AN SSSR)

This archive is not catalogued in the normal way. I have therefore attempted to identify each item according to the author or addressee, and whenever possible, date of composition.

Correspondence with Yudin (1933–4). Eight items (three from Gorky)
Preparations for the First Congress (March-August 1934)
K. L. Zelinsky, 'Vstrecha pisatelei s I. V. Stalinym' (26 October 1932)

Tsentral'nyi gosudarstveny arkhiv literatury i iskusstva SSSR (TSGALI)

Fond 457: A. Serafimovich

3/101 Meeting with *Agit-prop* on VAPP (23 October 1926)
4/27 Letter to the Editors of *Oktyabr'* (6 June 1930)

Fond 602: Krasnaya nov'

1/1758 Protocol of editorial board (20 November 1931)

Fond 969: First Moscow Oblas' Conference of Proletarian Writers

(5–8 February 1930)

Fond 1328: V. P. Polonsky

1/275 Letter from Pil'nyak (24 December 1926)
2/172 Letter from Friche (20 February 1929)

Fond 1698: Na literaturnom postu

1/843 Speech of Meyerhold (23 April 1931)
1/916 'United meeting' of VAPP and MAPP, AKhRR and other cultural associations (11 November 1927)
1/931 Meeting of the Communist Academy Institute LiYa (25 February 1930)

Houghton Library (Harvard University)

Trotsky Exile Papers (released in 1980)
T. 1897 Bukharin-Kamenev Conversation (late 1928)
T. 1901 Bukharin's Plenum Speech (July 1928)
T. 17208 'Quelques notes pour le SI sur l'assassinat de Kirov'
T. 17226 List of 'Enemies of the People' (February-June 1937)

Widener Library (Harvard University)

The Smolensk Archive

WKP 162 Central Directives on collectivisation
WKP 260 OGPU Reports on collectivisation
WKP 499 Secret Letter of the Central Committee (13 May 1935)
WKP 499 Secret Letter of the Central Committee (29 July 1936)

Public Record Office (London)

Russian Correspondence (1929–1939)

UNPUBLISHED DISSERTATIONS

Ermakov, B. T., 'Bor'ba K. P. za perestroiku raboty nauchnykh uchrezhdenii v gody pervoi pyatiletki' (Candidate's thesis, Moscow 1955).
Ferdinand, Peter, 'The Bukharin group of political theoreticians. Their ideas and their importance to the Soviet Union in the 1920's' (D. Phil., Oxford 1984).
Grakina, E. I., 'Iz opyta raboty KPSS po ukreplenyu sviazi teatra i zhizni v pervoi polovine 30-kh godov', (Candidate's thesis, Moscow 1966).
Katz, Zev, 'Party-Political Education in Soviet Russia' (Ph.D., London, 1957).
Romanovsky, A. K. 'Iz istorii podgotovki pervovo s"ezda sovetskikh pisatelei' (Candidate's thesis, Moscow 1958).
Scott, H. G. 'An Experiment in Sociology of Form: A Re-evaluation of the "crude sociologism" of V. F. Pereverzev' (Ph.D., Chicago, 1981).
Vaganov, F. M. 'Pravy uklon v VKP (b) i ego razgrom' (Doctoral thesis Moscow 1970).
Zak, L. M. 'Stroitel'stvo sotsialisticheskoi kul'tury v SSSR, 1933–1937' (Doctoral thesis, Moscow 1966).

PUBLISHED PROCEEDINGS

Writers' Congresses and Plenary Sessions
All published in Moscow unless otherwise indicated.
Voprosy kul'tury pri diktature proletariata: sbornik (1925)
Puti razvitiya teatra ed. S. M. Krylov (1927)
Tvorcheskye puti proletarskoi literatury (1929)
Protiv mekhanisticheskogo literaturovedeniya. Diskussiya o kontseptsii V. F. Pereverzeva (1930)
Tvorcheskaya diskussiya v RAPPe (1930)
Protiv burzhuaznoqo liberalizma v khudozhestvennoi literature (1931)
Sovetskaya literatura na novom etape: stenotchot 1-ovo plenuma Orgkomiteta (1933)
Pervyi vsesoyuznyi s"ezd sovetskikh pisatelei: 1934 (1934). Partly translated as *Problems of Soviet Literature* (London, 1935) and reissued as *Soviet Writers' Congress, 1934* (London, 1977).
Vtoroi plenum pravleniya soyuza sovetskikh pisatelei (1935)
Mezhdunarodnyi kongress pisatelei v zashchitu kul'tury (Paris, 1935; Moscow, 1936)
Vtoroi vsesoyuznyi s"ezd sovetskikh pisatelei (1954)

Party Congresses and Conferences

XVI konferentsiya VKP (b) (1962)
XVI s"ezd VKP(b) (1930)
XVII konferentsiya VKP(b) (1932)
XVII s"ezd VKP (b) (1934)
XVIII s"ezd VKP(b) (1939)

SECONDARY SOURCES

Many thousands of volumes were consulted. Only those most essential to the text have been included. M = place of publication Moscow; L = place of publication Leningrad. Items without an author's name are listed alphabetically under the first word of the title.

Abramsky, Chimen (ed.) *Essays in Honour of E. H. Carr* (London, 1974).
Adamovich, A., *Opposition to Sovietization in BeloRussian Literature* (New York, 1958).
Afinogenov, A., *Stat'i, dnevniki, pis'ma. Vospominaniya* (M, 1957).
Afinogenov, A., *Tvorcheskii metod teatra. Dialektika tvorcheskovo protsessa* (ML, 1931).
Akhmatova, Anna, *Stikhotvoreniya i poemy* (L, 1976).
Alekseev, M., *Drachuny* (M, 1982).
Alliluyeva, Svetlana, *Letters to a Friend* (London, 1967).
Annali, 1966 (Milan, 1966).
Anti-Stalin Campaign and International Communism, The (New York, 1956)
Antonov-Ovseyenko, Anton, *The Time of Stalin* (New York, 1983).

Assotsiatsiya khudozhnikov revolyutsionnoi Rossii: Sbornik vospominanii statei i dokumentov (M, 1973).
Averbakh, L. L., *Iz RAPPovskogo dnevnika* (L, 1931).
Averbakh, L. L., *Kriticheskiye stat'i* (M, 1932).
Averbakh, L. L., *Voprosy yunosheskogo dvizheniya i Lenin* (M, 1923).
Avtorkhanov, A., *Stalin and the Soviet Communist Party* (New York, 1959).
Babel, I., *Isaac Babel: The Lonely Years*, (London, 1966).
Babel, I., *Isaac Babel: You Must Know Everything* (London, 1970).
Bailes, Kendall E., *Technology and Society under Lenin and Stalin* (New Jersey, 1978).
Barber, John, *Soviet Historians in Crisis* (London, 1977).
Barooshian, Vahan D., *Brik and Mayakovsky* (The Hague, 1978).
Baxandall, Lee and Morawski, Stefan (eds), *Marx and Engels on Literature and Art: A selection of writings* (St Louis and Milwaukee, 1973).
Beaujour, E. K., *The Invisible Land: A Study of the Artistic Imagination of Iurii Olesha* (New York, 1970).
Beck, F., and Godin, W., *Russian Purge and the Extraction of Confession* (London, 1951).
Bel'chikov, N. F. (ed.), *M. Gor'kii o literature: Stat'i i rechi, 1928–1936*, 3rd ed. (M, 1937).
Belinkov, Arkady, *Sdacha i gibel' sovetskogo intelligenta: Yury Olesha* (Madrid, 1976).
Belomorsko-Baltiiskii kanal imeni Stalina: Istoriya stroitel'stva (M, 1934).
Berberova, Nina, *The Italics are Mine* (London, 1969).
Berger, J., *Shipwreck of a Generation: The Memoirs of Joseph Berger* (London, 1971).
Berlin, Isaiah, *Russian Thinkers* (London, 1978).
Beskin, O., *Kulatskaya khudozhestvennaya literatura i opportunisticheskaya kritika* (M, 1930).
Borland, Harriet, *Soviet Literary Theory and Practice in The First Five-Year Plan, 1928–1932* (New York, 1950).
Bowman, Herbert, E., *Vissarion Belinski 1811–1848* (Cambridge, Mass., 1954).
Bowra, M., *Poetry and Politics, 1900–1960* (Cambridge, 1965).
Braun, Edward, *The Theatre of Meyerhold* (London, 1979).
Britikov, A. F., *Masterstvo Mikhaila Sholokhova* (M, 1964).
Brodski, N. L. ed., *Literaturniye manifesty: ot Simvolizma k Oktyabryu* (M, 1929).
Brown, Edward J., *Mayakovsky: A Poet in the Revolution* (New Jersey, 1973).
Brown, Edward J., *The Proletarian Episode in Russian Literature, 1928–1932* (New York, 1953).
Browning, Gary, *Boris Pilniak: Scythian at a Typewriter* (Ann Arbor, 1985).
Broyde, Steven, *Osip Mandelstam and His Age* (Cambridge, Mass., 1975).
Brzezinski, Z. K., *The Permanent Purge* (Cambridge, Mass., 1956).
Bukharin, N. I., *Ekonomika perekhodnogo perioda* (M, 1920).
Bukharin, N. I., and Preobrazhensky, E., *The ABC of Communism* (London, 1922; reprinted 1969).
Bulgakov, Mikhail, *Romany* (M, 1973).

Bykovtseva, L., *Gor'kii v Moskve, 1931–1936* (M, 1968).

Cammett, John, *Antonio Gramsci and the Origins of Italian Communism* (Stanford, 1967).

Carr, E. H., *Socialism in One Country, 1924–1926*, vol. I (London, 1959).

Carr, E. H., *The Bolshevik Revolution*, vol. 1 (London, 1966).

Carr, E. H., *The Twilight of the Comintern 1930–1935* (London, 1982).

Chamberlain, W. H., *The Russian Revolution, 1917–1921*, vol. 1 (Cambridge, Mass., 1935).

Chayanov, A. V. *on the Theory of the Peasant Economy* (Homewood, Ill., 1966).

Chudakova, M. *Zhizneopisaniye Mikhaila Bulgakova* (M, 1988).

Chukovsky, K. I., *Sovremenniki: Portrety i etiudy* (M, 1962).

Chumandrin, M. F., *Dostoinstvo sily* (L, 1932).

Chumandrin, M. F., *Kriticheskaya otsenka moyei tvorcheskoi praktiki* (L, 1933).

Churchward, L. G., *The Soviet Intelligentsia* (London, 1973).

Clark, K., *The Soviet Novel: History as Ritual* (Chicago, 1981).

Cohen, Stephen, F., *Bukharin and the Bolshevik Revolution, 1888–1938: A Political Biography* (New York, 1973).

Cohen, Stephen, F. (ed), *An End to Silence* (New York, 1982).

Conquest, Robert, *Harvest of Sorrow* (London, 1986).

Conquest, Robert, *Stalin and the Kirov Murder* (Oxford, 1989).

Conquest, Robert, *The Great Terror*, (London, 1968).

Cooke, Raymond, *Velimir Khlebnikov: A critical study* (Cambridge, 1983).

Curtis, J., *Bulgakov's last decade: the writer as hero* (Cambridge, 1987).

Daniels, Robert V., *The Conscience of the Revolution* (Cambridge, Mass., 1960).

Davies, R. W., *Soviet History in the Gorbachev Revolution* (London, 1989).

Day, Richard B. (ed.), *N. I. Bukharin: Selected Writings on the State and the Transition to Socialism* (Nottingham, 1982).

Demetz, Peter, *Marx, Engels and the Poets* (Chicago, 1967).

Desai, P. (ed.), *Marxism, central planning, and the Soviet economy: economic essays in honor of A. Erlich* (Cambridge, Mass. 1983).

Dewhirst, M. and Farell, R. (eds) *The Soviet Censorship* (Metuchen, NJ, 1973)

Dramaturgiya: Sbornik (M, 1933).

Dremov, A. K., *Partiinost' literatury i sovremennost' ucheniya Lenina* (M, 1980).

Dunham, V., *In Stalin's Time: Middle-class Values in Soviet Fiction* (Cambridge, 1976).

Dve kritiki (Plekhanov-Pereverzev) (M, 1930).

Eastman, Max, *Artists in Uniform: a Study of Literature and Bureaucratism* (New York, 1934).

Ehrenburg, I., *Den' vtoroi* (M, 1933).

Ehrenburg, I., *Men, Years – Life* (4 vols): vol. 4, *The Eve of War* (London, 1963); vol. 6 *Post-War Years, 1945–54* (London, 1966).

Elsworth, J. D., *Andrey Bely* (Letchworth, 1972).

Erlich, V., *Russian Formalism: History-Doctrine*, 3rd. ed. (New Haven, 1981).

Ermolaev, Herman, *Mikhail Sholokhov and His Art* (Princeton, 1982).
Ermolaev, Herman, *Soviet Literary Theories, 1917–1934: The Genesis of Socialist Realism* (New York, 1977).
Ermolaev, Herman (ed.), *Maxim Gorky, Untimely Thoughts* (Princeton, 1982).
Fadeyev, A., *Aleksandr Fadeyev: Materiali i issledovaniya, Vypusk II* (M, 1984).
Fadeyev, A., *Kakaya literatura nuzhna rabochemu klassu?* (M L, 1932).
Fadeyev, A., *Na literaturnye temy* (M L, 1932).
Fadeyev, A., *Pis'ma, 1916–1956* (M, 1967).
Fadeyev, A., *Za khudozhnika materialista-dialektika* (M, 1931).
Fainsod, Merle, *Smolensk under Soviet Rule* (Cambridge, Mass., 1958).
Fedyukin, S. A., *Sovetskaya vlast' i burzhuaznye spetsialisty* (M, 1965).
Fedyukin, S. A., *The Great October Revolution and the Intelligentsia* (M, 1975).
Fedyukin, S. A., *Velikii oktyabr' i intelligentsia* (M, 1972).
Feuchtwanger, L., *Moscow, 1937* (London, 1937).
Fevral'sky, A. (ed), *V. E. Meyerhold: Stat'i, pis'ma, rechi, besedi* (M, 1968).
Fitzpatrick, S., *Education and social mobility in the Soviet Union, 1921–1934* (Cambridge, 1979).
Fitzpatrick, S., *The Commisariat of Enlightenment: Soviet Organisation of Education and the Arts under Lunacharsky, October 1917–1921* (Cambridge, 1970).
Fitzpatrick, S. (ed.), *Cultural Revolution in Russia, 1928–1931* (Indiana, 1978).
Fleishman, Lazar', *Boris Pasternak v tridtsatye godi* (Jerusalem, 1984).
Fogelevich, L. G. (compiler), *Osnovnye direktivy i zakonodatel'stvo o pechati*, 5th. ed. (M, 1935).
Forsh, Ol'ga, *Sumasshedshii korabl'* (1931).
France, A. K., *Boris Pasternak's translations of Shakespeare* (Berkeley, 1978).
Garrard, J. and C., *Inside the Soviet Writers' Union* (New York, 1990).
Geller, M., *Andrei Platonov v poiskakh schast'ya* (Paris, 1982).
Getty, J. Arch, *Origins of the Great Purges* (London, 1985).
Gladkov, Alexander, *Meetings with Pasternak: A Memoir* (London, 1977).
Glinka, G., *Na Perevale* (New York, 1954).
Gorky, A. M., *Letopis' zhizni i tvorchestva A. M. Gor'kogo*, vol. 3 (M, 1959).
Gorky, A. M., *O russkom krestyanstve* (Berlin, 1922).
Gorky, A. M., *Sobraniye sochinenii* (M, 1949–55).
Graham, Loren, *The Soviet Academy of Sciences* (New York, 1968).
Gramsci, A., *Selections from the Prison Notebooks* (London, 1971).
Gray, Camilla, *The Russian Experiment in Art, 1863–1922* (London, 1962).
Gudov, I., *Put' stakhanovtsa: Rasskaz o moei zhizni* (M, 1938).
Hackel, Sergei, *The Poet and the Revolution* (Oxford, 1975).
Haraszti, Miklós, *The Velvet Prison: Artists under State Socialism* (London, 1988) (London, 1990).
Hayward, M., (ed. Patricia Blake) *Writers in Russia, 1917–1978* (London, 1983).
Hayward, M. (ed.), *Dissonant Voices in Soviet Literature* (London, 1964).

Hayward, M., and Labedz, L. (eds), *Literature and Revolution in Soviet Russia, 1917–62* (Oxford, 1963).

Hughes, Olga, *The Poetic World of Boris Pasternak* (Princeton, 1974).

Il'in Ya (ed.), *Lyudi Stalingradskogo traktornogo* (M, 1933).

Isbakh, A., *Na literaturnykh barrikadakh* (M, 1964).

Ivanov, V. V., *The Position of the Author in the USSR* (M, 1934).

Ivanov-Razumnik, R. V., *Pisatel'sky sud'by* (New York, 1951).

Ivanov-Razumnik, R. V., *The Memoirs of Ivanov-Razumnik*, (Oxford, 1965).

Ivinskaya, Olga., *A Captive of Time: my years with Pasternak* (London, 1979).

Iz istorii sovetskoi esteticheskoi mysli: sbornik statei (M, 1967).

Jackson, Robert Louis, *Dostoevsky's Underground Man in Russian Literature* (The Hague, 1958).

Janecek, G. (ed.), *Andrei Bely. A Critical Review* (Lexington, 1978).

Joravsky, David, *Soviet Marxism and Natural Science* (London, 1961).

Joravsky, David, *The Lysenko Affair* (Cambridge, Mass., 1970).

Kalinin, M. I., *Ob iskusstve i literature* (M, 1957).

Kalinin, M. I., *O voprosakh sotsialisticheskoi kul'tury. Sbornik statei i rechei (1929–38)* (M, 1939).

Karaganov, A., *Zhizn' dramaturga: tvorcheskii put' A. Afinogenova* (M, 1964).

Karlinsky, Simon, and Appel, Alfred Jr. (eds) *The Bitter Air of Exile: Russian Writers in the West, 1922–1972* (Berkeley, Ca., 1977).

Karlinsky, Simon, *Maria Cvetaeva: her life and art* (Berkeley, Ca., 1966).

Katayev, Valentin, *Time, Forward!* (M, 1933; reprinted Indiana, 1976).

Kemp-Welch, A. (ed.), *The Ideas of Nikolai Bukharin* (Oxford, 1990).

Kerzhentsev, P. M., *Protiv fal'sifikatsii narodnogo proshlogo* (M, 1937).

Kerzhentsev, P. M., *Tvorcheskii teatr. Puti sotsialisticheskogo teatra* (Petrograd, 1918).

Khodasevich, V. F., *Nekropol: vospominaniya* (Brussels, 1939).

Khrushchev, N., *Khrushchev Remembers* (London, 1971).

Khrushchev, N., *The Last Testament* (New York, 1976).

Khvylovy, Mykola, *The Cultural Renaissance in the Ukraine* (Edmonton, 1986).

Khudaverdyan, K. S., *Kul'turnaya revolyutsiya v Sovetskoi Armenii* (Yerevan, 1966).

Kim, M. P. (ed.), *Kul'turnaya revolyutsiya v SSSR, 1917–1965 gg.* (M, 1967).

Kirpotin, V. Ya., *Literatura na novom etape* (M, 1933).

Kirpotin, V. Ya., *Proza, dramaturgiya i teatr: stat'i.* (M, 1935).

Kirshon, V. M., *O literature i iskusstve* (M, 1967).

Kirshon, V. M., *Stat'i i rechi o dramaturgii, teatre i kino* (M, 1962).

Kirshon, V. M., and Serebryansky, M., *Za bol'shevistskoye iskusstvo* (M, 1932).

Knei-Paz, Baruch, *The Social and Political Thought of Leon Trotsky* (Oxford, 1978).

Kolakowski, Leszek, *Main Currents of Marxism*, vol. 1 (Oxford, 1978).

Kopelev, Lev, *The Education of a True Believer* (New York, 1980).

Kopp, Anatole, *Town and Revolution: Soviet Architecture and City Planning 1917–1935* (New York, 1970).

Kosarev, A., *Bol'shevistskomu pokoleniyu–leninskoye rukovodstvo* (M, 1931).
Kostiuk, Hryhory, *Stalinist Rule in the Ukraine* (London, 1960).
Kratkii otchet o rabote Kommakademii za 1928/1929 gg. (M, 1929).
Krupskaya, Nadezhda, *Memoirs of Lenin* (London, 1970).
Krutikova N. I. (ed.), *V. I. Lenin o literature i iskusstve* (M, 1967).
Kunitz, Stanley, *Poems of Akhmatova* (London, 1974).
Lelevich, G., *Na literaturnom postu* (Tver, 1924).
Lenin, V. I., *Nasledye Lenina i nauka o literature* (L, 1969).
Lenin, V. I., *Polnoie sobraniye sochineniye* (M, 1958–65).
Leonov, L., *Sot'* (M, 1931).
Lewin, M., *Russian Peasants and Soviet Power: A Study of Collectivisation* (London, 1968).
Lewin, M., *Political Undercurrents in Soviet Economic Debates* (London, 1975).
Lewin, M., *The Making of the Soviet Union* (London, 1985).
Lifshits, M. A. *Marks i Engel's ob iskusstve* (M, 1933).
Lifshits, M. A., *The Philosophy of Art of Karl Marx* (London, 1973).
Literatura Ukraini: Materialy I-mu Vsesoyuznomu s"ezdu sovetskikh pisatelei (M, 1934).
Literaturnii fond SSSR: ustav (M, 1934).
Literaturovedeniya. Sbornik statei (M, 1928).
Litovski, O. E., *Tak i bylo* (M, 1958).
Livshits, B. K., *Polutoraglazyi Strelets* (L. 1933)
Lodimer, Christina, *Russian Constructivism* (New Haven, 1983).
Lorimer, F., *Population of the Soviet Union* (Geneva, 1946).
Luckyj, George, S. N., *Literary Politics in the Soviet Ukraine, 1917–1934* (New York, 1956).
Lukács, G., *K istorii realizma Stat'i po estetike* (ML, 1935).
Lukács, G., *Marks i Engel's o literature. Novye materialy.* (M, 1933).
Lukács, G., *Shiller kak estetik. Stat'i po estetike* (ML, 1935).
Luker, N., *Alexander Grin* (Letchworth, 1973).
Lunacharsky, A. V., *Sobraniye sochinenii*, vol. 8 (M, 1967).
Luria, A. R., *The Making of Mind: a personal account of Soviet psychology* (Cambridge, Mass., 1978).
Mace, James E., *Communism and Dilemmas of National Liberation* (Cambridge, Mass., 1983).
Machajski, J. W., *Umstvennyi rabochii* (New York, 1968).
Maguire, Robert, A., *Red Virgin Soil: Soviet Literature in the 1920's* (Princeton, 1978).
Maisky, I. (ed.) *Proletariat i literatura: sbornik statei* (L, 1925).
Makarenko, A. S., *The Road to Life* (London, 1936).
Maksimova, V. A., *Gor'kii-redaktor, 1918–1936* (M, 1965).
Malakhov, Sergei, *Protiv trotskizma i menshevizma v literaturovedenii* (M, 1932).
Mallac, Guy de, *Boris Pasternak: his life and art* (London, 1983).
Mandelstam, Nadezhda, *Hope Against Hope* (London, 1971).
Mandelstam, Nadezhda, *Hope Abandoned* (London, 1974).
Mandelstam, O., *The Complete Critical Prose and Letters* (Ann Arbor, 1979).

Mannheim, Karl, *Ideology and Utopia*, (undated, first published New York 1936).

Markov, P. A., *The Soviet Theatre* (London, 1934).

Markov, Vladimir, *Russian Futurism: A History* (London, 1969).

Markov, Vladimir, *The Longer Poems of Velimir Khlebnikov*. (Berkeley, 1962).

Materialy ko vtoromu plenumu soyuza sovetskikh pisatelei (M, 1935).

Mathewson, Rufus, W. Jr., *The Positive Hero in Russian Literature*, 2nd. ed., (Stanford, Calif., 1975).

Matsuyev, N. I., *Tri goda sovetskoi literatury: 1931–1933* (M, 1934).

Matsuyev, N. I., *Khudozhestvennaya literatura russkaya i perevodnaya, 1933–37* (M, 1940).

Mayakovsky, V., *Polnoye sobraniye sochinenii* (M, 1955–61).

McLellan, David, *Marx before Marxism* (London, 1980).

McLellan, David (ed.), *Karl Marx: Selected Writings* (Oxford, 1977).

McMillin, A., *Die Literatur der Weissrussen: a history of Byelorussian literature* (Giessen, 1977).

McNeal, Robert, H., *Stalin: Man and Ruler* (London, 1988).

McVay, Gordon, *Esenin: A Life* (London, 1976).

Medvedev, Roy, *K sudu istorii*, 2nd ed., (New York, 1974).

Medvedev, Roy, *Let History Judge* (London, 1972).

Medvedev, Roy, *Nikolai Bukharin: The Last Years* (New York, 1980).

Medvedev, Roy, *On Stalin and Stalinism* (Oxford, 1979).

Medvedev, Zhores A., *The Rise and Fall of T. D. Lysenko* (New York, 1971).

Mikitenko, I. K., *O sozdanii soyuza sovetskikh pisatelei* (Kharkov, 1934).

Mikitenko, I. K., *Na fronte literatury 1927–37* (Kiev, 1962).

Mints, I. (ed.), *Istoriya grazhdanskoi voiny* (M, 1935).

Mitrakova, N. M., *A. P. Platonov (1899–1951) Materialy k bibliografia* (Voronezh, 1969).

Muratova, K. D., *M. Gor'kii v bor'be za razvitiye sovetskoi literatury* (M. L, 1958).

Namier, L. B., *1848: The Revolution of the Intellectuals* (London, 1944).

Nikitenko, Aleksandr, *The Diary of a Russian Censor* (ed. H. Jacobson) (Amherst, 1975).

Nilsson, N. A. (ed.), *Art, Society, Revolution: Russia, 1917–1921*, (Stockholm, 1979).

Novitsky, P. I., *Sotsiologiya iskusstva. Programma kursa* (M, 1928).

Novitsky, P. I., *Sovremennye teatral'nye sistemy* (M, 1933).

O zadachakh RAPPa na teatral'nom fronte (M, 1932).

O'Connor, T. E., *The Politics of Soviet Culture: Anatolii Lunacharskii* (Ann Arbor, 1983).

Obogashchenie metoda sotsialisticheskogo realizma i problema mnogoobraziya sovetskogo iskusstva (M, 1967).

Ol'khovy, B. S. (ed.), *Puti kino* (M, 1929).

Orlov, A., *The Secret History of Stalin's Crimes* (London, 1954).

Ossowski, Stanisław, *Struktura klasowa w spotecznej świadomośći* (Lodz, 1957).

Oulanoff, H., *The Prose Fiction of Veniamin A. Kaverin* (Cambridge, Mass., 1976).

Pamiati Esenina (M, 1926).
Panfyorov, F., *Bruski: A Story of Peasant Life* (London, 1930).
Pashukanis, E. B., *Law and Marxism: A General Theory* (London, 1978).
Pasternak, Boris, *An Essay in Autobiography* (London, 1978).
Pasternak, Boris, *Safe Conduct: An Early Autobiography and Other Works* (London, 1959).
Pasternak, Boris, *Stikhotvoreniya i poemy* (M, 1965).
Pasternak, Boris, *The Correspondence of Boris Pasternak and Olga Freidenberg, 1910–1954,* (London, 1982).
Paustovsky, K., *The Restless Years: Memoires,* vol. 6 (London, 1979).
Pavlenko, P., *Golos v puti* (M, 1952).
Pel't, V. D., *Gor'kii-zhurnalist, 1918–1936* (M, 1968).
Pereverzev, V. F., *Tvorchestvo Dostoyevskovo* (3rd. ed. M, 1928).
Pertsov, V., *Mayakovsky: Zhizn' i tvorchestvo* (M, 1950).
Piksanov, N. K., *Sotsialisticheskii realizm: bibliograficheskii ukazatel'* (M, 1934).
Pim, V. F., *Vospominaniya o Litinstitute, 1933–1983* (M, 1983).
Piper, D. G. B., *V. A. Kaverin: A Soviet Writer's Response to the Problem of Commitment* (Pittsburgh, Pa. 1970).
Platonov, Andrei, *Collected Works* (Ann Arbor, 1978).
Plotkin, A., *Partiya i literatura* (L, 1960).
Polonsky, V. P., *Magnitostroi* (M, 1930).
Polonsky, V. P., *Ocherki literaturnogo dvizheniya revolyutsionnoi epokhi (1917–1927)* (M, 1928).
Postyshev, P. P., *Ot XVI do XVII s"ezda: Stat'i i rechi* (M, 1934).
Pravda o Gorl'kom (M, 1932).
Prawer, S. S., *Karl Marx and World Literature* (Oxford, 1976).
Preobrazhensky, E., *The New Economics* (Oxford, 1965).
Proffer, E. C., *Bulgakov: Life and Work* (Ann Arbor, 1984).
Pyman, Avril, *The Life of Aleksandr Blok:* vol. II, *The Release of Harmony: 1908–1921* (Oxford, 1980).
Raeff, Marc, *Russian Intellectual History: An Anthology* (New Jersey, 1978).
Reck, Vera T., *Boris Pil'niak: A Soviet Writer in Conflict with the State* (Montreal, 1975).
Report of the Court Proceedings in the Case of the Anti-Soviet Trotskyite Centre (M, 1937).
Report of Court Proceedings: The Case of the Trotskyite-Zinovievite Terrorist Centre (Moscow, 1936).
Rigby, T. H., *Communist Party Membership in the USSR, 1917–1967* (Princeton, 1968).
Rigby, T. H. *et al.* (eds), *Authority, Power and Policy in the USSR: Essays dedicated to Leonard Schapiro* (London, 1980).
Romano-Petrova, N., *Stalin's Doctor, Stalin's Nurse: A Memoir* (Princeton, N. J., 1984).
Rosenberg, W. G. (ed.), *Bolshevik Visions* (Ann Arbor, 1984).
Rozental', M. M., *Protiv vul'garnoi sotsiologii v literaturnoi teorii* (M, 1936).
Rudnitsky, K. L., *Rezhisser Meyerkhol'd* (M, 1969).
Ruud, Charles A., *Fighting Words: Imperial Censorship and the Russian Press, 1804–1906* (Toronto, 1982).
Schapiro, Leonard (ed. Ellen Dahrendorf), *Russian Studies* (London, 1986).

Schapiro, Leonard, *The Communist Party of the Soviet Union* (London, 1960).
Schapiro, Leonard, *The Origin of the Communist Autocracy* (London, 1955).
Schapiro, Leonard and Reddaway, P. (eds), *Lenin: The Man, the Theorist, the Leader* (London, 1967).
Selivanovsky, A., *Ocherki po istorii russkoi sovetskoi poezii* (M, 1936).
Serebryansky, M., *Literatura i sotsializm* (M, 1935).
Serebryansky, M., *Tema grazhdanskoi voiny v sovetskoi literature* (Rostov, 1935).
Serge, Victor, *Memoirs of a Revolutionary, 1901–1941* (Oxford, 1967).
Shaginyan, M. S., *Literatura i plan* (M, 1934).
Shaginyan, M. S., *Besedy ob iskusstve* (ML, 1937).
Shane, A. M., *The Life and Works of Evgenij Zamjatin* (Berkeley, Calif., 1968).
Shanin, Teodor, *The Awkward Class* (Oxford, 1972).
Shcherbina, V. P., *Problemy literaturovedeniya v svete naslediya V. I. Lenina* (M, 1971).
Sheshukov, S., *Neistovye revniteli: Iz istorii literaturnoi bor'by 20-kh godov* (M, 1970).
Shiller, F., *Engel's kak literaturnyi kritik* (M, 1933).
Shkapa, I., *Sem' let s Gor'kim* (M, 1964).
Shklovsky, V., *Gamburgskii schet* (L, 1928; M, 1989).
Shklovsky, V., *Mayakovsky and his Circle* (London, 1974).
Shklovsky, V., *Third Factory* (Ann Arbor, 1977).
Shklovsky, V., *Zoo, or Letters not about love* (Ithaca, N. Y., 1971).
Shukurov, M. Sh., *Bor'ba K. P. Uzbekistana za razvitiye sovetskoi literatury 1917–1936* (Tashkent, 1971).
Siegelbaum, Lewis, H., *Stakhanovism and the Politics of Productivity in the USSR, 1935–1941* (Cambridge, 1988).
Sliwowski, René, *Dawni i nowi. Szkice o literaturze radzieckiej* (Warsaw, 1967).
Sochor, Zenovia, *Revolution and Culture: the Bogdanov-Lenin Controversy* (Ithaca, 1988).
Solzhenitsyn, Alexander, *The GULag Archipelago* vols 1 and 2 (London, 1974).
Sovetskaya literatura na novom etape: sbornik (M, 1932).
Spravochnik partiinogo rabotnika (M, 1930), vol. VII (i).
Stakhanov, A., *Rasskaz o moei zhizni* (M, 1937).
Stalin, J. V., *Joseph Stalin: A Short Biography* (M, 1949).
Stalin, J. V., *Marxism and Linguistics* (M, 1951).
Stalin, J. V., *The Foundations of Leninism* (M, 1951).
Stanislavsky, Konstantin, *Stanislavsky on the Art of the Stage* (London, 1961).
Starosel'sky, Ya. V., *Problema yakobinskoi diktatury* (M, 1930).
Starr, S. Frederick, *Melnikov: Solo Architect in a Mass Society* (Princeton, 1978).
Stavsky, V., *Pis'mo nachinayushchemu pisatelyu* (M, 1934).
Stites, Richard, *Revolutionary Dreams: Utopian Visions and Experimental Life in the Russian Revolution* (Oxford, 1989).

Struve, Gleb, *Russian Literature under Lenin and Stalin, 1917–1953* (London, 1972).
Svirsky, Grigory, *Na lobnom meste* (London, 1979).
Swayze, H., *The Political Control of Literature in the USSR, 1946–1959* (Cambridge, Mass., 1962).
Terras, Victor, *Belinskij and Russian Literary Criticism* (Madison, Wisc., 1974).
Tertz, Abram, *On Socialist Realism* (New York, 1960).
Tregub, S., *The Heroic Life of Nikolai Ostrovsky* (M, n.d.).
Trotsky, L. D., *Literature and Revolution* (New York, 1925).
Trotsky, L. D., *Sochineniya*, vol. XXI (M, 1927).
Tsvetaeva, M., *Pis'ma k Anne Teskovoi* (Prague, 1969).
Tuck, Jim, *Engine of Mischief: An Analytical Biography of Karl Radek* (London, 1988).
Tucker, Robert C., *Stalin as Revolutionary 1879–1929* (London, 1975).
Tucker, Robert C. (ed), *Stalinism: Essays in Historical Interpretation* (New York, 1977).
Tumarkin, Nina, *Lenin Lives! The Lenin Cult in Soviet Russia* (Cambridge, Mass., 1983).
Usievich, Ye. F., *Pisateli i deistvitel'nost'* (M, 1936).
Usievich, Ye. F., *Tri stat'i* (M, 1934).
Usievich, Ye. F., *Za chistotu leninizma v literaturnoi teorii* (M, 1932).
Ustav Akademii nauk SSSR (M, 1936).
Vaughan James, C., *Soviet Socialist Realism: Origins and Theory* (London, 1973).
Viola, Lynne, *The Best Sons of the Fatherland: Workers in the Vanguard of Soviet Collectivization* (Oxford, 1987).
Vishnevsky, V. V., *Stat'i i vystupleniya* (M, 1961).
Volkov, S. (ed.), *Testimony: The Memoirs of Dmitri Shostakovich* (London, 1981).
Voroshilov, K. E., *Stalin i Krasnaya Armiya* (M, 1937).
Voroshilov, K. E., *Stalin i stroitel'stvo Krasnoi Armii* (M, 1941).
Vygotsky, L. G., *Mind in Society* (Cambridge, Mass., 1978).
Walicki, Andrzej, *A History of Russian Thought from the Enlightenment to Marxism* (Oxford, 1980).
Williams, Robert, C., *Culture in Exile: Russian emigres in Germany, 1881–1941* (Ithaca, N. Y., 1972).
Woehrlin, William, F., *Chernyshevski: the man and the journalist* (Cambridge, Mass., 1971).
Wolfe, Bertram, D., *The Bridge and the Abyss: The Troubled Friendship of Maxim Gorky and V. I. Lenin* (London, 1967).
Woroszylski, Wiktor, *The Life of Mayakovsky* (London, 1972).
Wright, A. Colin, *Mikhail Bulgakov: Life and Interpretations* (Toronto, 1978).
Yudin, P. F., *Marksizm-leninizm o kul'turi i kul'turnoi revolyutsii* (M, 1933).
Yudin, P. F. (ed.), *Pisateli k XVII parts'ezdu* (M, 1934).
Yuzovsky, Yu., *Spektakli i p'esy* (M, 1935).
Za platformu teatra RAPP (LM, 1931).
Za povorot na filosofskom fronte (M, 1931).

Zabolotsky, Nikolai, *Stikhotvoreniya* (New York, 1965).
Zak, L. M. (ed.), *A. M. Gor'kii i sozdaniye istorii fabrik i zavodov* (M, 1959).
Zamyatin, E., *A Soviet Heretic: Essays by Yevgeny Zamyatin* (Chicago, 1970).
Zelinsky, K. I., *Na rubezhe dvukh epokh: Literaturnye vstrechi, 1917–1920 godov* (M, 1959).

Index

Index